Banking Systems

second edition

Center for Financial Training

SOUTH-WESTERN
CENGAGE Learning

Australia • Brazil • Japan • Korea • Mexico • Singapore • Spain • United Kingdom • United States

SOUTH-WESTERN
CENGAGE Learning™

Banking Systems, 2nd Edition
Center for Financial Training

Vice President of Editorial, Business:
Jack W. Calhoun

Vice President/Editor-in-Chief:
Karen Schmohe

Vice President/Marketing: Bill Hendee

Executive Editor: Eve Lewis

Senior Developmental Editor: Enid Nagel

Editorial Assistant: Virginia Wilson

Consulting Editor: Marce Epstein

Assistant Marketing Manager: Linda Kuper

Content Project Management:
Pre-Press PMG

Technology Project Manager: Mike Jackson

Senior Manufacturing Buyer: Kevin Kluck

Production Service: Pre-Press PMG

Senior Art Director: Tippy McIntosh

Cover and Internal Design: Kim Torbeck,
Imbue Design

Cover Image: Corbis

Photography Manager: Amanda Groszko

For product information and technology assistance, contact us at
Cengage Learning Customer & Sales Support, 1-800-354-9706

For permission to use material from this text or product,
submit all requests online at **cengage.com/permissions**
Further permissions questions can be emailed to
permissionrequest@cengage.com

Library of Congress Control Number: 2009922200

Student Edition ISBN 13: 978-0-538-44928-1

Student Edition ISBN 10: 0-538-44928-4

Instructor's Edition ISBN 13: 978-0-538-44930-4

Instructor's Edition ISBN 10: 0-538-44930-6

South-Western Cengage Learning
5191 Natorp Boulevard
Mason, OH 45040
USA

Cengage Learning products are represented in Canada
by Nelson Education, Ltd.

For your course and learning solutions, visit **school.cengage.com**

Printed in China by China Translation & Printing Services Limited
3 4 5 6 7 8 9 12 11 10

Banking Consultants

Christine Bumgardner
President & CEO
Center for Financial Training
Western States
Denver, Colorado

Loyd Hoskins
Educational Consultant
Loyd Hoskins and Associates
Lakewood, Colorado

Marta W. Liimatainen
VP, Distance Learning
Center for Financial Training
Atlantic & Central States
Chesterfield, Massachusetts

Michael Meakem
President
Center for Financial Training
Atlantic & Central States
Norwich, Connecticut

Rita Maria A. St. John
VP/Banking Information Center Manager
Home State Bank
Loveland, Colorado

DeeDee Sebrin
Executive Director
Center for Financial Training
South Central States
Hot Springs, Arkansas

Daniel R. Sierchio
COO
Danson, Inc.
Consultant, Online Instruction
Center for Financial Training
Atlantic & Central States
East Hanover, New Jersey

Eric D. Walser
Manager, Internal Audit
MDC Holdings, Inc.
Denver, CO

Dan Wojcik
President
B & F Advisors
Little Rock, Arkansas

Educational Consultants

Joseph J. Bachan
Business Teacher
Portage High School
Portage, Indiana

Debra L. Beckwith
Business, Media, and Technology Instructor
Bonney Lake High School
Bonney Lake, Washington

Norma Brown
Marketing Instructor
Dutch Fork High School
Irmo, South Carolina

Melissa Faucett
Marketing and Finance Instructor
Carthage Technical Center
Carthage, Missouri

Carolyn S. Hunter
Teacher
Arkadelphia High School
Arkadelphia, Arkansas

Kathleen Lowry
Accounting and Financial Serv. Instructor
Gordon Cooper Technology Center
Shawnee, Oklahoma

Shelley G. Lynch
Business and Technology Teacher
Reading Memorial High School
Reading, Massachusetts

Gladys Montgomery
Business Department Chairperson
Charles H. Flowers High School
Springdale, Maryland

Mitzi Plunkett
Teacher, Cypress High School
Weston, Florida

Kenneth Reed
Business Teacher, Blackman High School
Murfreesboro, Tennessee

Cassaundra Thrasher
Teacher, Upson Lee High School
Thomaston, Georgia

CONTENTS

CHAPTER 1

The Business of Banking 2

Climbing the Ladder From Human Resource Assistant to Human Resource Specialist 3

1.1 Introduction to Banking 4

1.2 Role of Banks in the Economy 10

1.3 How the Banking System Works 17

1.4 Other Financial Institutions 26

CHAPTER 2

Development of the U.S. Banking System 36

Climbing the Ladder From Web Content Consultant to Documentation Manager 37

2.1 Creation of a National Currency 38

2.2 Banking Before 1913 43

2.3 Modern Banking 47

CHAPTER 3

The Federal Reserve System 58

Skills That Pay Dividends Understanding Public Policy and Its Impact on Business 59

3.1 Structure of the Federal Reserve System 60

3.2 Monetary and Fiscal Policy 67

3.3 Consumer Protection 74

3.4 Role in Determining Bank's Financial Health 81

3.5 International Banking and the Federal Reserve System 86

CHAPTER 4

Money and Interest 96

Skills That Pay Dividends Quantitative Skills 97

4.1 The Money Supply 98

4.2 Money Creation and Circulation 105

4.3 Interest and Interest Rates 111

CHAPTER 5

Deposits in Banks 120

Climbing the Ladder From Trust Associate to Trust Department Director 121

5.1 Deposit Accounts 122

5.2 Interest-Bearing Accounts 130

5.3 Flow of Deposits 135

5.4 Deposit Regulations 140

CHAPTER 6

Negotiable Instruments 150

Skills That Pay Dividends Public Speaking and Persuasion 151

6.1 Types of Negotiable Instruments 152

6.2 Presenting Checks for Payment 158

6.3 Processing Checks 165

6.4 Changing Forms of Payment 171

CHAPTER 7

Bank Loans   184

Climbing the Ladder   From Loan Service Clerk to Credit Card Risk Specialist   185

7.1   Consumer Loan Theory   186

7.2   Consumer Loans   193

7.3   Granting and Analyzing Credit   199

7.4   Cost of Credit   207

7.5   Bank Loans and Policy   214

CHAPTER 8

Mortgages   224

Skills That Pay Dividends   Ethics at Work   225

8.1   Mortgage Lending   226

8.2   Mortgage Loan Processing   234

8.3   Mortgages and the Law   239

8.4   Government-Backed Loans   245

8.5   The Mortgage Crisis   252

CHAPTER 9

Commercial Lending   262

Climbing the Ladder   From Commercial Banking Associate to Portfolio Manager   263

9.1   Commercial Loans   264

9.2   Commercial Credit Analysis   272

9.3   Small Business Loan Programs   279

9.4   The 2008 Financial Crisis   286

CHAPTER 10

Specialized Bank Services   296

Climbing the Ladder   From Associate Team Leader to Product Manager   297

10.1   International Banking   298

10.2   Insurance and Brokerage   307

10.3   Cash Management   316

10.4   Trusts   321

CHAPTER 11

Security, Fraud, and Ethics   330

Skills That Pay Dividends   Convey a Professional Image   331

11.1   Robbery Prevention and Response   332

11.2   Ethics in Banking   338

11.3   Fraud and Scams   344

11.4   Identity Theft   351

CHAPTER 12

Bank Marketing   362

Skills That Pay Dividends   Understanding Customer Motives   363

12.1   Define the Customer   364

12.2   Develop and Maintain the Customer   369

12.3   Public Relations   374

12.4   Customer Service   379

12.5   Marketing and Advertising   385

CHAPTER 13

Employment Opportunities **396**

Climbing the Ladder From Teller to District Manager 397

13.1 Organizational Structure 398

13.2 Human Resources 405

13.3 Employee Evaluation 411

GLOSSARY 422

INDEX 428

FEATURES

Banking Math Connection 18, 50, 87, 106, 131, 156, 209, 235, 275, 319, 346, 388, 401

Branching Out 71, 128, 190, 283, 366, 402

Communicate 8, 48, 82, 103, 137, 143, 166, 204, 227, 283, 308, 347, 386, 416

Ethics in Action 29, 48, 77, 113, 142, 163, 197, 240, 276, 323, 341, 376, 408

Flat World 13, 44, 108, 175, 256, 303, 349

Interesting Facts 5, 21, 49, 64, 68, 100, 126, 132, 153, 176, 196, 202, 236, 246, 253, 268, 299, 317, 322, 345, 352, 380, 402, 409

Net Bookmark 15, 41, 76, 112, 125, 177, 218, 255, 277, 300, 354, 372, 410

Tech Talk 22, 51, 88, 100, 136, 169, 203, 248, 267, 312, 334, 381, 413

ABOUT CFT

Center for Financial Training (CFT) is a network of more than 25 centers throughout the country that provide career enhancing training solutions to the financial services industry. Through innovative educational formats, CFT is the training partner for financial institutions that helps improve performance to meet the needs of tomorrow's challenging business environment.

INSIDE THE STUDENT EDITION

climbing the ladder

From Web Content Consultant to Documentation Manager

**CLIMBING THE
LADDER**
explores careers in
banking.

While his children slept on the flight bringing them home from a hectic week at a Florida amusement park, Reza reflected on his career. After college, he had accepted a position at a diversified financial institution. Working as a web marketing consultant for the annuity and mutual funds division, he was responsible for developing and executing online marketing initiatives. Reza supported multiple products that were advertised on a variety of websites. He developed web content and designed site layouts. Ensuring that the written and visual elements complemented each other and functioned smoothly were a critical part of this position.

Reza had realized that job security could be improved by having a broad base of experiences developed by working in a variety of areas. An expanded personal network was another advantage of multiple positions.

Next Reza had accepted a job as an implementation technical consultant in the credit card division. Reza was responsible for assessing data technology needs, file specifications, and delivery methods. He streamlined processes and met with internal customers to determine electronic reporting formats for products.

Realizing that he wanted to move higher in the organization, Reza routinely reviewed internal job postings for supervisory positions. He had been delighted to pass the rigorous interview process for a job as a business technology supervisor in his company's trust division. In this role, Reza was responsible for application systems analysis and programming activities. After leading teams to conduct feasibility studies and time and cost estimates, Reza assigned members of his group to complete various components of the projects.

Reza's stellar reputation as an effective supervisor had led to a job offer as a network security manager. His team was responsible for developing systems and procedures that protected host and network systems from unauthorized access. He managed the creation of firewall security standards and intrusion detection procedures. The team perpetually evaluated the information technology (IT) infrastructure to identify new areas of risk.

After the birth of his twins, Reza had decided to scale back on his hours at the office. By working in his current position as an online training documentation manager, Reza was able to work from home three days a week. The flexibility in his schedule helped him and his wife manage childcare needs. In this position, Reza is responsible for overseeing the content development of online training courses, updating existing online courses, and writing and maintaining operational procedures.

PHOTODISC

**Upper Rungs
to Consider**

Now that his children were older, Reza realized it was time to find a challenging onsite position. Management positions that Reza planned to look for included technology integration, IT project management, and network operations.

**Preparing for
the Climb**

Over the course of a long career, are there ways to occasionally scale back to handle temporarily demanding life needs? What is the best way to stay involved in your field to make it easy to reenter the field?

GOALS
outline the main
objectives of the
lesson.

TERMS
lists the new
terms defined
in the lesson.

9.4 The 2008 Financial Crisis

goals

+ Identify the root causes of the 2008 financial crisis.
+ Discuss self-regulation and its effects.

terms

+ risk averse
+ risk preferrer
+ credit default swap (CDS)
+ speculation
+ synthetic financial product

Banking Scene

Gloria Velez has had a successful few years running her own business. She has some extra money she'd like to invest. Although traditional investments, like CDs, are comforting to consider because of the low risk and guaranteed interest rate, she'd prefer to make more money faster. Gloria's heard about a great way to make money with credit default swaps. Although they sound lucrative, she's a little concerned about the uncertainty associated with them. What factors should she consider before making this investment?

BANKING SCENE
provides a motivating
introduction to the
lesson.

THE PROFIT MOTIVE • • • • • • • • • • • • • • • • • • •

Most people are interested in making money. Some people rely on traditional ways to produce income, which include working for a corporation, directly selling products or services to individuals or companies, or through making investments. If someone is **risk averse**, he or she would

SPECIAL FEATURES ENHANCE LEARNING

flat world...

The International Impact of the Mortgage Crisis

Just as a stone thrown in a pond makes a ripple effect throughout the water, the U.S. mortgage crisis has sent shockwaves through financial systems across the globe. In April 2008, the International Monetary Fund (IMF) estimated that the U.S. subprime mortgage crisis could cause global losses of about $1 trillion. The euro zone is the second largest economy in the world. In June 2008, the euro zone experienced an inflation rate of 4 percent. The central bank of the euro zone had targeted inflation to be about 2 percent. By July 2008, European banks with investments in securities backed by U.S. mortgages suffered losses.

There was a tightening of European lending and a rise in European interest rates as a result of these losses. Countries that exported products to the U.S. received fewer orders because U.S. consumers had less money available to spend on nonessential items.

Think Critically Investigate current ramifications of the mortgage crisis online. In this age of global financial interdependence, what steps can individual economies take to shield themselves from financial exposure due to investments in other countries?

> **FLAT WORLD** provides international banking connections relevant to today's current events.

tech talk

Fannie Mae DU and Freddie Mac LP

As underwriting of mortgage loans becomes increasingly automated, government-chartered agencies that work with private lenders have developed tools for their lending clients. Fannie Mae's Desktop Underwriter (DU) and Freddie Mac's Loan Prospector (LP) are two automated systems that are helping streamline the underwriting communications between agencies and the client lenders.

The desktop programs are based on statistical models of FHA underwriting data to create an automated scoring system specifically designed with FHA criteria in mind. As a result, these customized automated underwriting systems streamline the often cumbersome process of working through the agencies and the FHA. The systems are FHA approved and can return a routine underwriting decision and conditions within an hour. Lenders enter data from their own sites, using a standard Residential Loan Application. Although they are not the only ways to get FHA approval for Fannie Mae and Freddie Mac funds, these two software programs are the wave of an interconnected future in underwriting.

Think Critically What type of information had to be factored into the DU and LP programs in order for them to be reliable? What are some elements of the underwriting process that make it difficult to automate?

> **TECH TALK** provides information about new technology that is being used in banking.

Ethics in Action

According to reports throughout the media, Senator Chris Dodd, Chairman of the Senate Banking Committee in 2008, received interest rate reductions on two of his mortgages held by Countrywide. One rate reduction resulted in an annual interest savings of $2000. The other rate reduction resulted in a $17,000 reduction over the life of the loan. In June 2008, Senator Dodd indicated he had solicited multiple rate quotes from lenders and was unaware of any special treatment.

> **ETHICS IN ACTION** provides a real-world situation where students decide an ethical action.

Think Critically

What extra precautions are required of a politician during financial transactions? What probing questions would be wise to ask to avoid the appearance of favoritism?

branching out

Aisling

Banks have had branches in nontraditional locations, like grocery stores, for well over a decade. In addition to providing convenience to customers, these branches need to work to stay prominent in customers' minds. A variety of creative marketing approaches have been used by personnel at nontraditional branches. At one Ohio bank, tellers take to the supermarket aisles to interact with customers. By telling customers that they can receive $100,000 if they can identify the name of the bank located in the store, customers are prompted to recall the bank's name. If they correctly identify the name of the bank, the teller then gives them a $100,000 candy bar. Undoubtedly, receiving the candy sweetens their experience!

Think Critically How would you react if your grocery shopping experience included an individualized marketing effort by a bank? Do you think this is an effective way to engage customers?

BRANCHING OUT presents interesting and unique ways bank and companies provide banking services.

skills that pay dividends

Understanding Consumer Motives

People have a variety of reasons for buying products and services. Some of these reasons are based on thoughts and some are based on feelings.

Banking is a basic need in modern society. Intellectually, most people understand that they need a bank to deposit a paycheck, to hold their funds, to provide various checking and savings accounts, and to provide ATM services. How a bank is chosen depends on the personality and values of the customer.

An analytical customer may do a lot of research to compare products, service levels, and costs among competing banks. If an analytical customer values cost effectiveness and efficiency, they may select the bank that provides the best combination of both. This analytical customer takes a detached, objective approach to decision making.

Some customers take a more emotional approach when choosing a bank. A customer who either lived through the depression or who is worried about the lasting impact of the 2008 credit crisis may place a high premium on the security of their funds. This customer may gravitate to a bank with personnel that convey a strong sense of financial knowledge and financial responsibility. During banking transactions, this customer may often seek reassurance that their funds are safe.

A customer with a strong need either to feel like part of a community or to do business with people they know socially may place a higher premium on banking where one can develop strong personal relationships. This customer may not thoroughly comparison shop and may select, instead, to choose a bank where they feel they can trust the people they know.

When interacting with customers regarding product or service selection, ask them to rank what is most important to them in their selection process. Their answers will reveal whether they are more analytical, emotional, or a combination of both. Using their responses to frame your discussion, emphasize the qualities of your products or services that are most important to them. For example, efficiency- and value-driven customers might be influenced to buy from you if they hear about all of the free online services offered by your bank. Socially oriented customers might like to hear about outings to pro baseball games sponsored by your bank.

Customers make post-purchase evaluations. Followup with customers after a purchase to see if there's anything you can do to improve their satisfaction.

Develop Your Skill

In small groups, assign the role of an analytical customer and a social customer to group members. Assign the role of a bank representative, focusing on specific bank products, like a checking account or a CD, to other group members. The bank representatives should try to sell each type of customer their product by first asking the customer to list their decision priorities and then by framing the discussion around those priorities. Reflect on how the approaches and conversations are different based on the personality type of the customer. Be prepared to share your findings with the class.

SKILLS THAT PAY DIVIDENDS presents skills that are necessary for success in the banking industry.

PHOTODISC

SPECIAL FEATURES ENHANCE LEARNING

NET BOOKMARK incorporates Internet activities into every chapter.

NET Bookmark

All across America, families are being touched by the mortgage crisis. Access www.cengage.com/school/pfinance/banking and click on the link for Chapter 8. The Hope Now Alliance is an alliance of mortgage-related industries and service providers that is focused on keeping homeowners in their homes. The Treasury Department and HUD supported the formation of this alliance to help stabilize the mortgage market. Use the site to learn more about FHASecure and Project Lifeline. How can these programs help troubled homeowners?

www.cengage.com/school/pfinance/banking

Banking Math *Connection*

Private mortgage insurance (PMI) rates may vary, but a typical PMI rate is ½ of 1 percent of the borrowed principal. The formula for calculating the monthly PMI cost is

$$\text{Rate} \times \text{Principal} \div 12 = \text{PMI}$$

Calculate the monthly PMI cost for a principal balance of $140,000.

Solution

If PMI were required for a principal of $140,000, the calculation would be

$$\text{Rate} \times \text{Principal} \div 12 = \text{PMI}$$
$$0.005 \times \$140,000 \div 12 = \$58.34$$

BANKING MATH CONNECTION provides worked examples that reinforce and review math concepts.

interesting *facts*

NeighborWorks America was founded by Congress during the 1970s to support community-based revitalization. Their Home Ownership Centers provide mortgage assistance to underserved buyers. ◻

INTERESTING FACTS provides an interesting fact about the topic.

COMMUNICATE provides activities to reinforce, review, and practice communication skills

"communicate"

Interview someone who experienced either the Great Depression firsthand or a recent FDIC takeover of a financial institution. Find out ways that people coped with the economic crisis. Write a short report on what you learn and what your interviewee thinks should be learned from bank failures.

ONGOING ASSESSMENT

 checkpoint

List five loan products that were developed to support loosened loan qualification standards.

_____

_____

CHECKPOINT
Short questions within lesson to assist with reading and to assure students are grasping concepts.

assessment 8.5

Think Critically

1. What motivated lenders to shift from funding mortgage loans from locally held deposits to funding mortgages with Wall Street financing?

2. Strong relationships within a community help bankers increase their customer base. How would ongoing, personal relationships with customers impact a bank's decision regarding qualifying customers for appropriate loans?

3. Review the description of a AAA bond rating online. What do you think is an appropriate rating for a subprime mortgage-backed security?

4. Look for SIVA, SISA, NINA, or No Income, No Asset, No Employment loans online. Are they still available? List reasons explaining their current level of availability.

Make Academic Connections

5. **COMMUNICATION** The Humane Society, recognizing that the mortgage crisis is preventing people from keeping their pets, has instituted a grant program to help agencies reach out to pet owners with ideas for keeping their pets. These pets are suffering downstream effects of the mortgage crisis. What other parts of society, either living entities or businesses, are being affected by the crisis? Prepare a chart describing the affected entities and how they are affected. Share the chart with the class.

6. **THE RIGHT DECISION** During July 2008, the *Cleveland Plain Dealer* featured three local lending institutions that were in solid financial condition despite the mortgage lending crisis. They shared a common trait of maintaining conservative lending standards. The names of these banks are Valley Savings, First Federal of Lakewood, and Third Federal Savings. Research these banks online to see how they are doing today. How do you think their conservative approaches affected their longevity?

THINK CRITICALLY Provides opportunities to apply concepts.
MAKE ACADEMIC CONNECTIONS Provides connections to other disciplines.

CHAPTER ASSESSMENT Contains Chapter Summary, Vocabulary Builder, Review Concepts, Apply What You Learned, and Make Connections

chapter 8 **assessment**

Chapter Summary

8.1 Mortgage Lending
A. A mortgage is a note secured by real property.
B. Mortgage lenders provide many types of loan products for buying a home.

8.2 Mortgage Loan Processing
A. Monthly mortgage payments to lenders usually consist of principal, interest, taxes, and insurance (PITI).
B. Six steps in the mortgage approval process are application, documentation, underwriting, drawing documents, closing, and recording.

8.3 Mortgages and the Law
A. Consumer protection legislation applies to mortgage lending as well as other loans.
B. Lenders must comply with numerous housing-specific laws.

8.4 Government-Backed Loans
A. The government backs some loans by guaranteeing to repay the lender if the borrower defaults.
B. Mortgage programs like FHA loans, VA loans, and others make loans possible to people who might not otherwise qualify.

8.5 The Mortgage Crisis
A. Historically, mortgages were a sound, safe investment because they provided a reliable, steady income stream.
B. The mortgage crisis was caused by a combination of factors including an increased demand for mortgage-backed securities, lowered lending criteria, and bond ratings that were issued without due diligence.

Vocabulary Builder

Choose the term that best fits the definition. Write the letter of the answer in the space provided. Some terms may not be used.

a. adjustable rate mortgage
b. balloon mortgage
c. buy-down mortgage
d. escrow
e. Fannie Mae
f. fixed rate mortgage
g. foreclosure
h. Freddie Mac
i. Ginnie Mae
j. loan-to-value (LTV)
k. mortgage
l. mortgage-backed securities
m. mortgage origination
n. negative equity
o. PITI
p. point
q. redlining
r. shared appreciation mortgage (SAM)

____ 1. Value of loan compared to value of asset
____ 2. Prepaying part of the interest to get a lower mortgage rate
____ 3. When banks refuse to lend in certain neighborhoods
____ 4. Mortgage with changing interest rate
____ 5. A note secured by real property
____ 6. A value equal to 1 percent of loan principal
____ 7. A mortgage in which the entire remaining balance of the loan is due in one single payment
____ 8. Principal, interest, taxes, and insurance
____ 9. Conventional mortgage
____ 10. When the amount owed on a home is more than the current value of the home

Review Concepts

11. What is a mortgage?

12. What is a foreclosure?

Apply What You Learned

25. Under traditional circumstances, why does obtaining a mortgage initiate the most thorough credit review most consumers will ever undergo?

26. What factors does a lender judge in order to assess consumer capability?

Make Academic Connections

29. **BANKING MATH** Calculate the PMI (private mortgage insurance) for a principal balance of $125,500. Assume the PMI rate is ½ of 1 percent of the borrowed principal.

30. **TECHNOLOGY** Use the Internet to learn more about the impact of technology on the real estate and mortgage industries. Prepare an oral report on what you learn.

CHAPTER

I

The Business of Banking

I.I   Introduction to Banking

I.2   Role of Banks in the Economy

I.3   How the Banking System Works

I.4   Other Financial Institutions

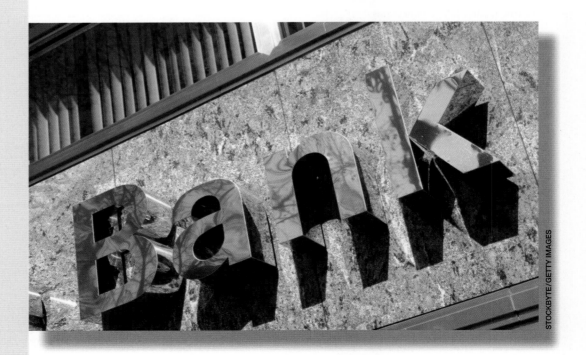

STOCKBYTE/GETTY IMAGES

From Human Resource Assistant to Human Resource Specialist

Leya, a banking human resources specialist, finished giving a brief welcoming speech to a group of administrative assistants recently hired. Their eager faces and attentive manner prompted her to reflect fondly on the beginning of her career.

Leya began her banking career as a human resources administrative assistant. This entry level position provided Leya the opportunity to demonstrate her project management skills. By effectively processing job applications, co-coordinating new employee orientation, administrating employee training schedules, and handling travel schedules and expense reports for managers, she had proven herself as a reliable employee.

Leya's experience with new employees helped her earn an entry level corporate recruiter position. Conducting reference checks, overseeing background investigations, and arranging pre-employment drug screening were among her routine duties. Leya also enjoyed publicizing job postings, following up on employee referrals, representing her bank at career fairs, and traveling to colleges for campus recruitment.

As Leya had a knack for recognizing talent and sending viable candidates forward for additional interviews, she was tapped for a position as a corporate recruiter. To ensure she carried out her duties effectively, and in compliance with the law, Leya obtained training in employment law as well as wage and hour regulations. She also received training regarding how to avoid discrimination in the hiring process.

Her duties as a corporate recruiter varied. She updated and maintained her bank's Open Requisition Report that contained job postings for all open positions. Leya managed the bank's New Hire Orientation Program. She also participated in final hiring interviews for management level employees. Developing employment agreements was another part of her job.

As a corporate recruiter, Leya conducted exit interviews for employees. She developed a continuous improvement program which incorporated comments of exiting employees to develop strategies for reducing turnover.

With the breadth of her prior experience to support her, Leya applied for and obtained her current position as a human resources specialist. Leya enjoyed her current duties, which included staying current on banking salary trends to ensure her company offered competitive salaries, developing best practices for employee career development, and facilitating smooth transitions of employees from acquired banks into her bank's organization.

Upper Rungs to Consider

Leya found her current position challenging and gratifying. In order to prepare for future job opportunities, she planned to investigate the job responsibilities for a human resources manager and for a corporate training manager.

Preparing for the Climb

Career manuals often suggest taking on pieces of jobs that you would like to have while you are still in your current role. Are there responsibilities or projects you could ask for, in your current job, that would give you experience in a job you would like to have?

PHOTODISC

1.1

goals

+ Define the business of banking.

+ Identify trends in modern banking.

terms

+ medium of exchange
+ financial intermediary
+ commercial bank
+ retail bank
+ central banks

Banking Scene

Edouard Ramirez has taken his first full-time job working as a summer lifeguard at a local pool. After receiving his first paycheck, Edouard has decisions to make about how to handle that money. Along with choices about budgeting and spending, Edouard must decide what to do with his check, such as how to cash it, where to put his money, how to gain access to it, how to use it effectively, and how to take advantage of the range of services available to modern consumers. Writing checks, using ATMs, learning about debit and credit cards, and investigating forms of saving and investment are all things Edouard wants to consider. How can he get this information?

WHAT IS A BANK? •

When you think of a bank, what image comes to mind? Do you see a nearby building where people deposit their paychecks? Maybe you visualize the automated teller machine (ATM) where people use a card to get cash fast, or you recall the bank statements that many people still get in the mail. Perhaps you see a tall tower with a logo or a name you recognize. If you're technologically savvy, you may imagine someone going over personal finances while on the Internet. Maybe you think of managing all of your accounts from the convenience of your home computer or laptop. Performing account management functions from your cell phone is another option.

However you think of banks, and they include all these ideas and more, don't lose track of one basic idea. A bank is a business. Banks sell their services to earn money, and they market and manage those services in a competitive field. In many ways, banks are like other businesses that must earn a profit to survive. Understanding this fundamental idea helps explain how banks work, and helps you understand many modern trends in banking and finance.

A Unique Business

Banks, of course, don't manufacture cellphones or repair automobiles. The services banks offer to customers have to do almost entirely with handling money for other people. Money is a **medium of exchange**, an agreed-upon

© JOHN CONNELL/CORBIS

interesting *facts*

The first automated teller machine (ATM) appeared at a Chemical Bank branch in Rockville Center, New York, in 1969. ▧

system for measuring the value of goods and services. Once, and still in some places today, precious stones, animal products, or other goods of value might be used as a medium of exchange. Roman soldiers were sometimes paid in salt, because it was critical to life and not easy to get. The word *salary* and the expression *not worth his salt* come from that practice. Anything with an agreed-upon value might be a medium of exchange. Today, many forms of money are used. Money simply shows how much something is worth, whether it is a new stereo or two hours of your labor. When you have money, a bank can act as your agent for using or protecting that money. A bank is a **financial intermediary** for the safeguarding, transferring, exchanging, or lending of money. Banks distribute the medium of exchange.

Because banks and money are essential to maintaining not only economies but entire societies, they are closely regulated and must operate by strict procedures and principles. In the United States, banks may be chartered by federal or state governments. Banks are usually corporations and may be owned by groups of individuals, corporations, or some combination of the two. In the United States, all federally chartered banks have been required to be corporations since 1863. A few states permit noncorporate banks, which are owned by partnerships or individuals. Around the world, however, banks are supervised by governments to guarantee the safety and stability of the money supply and of the country.

Types of Banks

Actually, a lot of businesses are involved in financial services. If you consider the definition of a bank to be a business that safeguards, transfers, exchanges, and lends money, many firms might qualify. Certainly banks perform these roles, but so do trust companies, insurance companies, stockbrokers, investment bankers, and other companies. Since the deregualtion of banks in in the 1980s, there has been a blurring of the line between "pure" banking and other providers of financial and investment services. Banks provide a multitude of financial services beyond the traditional practices of holding deposits and lending money. Consequently, not only has banking changed considerably, so have the people who work in the banking world.

- **Commercial banks** are the institutions commonly thought of as banks. Commercial banks do about 60 percent of the deposit and loan business in the United States, and provide familiar services such as checking and savings accounts, credit cards, investment services, and others. Historically, commercial banks offered their services only to businesses. Today, commercial banks seek the business of any worthy customer.

- **Retail banks** and other thrift institutions such as mutual savings banks, savings and loans, and credit unions, developed to help individuals not served by commercial banks. These institutions help customers save money, acquire loans, and invest. They also offer a wide range of financial services to a broad customer base.

- **Central banks** are the government banks that manage, regulate, and protect both the money supply and the banks themselves. Central banks serve as the government's banker. Central banks issue currency and conduct monetary policy. In the United States, the Federal Reserve System performs the central banking function. Although the Federal Reserve is technically owned by the banks themselves, the Board of Governors is appointed by the President with the consent of the Senate. The President also selects the powerful chair of the Federal Reserve.

Edouard Ramirez has a number of options for what he might do with his paycheck. He'll need to know more about banking to make wise decisions that fit his needs.

List four functions that define a bank.

BANKING TODAY •

Banking used to be thought of as a solid and slow-moving industry. Banking today is an exciting, fast-moving, around-the-clock, global activity. Changes in regulation, changes in technology, and changes in competition have pushed banking, like most other businesses, to become organizations that must respond rapidly to changing business conditions in order to survive.

Mergers

One of the most significant changes in banking in the last twenty years has been the number of mergers. A *merger* occurs when one or more banks join or acquire another bank or banks. Mergers increase the size of banks, giving them more resources. Mergers also decrease the number of banks.

The effects of mergers have been mixed. Banks are larger and ownership is concentrated. Fewer banks control more and more of the nation's money. About 25 large banks control 45 percent of U.S. assets, and the number of commercial banks has dropped to around 8,000 from more than 14,000 in the 1980s. Although there were about 14,000 banks in the 1980s, there are about 6,500 banks today. The largest banks control about 75 percent of domestic assets.

Top Ten Largest Banks Worldwide

(Ranked by size of assets)	
Bank	**Country**
UBS AG	Switzerland
Barclays PLC	United Kingdom
BNP Paribas SA	France
The Royal Bank of Scotland Group plc	United Kingdom
Crédit Agricole SA	France
Deutsche Bank AG	Germany
The Bank of Tokyo-Mitsubishi UFJ Ltd	Japan
ABN AMRO Holding NV	Netherlands
Société Generalé	France
Bank of America Corp. NA	United States

After a merger, some consumers face higher fees and find less community involvement and lending in local areas. People like to feel that their money is staying home. Mergers also created an opening, though, for a new wave of small local banks. Small banks have doubled the amount loaned to businesses in the last decade.

Banking is an international business as well, and becoming more so all the time. Technology has allowed instant communication as well as transfer of funds, so barriers of geography apply less than ever. U.S. commercial banks actively seek international business, putting together huge investment transactions overseas and engaging in investment banking prohibited in the United States.

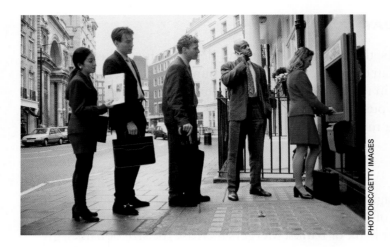

PHOTODISC/GETTY IMAGES

Technology

As with many industries, technology has changed everything. Perhaps no business has been more affected by the growth of computers and telecommunications than banking. Not only have accounting, auditing, and examining functions been taken over by fast and efficient technology, funds transfer, record keeping, and financial analyses have become instantaneous because of the powerful tools now available.

Technology's changes are not limited to bankers either. Consumers' relationships with their banks have changed also. Gone are the banker's hours of 9:00 a.m. to 3:00 p.m., for consumers want instantaneous access to banking services just as they do from other businesses. They want access to their money at any time. Automated teller machines (ATMs), networked computers that allow access from around the world, "smart" cards with embedded microchips, and online banking via the Internet are some of the technological innovations changing the face of banking.

Competition

Banking is a business, and as with any business, competition is an ongoing challenge. As government regulations have loosened, competition between banks has become fiercer. This fact has resulted in mergers and decreasing numbers of banks, but it has also made more services available to consumers, as banks compete to earn customers' financial business. Banks compete not only with other banks, but with other businesses that sell financial services, such as credit unions. Banks are more sales oriented than ever, with an emphasis on service, innovation, and marketing that could scarcely have been imagined 30 years ago.

 checkpoint

What three factors in modern banking have changed the industry?

assessment 1.1

Think Critically

1. What are ways a bank is like any other business? What are ways it is different from other businesses?

2. Name three ways you interact with your own bank. For each, explain how technology has changed the interaction between the bank and the customer.

3. Why do governments regulate banks?

4. What challenges do you think the trend toward mergers poses to banks? What skills will these challenges require of those making careers in banking?

Make Academic Connections

5. **COMMUNICATION** Banking has changed over the years. Interview a member of a previous generation to find out more. Prepare a list of questions that will generate memories about banking in earlier days. What were banks and banking like? In what specific ways have banks changed? Which of those changes were for the better? Which, in the opinion of your interviewee, were for the worse? Compare the results of your interview with those of classmates. Compile a class list or table showing the composite results.

6. **BANKING MATH** In international banking, exchange rates are used to compute the value of currencies between different countries. Locate the current exchange rates in a newspaper or on the Internet. Using these exchange rates, compute the value of $20,000 $US expressed in Canadian dollars, Mexican pesos, and Japanese yen.

1.2

goals

+ List banking activities that contribute to economic stability.

+ Explain how banking expands the economy.

terms

+ identity theft

+ creditworthy

Role of Banks in the Economy

Banking Scene

As Edouard Ramirez thinks about how to use his paycheck, he begins to notice money and banking in the world around him. On the radio and television, he hears ads mentioning automobile deals and interest rates, and financing or refinancing plans for houses. He sees people using checks, debit cards, and credit cards as well as cash at the grocery store. Some even use an ATM in the store. When Edouard notices a clerk examining a twenty-dollar bill at a fast-food place, he begins to wonder about the nature of money itself. What other ways do banking functions play a role in Edouard's life?

BANKS AND ECONOMICS •

Money is a medium of exchange and the basis of the modern economy. Banks play a huge role in the distribution of funds throughout society. Although there are many institutions involved in the movement of money today, banks remain fundamental to the flow of money that maintains local, national, and global economies.

Banks and other institutions play this critical role by performing services essential to the functioning of an economy. Safeguarding, transferring, lending, and exchanging money in various forms, along with evaluating creditworthiness of customers, are the main functions that banks perform. Each of these roles has a ripple effect in the economy that helps keep money moving.

Keeping Your Money Safe

Safeguarding the holdings of people may be the oldest bank function. Long before banks existed, people looked for ways to secure their valuables, whatever the medium of exchange. Many of these you may easily imagine. In some societies, such as Babylonia about 2000 B.C., people began to store money in temples, perhaps because they thought others would be less likely to steal from houses of gods. Ancient records indicate that about 4,000 years ago temples were in the business of lending and exchanging money. At that time, temples were acting as banks.

You may think of a bank vault or a safe-deposit box when you think of safeguarding money, and those on-site measures are certainly ways of protecting valuable assets. Yet there is much more to safeguarding money than simply storing it in a secure place.

PHOTODISC/GETTY IMAGES

- **Record keeping is an important part of securing your money.** Banks devote much time and attention to both the practice and technology of maintaining and storing accurate records. If banks expect you to let them hold and use your money, they know you expect them to keep careful track of it. The same principle applies to large transactions between banks and industry and between banking institutions and the government.

- **Identification is an important security function of banking.** Obviously, you don't want unauthorized people walking in and taking money from your account, but the issue of security and identification goes far beyond the local branch. Identifying theft is a growing concern in the economy, and bank officials work closely with technology experts and law-enforcement agencies to prevent various forms of **identity theft**. Identity theft occurs when someone achieves financial gain by using another person's personal information to unlawfully assume the identity of the other person. An identity thief conducts transactions illegally for personal gain. With the increased reliance on the Internet for financial transactions, identity theft protections extend beyond conventional checking accounts to include on-line banking, automatic bill pay, and online shopping.

- **Enforcement is a part of safeguarding money that involves catching those who attempt to take it.** Not only does this function involve physical security, but it also includes tracking down fraud, making collections, and pursuing legal actions against those who inflict losses on the bank. Robbers, white-collar embezzlers, or people who default on loans are all included in the group targeted by enforcement efforts.

- **Transfer security is important to banks.** Although cash is still an important part of bank transactions, most money moves merely on computer screens. High-tech security measures are increasingly more critical to banking operations between banks and customers, between banks and banks, and between banks and the government. As all financial intermediaries become more dependent on electronic banking, technological security takes a on a more significant role.

- **Sound business practices also safeguard your money.** Most of these involve good judgment and management of daily bank operations. Banks invest time and money to train employees in procedures and practices. Training goals include ensuring accuracy, encouraging good decision-making regarding creditworthiness of perspective customers, and teaching how to make sound financial decisions.

- **Federal and/or state bank examiners closely review the records of banks to protect consumers.** Their examinations include not only the accuracy of records but also the prudence of banks' policies. These thorough examinations may take a week or more for a small bank, and a much longer time for a larger institution.

You can see how these various ways of safeguarding your money work together within the local bank and the banking community at large to create a more secure financial environment. This system of checks and balances is important to the economy and to society.

✔ checkpoint

Name six ways banks safeguard your money.

SPREADING THE WEALTH ●

Banks are critical to the economy. Although there are many ways that money moves around the economy, banks play a central role in establishing the financial environment. Transferring money to provide growth and stabilizing the monetary supply are important functions performed by banks. Lending by banks makes money available to consumers and businesses to make purchases they might not otherwise be able to make, or at least not for a very long time. Banks also help determine the creditworthiness of prospective customers so that good money is not lost on bad loans.

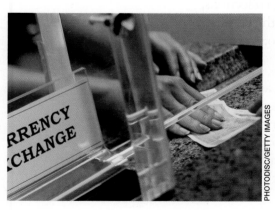

Transferring

Banks move money. They move it between banks, between banks and individual customers, between banks and industry, between banks and governments, and sometimes between governments. Sometimes the sums involved are huge. This motion of money throughout the nation and the world allows businesses to have access to capital. With capital to invest, businesses expand, job creation occurs, products get manufactured, services are performed, and the economy grows. This large-scale transfer of assets is a feature of the modern economy particularly in an age of fierce competition and globalization. Industries seek out financing wherever they can find it, and banks seek out investment opportunities wherever they may be.

In international banking, exchange rates measure the relative strength of one form of currency against another. These variable rates are often indications of the strength of a nation's economic position.

The ability to transfer sums of money between financial institutions safely and effectively depends on the stability of the institutions, the stability of the countries where the banks reside, and the security of the money supply itself.

Lending

Need a new car? Reach into your wallet and pull out $28,000. How about a new home? Do you have $246,000 in your piggy bank? Most people don't, of course, and bank lending is the main reason that people are able to own homes and cars without waiting forever to buy them.

Lending makes up most of a bank's business. Many bank deals are more complex than automobile or home loans. In fact, banks lend money to businesses and governments in a wide variety of ways, with loan duration

flat world...

The European Union and the Euro

In Europe, banking has changed dramatically in the past decade. European nations have been working since 1958 to provide a single market and single banking structure. The European Union (EU) consists of 27 nations. On January 4, 1999, these nations began using the euro, an agreed-upon currency with stable values among the nations. For example, a euro is always worth 6.55957 French francs, the same way a dollar is always worth ten dimes, regardless of the overseas value of a dollar.

Twenty EU member countries use the euro. A few nonmember nations also use the euro.

The implications for banking were huge. Although recognizing the primacy of a host country's banking laws, member nations accepted common rules and a common central bank, the European Central Bank (ECB), for the euro. All government debt, stock quotes, prices, and monetary policies were referenced in euros. Results have been mixed so far, as differing laws in countries have affected the flow of capital, but with the pressures of technology and globalization increasing, the EU may eventually bring about price stability, increased banking efficiency, and more services for member nations and their neighbors.

Think Critically
What are the advantages of using a common currency for member nations? Why might some nations be reluctant to do so? Do you think there will ever be a world currency? Why or why not?

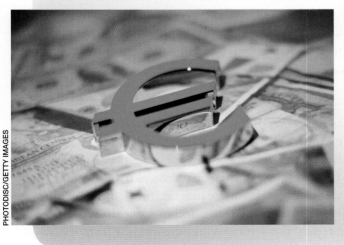

ranging from a single day to decades. A variety of loan products provide many choices for banks to transfer money in the economy. In the far-ranging and fast-shifting world of banking, strong management skill and a thorough understanding of finance are required.

Credit cards issued by banks are another form of lending, and they are not only good business for the bank, they help the economy. People buy things with credit, and keep merchandise moving and manufacturing producing at a more rapid rate than if transactions had to take place in cash. Although there is risk in the unwise use of credit cards by consumers, the judicious use of credit stimulates the economy.

Home loans still constitute an important part of the banking business, too. Loan decisions need to be made in a healthy, rational way to borrowers who are qualified for the loans they obtain. The mortgage loan crisis that began escalating in the summer of 2007 illustrates the fundamental importance of a healthy, stable mortgage market in the U.S. economy. As the mortgage crisis escalates, the ripple effect of loan defaults can be seen in all areas of the economy—from the impact on the personal lives of individual homeowners, to businesses that do not get paid, to municipalities that are faced with bearing the costs of maintaining the safety of abandoned properties.

People want to own their own homes and will work hard to do so. Matching appropriate loans to qualified buyers facilitates long-term home ownership. A healthy housing economy provides jobs for people who construct, furnish, and repair homes. Workers in construction industries want homes built, furnished, and repaired for themselves, and so the cycle of economic activity expands. Without bank lending, the cycle would be far smaller and slower. The automobile and housing industries have grown hand in hand with a solid banking industry, and the American economy has grown with it.

Creditworthiness

A **creditworthy** customer has a good credit rating, sufficient collateral for loans, and an ongoing income source sufficient to make timely loan payments. Evaluating the creditworthiness of customers, whether they are large industries, governments, or individual consumers, is a critical banking function that affects the economy. It is a good business practice for banks to evaluate loan applications carefully because their profits, and in some cases their survival, depend upon being repaid the principal and the interest from loans. If banks were to overextend themselves with uncollected loans, they could begin to fail, and if they fail, the economy is at risk. Bank failures played a role in the Great Depression. The mortgage loan crisis, which began in the summer of 2007, pushed the American economy to the brink of recession. Banking policies and regulations regarding creditworthiness and the ratio of loans to deposits help guarantee a secure financial environment. These policies also assure that businesses get paid for the things that consumers buy with bank funds.

Guaranteeing the Money

So what makes that piece of green paper that Edouard handed the cashier worth twenty dollars? The government guarantees the value of money, and the banks back up the guarantee. In the United States, banks and the government work together to form the banking system and to make sure the money supply is adequate, appropriate, and trustworthy. Much of this guarantee is backed through the central banking function of the Federal Reserve. Individual banks also work with the government to implement monetary policy, perform exchange functions for citizens, defeat counterfeiters of currency, and prevent identity theft.

In addition, banks guarantee their own policies. Networks of banks agree to honor credit cards. If you write a check on your account, you can be sure that the recipient of the check will get his or her money from your bank, providing you have sufficient funds in your account to cover the check amount. These actions make the transfer of money between citizens and businesses easy, which helps to keep the economy going.

The Substance of Society

The functions that banking institutions perform do more than move money through the economy. They also provide a common system. A great part of an economic system is psychological. It is your belief and trust in the financial system that makes you willing to borrow and pay later for a car, to invest money in businesses you've never seen, to deposit money in banks that is in turn loaned to people you don't know, or to take on a 30-year mortgage. Banks are at the heart of this financial system, and their effect on your life cannot be calculated.

NET Bookmark

Compare interest rates offered at local banks. Visit the website for MSN Money. Access www.cengage.com/school/pfinance/banking and click on the link for Chapter 1. Go to the Mortgage Loan Center. Search for mortgage rates by selecting your state, nearest city, type of loan, and feature that is most important to you. Are you surprised at the amount of variation in interest rates? Is there any reason you might choose an account with lower interest?

www.cengage.com/school/pfinance/banking

 checkpoint

How does lending stimulate the economy?

assessment 1.2

Think Critically

1. How do banks contribute to the stability of the society at large while safe-guarding the funds of their own customers?

_____

_____

_____

2. Governments don't routinely examine the books of many businesses. Poor business practices just put them out of business. Why should banks be treated any differently?

_____

_____

_____

3. In what ways have security issues for banks changed in the last 30 years?

_____

_____

Make Academic Connections

4. **TECHNOLOGY**   Banks have been using computer networks to transfer funds for some time. Customers can now get in on the act with online banking. Use the Internet or other reference materials to learn about secure servers. Summarize ways that Internet providers attempt to guarantee security and privacy.

_____

_____

_____

5. **HISTORY**   One banking function is guaranteeing the worth of money. One big historical change was the growth of paper money, which depended upon people believing that the paper was worth something. Research the history of paper currency. Choose an interesting example, and write a one-page report explaining the case.

6. **COMMUNICATION**   With a classmate, make a list of the most important services you want from a bank. Rank these services in order of importance. Compile a class list from the results of all pairs, and come to a consensus on the most important services wanted by customers.

How the Banking System Works

1.3

goals

+ Explain how banks acquire money to do business.

+ Identify new services that banks offer to stay competitive.

terms

+ depositor
+ spread
+ profit
+ asset
+ liquid asset
+ liability
+ return on assets (ROA)
+ return on equity (ROE)
+ equity
+ niche market
+ deregulation

Banking Scene

As he considers places to deposit his paycheck, Edouard Ramirez sees a bewildering array of offers from banks and other financial institutions. He recognizes that banks want his business, no differently from the electronics store where he bought an MP3 player or the grocery where his family shops. Unlike those stores, however, banks are selling services. He knows that banks are big businesses, but he wonders where they get their funds. He knows they make money on services, but how exactly does the bank earn its profit? What sources of information might Edouard use to find answers to these questions?

MONEY AT WORK

Despite their central role in the economy at large, banks are businesses. For their services, banks earn money in various ways. Banks also have income from other sources, but most of their money comes from lending— or, to be more precise, the loan interest paid by borrowers.

When banks lend money, they put it to work. The money that people borrow goes to buy products or services, to manufacture goods, and to start businesses. In this way, the money that banks lend works to keep the economy going.

The Spread

People who put money into banks are called **depositors**. Banks encourage deposits by protecting the money and by paying the depositor *interest*, a percentage of revenue earned on the principal over a period of time. The depositor thus earns some money from the deposits. Using the accumulated funds of many depositors, the bank makes loans to customers it considers likely to repay. The bank charges more interest on the money it lends than it pays depositors, so when the money is repaid, more comes in than went out. The difference between what a bank pays in interest and what it receives in interest is the **spread**, or *net interest income*.

	Revenue
−	Cost
=	**Profit**

The spread is not pure profit. The spread is income, or *revenue*, but costs have yet to be considered. Costs include maintaining the security of your money, personnel expenses, building maintenance costs, and so forth. **Profit,** or *net income*, is what's left of revenue after costs are deducted. What happens if a homeowner can't repay a loan? With the loss of these funds, the bank loses the ability to earn money on the loan.

What happens to your prior deposits if after two months a tree falls on your roof and you need to withdraw your $10,000 savings? The bank has loaned it to another homeowner, but it must have reserves to meet the obligation of your $10,000 withdrawal. It's not really the same money. The bank has other depositors, not all of whom, the bank hopes, need their money at once. Even if they did, the bank has a backup, the Federal Reserve System.

Other Funds

Banks have additional income sources. In addition to loan income, including credit-card interest, they also charge for various services. Charges include fees for rental of safe-deposit boxes, checking account maintenance, online bill payment, and ATM transactions. It is important to note that banks do not earn interest on money kept on hand for services such as ATM transactions. Thus, banks charge fees to offset lost interest. To keep pace with the rising cost of servicing accounts, fees for services have increased significantly. These service fees provide substantial revenues for banks.

Banks, like people and other corporations, make money on investments. Especially since the early 1980s, banks have become large and careful

Banking Math *Connection*

Calculate the one-year spread for a bank that receives a deposit of $10,000 from a customer and lends it out to a homeowner who needs to make some repairs. Assume the bank pays a straight 6% per year interest to the customer and charges 12% per year for the loan.

Solution

The formula for calculating the spread is

Income from interest − Interest paid to depositors = Spread
Income from interest: 12% × $10,000 = $1,200
Interest to depositor: 6% × $10,000 =   600
                                                   Spread = $600

The spread is $600. This is a simplified example and does not take into account compounding, declining balances, or other factors that affect deposits and loans in the real world.

investors in some types of securities and government bonds. Because banks can at times invest large amounts of money, they can do well, but they face the same risks as other investors. The speed of modern communication allows banks to move their investments quickly if necessary. Even a day or two of a large investment can yield a good return. Professional investment staffs work hard to make every dollar return a profit in the financial market.

Because most banks are corporations, banks may have funds from stockholder investments to use. Stockholders buy bank shares, hoping to receive a return on them and get a say in how the bank does business.

Assets and Liabilities

Why aren't deposits themselves a form of bank income? The money in them doesn't really belong to the bank. You may not like to think of your savings account as a problem for the bank, but it is one in theory. If depositors simultaneously want all their money from all their accounts, banks would be in trouble.

PHOTODISC/GETTY IMAGES

An **asset** is anything of value. In financial terms, that usually means money. A **liquid asset** is anything that can readily be exchanged, like cash. A **liability**, in financial terms, is a cash obligation. If you borrowed $5 from a friend for lunch, you have a liability of $5 and your friend has an asset of $5. The asset's liquidity depends on how quickly you've agreed to repay the sum and how reliable you are.

For banks, deposits are liabilities. Depositors have the right to request their funds, and the bank must pay them. Money the bank borrowed is also a liability, a debt to be paid.

A bank's assets are its loans and investments, which may be less liquid by contract than deposits. Deposits may have to be returned any time, but assets can arrive in small amounts over a long period.

Because banks have more money out working than they keep on hand, two principles of the banking business come into play.

- **A bank's liabilities exceed its reserves.** The money is loaned out, and the reserves don't match the total of deposits (liabilities). However, the money is out working, financing businesses and expanding the economy.

- **A bank's liabilities are more liquid than its assets.** A bank must give depositors their money if they request it. The bank's assets, however, may be less liquid because they are tied up in longer-term loans, so the bank can't get them as quickly. If many depositors need their money at once, the bank must either break its promise to depositors or pay until its reserves are gone. If the bank fails, unpaid depositors lose their money. In the United States, deposit insurance, backed by the government since 1934, has kept people from fearing the loss of their deposits. A "run on the banks," when people call for their money all at once, is rare.

Faulty Investment Strategies

A problem for banks has been faulty investment strategies. Especially in international banking, some banks have sometimes invested substantial amounts of money in questionable businesses or complicated financial products. If those businesses fail, the banks don't get their assets. A crisis in the Asian economy in the late 1990s nearly destroyed the Asian banking system, which was neither carefully funded nor controlled. A crisis in the U.S. mortgage lending markets, which began in the summer of 2007, impacted foreign investors with investments in the mortgage market. In the first quarter of 2008, fraudulent investments by a trader at a French bank resulted in a massive sell-off of faulty investments that impacted international financial markets.

Banking today is not as simple as earning interest on the spread. Rapidly changing conditions, complex factors, a 24-hour-a-day global economy, and financial interdependency among nations set the banking climate.

Tests of Bank Profitability

Information from financial statements, which report a bank's assets, liabilities, and net income, can be used to determine its profitability—a necessary condition for survival. Of the various profitability tests, two commonly used are *return on assets* and *return on equity*.

Return on assets (ROA) is the ratio of net income to total assets. It indicates how well bank management used its total amount of assets (loans and investments) to earn income. ROA is also interpreted as the amount earned for each $1 in assets.

As an example, Hometown Bank (HB) has net income of $10,000 ($220,250 revenue − $210,250 in expenses). HB has total assets of $171,500 and total liabilities of $100,000. HB's ROA is calculated using net income from the financial statement as follows:

Net income ÷ Total assets = Return on assets
$10,000　　 ÷ $171,500　 = 0.058 or 5.8% ROA (5.8 cents on the dollar)

Another important ratio is **return on equity (ROE)**, which measures how well a bank is using its equity (also called stockholders' equity). **Equity** represents net assets, or total assets, minus total liabilities. HB's ROE is:

Net income ÷ Total equity = Return on equity
$10,000　　 ÷ $71,500　 = 0.139 or 13.9% ROE (13.9 cents on the dollar)

ROA and ROE are of particular interest to stockholders (investors). ROA measures how efficiently the bank is using its assets to generate revenue. ROE represents the amount or return earned on each dollar invested. Investors can compare a bank's ROA and ROE to those of other banks to see how it performed relative to the other banks. A bank's ratios for several years can be reviewed to determine whether they have remained the same, increased, or decreased. A bank's ratios that decrease or stay the same are cause for concern.

✔ checkpoint

Name three sources of bank income. What is a bank's spread?

_____

_____

BANKS WORKING FOR YOU •••••••••••••••••••••••

Like any business, a bank must attract customers in order to make money. Banking has changed radically in the last 20 years, and it is now one of the most competitive businesses in the world. Today, large regional banks may have huge resources, and when these giants compete, consumers can sometimes be the winners. Smaller banks that target particular consumers work in **niche markets**, targeting particular customers in defined locations or by particular services. They use the flexibility that sometimes comes with smaller size to their advantage.

Although there are fewer commercial banks than there were ten years ago, there is an ever-wider array of services. It was not always so. You'll learn more about the history of U.S. banking in Chapter 2, but one consequence of the Great Depression of the 1930s was heavy regulation of banking. Banks could make good profits simply on the spread, for there were fewer financial options for consumers.

In the early 1980s, however, interest rates rose for all types of debts and investments. Banks were still paying only 5½ to 5¾ percent, as prescribed by law. Consumers, who could get 10 to 14 percent on other investments such as mutual funds, began removing their money from banks or depositing it elsewhere. Some banks (primarily savings and loans associations) had trouble, and with their problems the American economy was at risk. A series of laws passed in the early 1980s loosened the restrictions on bankers and let them compete in the open market like other financial businesses. This loosening of government control, called **deregulation**, changed the banking environment in the United States completely.

Changes in Traditional Services

One of the most obvious changes in banking was a new focus on consumers. Banks were not as customer-oriented as they are now and advertising was far different. They often kept the so-called "banker's hours" of 9:00 a.m. to 3:00 p.m., were closed on Saturdays, and were sometimes closed Wednesdays. That way of doing business is a fading memory, as banks keep doors and windows open longer and have branches in more places than ever. Innovations such as drive-up windows with extended hours took on more importance as banks scrambled to attract customers. Many banks are now open six days a week, and bank operations at most banks run twenty-four hours a day, seven days a week. Also, many banks have opened branches in

interesting *facts*

The word *bank* comes from the Italian word *banco*, or bench, from which money changers in medieval Italy carried on their business in the marketplace. ■

retail stores and shopping centers, making it more convenient for consumers to access their services.

In addition, changes in traditional services help keep customers. These are the promotions you may often see in banking advertisements today. Several types of checking accounts, for example, are typically available at a single institution, as banks tailor their offerings to match consumer needs. No-cost checking above a minimum balance, overdraft protection, interest-bearing accounts, no-frills checking accounts, or a custom-tailored mix of features let customers pick an account to suit their wishes and balances.

Traditional savings accounts still exist too, but so do other savings options. A variety of ways to compound interest maximizes the money customers can earn, or they may place funds in special accounts, such as money-market accounts that may offer higher interest rates.

Marketing is an ever more important matter to banks in today's environment. Bank personnel often become experts in certain services, and selling is now an important part of any banker's job. Small community banks often offer excellent personal service, important to survival in a niche market, on such personalized traditional services as trust accounts and safe-deposit boxes.

New Services

One of the biggest effects of deregulation was that banks got into new areas of business. Banks began offering financial services such as credit cards, innovative lending options, and technology-related services.

Credit Cards   Banks (or their holding companies) are facilitators in the credit card business in a big way. This profitable field is a form of lending that has greatly expanded in the last few years. Some economists worry that

tech talk

Intranet

You know about the Internet, of course, but do you know what an *intranet* is? An intranet is a private network that uses Internet software to store information for internal use by a company. Essentially, an intranet is a collection of web sites to which only specified users can gain access. Passwords, software security measures, and data encryption protect the intranets from unauthorized use. Intranets make it possible for employees to use the resources on them with standard Internet browsers. Banks routinely use intranets to provide a centralized source for everything from updated forms to training materials to their recent financial performance.

Think Critically   In an industry that needs to keep current with changes ranging from legal requirements to fluctuating interest rates, how can the use of an intranet streamline the operating efficiency of a bank?

the growth in this business comes at the expense of saving, perhaps a recipe for long-term trouble. Still, banks compete fiercely for this business and offer varying forms and types of credit-card accounts. Many banks change or negotiate rates with consumers, and special low-rate promotions are a daily fact of credit card life.

Innovative Lending New types of lending are also made available to consumers. A recent boom in second-mortgage loans has brought a wave of new business. These loans, called home-equity loans, are secured by the difference between the value of a home and the amount the homeowner still owes on it. The loans may take the form of a special credit card, a line of credit, or a single disbursement. They have become a popular form of credit because the interest on them is tax-deductible for the consumer.

Reverse mortgages allow consumers age 62 or older to utilize the equity from their homes by receiving payments from a lender based on the value of the equity. These payments can be received either in monthly installments, in a lump sum, or as a line of credit. Typically the equity does not need to be paid back until the home is sold.

Technology Tools Probably the flashiest new services banks offer involve technology. The revolution in computers and telecommunications affected banks dramatically and helped drive a reliance on Internet-based transactions. New and expanded services based on a blend of technologies are now available.

PHOTODISC/GETTY IMAGES

- **Automated teller machines (ATMs)** were the first of the high-tech revolutions for consumers. First appearing as novelties in the late 1960s, ATMs have made "banker's hours" irrelevant. Customers can now perform almost any banking function from an ATM, and have access to their accounts day or night. Networked ATMs have made it possible to do business with one's bank at any time from almost anywhere in the world. ATMs reduce transaction costs, encourage the use of the bank, and earn income from fees. ATMs are available in a variety of venues, including shopping centers, amusement parks, universities, airports, sports arenas, and workplaces. Because ATMs are everywhere, using an ATM, which often intimidated early customers, is today a common and casual act that most people take for granted.

- **Smart cards** are credit, debit, or other types of cards that have embedded microchips. Smart cards are useful for a wide variety of "electronic purse" applications, which allow the card to store a value. When the card is used, the stored value decreases. You may have used these already in grocery or video-rental stores. Gift cards, security cards, and customer loyalty reward cards are also examples of smart cards. Consumers should use smart cards cautiously. In November 2007, in conjunction with the start of the holiday shopping season, *Consumer Reports* placed an ad in *The New York Times* advising consumers that in the prior year consumers lost $8 billion dollars due to unredeemed gift cards. Although smart cards do provide many conveniences, consumers should take care to examine the fees and terms (including expiration dates) associated with the cards.

- **Payroll cards** are a specific type of smart card. Banks can facilitate salary payments between employers and employees. By using a bank as an intermediary, payroll cards enable an employer to load salary payments onto an employee's smart card. Employees can then access their pay even if they do not have a bank account.

- **Online banking** takes advantage of growing Internet use. Whether called Internet banking, electronic banking, home banking, or PC banking, online banking allows customers to perform banking transactions from their home computers. Everything from balance inquiries to bill paying to applying for a loan may be available online at any time. Some banks use Internet technology in intranets, and others simply provide a dial-in service to their mainframe computer. Online services can be complicated and costly to set up, and some consumers are not comfortable using computers for private matters such as banking. The future is bright for online banking, though, as security systems improve, software applications become more sophisticated, and a new generation of customers comfortable with the technology matures.

- **Mobile banking** has grown in popularity as reliance on sophisticated cell phones and related technology has grown. Consumers can execute a variety of banking transactions with mobile phones. Customers can check their account balances, make requests for payments, and even receive updates regarding their accounts on their mobile phones.

The new services and the new environment for banking offer both challenges and rewards to consumers and bankers alike. Opportunities to handle money more efficiently and effectively for both are increasing, and they offer possibilities unimagined just a few years ago. They also require a thorough understanding of how the system and its tools work, and how money moves in an increasingly complex economy.

 checkpoint

What changes have deregulation and competition brought to modern banking?

assessment 1.3

Think Critically

1. How does the fact that consumers have many choices for places to put their money affect the banking industry?

2. Savings deposits today are smaller by percentage than they once were. Why do you think some economists feel that this is a risk to the economy?

3. What reasons might some people have for not taking full advantage of today's banking services and technology?

4. How might smart-card technology reduce the number of cards in a consumer's wallet or purse?

Make Academic Connections

5. **BANKING MATH** If you had $8,400 placed in an account that earned 5½ percent interest, paid just once a year, how much money would be in the account at the end of four years, assuming you made no withdrawals of any kind from the account?

6. **TECHNOLOGY** Find out more about online and mobile banking. Visit the online site of three banks of your choice. Many online banking sites offer a demonstration of how the system works. List the services available on the sites, including whether mobile banking services are offered. Identify what is needed to enroll in online and mobile banking.

1.4

goals

+ Define depository financial institutions.

+ Explain nondepository financial institutions.

terms

+ depository intermediaries

+ nondepository intermediaries

+ wholesale bank

Other Financial Institutions

Banking Scene

Deciding how to manage his earnings, Edouard Ramirez has investigated various local banks and learned about their services. He has an uncle who works at a nearby college and is a member of the college's credit union. He mentions to Edouard that credit unions can perform many of the same functions of a bank, although some of the terms may be different. Edouard wants to learn more about credit unions. What other types of financial institutions act as intermediaries to help people handle money?

DEPOSITORY INTERMEDIARIES

A bank is a financial intermediary for the safeguarding, transferring, exchanging, or lending of money. There are two primary types of financial institutions. **Depository intermediaries** are those that get funds from the public and use them to finance their business. **Nondepository intermediaries** are those that do not take or hold deposits. They earn their money selling specific services or policies.

Depository intermediaries receive deposits from customers and use the money to run their businesses. These institutions may have other sources of income, but the bread and butter of their business is handling deposits, paying interest on them, and lending money based on those deposits. There are four main types of depository institutions. Although there are fewer differences today than in the past, some important distinctions remain.

Commercial Banks

You have been working with concepts and services based mostly on commercial banks throughout this chapter. One of the big distinctions between commercial banks and other depository institutions is that commercial banks are owned by stockholders who expect a profit on their investments. Today commercial banks may work with both businesses and individuals. Commercial banks that specialize only in business banking are sometimes called **wholesale banks.**

Savings and Loan Associations

Savings and loan associations (S&Ls) may go by various names. Building and loan associations, homestead banks, and cooperative banks are all names for savings and loan associations. Savings and loan associations receive most of their deposits from individuals. Chartered by either state or federal governments, these institutions grew by focusing on real-estate lending for people. Today, they offer most of the same services as commercial banks. Savings and loan associations are owned not by outside investors, but by depositors themselves, who receive shares of the company.

Mutual Savings Banks

Mutual savings banks are similar to savings and loan associations. They receive deposits primarily from individuals and concentrate also on private real-estate mortgages. Mutual savings banks are owned by depositors as well. These state-chartered banks are sometimes granted greater powers with regard to assets and liabilities than S&Ls, but usually not as much as those of commercial banks.

Mutual savings banks and savings and loan associations are sometimes called *thrift institutions*. Few remain as a result of a crisis in the industry in the 1980s. These institutions are regulated and protected by the state or federal government, which is not necessarily true of nondepository intermediaries.

Credit Unions

Credit unions also are owned by depositors, but there are a couple of key differences. First, users of credit unions must be members. Membership is usually based on some type of association, such as a common employer, a certain line of work, a geographical region, or even a social or religious

© LAWRENCE MANNING/CORBIS

affiliation. Second, credit unions are *not-for-profit* financial institutions that exist to benefit the members. Any money beyond costs is returned to the members in the form of dividends on savings, reduced fees for services, or lower rates for loans.

 checkpoint

What is a wholesale bank? What is the primary difference between credit unions and other depositor-owned financial institutions?

NONDEPOSITORY INTERMEDIARIES

As the name suggests, nondepository intermediaries don't take deposits. Instead, they perform other financial services and collect fees for them as their primary means of business. In many cases, these institutions are private companies. Although they may be regulated by the government, they are usually not backed or protected by the government.

Insurance Companies

You might not think of insurance companies as financial institutions, but they are. Insurance companies make money on the policies they sell, which protect against financial loss and/or build income for later use. The policies are not tangible and the protection they offer is financial, so the com-

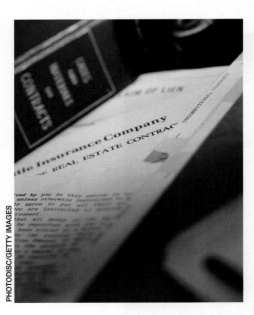

panies are performing a financial service. Some types of insurance policies have a cash value that can be redeemed at any time, and some policies let customers remove cash gradually. Although insurance companies do not typically make loans, in some cases the cash value of a policy may be used to secure a loan from elsewhere. Insurance premiums (costs) are not deposits. Private insurance companies try to earn a profit from the premiums beyond the cost of insurance payouts. Many professional money managers regard insurance as essential financial protection, but not a good investment.

Trust Companies/Pension Funds

Companies that administer pension or retirement funds also perform financial services. These companies manage money for a fee and promise in return to provide future income. Some pension funds are closely regulated, but others may not be. Growth for the contributor comes not from interest on deposits, but investments made by the administrator. These investments may yield a profit, but there is a risk of loss as well.

Brokerage Houses

Brokers are people who execute orders to buy and sell stocks and other securities. They are paid commissions. Their service is to help investors do as well as possible with their investments. Brokerage houses may offer advice or guidance, but are private companies who make a profit on the transactions.

Loan Companies

Loan companies, sometimes called finance companies, are not banks. They do not receive deposits, and they should not be confused with banks, savings and loan associations, or credit unions. They are private companies who lend money and make a profit on the interest. Loan companies sometimes make loans to customers when other institutions will not, but they charge higher interest rates to offset the risk.

Payday Loans

A specific form of loan company focuses on payday loans. These companies offer extremely short-term loans against an expected paycheck or other check at high interest rates. Other names for these loans include deferred deposit check loans, check advance loans or post-dated check loans.

Ethics in Action

Banks are required by law to offer their products and services on an equal opportunity basis. According to the Federal Trade Commission, the Equal Credit Opportunity Act (ECOA) ensures that all consumers are given an equal chance to obtain credit. This doesn't mean all consumers who apply for credit get it. Factors such as income, expenses, debt, and credit history are considerations for creditworthiness.

What the law guarantees is that all applicants be treated fairly. Applications for credit cannot be evaluated on the basis of sex, race, marital status, national origin, or religion.

Think Critically

Banks want to attract and keep customers. Why do you think a law like ECOA might have become necessary?

Payday loans usually require an upfront fee that is immediately deducted from the loan amount. Exorbitantly high interest rates are common for payday loans. Although disclosure of the effective annual percentage rate (APR) is required by law, consumers who utilize this type of loan may not fully understand the financial consequences of using this type of financing.

Many online sites are available to facilitate obtaining payday loans. Many even sweeten the offer by providing direct deposit of the loan to a consumer's banking account. However, these same loan providers often require authorization for automatic withdrawal of the funds from the consumer's bank account on a predesignated date. These companies also may perform some of the same services as currency exchanges.

Currency Exchanges

Currency exchanges do not make loans or receive deposits. Currency exchanges are private companies that cash checks, sell money orders, or perform other exchange services. They charge a fee, usually a percentage of the amount exchanged. Because their business depends on these fees, interest rates are usually higher than at banks or other financial institutions. Currency exchanges often locate in areas where no other financial intermediaries exist, and they offer the only financial services available to people in those areas.

A wide range of financial services is available from both depository and nondepository intermediaries. Most of the nondepository institutions are private companies earning money by performing specific services. You don't make deposits, earn interest, or have checking or savings accounts with them. Nondepository institutions are a part of the financial world and help move money through the economy. However, they are not part of the banking system and may not really be considered to be in the business of banking.

✔ checkpoint

Why is an insurance company considered a financial intermediary? What is the primary difference between depository institutions and most nondepository institutions?

assessment 1.4

Think Critically

1. Services from depository institutions have become similar since deregulation. Why is there any need for different forms of depository institutions?

2. Credit unions are not-for-profit institutions. They return profits to members. Why wouldn't everyone place their money only in credit unions?

3. Do you think payday loans and currency exchanges take advantage of those who do not have access to other forms of financial services? Why or why not?

4. How does the fact that the government backs many forms of depository institutions affect the confidence of consumers about their deposits?

Make Academic Connections

5. **SOCIAL SCIENCE** Until late in the twentieth century, the financial world was male territory and not ethnically diverse. Contact a large bank and learn what policies they have in place to guarantee and encourage equal opportunity careers, for both genders and all races, in the banking profession. List some of those policies.

6. **HISTORY** Although services offered seem similar today, there was once a great difference between thrift institutions and banks. Find out more about the way these institutions arose to meet a particular social need. Write a one-page report about the beginnings of savings and loans, credit unions, and mutual savings banks.

chapter 1 assessment

Chapter Summary

1.1 Introduction to Banking
A. Banks are financial intermediaries that safeguard, transfer, exchange, and lend money. Commercial, retail, and central banks are three main types.
B. Mergers, technology, and competition have reshaped banking.

1.2 Role of Banks in the Economy
A. Banks safeguard our money through various business practices that protect, record, and evaluate banking transactions and businesses.
B. Banks expand the economy by transferring and lending funds to creditworthy borrowers, thus supporting markets and providing economic stimulus for jobs.

1.3 How the Banking System Works
A. Banks make money on the spread between interest paid and received. Bank assets include earnings and investments. Deposits are liabilities. ROA and ROE are two ratios used to measure a bank's profitability.
B. Bank deregulation brought expansion of customer services. New services banks offer to stay competitive involve credit cards, new types of loans, smart cards, online banking, and mobile banking.

1.4 Other Financial Institutions
A. Depository intermediaries include banks, savings and loan associations, mutual savings banks, and credit unions. Most of these are backed by the government.
B. Nondepository institutions include insurance companies, trust companies, brokerage houses, loan companies, and currency exchanges. Most of these are private firms not part of the national banking system.

Vocabulary Builder

Choose the term that best fits the definition. Write the letter of the answer in the space provided. Some terms may not be used.

a. asset
b. central banks
c. commercial bank
d. creditworthy
e. depositor
f. depository intermediary
g. deregulation
h. equity
i. financial intermediary
j. identity theft
k. liability
l. liquid asset
m. medium of exchange
n. niche market
o. nondepository intermediary
p. profit
q. retail bank
r. return on assets (ROA)
s. return on equity (ROE)
t. spread
u. wholesale bank

____ 1. The difference between interest paid and interest received
____ 2. A private company that does not receive deposits but sells financial services
____ 3. Government banks that regulate and manage money supply
____ 4. The ratio of net income to total assets
____ 5. Most common form of government-backed corporate bank
____ 6. To banks, deposits represent this type of obligation
____ 7. The loosening of government control
____ 8. Anything of value that can be readily exchanged
____ 9. Revenue minus cost
____ 10. An agreed-upon system for measuring value of goods and services
____ 11. Net income ÷ Total equity
____ 12. Total assets − Total liabilities

Review Concepts

13. Why are banks called financial intermediaries?

_____

_____

_____

14. List four functions that banks perform.

_____

_____

_____

15. Name three trends in recent banking history.

_____

_____

_____

16. List four ways that banks safeguard money.

_____

_____

_____

17. How do banks help expand and maintain the economy?

_____

_____

_____

18. Why is a deposit considered a liability for a bank?

_____

_____

_____

19. How might investors evaluate a bank's ROA and ROE ratios?

_____

_____

_____

20. What has been the effect of competition between banks?

_____

_____

21. Name five types of technological innovations in banking.

_____

_____

22. Name two types of thrift institutions.

_____

_____

23. What is a nondepository financial institution?

_____

_____

_____

Apply What You Learned

24. Why are banks regulated and protected by government?

_____

_____

25. What are advantages and disadvantages of mergers in banking?

_____

_____

_____

_____

26. How did deregulation ultimately result in more banking services for consumers?

_____

_____

27. Would consumers be better off if all public utilities, including electric and gas companies, were deregulated so that the marketplace could set prices?

_____

_____

28. Consumer debt is higher than ever in the United States. What would happen if people suddenly simply stopped borrowing from banks?

_____

_____

29. How has the U.S, mortgage crisis affected both the U.S. economy and the international economy?

_____

_____

_____

_____

30. If private, nondepository loan companies charge higher interest than depository institutions backed by government, how do they stay in business?

Make Academic Connections

31. **PROBLEM SOLVING**   Most insurance is bought to protect against the possibility of loss, except life insurance. Everybody who buys life insurance eventually dies. Explain how life insurance works.

32. **ADVERTISING**   Analyze five bank advertisements from a variety of media, such as newspapers, magazines, radio, television, billboards, and the Internet. What do banks do to get your business? Keep a journal for one week, noting each advertiser, the services being advertised, and a basic description of each ad. Make a chart that shows your analysis.

33. **BANKING LAW**   *Usury* is the practice of charging extreme interest rates. From your library or the Internet, find out more about usury limits, what they are, how they work, and what the usury limits are in various states. Write a one-page report summarizing what you learn.

34. **ETHICS**   ATM fees are a source of revenue for banks. If you use an ATM from a bank different from your own, you may be charged a fee for the transaction both by the bank that owns the machine and by your own bank for processing the transaction. Does this seem fair to you? Why or why not?

35. **ETHICS**   Some lenders target the neediest consumers. The recent mortgage crisis was fueled, in part, by qualifying borrowers for loan amounts that exceeded their realistic ability to meet monthly payments. Likewise, payday loans charge exorbitant interest rates with high processing fees. Are the terms and conditions offered by these lenders fair and reasonable? Why or why not?

36. **CAREERS**   Visit the web site of a large regional bank. Find out what opportunities the bank offers to prospective employees. Make a list of some of the positions available and the training and experience required.

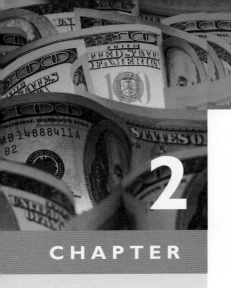

Development of the U.S. Banking System

2.1	Creation of a National Currency
2.2	Banking Before 1913
2.3	Modern Banking

ROB BARTEE/INDEX STOCK IMAGERY

From Web Content Consultant to Documentation Manager

While his children slept on the flight bringing them home from a hectic week at a Florida amusement park, Reza reflected on his career. After college, he had accepted a position at a diversified financial institution. Working as a web marketing consultant for the annuity and mutual funds division, he was responsible for developing and executing online marketing initiatives. Reza supported multiple products that were advertised on a variety of websites. He developed web content and designed site layouts. Ensuring that the written and visual elements complemented each other and functioned smoothly were a critical part of this position.

Reza had realized that job security could be improved by having a broad base of experiences developed by working in a variety of areas. An expanded personal network was another advantage of multiple positions.

Next Reza had accepted a job as an implementation technical consultant in the credit card division. Reza was responsible for assessing data technology needs, file specifications, and delivery methods. He streamlined processes and met with internal customers to determine electronic reporting formats for products.

Realizing that he wanted to move higher in the organization, Reza routinely reviewed internal job postings for supervisory positions. He had been delighted to pass the rigorous interview process for a job as a business technology supervisor in his company's trust division. In this role, Reza was responsible for application systems analysis and programming activities. After leading teams to conduct feasibility studies and time and cost estimates, Reza assigned members of his group to complete various components of the projects.

Reza's stellar reputation as an effective supervisor had led to a job offer as a network security manager. His team was responsible for developing systems and procedures that protected host and network systems from unauthorized access. He managed the creation of firewall security standards and intrusion detection procedures. The team perpetually evaluated the information technology (IT) infrastructure to identify new areas of risk.

After the birth of his twins, Reza had decided to scale back on his hours at the office. By working in his current position as an online training documentation manager, Reza was able to work from home three days a week. The flexibility in his schedule helped him and his wife manage childcare needs. In this position, Reza is responsible for overseeing the content development of online training courses, updating existing online courses, and writing and maintaining operational procedures.

Upper Rungs to Consider

Now that his children were older, Reza realized it was time to find a challenging onsite position. Management positions that Reza planned to look for included technology integration, IT project management, and network operations.

Preparing for the Climb

Over the course of a long career, are there ways to occasionally scale back to handle temporarily demanding life needs? What is the best way to stay involved in your field to make it easy to reenter the field?

PHOTODISC

2.1

goals

+ Identify different types of currency.

+ Explain how currency evolved through the early days of the United States to what it is today.

terms

+ currency

Creation of a National Currency

Banking Scene

When Katie Conlon finished high school, an aunt gave her a $100 bill for graduation. While writing a thank you note to her aunt, Katie took a good look at the bill. She had never thought too much about cash. How and why did currency start circulating in the United States? What part of the government prints money? Katie started checking the Internet to learn more. What websites would be good places to start looking?

WHAT IS CURRENCY? •

Money is a *medium of exchange* for people to use to trade things of value. Anything from fur to grain to metal can fill that role. In most places of the world, some form of money is the agreed-upon medium of exchange. So what is meant by the term "currency"?

Most people associate the word with paper money, and they're right. Strictly speaking, **currency** is all media of exchange circulating in a country. This definition includes coins as well as paper money. In today's society it also includes credit instruments, such as bonds, checks, and even some types of loan papers.

Classifying Currency

To keep terms straight, most economists make some other distinctions, dividing the term currency between coins, called *metallic currency*, and paper money or credit instruments, called *paper currency*. There are further terms for paper currency, depending upon who issued it. *Government currency* is money printed by a government. In some countries, banks issue notes against their reserves called bank notes, which are referred to as *bank currency*. Checks are also a form of currency, and they are called *deposit currency*, because that is how their value is redeemed.

Shifting Meanings

As with many financial concepts, the idea of currency has changed. Before World War I (1914–1918), many countries had governments that did not issue paper money. Paper currency meant only notes issued by large banks.

In the United States, however, paper currency meant the money that the government printed, and nothing else. Following the war, the idea of currency began to take on the broader sense in use today. In part, this wider sense was the result of changes in banking and economics that circulated a lot more forms of valuable paper, including the various credit instruments comprising the idea of currency today.

 checkpoint

What is currency?

_____

_____

THE GROWTH OF AMERICAN CURRENCY

An account of the earliest days of American currency is generally a history of a mixture of types of money—not unlike the mixture of people who came to populate the country. In the early days, some settlers used shells and nails to trade for what they needed, making them a kind of coinage. Pretty quickly, though, various types of money, both coins and paper, were circulating among the settlements that would one day rise up and create a nation.

Colonial Cash

Coins were the most common medium of exchange. Some British-type coins were minted on American soil as early as the 1650s, but few colonists trusted them. Foreign money was much more common. Though the

KEN CAVE/SHUTTERSTOCK

colonies did use English pounds and shillings, a Spanish dollar called the *real* was the most popular. Higher in silver content than other coins, the real was the most trusted form of currency in America. Early American coins were imitations of reals.

There was always some form of paper money in the colonies too. Much of it consisted of English or other foreign bank notes. Most of this paper money could be redeemed for coins, which were trusted far more than paper certificates.

During the Revolutionary War, the Continental Congress issued paper money to buy desperately needed supplies. Few people had any confidence in this currency. In fact, the scornful phrase "not worth a continental" referred for many years to any worthless item.

Currency in the United States

After the Revolutionary War, the new United States decided to replace the many colonial coins then circulating. The Mint Act of April 1792 authorized $10, $5, and $2.50 gold coins; $1, 50¢, 25¢, 10¢ and 5¢ silver coins; and 1¢ and 1/2¢ copper coins. The U.S. mint began operation in 1794, but many of the foreign coins remained in common circulation well into the 1830s.

The U.S. government did not print paper money itself until 1861. Before then, bank notes from two chartered Banks of the United States and from many different state banks were the only paper currency.

The many types of currency often caused problems. During the crisis of the Civil War, people became so concerned about the value of money that some stores even issued their own currency. The National Currency Act of 1863, later rewritten as the National Banking Act of 1864, established standards for currency. It also taxed state bank notes, making them unprofitable. State banks gradually got out of the business of issuing currency, and a system of national currency came into being. Problems with the money supply still persisted, though, and in 1913 the Federal Reserve Act established the basic banking system in use today.

U.S. Government Paper Currency Today

Amount	Portrait on Front
One dollar note	George Washington
Two dollar note	Thomas Jefferson
Five dollar note	Abraham Lincoln
Ten dollar note	Alexander Hamilton
Twenty dollar note	Andrew Jackson
Fifty dollar note	Ulysses S. Grant
One hundred dollar note	Benjamin Franklin

Five hundred, one thousand, five thousand, and ten thousand dollar notes have been unavailable from the Treasury since 1969. Last printed in 1945, these large denominations are still legal tender, although most are in the hands of collectors.

Sometimes there is a need for currency to evolve to reflect the state of the economy it serves. In 2006, there was a debate in the United States whether to discontinue the penny. A number of factors propelled this debate forward. As the price of zinc escalated, it cost one-and-a-half cents to produce a one-cent penny. As the cost of living increases, the relative value of the penny decreases. Despite these quantitative arguments, the penny continues to circulate in the United States economy.

More Than a Medium of Exchange

Currency does more than serve as a medium of exchange. Currency can provide a means for a country to provide recognition for individuals or events that are of historical significance to a country. For example, from 1999–2008, the U.S. Mint issued quarters commemorating each of the 50 U.S. states.

Sometimes the past is honored in the present. Access www.cengage.com/school/pfinance/banking and click on the link for Chapter 2. Visit the United States Mint site and learn about the $1 coin series that will commemorate personal contributions of Native Americans. The series is scheduled to begin in 2009 and run until at least 2016. How do you think Native Americans and the rest of American society will feel about these coins? Are there other groups or events you think worthy of similar commemoration?

www.cengage.com/school/pfinance/banking

Each state governor was allowed to decide how the quarter design process would work in his or her state. One state, Massachusetts, even held a competition among elementary school students to allow children the opportunity to participate in the design of the state's commemorative quarter. In addition to highlighting the particular characteristics of each state, the quarters also created additional demand for coinage. Collectors often strive to obtain the complete series of the coins, which they save in their personal collection. Coins that remain in private collections are removed from circulation, thus increasing the need for additional coins.

In contrast to the somewhat frequent design changes of U.S. coins, the portraits featured on United States paper currency have remained constant since 1928. Individuals of historical significance, who are no longer alive, are featured in the portraits. To meet evolving security needs, in 1996 some design changes were made to dollar bills to combat counterfeiting.

✔ checkpoint

What was the most common medium of exchange in Colonial America? When did the U.S. government begin to issue paper currency?

assessment 2.1

Think Critically

1. Why was early American currency a mixture of forms of money?

2. Outline the early history of money in the U.S. economy.

3. Why might people have distrusted the value of paper currency issued by the Continental Congress during the Revolutionary War?

4. Why might currencies issued by the many state banks have caused confusion before the Civil War?

5. List some reasons that might prompt design changes in currency.

Make Academic Connections

6. **HISTORY**   Another form of currency that didn't hold its value was currency issued by the Confederate States of America during its rebellion from the Union in the Civil War. Use the library, the Internet, or other research sources to learn more about Confederate currency. Write a one-page report that explains the problems that the Confederate States had with its currency and why it couldn't hold its value. What are specimens of Confederate currency worth today?

7. **SOCIAL STUDIES**   The U.S. Bureau of Engraving and Printing is responsible for printing currency for the U.S. government. Incorporated in the design of each note are symbols that represent ideas from American philosophy and identifying features of the particular note. Visit the Bureau's website at www.bep.treas.gov/ to learn more. Choose a note of some denomination, and create a chart or graphical representation that interprets and explains the symbols and features and what they mean.

8. **TECHNOLOGY**   Both metallic and paper currency are so common in society that hardly anyone gives them a second glance. Did you ever wonder how they are produced? Research sources of your choosing and create a written, oral, or computer presentation that explains the process used to make either paper or metallic currency.

Banking Before 1913

2.2

goals

+ Identify the reasons for the establishment and expiration of both the First and Second Banks of the United States.

+ Describe the continuing problems that led to the Federal Reserve Act.

terms

+ Federal Reserve Act

Banking Scene

When Katie Conlon moved from her home in New Jersey to attend college in Bloomington, Indiana, she wanted to set up a bank account in town. She saw advertisements for many banks, but two banks caught her eye. BankOne, a national bank, and the Peoples State Bank both offered services that looked more or less the same. What is the difference between a state bank and a national bank? How could she find out?

BANKS IN THE YOUNG UNITED STATES • • • • • • • • • • • •

In many ways, democracy in the new United States of America was an experiment. Never before had a country attempted such an enterprise. The young nation had to work its way through many problems of government, trying to find the right balance between the role of the government and the freedom of individuals. In a similar way, banking in the early United States also had an experimental quality. Some of the history of U.S. banking was a process of trial and error, and some of the issues were the result of struggles between competing ideas—just as in the nation at large.

The First Bank of the United States

George Washington's Secretary of the Treasury, Alexander Hamilton, believed that without a strong central government and a strong bank, the new nation would eventually fail. Hamilton encouraged the new government to accept and pay with interest not only the debts of the Revolutionary War, but also to assume responsibility for debts of individual states incurred in the struggle. In this way, the federal government established itself as the final authority for the economic security of the new nation.

Hamilton also urged the creation of a Bank of the United States. Thomas Jefferson, who believed creating such an institution gave too much power to too few people, fiercely opposed him in this idea. Over Jefferson's objections, the bank was chartered in 1791.

The first Bank of the United States was not an institution of government. The bank was privately held. Although the government owned about 20 percent of the bank, the rest was in the hands of private investors and foreign governments, to the continuing unhappiness of those who opposed it.

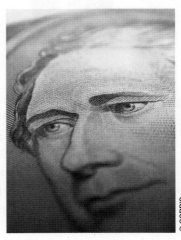

© CORBIS

As the chief depository of the U.S. government, the bank gained power. By 1805, the bank had eight branches. Its bank notes became the most common form of currency circulating in the United States. It exercised control on state-chartered banks, not by law but by demanding that state banks redeem their bank notes with gold or silver when they were deposited in the First Bank of the United States. Thus, the bank almost accidentally performed the role of a central bank. As the nation grew westward, more people resented the control of powerful Eastern bankers. When the bank's charter expired in 1811, there was not enough political support to renew it.

The Second Bank of the United States

Within five years, conflicting state bank policies and changing economic conditions caused Congress to reconsider. In 1816, Congress granted the second Bank of the United States a twenty-year charter. After a slow start, the bank began to do well under its president, Nicholas Biddle.

Biddle deliberately improved upon the central banking functions of regulating credit and the money supply, but had to do so by restraining state banks, who then saw the U.S. bank as an enemy. A new class of entrepreneurs and developers who thought regulation of money and credit supply not in their interest was gaining power. Rising resentment of what people saw as an aristocracy again spelled trouble for the bank.

President Andrew Jackson took office in 1828 and was an unyielding opponent of the bank. Jackson's chief rival, Senator Henry Clay, tried to renew the bank's charter four years early in 1832, hoping to make the renewal an election issue. Jackson vetoed the bill, arguing that the bank represented "the advancement of the few at the expense of the many." The bank did indeed become a campaign issue, but Jackson trounced Clay in the election.

The bank's charter still had four years to run. Determined to kill the bank that he saw as unconstitutional, Jackson forced the withdrawal of government funds from it, moving money instead to a number of state banks, which came to be called his "pet banks." The Second Bank of the United States weakened and died when its charter expired in 1836.

flat world...

The Bank of England

The Bank of England, one of the oldest central banks, was nationalized in 1946. The bank advises the government on monetary issues, but its freedom to act independently is limited. The bank implements the chosen monetary policy and performs other central banking functions, such as funding public borrowing, issuing bank notes, and managing reserves. It also deals with international banking issues on behalf of the government.

Think Critically
What are advantages of a central banking system entirely under the control of the government? What are the disadvantages?

✔ **checkpoint**

Why did the two first U.S. National banks fail?

_____

_____

STEPS TOWARD CENTRAL BANKING • • • • • • • • • • • • • •

In the absence of a national banking system, state banks grew in number and influence. Private banks sprang up, each with its own policies and currency. This fragmented system supplied money for the economy, but without some overriding control, chaos with credit and the money supply reigned. The Independent Treasury System, a network of federal offices that handled U.S. government money, could not manage the banking system adequately.

The National Banking Act of 1864

After the Civil War, rampant inflation threatened the entire economic system. The National Banking Act of 1864 was enacted. It established the office of the Comptroller of the Currency to issue charters to national banks. These banks were authorized to issue national bank notes. Each time a bank issued national currency, it was required to purchase an equivalent amount of U.S. Government bonds. This caused problems as the country was in a growth period and banks had to decide whether they were going to issue currency or make loans with the money they had on hand. State bank currencies died out because high taxes were assessed on them. To survive, state banks expanded their deposit functions and other services.

Continuing Issues Although the National Banking Act helped by establishing a national currency, it still did not address regulation of the credit and money supply, nor did it guarantee the safety of banks. Money supply problems occurred repeatedly, including crises and bank failures in 1873, 1883, 1893, and 1907. In 1913, the **Federal Reserve Act** created a system to stabilize the banking system. As part of the central banking system, the Federal Reserve provided a check collection system and flexible currency.

✔ **checkpoint**

What was the purpose of the National Banking Act of 1864?

_____

_____

assessment 2.2

Think Critically

1. Do you agree with Hamilton or Jefferson about the creation of a private bank to handle government banking? Explain your reasoning.

2. How did conflicting political views ultimately cause the demise of the first two Banks of the United States?

3. Prior to the Federal Reserve Act of 1913, what factors made the banking system and the economy unstable?

Make Academic Connections

4. **TECHNOLOGY** Counterfeiting is an ongoing problem associated with paper currency since the government first began printing it. Visit the U.S. Bureau of Engraving and Printing's website at www.bep.treas.gov/ to learn about anticounterfeiting measures. What challenges does modern technology present and what steps does the Bureau take to meet them?

5. **HISTORY** The battle between Hamilton and Jefferson over the Bank of the United States led to the formation of political parties. Find out how. In what way did the disagreement between Hamilton and Jefferson over the bank reflect two fundamentally different views of the union of states? How did this tension affect the growing economy of the United States?

6. **COMMUNICATION** In some ways, the argument over power and influence of monetary policy that raged in the early 1800s is still with us. Conduct a poll of classmates, friends, relatives, or your community members to find out whom the public thinks controls the economy. Ask how their opinions have changed as a result of the banking crisis of 2008. Compile your results as a class, interviewing at least 50 total subjects.

Modern Banking

2.3

goals

+ Explain why Congress established the Federal Reserve System.
+ Identify recent challenges faced by the banking system.

terms

+ reserve liquidity
+ Great Depression
+ margin
+ bank run
+ Federal Deposit Insurance Corporation (FDIC)
+ inflation
+ stagflation
+ recession

Banking Scene

Before she left for college, Katie Conlon visited her grandmother, who had given her a check toward her education and told her to put it in a "good, safe bank." Then her grandmother told Katie stories of her own childhood during the Depression, including how her father had lost his savings when a bank went out of business. "Could that happen today?" Katie wondered. What are good resources to learn about the Great Depression?

A TRUE NATIONAL BANKING SYSTEM • • • • • • • • • • • • • •

In the half century before the Federal Reserve Act of 1913, America transformed itself into an industrial powerhouse. This massive industrialization sometimes caused problems with the banking system as the demand for credit and money was high. *Reserves* are a percentage of deposits that are set aside to help with liquidity drops. The National Banking Act of 1864 put a reserve system in place, with small banks able to borrow reserves from city banks, which could in turn borrow from central reserve city banks. However, this structure was not flexible. Sudden economic downturns could cause a chain reaction, with a few banks causing stress on the entire system because there was not enough **reserve liquidity,** or ways to convert the reserves readily to cash.

The Federal Reserve Act of 1913

After a severe economic panic in 1907, Congress formed a bipartisan group (made up of members from both political parties) to study the problem. The Federal Reserve Act in 1913 founded a system of central banking that was both adaptable and flexible. A board of directors controlled district reserve banks from which member banks could borrow money to meet demand. The original Federal Reserve Board consisted of presidential appointees, the Secretary of the Treasury, and the Comptroller of the Currency. Ten-year terms for appointed members removed the responsibilities of the board from partisan politics.

The Federal Reserve handled the government's central banking function, conducted bank examinations, and decided whether banks could borrow money from the Federal Reserve, based on whether the banks were

Ethics in Action

At the time of its founding, the Federal Reserve was hotly criticized by many who felt that its makeup was dominated by bankers, who would act only in their own interests and ignore the "common man." The final structure of the Reserve represented a compromise on these issues.

Think Critically

If you were a member of the Federal Reserve Board, how would you separate your own interests from the good of the country's economy?

being run responsibly and whether extending the loan would put stress on the banking system at large. In this way, banks came under the control of an organization whose job was to monitor and protect the entire banking system. It was also in the interest of member banks to conduct their own operations in such a way as to satisfy the Reserve Board. Thus, the United States at last had a federal institution to manage monetary policy.

The Federal Reserve has changed since its beginning in 1913, both in structure and in operation, largely as a result of the crisis of the Great Depression. Today, the Federal Reserve plays a key role in the economy.

Banks in Crisis

The **Great Depression**, which began in 1929 and extended worldwide until about 1939, was the worst and longest economic crisis of Western industrialized nations during the twentieth century. The stock market crash in October of 1929 brought about near-collapse of the economic system in the United States and other nations. Many banks and their customers were its victims.

Ironically, the failure was caused in part by success. The economy was roaring in the 1920s, and the stock market was booming. The market was so attractive, in fact, that everyone wanted in, whether they had the money available or not. People and companies borrowed money to buy stocks or bought them on credit. Many stocks were bought on **margin,** or for a fraction of their price, then resold at a profit, without the full purchase price of the stock ever having been paid. This practice led to risky investments and speculation. When the market began to fall in September 1929, nervous investors began to sell their stocks. In October, the panic spread, everyone tried to dump stocks, and the market collapsed. There was no money to pay what was owed on margins or on anything else.

In addition, many banks had also invested in the stock market. Those banks that did not fail outright were pressed to their limits and had no money for further loans or investments. Businesses failed, and people were forced out of work. They could not pay back loans from banks, further worsening the position of financial institutions. Hence, the entire economy

^{**"communicate"**}

Interview someone who experienced either the Great Depression firsthand or a recent FDIC takeover of a financial institution. Find out ways that people coped with the economic crisis. Write a short report on what you learn and what your interviewee thinks should be learned from bank failures.

spiraled rapidly downward. American ties to Europe and continuing economic problems after World War I spread the depression worldwide.

People rushed to their banks to withdraw what money they could. Deposits are liabilities, and no bank keeps enough reserves to cover all liabilities. When many people try to withdraw their money at once, a **bank run** takes place, and many such runs occurred.

Bank failures threatened the entire nation and depositors in most failed banks completely lost their money. On March 6, 1933, after a series of major bank failures, newly elected President Franklin D. Roosevelt closed all banks by proclamation. He declared a *bank holiday* in order to save the remaining assets of banks still in business and to let people calm down, as he tried to assure them that the government could help.

STOCK MONTAGE/INDEX STOCK IMAGERY

The Banking Acts of 1933 and 1935

Within four days after President Roosevelt declared the bank holiday, Congress passed the Emergency Banking Act of 1933. This law, also called the Glass-Steagall Act, massively reformed the nation's banking system. Among other things, it separated commercial banking from investment banking to protect assets, and it required bank holding companies to be examined by the Federal Reserve. Perhaps most importantly, it established the **Federal Deposit Insurance Corporation (FDIC)**, which guarantees deposits against bank failures up to $100,000 per depositor, per bank and sometimes even more for special kinds of accounts or ownership categories. These actions restored public confidence in the nation's banking system. Banks reopened, and three quarters of them survived.

The Banking Act of 1935 made further refinements by expanding the monetary controls of the Federal Reserve and changing the structure of the Federal Reserve Board. The Secretary of the Treasury and the Comptroller of the Currency were removed, and board member terms were lengthened. These two acts, with some modifications made later, prevented the massive banking failures of the 1930s from recurring during the twentieth century.

 checkpoint

What brought about the creation of the Federal Reserve in 1913? What is a bank run?

RECENT BANKING •

The basic banking system remained unchanged until 1980. During the 1980s and 1990s, several acts were passed that affected banking. Changes in the way the Federal Reserve deals with Congress and in the way it prices its services to member banks fine-tuned the system. The Reserve and its chair became more independent of government. Its primary goal is to promote general economic health more than any particular policy. Challenges posed by inflation, recession, and modernization have changed banking dramatically from the business it was in Roosevelt's time.

Inflation and Banking

Inflation contributed to bank changes that occurred in the 1970s and 1980s. **Inflation** is a rise in general prices, including a rise in the supply of money and incomes. You might think that an increase in money supply and incomes is a good thing, but what tends to happen is that prices go up as well. A sustained increase in costs and money supply leads to money having less purchasing power. For example, in 1932 a wool sweater cost $1.00 and a gas stove cost $19.95. A factory worker earned about $17.00 per week and an accountant earned $45.00. The problem is that in periods of severe inflation, prices tend to rise faster than earnings. When earnings catch up, the overall

Banking Math *Connection*

Did you get a 13% raise this year? Most people didn't. If inflation is running at 13%, you need a raise of that rate just to break even. If inflation continues to rise for a few years, it can have a ruinous effect. Calculate the cost of 13% inflation for five years on the cost of a $15,000 car.

Solution

The formula for calculating one year's rise is

(Original cost × Inflation rate) + Original cost = Year one cost
($15,000 × 0.13)   + $15,000   = $16,950

To calculate for five years, you can't just multiply 13% by five (65%) and use that as the rate, because the original cost changes (compounds) every year. The calculation must be repeated five times, using the year one cost in place of the original cost for year two, and so forth.

($16,950.00 × 0.13) + $16,950.00 = $19,153.50   Year 2 cost
($19,153.50 × 0.13) + $19,153.50 = $21,643.46   Year 3 cost
($21,643.46 × 0.13) + $21,643.46 = $24,457.11   Year 4 cost
($24,457.10 × 0.13) + $24,457.10 = $27,636.53   Year 5 cost

cost of living has risen, and so it becomes true that "a dollar isn't what it used to be." How well could that accountant live on $45.00 per week today?

Although there are many theories about what causes inflation, economic problems usually go with it. In periods of runaway inflation, no one can keep up, because the value of money does not match the value of goods. It takes more and more money to buy fewer and fewer things. In addition, money put aside earlier no longer has the buying power it had when it was saved.

Just such a cycle occurred in the 1970s and 1980s. Prices, wages, and interest rose rapidly, partly because of an excess of easy credit and money supply. During this same period, banks struggled because the law limited the amount of interest they could pay. Faced with more attractive options, depositors put their money elsewhere, and banks again began to have trouble. Although inflation was rising, the economy as a whole was not doing especially well, producing an unusual circumstance called **stagflation**. A combination of a stagnant economy, high inflation, and high unemployment lead to stagflation. During the 1970s, inflation was about 14 percent per year.

To combat inflation, the Federal Reserve tightened the money supply and allowed interest rates to rise. A severe recession followed, but inflation fell and has remained low. A **recession** occurs when there is a decline in total production lasting a minimum of two consecutive quarters (at least six months). The 1990s saw the longest period of sustained growth in U.S. history.

Root causes of stagflation during the 1970s included the rising cost of energy and food. By the end of 2007, there was concern that the U.S. economy, subjected to sharp increases in prices for energy and food, was heading toward stagflation. The spillover effect of the subprime mortgage crisis also caused consumers to slow down their spending. However, as the 2007 unemployment rate was about half of what it was during the early 1980s, economists have not officially concluded that the 2007 economy was experiencing stagflation.

tech talk

Document Management System (DMS)

Information in banking is a moving target. Laws and regulations change. Interest rates change. Bank account offerings and fees change. How can a bank efficiently inform employees about changes? How can customers access current offerings at a bank? A document management system (DMS) provides a streamlined approach for managing and updating documents. A DMS has a repository, a content server, and content applications. Together they provide information storage, information management, and end user access.

Think Critically
Do an Internet search for document management systems in the banking industry. Review the products vendors offer. Study how a DMS could improve efficiency in one of your particular areas of interest. Share your findings with the class.

PHOTODISC/GETTY IMAGES

Deregulation

Laws, including the Monetary Control Act of 1980, were passed in the early 1980s to let banks compete more freely with other financial firms, opening the doors to the services available today. Not all of the effects of deregulation were good, however. Some financial institutions were allowed to make unwise loans and investments. Many savings and loan institutions (S&Ls) took advantage of new regulations to invest in commercial real estate and speculative loans. When the recession of the mid-1980s struck, these S&Ls failed. Because the Federal Savings and Loan Insurance Corporation (FSLIC), similar to the FDIC for banks, could not cover all the losses, the government intervened. U.S. taxpayers had to pay for the policies of both the government and the officers of the failed S&Ls.

The mortgage crisis that came to the forefront during the summer of 2007 can be attributed, in part, to a loosening of lending oversight standards. By trying to encourage a growth in homeownership through creative lending strategies, many participants in the mortgage industry helped fuel the growth and distribution of risky mortgage products. Because homeowners were given access to mortgages that exceeded their realistic ability to make payments, they began to finance more of their daily expenses through the use of credit cards. As other investment products were developed based on both poorly-performing mortgage products and on credit card debt, when the mortgages began to fail and when people stopped making credit card payments, the investment products based upon them failed also. As the number of non-performing investment products grew, it became increasingly difficult for consumers to access credit. This led the U.S. government to institute a $700 billion bailout package to help troubled lenders. An in-depth explanation of the mortgage crisis, the credit crisis, and the subsequent Emergency Economic Stabilization Act of 2008 is provided in Chapters 8 and 9.

The Revolution Continues   During the first decade of the twenty-first century, various economic downturns prompted the Federal Reserve to drop interest rates multiple times in hopes of stimulating the economy. Evolving technology facilitated the passage of *Check Clearing for the 21st Century Act (Check 21)*, which allowed using substitute checks to process checks electronically. Mergers changed the banking industry constantly. The mortgage crisis, the credit crisis, and Federal intervention to rescue large financial institutions on the brink of failure all contributed to changes in banking. Although much of the basic structure of the banking system remains essentially as it was in 1913, the business of banking, with its rapid communication, its global information exchange, and its marketing focus, little resembles the banking industry of an earlier age.

✔ checkpoint

Why is inflation a potentially serious economic threat? Why were banks deregulated in the early 1980s?

assessment 2.3

Think Critically

1. Why couldn't Congress just allow a free market to determine monetary policy?

2. Why do you think the Federal Reserve Act attempted to remove the members of its board from the pressures of partisan politics?

3. How did consumer fear help cause the bank failures of the Great Depression?

4. Why is inflation particularly hard on those who save money well?

Make Academic Connections

5. **BANKING MATH**   Inflation is still with us, although the rates are far lower than they were 30 years ago. Anticipating inflation is part of financial planning. If this year's inflation rate is 2.7%, and you placed $2,000 in a savings account at the beginning of the year earning 2% interest, how much must you deposit in the account at the end of the year to hold the same purchasing value?

6. **POLITICAL SCIENCE**   Find out more about how Roosevelt reshaped society during the Great Depression. Although controversial, Roosevelt's efforts brought about the government you recognize today. Choose research materials to write a paragraph about how Roosevelt transformed the nation, listing some of the reforms.

chapter 2 **assessment**

Chapter Summary

2.1 Creation of a National Currency

A. Currency includes all circulating media of exchange in a country. It may include metallic currency (coins) and paper currency (government currency, bank currency, deposit currency, and other credit instruments).

B. There were many forms of currency in early American history. After the Revolutionary War, bank notes from many sources circulated. After the Civil War, forms other than U.S.-issued currency were taxed out of existence.

2.2 Banking Before 1913

A. Both the First and the Second Banks of the United States were private institutions that ultimately died. Banks were largely unregulated until the Civil War.

B. The National Banking Act of 1864 eliminated many forms of currency and moved toward a central banking system. Money supply problems persisted.

2.3 Modern Banking

A. Congress established the Federal Reserve in 1913. It was the first official central banking system in U.S. history.

B. The Great Depression brought many bank failures. Banking reform acts saved the industry. Challenges from inflation and changes from technology characterized latter twentieth-century banking.

Vocabulary Builder

Choose the term that best fits the definition. Write the letter of the answer in the space provided. Some terms may not be used.

a. bank run
b. currency
c. Federal Reserve Act
d. Federal Deposit Insurance Corporation (FDIC)
e. Great Depression
f. inflation
g. margin
h. recession
i. reserve liquidity
j. stagflation

____ 1. Ways to quickly convert banks' reserves to cash

____ 2. Combination of a stagnant economy and high inflation

____ 3. Legislation that created a system to stabilize the banking industry

____ 4. A decline in total production lasting a minimum of two consecutive quarters (at least six months)

____ 5. Circumstance when many depositors withdraw money at once

____ 6. All media of exchange circulating in a country

____ 7. Agency that guarantees bank deposits

____ 8. Worst economic crisis in U.S. history prior to the 21st century

____ 9. Collective rise in money supply, incomes, and prices

____ 10. Stocks bought for a fraction of their price, then resold at a profit, without the full price of the stock ever having been paid (encouraging risky investments and speculation)

Review Concepts

11. Why did Alexander Hamilton urge the founding of the first Bank of the United States?

_____

_____

_____

12. Why did Thomas Jefferson oppose founding the First Bank of the United States?

_____

_____

_____

13. How did the First and Second Banks of the United States exert control over other banks?

_____

_____

_____

14. Why did the First and Second Banks of the United States fail?

_____

_____

_____

15. How were banks regulated between 1836 and the Civil War?

_____

_____

_____

16. Why did state banks eventually stop issuing their own currency?

_____

_____

_____

17. Why did Congress establish the Federal Reserve system?

_____

_____

_____

18. What caused massive bank failures during the Great Depression?

_____

_____

_____

Apply What You Learned

19. In what ways does the disagreement between Hamilton and Jefferson about banking policy still exist today?

_____

_____

_____

20. Outline the history of banking in the U.S. economy.

_____

_____

_____

_____

Make Academic Connections

21. **BANKING MATH**   Calculate the loss of real value in a $10,000 savings account if inflation is 10% a year for 3 years versus the loss of real value if inflation remains around 3%. How much less would that savings account be worth if inflation goes up? (For this exercise, do not consider interest paid.)

_____

_____

_____

_____

_____

_____

22. **MEDIA**   Collect stories about interest rates, the Federal Reserve, inflation, banking, the effects of the mortgage crisis, and current economic conditions from various news media. Take notes from stories on electronic media such as radio, television, and the Internet. Use these notes in a class discussion about economic trends.

23. **HISTORY**   Thomas Jefferson was an American hero, but his opponent on the bank issue was also a fascinating man. Use research materials of your choice to write a two-page character sketch of Alexander Hamilton, focusing not only on biographical facts but on traits that made him both an effective and resented spokesperson for his opinions.

24. **ART**   Use printouts from the Internet or photocopies of library materials to create a collage of images from the Great Depression. In your collage, try to convey a sense of the economic conditions of the time.

25. **CURRENT EVENTS**   Research the ramifications of the subprime mortgage crisis of 2007/2008. List the impact on U.S. municipalities, the U.S. economy, and international economies.

26. **GOVERNMENT AS A BUSINESS**   *Seigniorage* is term used to describe the profit the government makes from manufacturing coins. As part of the effort to support their goal of being self-supporting, the Mint calculates the profit on each coin produced. The Mint also strategizes about how to respond to competitive threats that will decrease the demand for currency. Review the most recent annual report for the Mint at http://www.usmint.gov/about_the_mint/. List defined competitive threats and list which coins are profitable and those that are not. Be prepared to discuss with the class the two focuses of the mint. First, the mint serves the needs of the public by managing and issuing coins. Second, the mint views the public as their customer.

27. **CURRENT EVENTS**   The mortgage crisis that began in the summer of 2007 began because it became increasingly easier for buyers to qualify for loans. Research lending standards online and provide a brief description of how lending standards were lowered over time.

28. **CURRENT EVENTS**   One method the U.S. Treasury uses to avoid counterfeiting currency is to educate the public about the features of currency. Visit the Department of the Treasury Bureau of Engraving and printing website at www.moneyfactory.gov/newmoney/ to learn about security features released as recently as March 2008. Compare the security features listed on the website to an updated $5 bill and an older $5 bill. List the ways that you can use the new security features to quickly note a potential counterfeit bill.

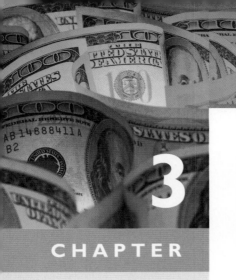

CHAPTER

3

The Federal Reserve System

3.1   Structure of the Federal Reserve System

3.2   Monetary and Fiscal Policy

3.3   Consumer Protection

3.4   Role in Determining Banks' Financial Health

3.5   International Banking and the Federal Reserve System

© CORBIS

skills that pay dividends

Understanding Public Policy and Its Impact on Business

Money flows through the economy. It allows people to trade products and services at a fair value. With money as a medium of exchange, products and services can be exchanged directly between individuals, businesses, and governments without the intervention of third parties.

Government exists to protect people from each other, to protect people from private interests, and to further the ideas that society holds valuable. Government also provides the legal framework to ensure that protections are provided in an organized way. Through legal requirements, the government mandates accountability. Individuals and corporations are legally responsible for their actions and they are required to comply with existing laws.

It is important to understand how these concepts intersect to achieve the goal of economic stability in a thriving society. One example of government policy impacting business is energy conservation. Increased public concern over the condition of the environment and the impact of global warming has been steadily gaining momentum.

In 1992, the Environmental Protection Agency (EPA) began a program called Energy Star, which is a voluntary labeling program. Products that are energy efficient and reduce the emission of greenhouse gases can earn an Energy Star rating.

In 1996, the United States Department of Energy (DOE) entered into a joint partnership with the EPA for the Energy Star program. This joint effort resulted in a substantial increase in the number of products that are eligible for an Energy Star rating.

In 2007, it was estimated that households using Energy Star products could save about 30% on their annual utility bills. Nationally, this represents a savings of $16 billion on consumers' utility bills.

Another method of promoting energy conservation is through tax incentives. Hybrid vehicles, which are powered by both batteries and fuel, achieve higher fuel efficiency and lower emissions than standard vehicles. To encourage consumers to begin using hybrid vehicles, the government developed an Alternative Motor Vehicle Credit.

This credit is structured to jump start purchases of hybrid vehicles by providing the largest amount of credit to consumers who purchase the vehicles closest to their release dates. The tax credit allows consumers to reduce the amount of federal tax owed by the amount of the credit.

The money consumers save through utility bill reductions and tax credits is money they have available to spend or invest. Government policies, which reflect the goals of the voting public, are designed to influence consumer behavior through financial incentives.

When government policy subsidizes an industry, as is the case for hybrid vehicles, it is impacting the growth and development of the industry. If consumers are eager to help the environment and receive a tax credit, they will purchase hybrid vehicles. This increases demand for hybrid vehicles and encourages more companies to manufacture hybrid vehicles.

Develop Your Skill

Research the tax incentives homeowners with mortgages receive. Determine whether mortgage tax credits subsidize the real estate market.

PHOTODISC

3.1

goals

+ Identify the organization of the Federal Reserve System.

+ Explain how the Federal Reserve influences banks and the economy.

+ Describe proposed reorganization of the Fed.

terms

+ member bank

+ District Reserve Bank

Structure of the Federal Reserve System

Banking Scene

After opening an account at People's State Bank, Kareema stopped at a fast food drive-thru for a soft drink. Waiting to pay, she happened to glance at the bill in her hand. At the top of her bill, she saw the words "Federal Reserve Note." Why, she wondered, are these bills called Federal Reserve notes? Kareema resolved to find out more about the Federal Reserve System. Where might she start?

STRUCTURE OF THE FED •

The Federal Reserve was created in 1913 to respond to problems with the nation's changing money supply. Now you will look more closely at the modern Federal Reserve System, learn who makes it up, what the system does, and how it does it. The "Fed," as it is often called, functions as the government's banker, providing a range of financial services both to the government and to all financial institutions. It also supervises banks, conducting examinations to identify risk or bookkeeping problems. The Federal Reserve manages monetary policy as well, hoping to benefit not only banks but also the economy at large.

The Federal Reserve is a uniquely American approach to central banking. It is a combination of public and private policymakers working together to control the nation's monetary policy, supervise banks, and provide financial services to the government and banks. The Federal Reserve is set up like a private corporation, with member banks holding stock in their District Reserve Bank. The President of the United States nominates candidates for the Board of Governors. The U.S. Senate confirms nominees. Congress compromised on a mix of private and public interests for the Federal Reserve, and that mix is intended to serve the interests of the nation at large. The Federal government appropriates no money for the Federal Reserve. Its income is derived from financial services and interest on loans to its member banks. Any money made

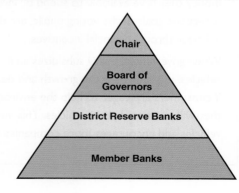

above the cost of providing services is turned over to the U.S. Treasury. Think of the structure of the Federal Reserve as a pyramid, with member banks as the base, District Reserve Banks in the middle, the Board of Governors near the top, and the Chairman at the very peak. Each of these levels depends upon information and action from other parts to hold up the system.

Member Banks

Any bank that is part of the Federal Reserve System is known as a **member bank**. All national banks must be member banks of the Federal Reserve System. They must purchase stock in the District Reserve Banks in their regions. This stock cannot be bought or sold, and it does not offer control of the District Reserve Bank. It does convey voting rights, however, for directors of the District Bank, and it also pays a 6 percent dividend. State-chartered banks are not required to be members of the Federal Reserve System, although they may choose to do so if they meet requirements. Investment banks are currently not required to be member banks.

District Reserve Banks

District Reserve Banks carry out banking functions for government offices in their area, examine member banks in the district, decide whether to loan banks funds, recommend interest rates, and implement policy decisions of the Board of Governors. There are twelve regional District Reserve Banks, located in Atlanta, Boston, Chicago, Cleveland, Dallas, Kansas City, Minneapolis, New York, Philadelphia, Richmond, San Francisco, and St. Louis. As of October 2007, there were 25 branch offices supporting the regional offices. The district and regional branches are shown at the right.

Each district bank is governed by a nine-member board of directors, six of whom are nonbankers elected by member banks. The Board of Governors selects the three other board members. Each board also elects the president of its district bank, subject to approval by the Board of Governors.

District Bank	Branch Bank
1. Boston, MA	
2. New York, NY	Buffalo, NY
3. Philadelphia, PA	
4. Cleveland, OH	Cincinnati, OH
	Pittsburgh, PA
5. Richmond, VA	Baltimore, MD
	Charlotte, NC
6. Atlanta, GA	Birmingham, AL
	Jacksonville, FL
	Miami, FL
	Nashville, TN
	New Orleans, LA
7. Chicago, IL	Detroit, MI
8. St. Louis, MO	Little Rock, AR
	Louisville, KY
	Memphis, TN
9. Minneapolis, MN	Helena, MT
10. Kansas City, MO	Denver, CO
	Oklahoma City, OK
	Omaha, NE
11. Dallas, TX	El Paso, TX
	Houston, TX
	San Antonio, TX
12. San Francisco, CA	Los Angeles, CA
	Portland, OR
	Salt Lake City, UT
	Seattle, WA

The Twelve Federal Reserve Districts

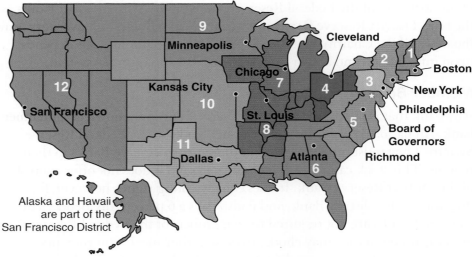

The Federal Reserve officially identifies Districts by number and Reserve Bank city.

In the 12th District, the Seattle Branch serves Alaska, and the San Francisco Bank serves Hawaii. The System serves commonwealths and territories as follows: the New York Bank serves the Commonwealth of Puerto Rico and the U.S. Virgin Islands; the San Francisco Bank serves American Samoa, Guam, and the Commonwealth of the Northern Mariana Islands. The Board of Governors revised the branch boundaries of the System in February 1996.

Source: Federal Reserve System

Board of Governors

The President of the United States selects members of the Board of Governors, subject to consent of the Senate. Each of the seven governors serves a 14-year term, one beginning January 31 of every even-numbered year so that terms are staggered. The Board of Governors is the policy-making arm of the Federal Reserve Board, and its decisions control monetary policy. The Board of Governors oversees the District Reserve Banks and also controls mergers, bank holding companies, U.S. offices of international banks, and the reserves of depository institutions.

The Chair

The President also selects the chair and vice-chair of the Federal Reserve from the membership of the Board of Governors, subject to confirmation of the Senate. The chair and vice-chair each serve a four-year term, but no limit is set on the number of terms. The current chairman, Ben Bernanke, has served since February 2006. The Chair is a visible symbol and powerful spokesperson of Federal Reserve policies.

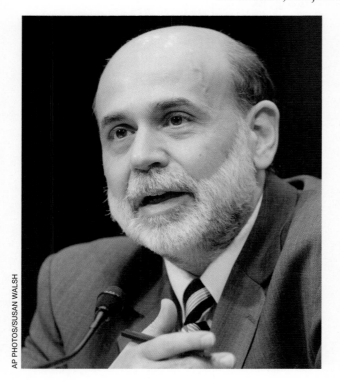

The Federal Reserve structure allows for both central control of monetary policy and regional control of district and member banks. Thus, the Federal Reserve, though a central bank, has a decentralized structure that bases policies on both national and regional concerns through close communication.

 checkpoint

What are the four structural elements of the Federal Reserve?

FUNCTIONS OF THE FED

The Federal Reserve serves as the central banking authority of the United States, managing the banking system of the country. The five main functions of the Federal Reserve are to serve as the government's bank, to ensure that the financial system remains stable through judicious use of monetary policy, to supervise and regulate bank operations, to protect consumers' credit rights, and to serve as a bank for other banks.

The Government's Bank

The U.S. government performs many financial actions through the Federal Reserve. Tax payments to the Internal Revenue Service go to accounts in Federal Reserve banks. From these accounts, the government makes payments to employees, to Social Security recipients, to military personnel, and for other expenses associated with the government.

In addition, Federal Reserve banks perform some services for the government that add directly to its income. The Federal Reserve is responsible for selling and redeeming various government securities, such as savings bonds, treasury bills, treasury notes, and treasury bonds.

The Banks' Bank

One of the main reasons the Federal Reserve was created was to serve as a reserve bank for other banks to ease shortages of cash or to credit banks that have an excess. The Federal Reserve also processes payments between banks. Originally, this function developed to speed the collection of checks, but the task expanded to processing payments for other large accounts, such as payroll accounts and payments for large manufacturing orders. Today, this role also includes not only paper checks, but also electronic funds transfers, the means by which most large transactions move.

Bank Supervision

The Federal Reserve supervises and regulates all member banks. Agencies such as the Office of the Comptroller of the Currency and the FDIC participate in regulatory activities as well. State banking authorities also

interesting *facts*

conduct supervisory activities, so that banks, whether members of the Fed or not, are supervised to ensure responsible banking practice. For international banks operating in the United States, the Federal Reserve ensures fair competition and communicates with central banking authorities in other countries to promote consistent policies.

Protecting Consumers

Consumer protection is another function of the Federal Reserve. Bank examiners monitor whether customers are treated fairly in terms of fees, prices, penalties, and even advertising. Banks must show that they offer and perform their services, including making loans, on an equal opportunity basis.

 checkpoint

What are the primary functions of the Federal Reserve?

PROPOSED REORGANIZATION OF THE FED

The financial crisis which the United States began to experience in the latter half of 2007 helped spur discussion regarding whether the banking regulation system should be reorganized. A number of federal agencies, including the Fed, regulate portions of the banking industry. There is some overlap between agencies and there are some areas not covered by federal oversight. For example, the Fed, the FDIC, the Office of the Comptroller of the Currency and the SEC are all involved in banking regulation. Other agencies are also involved in their regulation.

In response to the need for reorganization, the Treasury Department released a proposed plan for reorganizing the management of domestic financial markets. This plan acknowledged that, given the evolving nature of financial markets and the way that financial institutions overlap in products offered, a new system was required to respond quickly to market needs. For example, as financial institutions routinely sell diverse products covering securities, banking, and insurance, regulation needed to be positioned to manage those areas in a cohesive fashion. Following are some highlights of the report.

President's Working Group on Financial Markets (PWG)   Originally established in 1988, this group was responsible for communicating across agencies to help ensure a healthy stock market that inspired investor confidence. Inter-agency communication was achieved by having leadership representatives from the Treasury, the Fed, the SEC, and the Commodities Futures Trading Commission serve on the PWG committee. In March 2008, the Treasury recommended expanding the PWG committee to include representatives from the Office of the Comptroller of the Currency, the FDIC, and the Office of Thrift Supervision. This broader-based committee should help achieve the expanded goals of the PWG, including lessening system-wide risk to financial markets, improving the integrity of financial markets, improving protection for consumers and investors, and enhancing the competitiveness of financial markets.

Mortgage Origination Commission (MOC)   This proposed commission would be an inter-agency group with responsibility for developing federal legislation requiring states to develop consistent licensing and training requirements for participants in the mortgage industry. Also, states would have a way to enforce federal laws for mortgage originators that are not part of a regulated financial institution. (Independent mortgage originators developed a majority of the subprime mortgage loans.)

Payment and Settlement Systems Oversight   Used to transfer funds between businesses, financial institutions, and consumers, the payment and settlement systems help lubricate the economy by making sure money is accurately sent and received. The proposed revisions would include a uniform method for regulating these systems.

Insurance   Historically operated under state regulation, the proposed plan recommends establishing an organization to federally regulate insurance providers who opt in to the federal program. Federal oversight would help meet the needs of companies that provide insurance on either a national or international basis.

Futures and Securities   Separating the regulation of futures and securities, which made sense in the 1930s when the regulations were established, does not make sense in today's market. As products and markets have converged and as international trading has increased, there is a need to regulate futures and securities together. To achieve this objective, the proposal recommends merging the Securities and Exchange Commission (SEC) and the Commodity Futures Trading Commission (CFTC). One regulatory body would provide a more agile response to the changing needs of the marketplace.

As this report was first released in March 2008, and as the report in its entirety recommends a multitude of changes that cut across many federal, state, and private entities, it will be some time before the recommendations can be considered and acted upon.

checkpoint

Why is consideration of reorganizing the Fed such a complicated task?

assessment 3.1

Think Critically

1. Why do you think only national banks are required to be members of the Federal Reserve System?

2. Why are Federal Reserve District Banks distributed across the nation?

3. Why did the Treasury Department feel the need to initiate reorganization of the management of domestic financial markets?

4. List five areas of economic management that are facing possible reorganization based on the Treasury Department's recommendations.

Make Academic Connections

5. **EDUCATION** Visit the Federal Reserve Board of Governors' website at www.federalreserve.gov. From the Site Map link, find the District Reserve Bank that serves your area. Find and visit that bank's site, and discover what materials it makes available for citizen education. List those resources here.

6. **BIOGRAPHY** One of the most influential Federal Reserve chairs in recent history has been Alan Greenspan. Use resource material of your own choosing, and write a one-page report on the life and career of this powerful figure. Include reflections on his comments in the fall of 2008 when he acknowledged that relying on the "self-interest of lending institutions" to behave in a way that made businesses self-sustaining was a gross miscalculation and contributed to the 2008 financial crises.

Monetary and Fiscal Policy

Banking Scene

Kareema was delighted to get so many outfits for the fall on sale. She'd heard a lot of talk regarding how "money was tight." This was causing many customers to cut back on their spending. Because fewer people were buying clothes, she could get many discounted items. She was happy to get the sale prices, but she wondered what it meant that "money was tight." How can she learn more about the supply of money in the economy? Which government agencies influence the supply of money? Where should she begin her research?

3.2

goals

+ Explain how the Fed impacts monetary policy.

+ Identify how fiscal policy affects the economy.

+ Explore criticisms of monetary and fiscal policy.

terms

+ Federal Open Market Committee (FOMC)

+ Taylor rule

+ adverse feedback loop

MONETARY POLICY

The most famous function of the Federal Reserve is conducting monetary policy. The goals of the Federal Reserve's monetary policy are to maintain economic growth, to stabilize prices, and to keep international payments flowing smoothly. Federal Reserve actions affect the amount of reserves banks hold, as well as the money supply, which in turn affects the economy.

Open Market Operations   The Fed buys and sells securities issued by the Treasury Department or other government agencies. These are called *open market* sales because the Fed does not control with whom it is doing business in the sales, but trades at a profit or loss in order to accomplish monetary control. These transactions affect the *federal funds rate*, the rate at which banks borrow from each other. When the Fed wants to increase reserves, it buys securities. When it wants to decrease reserves, it sells them. Although this is the most powerful tool of the Fed, these adjustments are short-term and may take place within either days or hours.

Primary Dealers   There is a select group of 20 dealers that the Fed works with to buy and sell securities. These primary dealers must be either broker-dealers that are registered with the SEC or commercial banks that are regulated by supervisors of federal banks. To qualify as a primary dealer, certain capital standards must be met and a certain volume of business must be maintained. Primary dealers engage in a competitive bidding process each time new securities are offered on the open market.

Setting Reserve Requirements   The Fed adjusts the portion of total deposits that banks must keep on hand in their vaults or at the Federal Reserve. Higher reserve requirements result in less money in circulation. Reserve requirement changes are the least frequently used monetary tool of the Fed because changing the reserve requirements fundamentally affects the operations of banks.

Adjusting the Discount Interest Rate   The Fed indirectly affects interest rates at large. The *discount rate* is the rate of interest that the Federal Reserve charges banks for short-term loans. Other interest rates often rise or fall with the discount rate. The **Federal Open Market Committee (FOMC)** makes discount rate decisions. The committee consists of the seven-member Board of Governors (which includes the Chairman of the Federal Reserve), the Chairman of the New York District Reserve Bank, and presidents of four other District Reserve Banks who serve on a rotating basis. Although legally required to meet four times annually, the FOMC generally meets about eight times per year. Policy changes, when needed, are decided during the meetings.

The Federal Reserve determines necessary interest rate changes in response to economic conditions. A staff compiles and analyzes large amounts of data for support. Economics is an inexact science. The Federal Reserve had avoided the catastrophes of the 1930s until 2008. As a result of the financial crises of 2008, challenges abound for the Fed and other financial regulatory agencies.

Adjusting Monetary Policy

Tinkering with monetary policy does not occur in a vacuum. FOMC members provide input, through discussion and votes on actions. The market then responds to FOMC actions. During early 2008, market observers had hoped the Fed would cut interest rates by one percent. They thought a one percent cut would help keep inflation at bay. However, the Fed decided to cut rates by three quarters of a percent. (Combined with prior interest rate reductions, this cut led to a two percent rate cut in a two-month period.)

Illustrating that setting monetary policy is not an exact science, two members of the FOMC voted against the three quarter percent interest rate reduction. Even experts do not always agree on the most effective course of action. The three quarter percent rate cut was enough, in the short term, to help improve stock market performance and to improve the international value of the dollar. In essence, the markets gained confidence and responded favorably to the Fed's efforts to help stabilize the economy through interest rate reductions. Adjusting interest rates is one of the many components of monetary policy. Predicting the impact of these adjustments is not straightforward.

Developing Monetary Policy

Did you ever consider all the parties who review, analyze, and try to predict the overall state of the economy? In addition to government staffers and investors, college professors also are interested not only in the economy's performance, but in what drives that performance.

A Stanford University professor, John Taylor, published the Taylor rule in 1993. In simplified terms, the **Taylor rule** provides ideas for how to use short-term interest rates to achieve the goals of a central bank. These goals include keeping the economy stable and controlling inflation.

The Taylor rule recommends looking at how the economy is performing relative to three targeted indicators. Inflation, full employment, and short-term interest rates are the indicators. When inflation is high or when the economy is above its targeted full employment rate, the Taylor rule suggests that having a high interest rate, which in turn would decrease the money supply, is a good mechanism for restoring the economy to its targeted levels.

The rule provides a simplified method for assessing and forming monetary policy. Although the rule has some limitations, including not being comprehensive enough to capture the essence of a complex economy and not being able to incorporate decisions that might be made to manage specific risks, it is often included as part of the analytical and decision-making process of those who set monetary policy.

New Tools to Manage Monetary Policy

In order to help combat the financial crisis that began to appear in the economy during the summer of 2007, the Fed developed three new tools to help manage monetary policy. Term Auction Facility (TAF), Term Securities Lending Facility (TSLF), and Primary Dealer Credit Facility (PDCF) are the new tools.

There are a number of factors that set these tools apart from each other. The fees charged to the borrower for using the tools, how long the loan will last, the type of financial institution that can use the loan, and the type of collateral that can be used to secure the loan all contribute to the differences between the loans.

- **Term Auction Facility (TAF)**   Commercial banks can borrow money from the Fed for a maximum of 28 days. Types of collateral for these loans can vary.

- **Term Securities Lending Facility (TSLF)**   Treasury securities can be borrowed by primary dealers. The loans, which last up to 28 days, can be secured by a broader range of collateral than TAF loans.

- **Primary Dealer Credit Facility (PDCF)**   Primary dealers can take out loans for up to 120 days. A larger group securities than the TSLF securities will be accepted as collateral.

To avoid having these loans increase the total amount of money in the economy, each time the Fed issues one of these loans, the Fed sells an equal amount of Treasury securities. The TSLF and PDCF were initially planned as short-term measures.

✔ checkpoint

Why is it hard to predict the impact of monetary policy adjustments?

FISCAL POLICY

Just as the Federal Reserve System dominates monetary policy, Congress and the President control fiscal policy and are considered co-equal with the Fed in economic decision making. Congress and the President attempt to smooth economic ups and downs by manipulating the federal budget to create enough demand for goods to keep people working but not so much as to cause inflation. This process controls the total demand for goods and services by managing government spending and the amount of taxes collected. This economic management is called fiscal policy. Administered independently of the Fed's monetary policy, fiscal policy involves adjusting budgetary deficits or surpluses to achieve desired economic goals.

"Priming the Pump" in an Economic Downturn   When the economy experiences high unemployment and little or no business growth, the federal government attempts to add jobs and stimulate business by "priming the pump," or cutting taxes. Theoretically, doing so gives businesses and individuals more money to spend, which results in increased demand for goods and services. Expanded demand causes industries to manufacture more products, hire additional employees, and invest in new buildings and equipment. The expansion thus stimulates the economy. This policy is often referred to as *Keynesian economics* for John Maynard Keynes, who is credited with developing it to address the economic crisis during the Great Depression.

In addition to cutting taxes, which impacts workers' current and future paychecks, sometimes the government issues tax rebates. In effect, rebates provide a retroactive reduction in the level of taxation. They provide a partial refund on previously paid taxes.

During the second quarter of 2008, U.S. the government started issuing tax rebates. By using the rebates to pump $168 billion into the economy, the government hoped to stimulate the slow U.S. economy.

According to economists, tax rebates do not always provide the anticipated stimulus. While studying the affects of a 2001 tax rebate, which ranged in value from $300 to $600, Matthew D. Shapiro and Joel Slemrod, both University of Michigan economists, concluded that only about 20 percent of people spent their rebates on new purchases. A majority of taxpayers either put their rebate money into savings or used it to pay off debt.

Slowing the Boom Economy   In contrast, when the economy is prosperous, demand can exceed supply. This causes prices to increase and, unless stopped, leads to *inflation* when rising prices decrease the value of money. When this happens, the government uses the opposite policy. It cuts spending, raises taxes, or uses a combination of the two. As a result, consumers and businesses have less money to spend, reducing demand and stabilizing prices.

 checkpoint

Explain Keynesian economics.

CRITICISM OF MONETARY AND FISCAL POLICIES ● ● ● ● ● ● ●

Both monetary and fiscal policies have their critics. The two policies often work at cross-purposes. In general, monetary policies seek to control inflation and tolerate relatively high unemployment to achieve their goal. In contrast, fiscal policy appeals to politicians who want to keep the economy vigorous and growing even at the cost of moderately higher prices.

Monetary policy is relatively more agile than fiscal policy. It is easier for the Fed to change bank reserve requirements than to go through the fairly cumbersome process of changing legislation to alter taxes. It is quicker for the Fed to adjust the amount of money flowing into the economy, by buying or selling dollars on the open market, than altering the level of taxes.

branching out

Skip the Bank, Come to the Store

Retailers were licking their chops hoping to feast on the tax rebate checks that the U.S. government began to distribute during April 2008. The checks were part of a $168 billion dollar economic stimulus package. In an effort to capture the entire rebate check from as many customers as possible, retailers developed a variety of incentives. A number of grocery chains offered a 10% bonus for rebate checks used to buy gift cards—therefore a $600 rebate check could be redeemed for $660 of groceries. Some department and clothing stores offered similar bonuses. One electronics retailer, happy to settle for a portion of the rebate check, required that a portion of the check be used for a purchase at its store. It would then load the remaining balance onto a prepaid credit card that could be used at other retailers.

Think Critically
Is it ethical for retailers to try to get consumers to tie up their stimulus checks with just one store? How would being obligated to spend a large portion of a rebate check at just one store impact the speed with which the stimulus is felt in the economy?

Monetary policy has a downside. If the flow of cash into the economy is too severely restricted, consumers and businesses cannot afford to borrow. This results in a decline in spending and investments, leading to a failure to sell products—especially "big ticket" items such as new homes, automobiles, and appliances. Factories close. As the economy cools off, more and more workers are laid off, and the downward plunge picks up momentum. This cycle is often called an **adverse feedback loop**.

A recent adverse feedback loop began to occur during the fourth quarter of 2007. By the end of that year, about 8 percent of home loans were either late in payments or in the midst of foreclosure. Some banks wanted to have a smaller portion of their assets tied up in home mortgages. Because the market was unstable and so many home loans were in default, banks began to ask for larger down payments. They also began to cut way back on home equity loans.

With less money available to spend, consumers began to change their consumption patterns. Buying habits at the grocery store changed. Instead of buying convenient, single-serve packages, they bought in bulk. Entrees shifted from expensive meats to less expensive pastas. Other buying patterns also shifted. Instead of buying designer clothing, store brands were bought. In lieu of going out to the movies, DVDs were rented.

Although consumers who are caught in an adverse feedback loop may continue to meet their basic needs, they do so in the least expensive way possible. This reduces the total amount of money flowing through the economy.

Fiscal policy has created deep misgivings and endless controversy. Many economists doubt that the Federal government can regulate the economy by raising or lowering taxes and expenditures. In addition to being clumsy and time-consuming, these methods involve enormous uncertainties. Fiscal policy is especially difficult to use for stabilization because of the gap between the recognition of its need and its implementation by the President and Congress. For example, the tax cut proposed by President John F. Kennedy in 1962 to stimulate the economy was not legislated until 1964.

Both policies are based on predictions. Even made by experienced economists, predictions are just that—forecasts of what *could* happen.

 checkpoint

What is an adverse feedback loop?

assessment 3.2

Think Critically

1. How does increasing a bank's required reserve result in less money circulating in the economy?

_____

_____

2. Why doesn't the government legislate the value of money and set interest rates by law?

_____

_____

3. Explain the Taylor rule.

_____

_____

_____

4. List and define three new tools for managing monetary policy.

_____

_____

_____

Make Academic Connections

5. **PREFFERRED VENDORS**   The website of the Federal Reserve Bank of New York lists current primary dealers. Review the list and determine whether the status of any primary dealers has been or will be impacted by changes that have occurred in overall market conditions. List your thoughts below.

_____

_____

_____

6. **RESEARCH**   A tax rebate was issued in April 2008. Go online to research the effect of the rebate on the economy. Be prepared to discuss with the class whether you believe rebates are an effective stimulus tool.

_____

_____

3.3

goals

+ Explain the various acts that protect consumer rights.

+ Understand how enforcement responsibilities are shared across agencies.

terms

+ Truth in Lending Act (TILA)

+ Equal Credit Opportunity Act (ECOA)

+ Fair Credit Reporting Act (FCRA)

+ Fair Debt Collection Practices Act (FDCPA)

+ Government Accountability Office (GAO)

Consumer Protection

Banking Scene

Kareema decided to open a new credit card to take advantage of the customer reward program at her favorite clothing store. She was shocked to see all the forms and all the fine print she had to read and sign off on before getting a credit card. There was a lot of discussion regarding interest rates and finance charges. Kareema wondered why there was so much information on the forms. Who decides what information should be included on the forms? Where can she get help to understand what's on the forms?

CREDIT TRANSACTION PROTECTION

An important role of the Fed is to protect consumers. This protection is ensured when the Fed establishes and enforces regulations that promote fairness in the treatment of consumers by private businesses. Financial transactions of consumers are usually protected by consumer protection laws. Protected credit transactions run the gamut from debit cards, car leases, and mortgage loans to ATM transactions.

Credit policies are not always easy to understand. In the past lenders sometimes made it purposefully difficult. In a wave of consumer protection legislation during the 1960s, '70s, and '80s, Congress enacted several important laws to guarantee the rights of consumers. These disclosure laws require that details of lending agreements be specified in writing. Other important laws require far more than disclosure, guaranteeing equal access to credit for qualified consumers, accurate credit reporting, and freedom from unfair or deceitful collection practices. Banks are required not only to conform to federal and state laws, but also to document their compliance.

Truth in Lending

Credit cards are the most common form of open-end credit account that are not secured by a home. The **Truth in Lending Act (TILA)**, Title I of the Consumer Credit Protection Act of 1968, was landmark legislation. Amended many times, it guarantees that all information about costs of a loan is provided in writing to consumers. Items that must be disclosed include the following.

- Total sales price
- Amount financed
- Annual percentage rate (APR)
- Variable rate information
- Total payments

- Schedule of payments
- Prepayment policies
- Late payment policies
- Security interest

In addition, the act provides for a right of rescission, which allows a consumer to change his or her mind about a loan until midnight of the third business day following the signing of papers. The law also prescribes complaint procedures and penalties.

Legislation to update TILA was pending as of May 2008. These pending amendments involve ensuring that interest rate increases, discounted promotional rates, and all payments are applied fairly.

Equal Credit Opportunity Act

The **Equal Credit Opportunity Act (ECOA)** prohibits the use of race, color, religion, national origin, marital status, age, receipt of public assistance, or exercise of any consumer right against a lender as a factor in determining creditworthiness. If a credit request is denied, the law also requires that the lender provide the reasons for the denial upon request.

Fair Credit Reporting Act

The **Fair Credit Reporting Act (FCRA)** aims to protect the information that credit bureaus, medical information companies, and tenant screening services may collect. First enacted in 1971, the legislation provided the first legal oversight of the credit information industry. The FCRA establishes the following rights, some of which were added in 2003.

- Consumers must be told what is in their file and who has had access to the information.

- Consumers must be told if information in their file has been used against them.

- Consumers can dispute inaccurate information in their reports. The agency must investigate disputes within 30 days.

- Inaccurate information must be corrected or deleted.

- Credit bureaus cannot report information more than seven years old in most cases, or more than ten for bankruptcies.

- Access to consumer files is limited.

- Consumers must authorize the release of reports to employers.

- Lenders cannot obtain medical history or use medical history to determine a credit applicant's worthiness of obtaining a loan.

- Consumers can seek damages for violations of the law.

- By standardizing the information included on credit reports, bias is removed from the reports. These unbiased credit reports enable a broader spectrum of consumers to receive credit.

Legislation to update FCRA was pending as of 2008. A summary of these pending amendments follow.

- A company cannot share customer contact information with its affiliates unless the consumer is offered an easy way to opt out of the solicitation. This rule has been finalized.

- All businesses that hold a consumer account must develop an identity theft prevention program to proactively thwart attempted identity theft.

- *Risk-based pricing* is when a business offers less favorable credit terms to a consumer with a relatively weaker credit score. This proposal would require businesses that use risk-based pricing to provide a risk-based pricing notice to the consumer before the consumer commits to the transaction.

Fair Debt Collection Practices Act

The **Fair Debt Collection Practices Act (FDCPA)** protects consumers from unfair collection techniques. Third-party collectors may not use deceptive or abusive tactics as they try to collect overdue bills. Such collectors may not contact debtors at odd hours, call repeatedly or in a harassing manner, or threaten them in any way, even with legal action, unless it is actually contemplated. Nor may collectors reveal the debts or collection actions to other people, such as employers, in an attempt to embarrass the debtor. Penalties are prescribed for violations of the act.

✔ checkpoint

Name four important pieces of consumer protection legislation.

_____

_____

OTHER LEGISLATION •

The preceding four laws are the foundation of consumer protection, but there are many other laws that apply as well.

- **Fair Credit Billing Act**   An amendment of TILA, it specifies fair procedures for resolving billing disputes and prevents creditors from taking adverse action until the dispute is resolved.

Ethics in Action

FCRA, like many consumer protection laws, focuses on privacy rights of individuals. Privacy rights are an inherent part of the American psyche. The 2001 Patriot Act, enacted as a way to help combat the potential financing of terrorism, put into effect a number of policies that enabled government agencies to obtain personal financial information about citizens. By issuing requests either through the Foreign Intelligence Surveillance Act (FISA) or through national security letters (NSLs), government agencies are authorized to obtain this personal financial information without the knowledge of affected citizens. The financial institutions providing the financial information to the government are prohibited from revealing the requests to affected account holders. Although the Patriot Act was reauthorized by Congress in 2006, certain provisions to the Act are being challenged in court. The premise of the challenges is whether the First Amendment rights of citizens are being unlawfully violated. Litigation on this issue is pending.

Think Critically

Is it ethical for the government to obtain confidential information about citizens without the knowledge of citizens? When do national security concerns supersede individual privacy rights? How should oversight of government agencies occur in this situation?

- **Fair Credit and Charge Card Disclosure Act**   Also an amendment of TILA, it requires credit and charge card issuers to provide information about open-end credit in direct mail or telephone solicitations. Credit card issuers must advise consumers of all fees prior to assessing the fees.

- **Home Equity Loan Consumer Protection Act**   Also amending TILA, it requires lenders to make appropriate disclosures about open-end loans that are secured by homes and places limitations on such plans.

- **Credit Repair Organization Act**   Prohibits credit repair companies from misleading consumers about their services and costs and requires agreements to be in writing.

- **Gramm-Leach-Bliley Act**   Compels banks and other financial institutions to protect the privacy of consumers. Institutions must develop written policies, notify consumers of them, and allow consumers the opportunity to "opt out" before a bank can sell some forms of personal information to others.

In addition to these federal regulations, many states have enacted similar laws intended to protect the rights and privacy of consumers.

Housing and Real Estate

A number of acts have been passed to ensure consumer protection in real estate and housing. These acts include the Flood Disaster Protection Act of 1973, the Real Estate Settlement Procedures Act of 1974, the Home Equity Loan Consumer Protection Act of 1988, and the Home Ownership and Equity Protection Act of 1994. Requiring flood insurance for designated areas, mandating that real estate settlement costs be disclosed to consumers, and protecting against exploitative real estate lending practices are protections provided under these acts. Lenders are also required to clearly list all terms for home equity loans and to limit rates and fees on home equity loans.

Educating the Public on Their Rights

The Fed offers a variety of brochures on its website aimed at educating consumers, in easily understandable language, about their rights. The brochures span topics from shopping for a mortgage, identity theft protection, and understanding credit scoring to information on leasing a car. To serve as broad an audience as possible, and to keep pace with the changing demographics in the U.S., many of these brochures are also offered in Spanish.

checkpoint

Name three other pieces of lending legislation.

ENFORCEMENT OF POLICIES OUTLINED IN ACTS ● ● ● ● ● ● ● ●

Authority for enforcing consumer protection acts varies with the individual law and the government agency associated with it.

Shared Responsibilities

In addition to the Federal Reserve Board, agencies that share enforcement responsibilities include the Federal Deposit Insurance Agency (FDIC), the Securities and Exchange Commission (SEC), the Office of Thrift Supervision (OTS), the Federal Trade Commission (FTC), the National Credit Union Administration (NCUA), the Office of the Comptroller of Currency (OCC), and the Commodity and Futures Trading Commission. These agencies have specific areas of responsibility and work together jointly on various aspects of enforcement.

©DANIEL GILBEY/SHUTTERSTOCK

In addition, audits are conducted to test compliance at banks and other financial institutions. Examiners typically review randomly selected loan files for completeness of documentation. They also watch for patterns of credit granting and denial, look at the way disputes are resolved, and check to see that privacy regulations are being observed.

One such audit was conducted in January 2008 by the **Government Accountability Office (GAO)**. The GAO is the auditing arm of Congress that helps ensure that federal laws and policies are implemented properly. The 2008 audit was a comprehensive study of the banking industry's compliance with the fee disclosure requirements of the Fed.

The report indicated that for over 20 percent of the branches included in the survey, it was difficult to easily obtain complete information about account terms and conditions. In response to the issuance of the report, numerous government agencies with oversight and implementation responsibilities have pledged their support to make sure customers can easily obtain all banking fees and terms.

Why are so many agencies involved in enforcing consumer protection?

assessment 3.3

Think Critically

1. What factors brought consumer protection laws into being?

_____

_____

_____

2. How might incomplete disclosure in an advertisement about a car loan have misled consumers before passage of the Truth in Lending Act? Give an example.

_____

_____

_____

3. Why is it in a bank's best interest to provide complete disclosure in a lending agreement and documentation of compliance with all lending laws?

_____

_____

_____

4. Some bankers feel that the banking industry is overregulated. What probably leads them to feel this way?

_____

_____

_____

Make Academic Connections

5. **COMMUNICATION** Work in teams to conduct a poll of at least 30 people. Find out how many of them have examined their credit reports in the last 12 months. How many of them have been the victim of an erroneous entry in a credit report? How many are aware of key provisions of FCRA?

6. **PROBLEM SOLVING** Conduct research to learn what information you should include in a letter of dispute to a consumer reporting agency. Draft a sample letter to a consumer reporting agency disputing a charge for an unpaid dental bill from a dentist of whom you've never heard.

7. **CONSUMER AFFAIRS** Review the privacy policy of a local bank's website. Report your findings.

Role in Determining Banks' Financial Health

goals

+ Explain the regulatory process and how it works.

+ Review how regulations affect the banking business.

terms

+ charter

+ Call report

+ System to Estimate Examinations Ratings (SEER)

+ CAMELS

Banking Scene

Kareema was visiting her Grandma and they decided to order pizza. Grandma said she was short on cash and was going to run to the bank. One minute later, Grandma reappeared with cash. Puzzled, Kareema asked her how she got to and from the bank so quickly. With a wry smile, Grandma indicated that the "bank" was a secret stash under her mattress. Having lived through the Great Depression and the crash of the banks, Grandma was leery of banks. Kareema wondered how banks stayed secure today. What safeguards are in place to keep banks secure?

OVERSIGHT RESPONSIBILITIES OF THE FED

The banking crisis that began during the second half of 2007 caused many people to be quite concerned with the stability of the nation's financial markets. Indeed, for individuals who have (or had) friends or relatives who lived through the Great Depression of the 1930s, anxiety about the stability of banks may have been heightened.

How does the Fed work to promote the stability of the banking system? Congress gave the Fed the jobs of regulating and supervising the banking system. The Board of Governors writes banking regulations. These regulations provide a blueprint of appropriate business practices for banks.

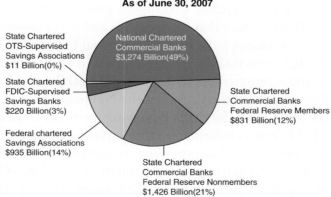

Federal Deposit Insurance Corporation
Summary of Deposits
Deposits of FDIC-insured Commercial Banks and Savings Institutions
By Charter Class
As of June 30, 2007

National Chartered Commercial Banks $3,274 Billion(49%)

State Chartered OTS-Supervised Savings Associations $11 Billion(0%)

State Chartered FDIC-Supervised Savings Banks $220 Billion(3%)

Federal chartered Savings Associations $935 Billion(14%)

State Chartered Commercial Banks Federal Reserve Members $831 Billion(12%)

State Chartered Commercial Banks Federal Reserve Nonmembers $1,426 Billion(21%)

Excludes U.S. branches of foreign banks and OTS trust institutions that are not required to file the Branch Office Survey
Source: Federal Deposit Insurance Corporation

Enforcing the rules is the responsibility of the 12 Reserve banks. Enforcement of a variety of financial institutions is required. International corporations that do banking in the U.S., state-chartered member banks, and bank holding companies are under the supervision of Reserve banks.

The Fed has help supervising banks. The FDIC, the OTS, and the OCC also supervise banking institutions. The pie chart on page 81 helps clarify supervisory roles and relative dollar volumes.

The Review Process

The Reserve banks ensure that each bank complies with state and federal legal requirements. They also make sure that each bank adheres to its own internally developed methods for conducting business. Most importantly, the Reserve banks make sure that each bank has sufficient reserves to handle outstanding loans and the risks associated with those loans.

Banks are given permission to operate as a business based on their **charter**, which is a legal approval to operate a business as a bank. Charters are issued by a government authority. The specific agency that issued the charter is responsible for regulating the bank. The table below clarifies some of these relationships.

Supervising Authority	Type of Institution
Federal Reserve	State banks (that have joined the Fed)
	Bank holding companies
Office of Thrift Supervision	Savings and loan associations
	Thrift holding companies
Comptroller of the Currency	National banks
Federal Deposit Insurance Corporation	State banks (that have not joined the Fed)

Size and structure of the financial institutions dictate the frequency of on-site reviews. Member banks, which are state banks that have chosen to become members of the Fed, usually receive an on-site review annually. Small banks, with assets of less than $250 million, might only be reviewed every 18 months. For some state member banks, the Fed may alternate on-site reviews with the overseeing state.

Processes and technologies are in place to streamline the off-site monitoring of banks. Actual reports that banks must complete on a regular basis vary by the size and scope of the bank. Larger banks with more diversified activities are required to complete more reports.

To make sure that bank reports and supervision are performed in a uniform manner, the Federal Financial Institutions Examination Council (FFIEC) was established by Congress in 1978. Membership on the council includes representatives from the Federal Reserve Board of Governors, the Comptroller of the Currency, the National Credit Union Administration, the FDIC, and the OTS. By having members from a variety of agencies, the FFIEC fosters information sharing between state and federal agencies with the common goal of providing consistent methods for banking supervision.

Each quarter, banks are required to complete a Consolidated Reports of Condition and Income, or **Call report**. This report is the basis for the *Uniform Bank Performance Report*. By comparing current financial ratios to past financial ratios, the Uniform Bank Performance Report highlights any changes in a bank's performance. Declines or startling changes in performance trigger investigation by the supervising agencies.

The **System to Estimate Examinations Ratings (SEER)** is an automated system that analyzes and compares historical supervisory ratings of banks with their Call report data. SEER provides an additional method of capturing changes in financial performance that may require supervisory intervention. SEER data can also be used to track trends within the banking industry.

 checkpoint

Why is the authority that issued a bank's charter important in the ongoing operations of the bank?

THE SCORE CARD

After each on-site review is completed, the Fed issues a rating for the bank. Examiners use the **CAMELS** system to evaluate six criteria of safety and soundness. Each letter stands for one of the criteria: **C**apital adequacy, **A**sset adequacy, **M**anagement, **E**arnings, **L**iquidity, and **S**ensitivity to risk. Risk evaluation measures whether a bank makes good decisions in lending money. CAMELS ratings are not public information. The agency that issues the rating has proprietary rights to the rating. Banks cannot release their CAMELS rating to third parties without first obtaining approval from the agency that issued the rating. This issue became prominent when insurance companies began to ask banks for their CAMELS rating prior to providing them with insurance.

Maintaining Balance in the Banking System

Banks are required to get permission from the Fed before they can acquire another bank, introduce new products, or diversify. This mandatory approval process enables Reserve banks to make sure that regulatory requirements are met. The permission process also gives the Fed an opportunity to ensure there will be sufficient competition in the regional market.

Trust Generates Trust

Remember, it takes a great deal of mutual trust for all parties in an economic system to keep investing in a system. Each investor needs to be assured that every other investor will act within a predefined and universally accepted way. Banking regulations make a code of conduct explicit and mandatory. This gives investors assurance that their money will be carefully and honestly managed. This trust allows money to keep flowing through the system. Regulations can be revised to reflect needs of society and still maintain the safeguards necessary for ethical and safe practices.

Regulations that Encourage Private Investors to Aid Ailing Banks

A variety of privately financed entities, including private equity firms, hedge funds, and mutual funds, were willing to provide capital to distressed banks during the recent mortgage and credit crises. Regulations that were in place during April 2008 allowed these investors access to the banks' books, including some confidential banking records. By being allowed to carefully examine banks' financial status before investing in them, privately financed companies could obtain a solid understanding of actual financial positions of the bank. Knowing what they were getting into allowed private equity firms the ability to negotiate the terms of their investment and to invest with a clear understanding of any risks associated with their investment.

During the savings and loan crisis that occurred during the late 1980s and early 1990s, private investors did not have the same level of open access to the books of banks. This lack of access discouraged private investment firms from providing capital to help save failing savings and loans.

Future Regulations that May Facilitate Private Investment

Some market watchers think the government should make additional regulatory changes to further encourage private equity investors to help save banks.

Current regulations cap the percent that a private equity firm can invest in a bank at less than 10 percent of shares. There is a belief that by increasing that cap, private equity firms would be more willing to invest in banks. An increased percentage of ownership would provide stronger shareholder voting power. With stronger voting power, firms would feel they have more control over future management of the bank.

Another recommended change would impact banking acquisitions. Currently, when one bank acquires another, any bad loans held by the acquiree must be written off immediately by the acquiring bank. This requires a lot of upfront capital from the acquiring banks. Similarly, a large amount of capital for bad debt is a disincentive for many potential investors.

The recommended change would allow bad debt held by the acquiree to be written off over time. This would lessen the amount of capital an acquiring bank would need to provide. By lessening the immediate financial exposure of the acquiring bank, the proposed change would lower the hurdle for acquiring a bank.

Why is society interested in encouraging banks to help other ailing banks?

assessment 3.4

Think Critically

1. What is a charter?

_____

_____

2. What does the acronym CAMELS represent?

_____

_____

3. How does the Uniform Bank Report help regulators?

_____

_____

4. Why is trust necessary in the banking system?

_____

_____

_____

Make Academic Connections

5. **LOCAL REGULATION** Interview a local bank representative and ask about the review process at his or her bank. Find out which regulatory agencies participate in the review and the frequency of the reviews. Inquire how the bank's asset level affects the frequency of the review schedule. Summarize your findings below.

_____

_____

_____

6. **RESEARCH** Copies of Call reports are available to the public at the FFIEC website. Go to cdr.ffiec.gov/public and look up the most recent Call report for your bank. Scan the report to obtain an idea of the completeness of the data collected. Does the thoroughness of the data collected make you, as a consumer, feel more confident that your bank is closely regulated? Be prepared to discuss your thoughts and feelings with the class.

_____

_____

3.5

goals

+ Explain the role of the Fed in international banking.

+ Discuss how the Fed works to keep the dollar strong.

+ Review how countries work together to provide a stable international banking economy.

terms

+ Strength of Support Assessment (SOSA)

+ ROCA score

+ fixed exchange rate

+ flexible exchange rate

+ balance of payments

+ Federal Reserve System Open Market Account (SOMA)

+ U.S. Treasury Exchange Stabilization Fund (ESF)

International Banking and the Federal Reserve System

Banking Scene

Kareema had spent a few years saving money for her upcoming vacation to Europe. She had carefully planned her budget to cover transportation, lodging, food, admittance to attractions, and some spare money for spontaneous "fun" activities. She had recently read that the value of the dollar had declined relative to the euro. She began to worry about her expenses. Realizing the dollar would buy less on her trip, she was examining her budget to see where she could cut back. Why did the dollar weaken?

AN INTERDEPENDENT GLOBAL ECONOMY

Globalization has led to increased interdependency between nations. Food, raw materials, medicines, electronics, and vehicles are just a few of the products that flow between borders. Money is required to enable these transactions. A mutually acceptable method needs to be in place so that nations that use different currency can exchange funds across international borders.

Just as products flow across borders, financial instruments flow across borders. U.S. monetary policies affect the global economy just as financial actions of the global economy affect the U.S. economy. Foreign-owned banks operate in the U.S. and U.S.-owned banks have offices in foreign countries. The Fed works, sometimes in conjunction with other U.S. agencies or with central banks of other countries, to promote stability in international financial markets. Efforts include supervising international banking, minimizing disruptions in currency value, and sponsoring internationally focused learning sessions.

Supervision of International Banks

There are multiple ways that the Fed regulates foreign banking. U.S.-chartered banks that operate in foreign countries are regulated by the Fed. Banks that are chartered in a foreign country and transact business in the U.S. are also regulated by the Fed.

Federal Regulation of foreign banks was formalized with the International Banking Act of 1978 (IBA). To ensure a level playing field between international banks and domestic banks, this act gave the same powers to foreign banks that U.S. banks have. On the flip side, foreign banks are subjected to the same restrictions as U.S. banks.

Nearly 20 years later, this act was amended with the passage of the Foreign Bank Supervision Enhancement Act of 1991 (FBSEA). Under FBSEA, foreign banks are required to obtain the approval of the Fed before opening offices in the U.S. In determining whether to approve these applications, the Fed considers how stringently the bank is regulated in its country of origin, the overall financial health of the bank, and whether the bank and its country of origin actively seek to fight money laundering.

Sometimes the Fed partners with other U.S. supervisory agencies to carry out regulations. Two sets of rankings have been established to help with this process. The **Strength of Support Assessment (SOSA)** reflects how well a foreign bank is able to provide appropriate guidance, oversight, and financial backing to its U.S. offices. A composite score of performance in four distinct areas is a **ROCA score**. The areas included in this score are risk management, operational controls, compliance, and asset quality.

Stabilizing Currency Values

Promoting full employment, price stability, and economic growth is the common goal of many monetary authorities in various countries.

Banking Math *Connection*

With a flexible exchange rate, currency values change relative to other currencies. The following chart shows the values of a few currencies relative to the dollar as of August 2008. These rates were listed in the Foreign Exchange Rates section of the Federal Reserve. Find how many euros equal 1 U.S. dollar.

Country	Denomination	$US August 2008
Australia	dollar	0.8815
EMU members	euro	1.4955
India	rupee	42.9057

Solution

$$\frac{1 \text{ euro}}{1.4955 \text{ \$US}} = \frac{x \text{ euro}}{1 \text{ \$US}}$$

$$1.4955 x = 1$$
$$x = 1 \div 1.4955$$
$$x = 0.67 \text{ euros}$$

Therefore, 1 $US will buy 0.67 euros.

Foreign exchange methodologies have changed through the years. From about the mid 1940s until the early 1970s, the U.S. dollar was at the center of international currency exchange. Under a fixed-rate exchange system, the U.S. needed to maintain the dollar price of gold at about $35 per ounce. The U.S. would buy and sell dollars to stay at or near the $35 rate. In turn, other countries were required to maintain the value of their currency relative to the U.S. dollar at a set amount. Only a one percent variation in value was allowed.

A **fixed exchange rate** is a bit of an artificial system. A monetary valuation of one country's currency is tied to the valuation of another country's currency. Sometimes the decision is made to maintain the international currency value at the expense of some other monetary goal—like maintaining full employment, price stability, or economic growth.

A **flexible exchange rate** enables currencies to fluctuate based on market conditions. However, to fully understand flexible exchange rates, an understanding of balance of payments is necessary.

Balance of Payments

Countries monitor the total amount of goods and services that leave their country. They also monitor the amount of goods and services that enter their country. Each country looks at the overall total of its imports and exports. It also monitors the amount of goods and services it trades with individual countries. The **balance of payments** is a record of all the exchanges of goods and services that occur between two countries for a specified time period.

A flexible exchange rate allows currency values to move up or down in response to changes in the balance of payments. If Country A sends more goods and services to Country B than it receives from Country B, then Country A has a surplus in the balance of payments with Country B. As a result of this surplus, Country A's exchange rate increases relative to Country B's. Therefore, Country A's currency can buy Country B's goods more cheaply. Likewise, Country B will find it more expensive to buy the goods of Country A.

tech talk

Electronic Funds Transfer

Like many businesses and private individuals, the Federal Reserve System uses electronic funds transfer (EFT) to make and receive payments. The Fed has its own system, called Fedwire, with special capabilities. Fedwire connects the Federal Reserve, the Treasury, other government agencies, and more than 9,500 financial institutions. In 2000, an average of 430,000 daily payments totaling about $1.5 trillion took place over the Fedwire network. The Federal Reserve by law must charge for its Fedwire services and prices them according to cost.

Think Critically
In what ways does Fedwire strengthen the entire Federal Reserve System? Why might the law mandate a charge for this service?

checkpoint

How would a balance of payment deficit affect Countries A and B?

KEEPING THE DOLLAR STRONG • • • • • • • • • • • • • • • • • •

In the mid 1970s, the method for managing international currency stability changed to flexible exchange rates in the U.S. The Fed helps maintain the international value of the dollar through foreign currency operations. The FOMC provides guidance to the Fed when it buys or sells U.S. dollars. The goal of stabilizing the international value of the dollar is to maintain a stable currency value to encourage international trade. Countries who wish to conduct business with the U.S. want a clear understanding of the profits and/or risks associated with the trades. Knowing that the value of the dollar will remain relatively stable allows foreign investors to predict the amount of profit or risk they will experience.

How do actions of the Fed stabilize the dollar? If the value of the dollar is falling, the Fed may purchase dollars by selling foreign currency. This tightens the supply of dollars on the open market, which causes the value of the dollar to increase. If the value of the dollar is high and the Fed wants to lower it, the Fed may buy foreign currency with U.S. dollars. This increases the supply of U.S. dollars in the marketplace, which lowers the value of the dollar. The Fed seeks to maintain a steady balance of Federal Reserve balances. When the Fed sells foreign currency, it *sterilizes* the impact of the sale by purchasing an equivalent amount of U.S. currency. Sterilization is necessary to maintain the federal funds rate at the target set by the FOMC. The account the Fed maintains international reserves in is the **Federal Reserve System Open Market Account (SOMA)**. The account the Treasury maintains international reserves in is the **U.S. Treasury Exchange Stabilization Fund (ESF)**.

As the U.S. Treasury and the Fed work in close cooperation on decisions and policies affecting foreign currency issues, they also share responsibility for maintaining the levels of foreign exchange reserves in the U.S. This shared responsibility results in a generally equal division of reserve holdings. For example, at the end of June 2007, the Federal Reserve had nearly $21 billion dollars in its SOMA account and the Treasury had a nearly equal amount in its ESF account.

checkpoint

Why is the Fed interested in stabilizing the value of the dollar?

INTERNATIONAL COOPERATION

Many countries realize their dependence on and vulnerability to international market conditions. In addition to trading products across borders, countries or citizens from one country may directly invest in businesses in another country. One example of this direct investment is when foreign investors purchased mortgage-backed securities during the U.S. mortgage crisis. These investors were hoping to make a profit by purchasing the securities at a discount. By doing this, foreign investors held a significant number of U.S. mortgages.

To foster a spirit of trust, and to develop laws that ensure transactions are carried out in good faith and honestly, a number of organizations have formed over the years that are designed to make banking safe and mutually beneficial across international borders.

International Monetary Fund (IMF) Representatives from 185 member countries work together to promote economic growth among member countries. The IMF takes actions to encourage the stability of the financial exchange markets. Sometimes the IMF will lend money to a country that needs help with its balance of payments. The IMF also seeks to avoid money laundering in an effort to avoid financing terrorism.

Bank for International Settlements (BIS) With about 140 customers, the BIS is a bank for central banks. Serving only countries (and not private entities), it focuses on fostering international monetary and financial stability. A variety of products aimed at helping central banks invest and manage their foreign assets is offered by BIS.

Asia Pacific Economic Cooperation (APEC) The 21 members of APEC are referred to as "member economies." APEC encourages economic growth in the Asia-Pacific Region. The U.S. is a member of APEC.

International Banking Seminars Since 1997, the Federal Reserve Bank of Chicago has organized international conferences on banking. By bringing together people who develop policy and people who do economic research, the seminars provide a cross section of ideas regarding issues that cut across many aspects of international banking. Recent seminars have focused on "Globalization and Systemic Risk," "International Financial Instability: Cross Border Banking and National Regulation," and "Credit Market Turmoil of 2007–2008: Implications for Public Policy."

 checkpoint

How does bringing together policy makers and researchers to examine a common topic facilitate smooth transactions for international banking?

assessment 3.5

Think Critically

1. Explain the key concepts of the International Banking Act of 1978.

_____

_____

2. What does the acronym ROCA mean and how does it relate to SOSA?

_____

_____

_____

3. What is the balance of payments?

_____

_____

4. Name the account for international reserves maintained by the Fed and by the Treasury.

_____

_____

Make Academic Connections

5. **EDUCATION**   Visit the website of the Chicago Federal Reserve at www.chicagofed.org/news_and_conferences/conferences_and_events/2008_international.cfm. Review recent seminars on international banking and see what seminars are planned for the future. Be prepared to discuss how the seminars reflect past, current, and future concerns of the industry.

6. **CURRENT EVENTS**   During the third quarter of 2007, the international value of the dollar fell. During that time, one euro could buy $1.4065. Prior to that time, one euro could not buy more than $1.4. One result of the falling dollar value was that products manufactured in America were less expensive to citizens of countries whose currency was strong relative to the dollar. This increased American exports. Research the current international value of the dollar relative to the euro. List it below. Also list how the dollar's international value affects the overall economy.

_____

_____

_____

_____

chapter 3 assessment

Chapter Summary

3.1 Structure of the Federal Reserve System

A. The Chair oversees the Federal Reserve Board, which oversees the 12 District Reserve Banks, which monitor and serve the member banks.

B. The Fed is the U.S. government's bank, a bank for banks, and a supervisory organization.

3.2 Monetary and Fiscal Policy

A. Monetary policy adjusts bank reserves and influences interest rates for economic stability. The Federal Reserve is the author of monetary policy.

B. Fiscal policy is the Congress and President's way to control the economy.

3.3 Consumer Protection

A. Four main laws (TILA, ECOA, FCRA, and FDCPA) provide the foundation for consumer protection in lending.

B. Banks are required to document their compliance with all applicable state and federal regulations.

3.4 Role in Determining Banks' Financial Health

A. The Fed, the FDIC, OTS, and OCC share oversight duties.

B. Quarterly Call reports summarize banks' performance.

3.5 International Banking and the Federal Reserve System

A. The Fed supervises U.S. banks with offices abroad and foreign banks with offices in the U.S.

B. The Fed and the Treasury work to keep the dollar strong.

C. Multiple organizations foster international economic development.

Vocabulary Builder

Choose the term that best fits the definition. Write the letter of the answer in the space provided. Some terms may not be used.

a. adverse feedback loop
b. balance of payments
c. Call report
d. CAMELS
e. charter
f. District Reserve Bank
g. Equal Credit Opportunity Act (ECOA)
h. Fair Credit Reporting Act
i. Fair Debt Collection Practices Act (FDCPA)
j. Federal Open Market Committee (FOMC)
k. Federal Reserve System Open Market Account (SOMA)
l. fixed exchange rate
m. flexible exchange rate
n. Government Accountability Office (GAO)
o. member bank
p. ROCA score
q. Strength of Support Assessment (SOSA)
r. System to Estimate Examinations Ratings (SEER)
s. Taylor rule
t. Truth in Lending Act (TILA)
u. U.S. Treasury Exchange Stabilization Fund (ESF)

____ 1. A report banks are required to complete quarterly that reflects their performance

____ 2. A rating of how well a foreign bank is able to provide appropriate guidance, oversight, and financial backing to its U.S. offices

____ 3. A record of all the exchanges of goods and services that occur between two countries for a specified time period

____ 4. Protects consumers from unfair collection techniques

____ 5. Guarantees that all information about a loan is provided in writing

____ 6. When the monetary valuation of one country's currency is tied to the valuation of another country's currency

____ 7. The government body that makes decisions about discount interest rates

____ 8. A theory about using short-term interest rates to achieve the goals of a central bank

____ 9. Legal approval to operate a business as a bank

Review Concepts

10. Name the four organizational components of the Federal Reserve System.

_____

_____

11. What four functions does the Federal Reserve perform?

_____

_____

12. Describe the structure and purpose of the FOMC.

_____

_____

_____

13. How does Keynesian economics relate to fiscal policy?

_____

_____

_____

_____

14. Explain the role of an adverse feedback loop in the recent credit crisis.

_____

_____

_____

_____

15. How does the balance of payments impact a flexible exchange rate?

_____

_____

_____

_____

16. Why is it significant which government agency issued a bank's charter?

_____

_____

17. How does the SEER report help regulators?

_____

_____

18. Why is the government interested in helping private investors aid banks that are struggling?

_____

_____

_____

_____

19. Describe the membership and objectives of the IMF.

_____

_____

20. Why did the U.S. transition from a fixed exchange rate to a flexible exchange rate?

_____

_____

_____

Apply What You Learned

21. What is the advantage of distancing the Federal Reserve System from politics?

_____

_____

_____

_____

22. Why is inflation a constant concern of the Federal Reserve Board?

_____

_____

_____

23. Describe the differences between monetary and fiscal policy.

_____

_____

_____

24. As of August 2008, the Australian dollar was worth $0.8815 U.S. dollars and the Indian rupee was worth $42.9057. How many Australian dollars and Indian rupees would a U.S. dollar have bought at that time?

_____

_____

25. Name four consumer protection laws related to lending.

_____

_____

_____

26. How would it help the banking industry if the amount a private equity firm could invest in a bank was increased beyond 10 percent?

_____

_____

_____

Make Academic Connections

27. **POLITICAL SCIENCE**   If inflation is such a concern, why not just stabilize the economy by imposing wage and price controls? Wages and prices have occasionally been frozen before in emergency situations. Should wage and price controls be permanently established? Write a paragraph that summarizes your opinion.

_____

_____

_____

_____

28. **SOCIAL STUDIES**   Choose one of the laws discussed in lesson 3.3, Consumer Protection. Prepare a detailed report on its history, its provisions, and its effect on the lending industry. Write a three-page report on what you learn.

_____

_____

29. **CURRENT EVENTS**   Consumer protection also applies to student loans. In September 2008, the *New York Times* reported that seven student loan companies were required to develop a $1.4 million dollar fund to help educate students and their parents on student loans. The companies were cited for misleading advertising practices, including sending students marketing materials that looked like they came from the federal government. Research any new cases where the government intervened to protect consumers' rights. Prepare a one-page report to summarize your findings.

_____

_____

Money and Interest

4.1	The Money Supply
4.2	Money Creation and Circulation
4.3	Interest and Interest Rates

PHOTODISC/GETTY IMAGES

skills that pay dividends

Quantitative Skills

The choice of computing methods—from calculators, to cell phones, to spreadsheets, to online services—has made it extraordinarily easy for you to enter data into a computing device and get an answer. Whether doing multiplication to calculate the cost of buying enough pizzas for a Little League team or performing complex analytical functions to determine the economic performance of a business, you can get a machine to provide an answer.

Do people using electronic calculators understand the concepts behind the computations? If electricity failed and batteries were not available, could most people manually calculate the answers? Maybe not, given that the 2006 scores of U.S. students in an International Student Assessment indicated that 15-year-old U.S. students performed less well on math than peers from 23 other countries.

The ability to mentally perform a "ballpark" calculation for financial transactions enables you to think on your feet. You will be able to quickly assess the reasonableness of the results you see on your screen. By having a rough idea of what an answer should be, you can catch errors before they progress very far.

In the banking industry, percentages are used in a variety of ways. Calculations that use percentages include simple interest and mutual fund performance.

Simple interest is calculated by multiplying the beginning amount, or principal, by the interest rate and by the length of the investment. The interest rate is expressed as a percentage. The length of the investment is expressed, in decimal form, in relation to a year. A three-month investment is 25 percent of a year, or 0.25 years. A 21-month investment is 1.75 years.

Mutual funds are comprised of a variety of distinct investments that have various degrees of risk and varying maturity dates. Typically the investments are spread out across a number of different industries to minimize the exposure caused by a downturn in any specific industry. The performance of each investment in each industry contributes to the performance of the fund as a whole.

Mutual funds may express their returns based on the performance of each industry in the fund. For example, the fund may state that 50 percent of its results are based on performance of the airline industry, 30 percent on the performance of the pharmaceutical industry, and 20 percent on the performance of the software industry. Stated another way, half of the fund is invested in the airline industry, a bit less than a third is invested in the pharmaceutical industry, and one fifth of it is invested in the software industry.

Develop Your Skill

Create a quiz on percentages that has ten values and ten percentages to calculate. Exchange papers with classmates and complete the quizzes. Grade the quizzes and see who earned the greatest percentage of correct answers.

PHOTODISC

4.1

goals

+ Explain how the money supply is measured.

+ Describe the two types of money.

terms

+ money supply

+ liquidity

+ aggregate measures

+ commodity money

+ fiat money

+ fractional reserve system

The Money Supply

Banking Scene

When Elizabeth Axtell paid for her gasoline fill-up, she received a ten dollar bill as change. She happened to notice that on the bill someone had written, "Happy Birthday, Betty!" This greeting on the bill caused her to think of all the places the bill had traveled and all the people who had handled the bill. As she put the bill away, she wondered how much money there is circulating out there at any given moment, and she resolved to learn more about it. How might Elizabeth begin to define "out there"?

WHAT IS THE MONEY SUPPLY? • • • • • • • • • • • • • • • •

As you learned about the creation of a national currency and problems throughout the nineteenth and early twentieth centuries with the money supply, did you wonder where money comes from? Why can't the government just print more money? What would happen if it did?

The Federal Reserve was established to solve currency problems and manage the money supply. Its adjustments are indirect, and because banks are private institutions, it doesn't simply command the money supply. The Federal Reserve influences the conditions under which banks do business and sees that those banks abide by banking regulations. You may be surprised about what money really is in the United States. You will get a sense of how much money is out there, what it is doing, and how its movements are measured. You will also learn more about how banks and the Federal Reserve work together to create and manage money.

The Concept of Money Supply

Even after state currencies disappeared and a national monetary system was in place, serious problems with the banking system occurred in 1873, 1883, 1893, and 1907, resulting in bank failures and large-scale economic problems. The crisis in 1907 caused Congress to commission a study group, which ultimately led to the establishment of the Federal Reserve.

The source of these problems was the money supply. The **money supply** is defined as the liquid assets held by banks and individuals. These assets include all the money in circulation as well as money held in banks or in other financial institutions. This money is moving in the economy from

PHOTODISC/GETTY IMAGES

place to place and person to person. The flow of money—and the amount of it flowing—has a direct effect on how the economy performs.

The basic idea is simple: if there is too much money around, prices rise to the point of inducing problematic inflation. If there is too little money around, there is not enough to meet needs and a "credit crunch" slows the economy. If the economy slows too much, commerce spirals down, jobs are lost, less and less money moves, and so forth. The trick is to keep the money supply and economy growing at a stable rate so that wealth spreads, yet without inducing inflation. Unfortunately, there are so many factors in a complex economy that providing steady growth is not easy.

Expanding the Money Supply

Why might extra money in the economy cause inflation? Assume you have an income of $4,000 per month that meets your basic needs. Suddenly, your income jumps 15 percent to $4,600. What would you do with the extra money? Most people would probably buy things. That seems good, doesn't it?

Now assume you own an electronics store. If a large rush of customers came in demanding DVD players, how would you respond?

Consider the following questions: What would happen to prices of DVD players? Why? What would happen to the supply of DVD players? What effect might that have on prices? If prices for all goods and services also went up, what would be the net effect on your 15 percent increase in income compared to what it actually buys?

The supply of DVD players will decrease, thus causing prices to rise. If prices for all goods and services go up, the 15 percent increase in income will actually buy less. If this trend continues for a period of time, it can result in inflation.

Measuring the Money

Defining the money supply as all the money in circulation, all the money held by banks, and all the money held by individuals may not be detailed enough to track the ebb and flow of money. **Liquidity** is a measure of how quickly things may be converted to something of value like cash. Liquidity is variable, depending on the nature of the asset or liability. Your savings account is not as liquid as coins in your pocket, but more liquid than a certificate of deposit that doesn't mature until next June.

All the money in all types of accounts is part of the money supply. However, some types of money are more liquid than others. To estimate money's movement, economists and the Federal Reserve use various measures. These measures, called M1, M2, and MZM, take into account various types of money and various circumstances of liquidity.

Measure	Explanation
M1	Money that can be spent immediately. M1 includes currency (paper and metallic) and various types of checking accounts, including nonbank travelers' checks, standard checking accounts, and NOW (interest-bearing) accounts.
M2	All the money in M1 plus short-term investments, such as small savings accounts (less than $100,000), money market accounts, and money market mutual funds.
MZM	Money at zero maturity. Represents all available liquid money. It is M2, minus time deposits, and includes all money market funds.

As a result of the Humphrey-Hawkins Act, also known as the Full Employment and Balanced Growth Act of 1978, the FED set semi-annual target rates for the money supply. Investors interpreted these target rates as an indicator of what the FED planned to do with the money supply. For example, if the FED released a low M1, investors might think short-term interest rates would be decreased to increase the money supply. (When consumers earn less return on the money in savings accounts, they may decide to take money from savings and make a purchase. This releases more money into the economy.) As of July 2000, the FED stopped setting target ranges for the money supply.

tech talk

Measuring Nontraditional Forms of Money

How do "electronic money" and automated payment systems affect the money supply and monetary policies? These nontraditional forms can alter the measurement of the money supply, which in turn could shift the way monetary policy is implemented. Most consumer electronic money falls easily into the M1 demand-deposit category, and it has already begun to be measured as such. But as these services grow, they may alter the definition of certain monetary instruments. Economists rely less on the M1 and M2 measures than they once did, and some think they are relatively unimportant.

Think Critically
Why are the M1 and M2 measures becoming less important? How does changing technology also alter the Federal Reserve's supervisory task?

Taken together, these **aggregate measures**, which add up the components of the money supply, are used to estimate the size of the money supply. M1 is sometimes referred to as the "base" money supply. M2 and MZM give some indication of potential demand on the money supply. Historically, it was believed that increasing growth of the money supply accompanied a strengthening economy, while decreasing growth of money implied a slowing economy.

Over time, M1 and M2 became less reliable indicators of financial performance. As financial offerings expanded, with the introduction of products like NOW accounts, the relationship between economic performance and the values of M1 and M2 weakened. NOW accounts allowed consumers to earn interest on service-free checking accounts so long as they maintained a minimum balance. Shifts in the economy, including changes in interest rates, prompted customers to shift their investment strategies. As investments moved from traditional savings accounts to the stock market, the value of M2 decreased. Stocks and bonds are excluded from M2 measurements. Therefore, although consumers still had their money working for them, the value of the money was not reflected in M1 or M2.

A fourth measure of the money supply, M3, was in use from 1971 until March 2006. M3 was the most comprehensive measure of available money and included all the money in M1 and M2 plus large deposits, such as agreements among banks and institutional money market funds. A surge in M3 indicated an excessive amount of money was available. As access to money became easier, costs rose and inflation occurred. Some who study economic trends believe that an unusually rapid growth of M3 was a predicator of a possible depression.

None of these measures is a safe predictor of inflation. Other factors such as supply, demand, labor, resources, and political events also play a role in determining the rate of inflation.

What makes up the money supply? Why do economists use different measurements to track the money supply?

THE NATURE OF MONEY

To understand where the money supply comes from, how it moves, and how banks and the Federal Reserve influence it, you need to understand what money in the United States really is. Although the monetary system has remnants from long ago, it is also a modern "agreement" dating from the 1930s. Two essential ideas dominate the monetary system. One is the idea of *fiat money*, and the other is the idea of a *fractional-reserve system*.

Two Types of Money

Why does money have value? Money is a medium of exchange—something with an agreed-upon value used for trade. Today that agreed-upon value is strictly a convention of the government and has no necessary relationship to the value of gold, silver, bushels of grain, feathers, or any other commodity. A dollar is worth a dollar because everyone agrees that it is, not because it is backed by an amount of precious metal somewhere. Historically, there are two types of monetary systems.

Commodity money is based on some item of value—for example, gold or precious stones. Coins, the oldest form of currency, had some value because of the metal in them. Bank notes were originally issued to represent holdings of precious metal and became the first paper currency. The notes had value because they could be exchanged for an actual amount of a valuable commodity. Although many of the symbolic ideas and concepts associated with commodity money remain in play, commodity money is not generally in use today.

Fiat money is money that is deemed legal tender by the government, and it is not based on or convertible into a commodity. The word *fiat*

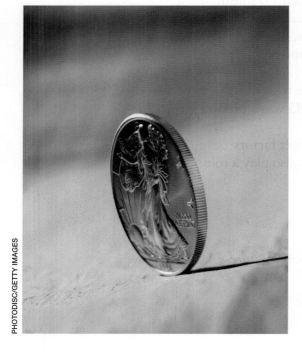

refers to any order issued by legal authority, and in the case of money, the authority is the Federal Reserve as created by Congress. Take a look at a dollar bill. It announces that it is a Federal Reserve note. During 2007, it cost about 6.2 cents to produce a dollar bill, and you cannot take Federal Reserve notes to the bank and exchange them for gold or silver. What makes Federal Reserve notes valuable is that they are the only kind of money the government will accept for payment of taxes and for payments of debts related to court actions. They are, in short, the official currency of the United States.

Fiat money makes sense as a medium of exchange. If you and some friends agreed to use certificates you made for value between you, and you all abided by that convention, your currency system would work. Saran might be willing to trade you a DVD for two of the certificates, which you might then give Luisa for an hour of raking leaves. Luisa might use them to buy a basket of flowers from Dawn for Saran, and Dawn might offer you two certificates to care for her dog while she's away. As long as you all agree on the relative values, the system works. In the case of the national system, the government enforces what is acceptable currency, and the Federal Reserve, banks, and market influence its value. In any case, there is no longer silver in a quarter, though everyone agrees that it is worth 25 percent of a dollar.

The Fractional-Reserve System

One of the key concepts in understanding how money is created and manipulated arose almost a thousand years ago. Some people say "modern" banking began in England around 1200. At that time, people began to pay goldsmiths to store precious metals safely. The goldsmiths charged a fee for this service. When people left gold or silver, the goldsmiths gave them receipts, indicating that the holder of the receipt had deposited a certain quantity. Soon, people began to use these receipts as a medium of exchange, because trading them was a lot simpler than going to the goldsmith, getting the gold, and giving it to the person owed. It was easier just to give the receipt. These receipts were the first bank notes in England, and became a form of paper currency.

The goldsmiths quickly got into the business of lending the gold and silver they had on deposit, charging interest for the loans. That business was good, so goldsmiths began to pay interest to attract deposits. This business practice initiated the *spread* in banking.

The goldsmiths also noticed something else. Not everyone wanted their gold back at the same time. Therefore, the goldsmiths adopted a **fractional-reserve system** whereby they needed to keep back, or reserve, only a fraction of the total gold that had been deposited—just enough to cover those who might want to withdraw their gold. They could also lend notes, thus making more money without actually having gold to back it up. The paper notes in circulation eventually exceeded the reserves of gold that the goldsmiths actually held. In effect, money was "created" without changing the amount of gold.

Although what the goldsmiths noticed was based on a system of commodity money, some of the same principles apply today. First, even though Federal Reserve notes are fiat money, money is created in more or less the same way. Second, a fractional-reserve system is still in use today, and adjusting its requirements is one way that the Federal Reserve controls the money supply.

 checkpoint

What is fiat money? What is meant by fractional reserve?

"communicate"

Interview several people from various walks of life. Ask them what they think makes our money valuable. Write a short report listing the various opinions (right or wrong), and share the ideas with your class.

assessment 4.1

Think Critically

1. Why are there more elements to the money supply than just the money that is actively circulating?

2. Why do different parts of the money supply need to be measured differently?

3. Why must the government enforce the value of fiat money by requiring its use for settling private debts in court or for transactions with the government?

4. What would have happened to the English goldsmiths if for some reason everyone had wanted their gold back at the same time? What could the goldsmiths have done?

Make Academic Connections

5. **HISTORY** Besides fiat money, the U.S. government has issued other types of money, such as silver certificates. Find out what a silver certificate is, when the last one was issued, and what one is worth today. Record your findings here.

6. **BANKING MATH** The Federal Reserve requires banks to hold a reserve on customer deposits subject to checking. Required in 2007, for example, was a reserve of 3 percent on the first liabilities between $9.3 million and $43.9 million and 10 percent on all amounts above that. If a bank had $91 million in such deposits, what was the amount of required reserves?

Money Creation and Circulation

Banking Scene

As Elizabeth Axtell pulls away from the gas station, she thinks about how currency circulates. She also begins to wonder more about the origin of money. She knows the government prints it, of course, but under what circumstances? How does the money supply grow? What would you tell her?

goals

+ Describe how money is created by bank activities.

+ Explain how money circulates in the U.S.

terms

+ primary reserves

+ secondary reserves

+ excess reserves

+ multiplier effect

HOW MONEY IS CREATED

How money is created and how currency is printed are two different things. The Bureau of Engraving and Printing performs the task of printing currency. No matter how much the Bureau prints, it isn't actually considered part of the money supply until a commercial bank or other financial institution calls for it in exchange for amounts on deposit in the reserve account of the Federal Reserve. Money is actually created by the interaction of the demand for it, banks' use of it, and the Federal Reserve's supply and control of it.

Banks and other financial institutions play a key role in the creation of money by transacting their business. Banks earn much of their profit by lending. The lending function, however, does much more than earn money for the bank and its stockholders. Because of the function of the Federal Reserve and the banking system as a whole, banks actually "create" and circulate money as they do business.

Deposits and Reserves

Your deposits are liabilities for the bank that holds them, because the bank will have to give your money back to you. In order to guarantee that the bank will have money on hand to cover its liabilities, the Federal Reserve requires banks to hold money in reserve. Only a portion of the total amount of deposits is required to be reserved. **Primary reserves** consist of *vault cash* (cash on hand) and the required percentage amounts on deposit in the Federal Reserve District Bank. A bank may have other reserves as well, called **secondary reserves**, including securities the bank purchases from the federal government and deposits that are due from other banks. Secondary reserves are used to meet liquidity needs, which include customer requests for withdrawal amounts and money needed for new loans.

Excess reserves are reserves held by a bank beyond its reserve requirement. Excess reserves, which are amounts that exceed Primary and Secondary reserves, are the resources a bank uses to create money through its business transactions. These excess reserves are amounts for which there is no immediate demand. The bank may go into the Fed Funds market and put them to work overnight by lending them to another institution that has a need for them. Or the bank may purchase a repurchase agreement from the Federal Reserve if the FRB is making such an offer through it's Open Market Operations.

The Multiplier Effect

To understand the role banks play in creating money, consider again the fractional-reserve system. Remember that a bank needs to keep on hand only part of its total liabilities, and that liabilities always exceed reserves. This fractional-reserve system works just as it did for the goldsmiths long ago. Money on deposit, minus the reserve requirement, can be loaned to customers. When it is, new deposits are created. These new deposits go out to customers as loans and create more deposits, thus expanding the amount of money in the system. This phenomenon is called the **multiplier effect**.

Suppose you deposit $1,000, and the bank has a 10 percent reserve requirement. That leaves $900 that may be loaned out to someone. That $900 may be used to buy something, and the seller will probably end up depositing that $900 in another bank. (It could be the same one, but use a different one for the sake of the example.) Of the $900 deposited in the second bank, 10 percent is reserved, leaving $810, which the second bank will lend and will thus end up deposited in a third bank. Your original $1,000 deposit has

Banking Math *Connection*

Calculate the total amount of money "created" from a deposit of $15,000 as it moves through four cycles of deposit. Assume a reserve rate of 10 percent.

Solution

The formula for calculating the money available from a deposit is

$$\text{Deposit} - \text{Reserve} = \text{New Deposit}$$

Repeat the operation for each deposit, then total the new deposits.

Deposit 1: $15,000 − $1,500.00 = $13,500.00   0.10 × $15,000 = $1,500.00
Deposit 2: $13,500 − $1,350.00 = $12,150.00   0.10 × $13,500 = $13,500.00
Deposit 3: $12,150 − $1,215.00 = $10,935.00   0.10 × $12,150 = $12,150.00
Deposit 4: $10,935 − $1,093.50 = $ 9,841.50   0.10 × $10,935 = $1,093.50

Total Deposits = $46,426.50

These four deposits result in the "creation" of more than $46,000 available for use in the money supply.

resulted in deposits in three separate banks totaling $2,710. Of this total, $1,710 was "created" by the transactions.

Now, of course, your bank must have enough total reserves to cover the $900 check it wrote for the loan when the second bank presents that check for payment. Your bank must also be prepared to give your original $1,000 back to you if you decide to withdraw it. It may use excess reserves for this money, or money from its cash flow of other business, or it may borrow from the Federal Reserve or other sources. Estimating the amount of reserves needed at a particular point in time is critical to banking, although it is impossible to do so with complete accuracy. The bank can't absolutely know when you will want your money, and it can't absolutely know when someone wants a loan. Banks follow the money supply and the economy as closely as they can in order to anticipate their liabilities and reserve needs. In order for all these transactions to pay off, the bank must be making a solid profit on the money it lends. That $900 loan and others like it must earn enough income to defray the costs of creating money. Banks that make poor judgments about the type and amount of loans they extend may find themselves in trouble. If enough banks get into trouble, the whole system could be in jeopardy. Overseeing sound banking practices is one of the important functions of the Federal Reserve, as shown by this example.

✔ checkpoint

Why must banks keep money on reserve? What is the multiplier effect?

How Money Circulates •

Banks move money. Not only do they move money, they create it by making deposits in other financial institutions so the monetary system as a whole expands.

Transfers and Circulation

As you considered the multiplier effect in the last section, did you get the sense that there's a lot going on as money moves? If you did, you're right. That simplified example showed only one small deposit at work. It did not consider the millions of customer and commercial transactions taking place every day, nor did it consider transactions flowing from banks and the Federal Reserve that make up the reserves any of the banks were holding. It also did not show the effect of the loans themselves on the economy, what products might have been purchased with the borrowed money, or what jobs depended upon them, so that the people holding those jobs could also make deposits—and thus fuel more expansion. All these transfers and transactions, as well as simpler movements of currency, such as bills passing as change, constitute the circulation of money.

If you look again at the elements of the money supply, M1, M2, and MZM represent so many potential transactions that the circulation of money is a complex phenomenon. Of course, most large transactions do not actually involve the movement of physical currency. Most, including creation of deposits at banks and at the Fed, involve *ledger entries*. A record of the transaction appears, just as you record your deposits and spending in your checking account. Many of these records are now entirely paperless.

The Fed and Fiat Money

It is important to remember what money is and isn't. When banks "create" money with deposits, it comes from somewhere. Where it comes from is the theoretical idea of the money supply, which is possible because of the fiat system. The Federal Reserve manages this fiat system, and it adjusts required deposits in bank accounts at the Federal Reserve to affect the money supply and banking system accordingly. The Fed has the option of contracting the money supply by raising reserve requirements if the economy seems to be overheating. If banks must hold more in reserve, there is less available to lend. Similarly, by lowering reserve requirements, the Fed expands the money supply by making more money available to create deposits. Although these options are available, the Fed very seldom uses changes in reserve requirement rates to implement monetary policy. Open market operations is the tool used most frequently by the Fed to implement monetary policy. The Fed also influences bank activity by control of interest rates.

flat world...

U.S. Currency Abroad

Of the $828 billion worth of Federal Reserve notes estimated to be in circulation during 2007, about two-thirds were held by people from abroad. Though their governments have their own money and may not be part of our fiat system, many people around the world use U.S. Federal Reserve notes and coins as a medium of exchange for both local and international business.

Think Critically   Why might U.S. currency be seen as valuable in other countries? Why might people who have no direct business with anyone in the United States value U.S. currency?

When investor confidence is shaken because of the perception of a high degree of turmoil in the economy, the Fed can take steps beyond adjusting both the reserve requirements and interest rates.

In March 2008, the Fed took the unusual step of facilitating the sale of Bear Stearns to J.P. Morgan Chase. By providing up to $30 billion dollars in financing for Bear Stearns' hard-to-move assets, like securities based on mortgages, the Fed helped the sale go through. In this particular transaction, the Fed agreed that if the value of the hard-to-move assets declined, then the Fed would incur the loss. This guarantee shielded the buyer, J.P. Morgan Chase, from exposure to loss from the hard-to-move assets. This financial protection from loss helped the deal go through.

Because Bear Stearns was such a large player in financial markets, and because of the potential ripple effect to other financial entities if Bear Stearns went under, the Fed took this action to try to stabilize the economy. A stable economy helps keep the money supply balanced.

Money as an IOU

Did you know that you hold an IOU from the government? A dollar bill in your hands represents an obligation of the government to provide something

© TONY MATTHEWS/SHUTTERSTOCK

of value to you. Because it is fiat money, the government promises not a quantity of gold, but a pledge that the note will be good in the United States. The thing of value being provided to you is the guarantee that it will be accepted for payment of taxes and settlement of debts.

Because money is an IOU in this way, it is also a liability on the Federal Reserve's books. When the Federal Reserve makes a loan and thus creates a deposit in a bank's account at the Reserve, it has "created" more currency (and may call for actual paper money to support it). Required by law to balance the books, the Fed buys and holds *treasury securities* from the government itself as pledge against the IOUs it has issued. These securities are what back your currency, although they would be paid in Federal Reserve notes. Because the fiat money system is a closed system, the full faith and credit of the U.S. government is what actually backs your bill. As long as the government is operating and able to maintain the system, its IOU to you (its money) will be a valuable medium of exchange.

✔ checkpoint

What circulates money in the United States? What backs the currency in circulation in the United States?

assessment 4.2

Think Critically

1. Why can't banks and the Federal Reserve just create money at will so that all people will have what they need?

2. Why do some people say that money is "borrowed into existence?"

3. Why is the stability of the U.S. government such a large factor in the monetary system?

Make Academic Connections

4. **BANKING MATH**   Revisit the Banking Math Connection on page 106. Recalculate the amount of new deposits created as a result of an original deposit of $15,000, and a required reserve rate of 12 percent instead of 10 percent. How much less money does this reserve rate create in deposits? Why would making such a change slow the economy?

5. **BIOGRAPHY**   Other factors influence the money supply as well, including government actions and policies. Two giants in economics, John M. Keynes and Milton Friedman, had differing opinions. Choose one of these men and write a one-page biographical sketch, outlining his principal ideas.

6. **COMMUNICATION**   With a classmate, discuss ways that the information in this chapter has changed your understanding of currency. Summarize your discussion.

Interest and Interest Rates   4.3

goals

+ List factors that affect interest rates.

+ Explain which factors the Federal Reserve affects.

terms

+ federal funds rate

+ discount rate

+ prime rate

Banking Scene

When Elizabeth Axtell bought her car, she shopped for a loan as well as a vehicle. Most car dealers finance through a bank or through the carmaker's financial company, and rates should be compared. A week after selecting her rate, she saw that the rate had jumped. Though she felt satisfied with the deal she got, she wondered why interest rates change.

INTEREST RATES AND BUSINESS

In the discussion of how money is created to expand the economy, little mention of interest rates has appeared. Yet interest rates are the primary way banks make money and the focal point of almost everything they do. Bankers are not creating money purely from the goodness of their hearts. Banks are businesses, and businesses depend on profit to survive. The money supply and the economy are linked closely to interest rates. Generally, when rates are high, money is said to be "tight" and business tends to slow, because it costs more to acquire capital. When rates drop, more credit is accessible, and the economy tends to gather speed. Interest rates play a critical role in determining what the economy is doing.

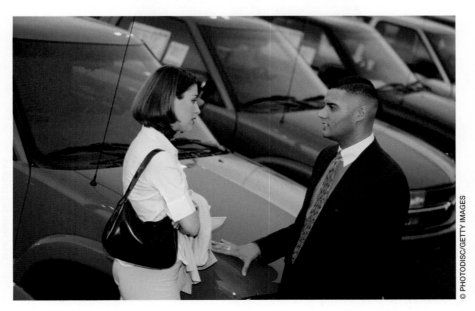

© PHOTODISC/GETTY IMAGES

NET Bookmark

In an ongoing effort to stimulate the economy in the wake of the mortgage crisis, the Fed lowered the federal funds target rate seven times between June 2006 and April 2008. Access www.cengage.com/school/pfinance/banking and click on the link for Chapter 4. Visit the Federal Reserve site and review whether the federal funds rate is increasing or decreasing. Is the rate trend (either increasing or decreasing) having the intended effect on the economy? Given the current state of the economy, do you think the next rate move will be increasing or decreasing?

www.cengage.com/school/pfinance/banking

Factors Affecting Interest Rates

Contrary to what many people believe, the Federal Reserve does not decide interest rates. Its actions influence them, and the Fed does indeed attempt to nudge rates up or down in the interest of its monetary policy, but forces that determine interest rates are not completely under the Fed's control.

Market forces determine most interest rates. Banks are free to charge whatever rates they want for most of their transactions with customers (within legal limits), but it is a balancing act. Setting a higher rate for a loan does bring in more income, but it also tends to drive away business. Banking is more fiercely competitive than ever, and the lower the rate banks can charge, the more customers they are likely to have.

The economic conditions at large help determine interest rates too. If the demand for capital is high, interest rates tend to rise like any other prices. If they rise too far, demand falls off. The inflation outlook influences rates as well, as both savers and investors look for higher rates when they fear that inflation will erode the value of what they earn. Bankers are no different from any other investors in this regard.

© ARCHMAN/SHUTTERSTOCK

The cost of money itself is a factor, and here the Federal Reserve's monetary policy matters. The Federal Reserve impacts two rates.

The **federal funds rate** is the amount of interest charged for short-term, interbank loans. The Fed influences the federal funds rate by setting a target rate. If the banks are selling federal funds for a rate that is in excess of the target, the FRB Open Market Operations will enter the market and sell repurchase agreements for U.S. Government securities that it owns at a higher rate. This action reduces the ability of banks to create money.

Banks are constantly monitoring and adjusting their reserves to make sure they can cover their liabilities, both those required by the Federal Reserve and those that occur in day-to-day banking. They often borrow or lend funds to each other to make those adjustments.

The **discount rate** is the interest rate that the Federal Reserve sets and charges for loans to member banks. The Fed controls the discount rate. This rate is not to be confused with the **prime rate**, which is the rate that banks charge their best and most reliable customers. The prime rate is usually the same among major banks, and movement in it often follows movement of the discount rate, but they are not the same thing.

Changes in these rates affect the amount of money banks are willing to borrow to maintain reserves. If rates rise, it discourages borrowing, so lending activity slows. When rates fall, banks may feel safe to lend more to earn more. The goal of these rates is to implement monetary policy by affecting reserves, which in turn affect the money supply, which affects the economy.

 checkpoint

What interest rates does the Federal Reserve control or affect?

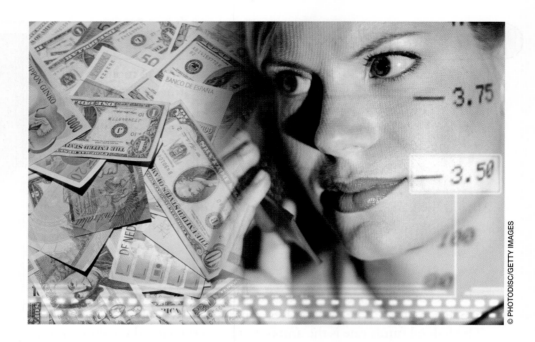

MONETARY POLICY AND INTEREST RATES

The goals of the Federal Reserve's monetary policy are to maintain economic growth, to stabilize prices, and to help international payments flow. Adjusting reserves, setting the discount rate, and influencing the federal funds rate are its tools for achieving policies.

The Federal Reserve sets the discount rate, but it only influences the federal funds rate. Using open market operations, the Fed buys and sells government securities, paying for them by making a deposit in the selling bank's Federal Reserve account. When it sells the securities to commercial banks, it withdraws their cost from the commercial bank's account at the Federal Reserve. In this way, reserves are increased or decreased, affecting the rate that banks charge each other for interbank loans. The Federal Reserve may buy or sell securities to yield a higher rate than the federal funds rate in order to achieve its goals, without taking gain or loss into consideration.

 checkpoint

How does the Federal Reserve influence the federal funds rate?

_____

_____

_____

assessment 4.3

Think Critically

1. Why do you think so many people believe that the Federal Reserve controls interest rates?

2. Why does the prime rate so often move up or down with the discount rate?

3. Why would it not be a good idea if the government completely controlled the money supply?

4. How does the Fed's use of open market operations reflect a free-enterprise economy?

Make Academic Connections

5. **COMMUNICATION** Poll people outside your class to see what they think is the dominant factor affecting interest rates. Make a table that shows your survey results. What percentage of the total number of people you poll thinks the government sets interest rates?

6. **PROBLEM SOLVING** Visit the St. Louis Federal Reserve Bank's web site listing of prime interest rates from 1929 to the present located at www. stls.frb.org/fred/data/irates/prime. Make a graph showing average interest rates for five-year periods. What might you infer about the economy at various times from the data on your graph?

chapter 4 assessment

Chapter Summary

4.1 The Money Supply

A. The money supply consists of liquid assets held by banks and individuals. The supply includes money in circulation and money held by banks and other financial institutions. Various measures track the money supply.

B. The United States uses a fiat system of money in which the value of money is declared and guaranteed by the government. The system still operates on a fractional-reserve system, left over from commodity money systems.

4.2 Money Creation and Circulation

A. Banks use their excess reserves to create money. By loaning the money not required to be reserved, new deposits are created. The multiplier effect expands the amount of money in the money supply.

B. Money circulates by means of the millions of transfers associated with the various elements of the money supply that occur daily, including consumer transfers, interbank transfers, and Federal Reserve-to-bank transfers.

4.3 Interest and Interest Rates

A. Market factors control interest rates, although the Federal Reserve influences them.

B. Federal Reserve activities affect the cost of money to banks, thus affecting the size of reserves and the money supply.

Vocabulary Builder

Choose the term that best fits the definition. Write the letter of the answer in the space provided. Some terms may not be used.

a. aggregate measures
b. commodity money
c. discount rate
d. excess reserves
e. federal funds rate
f. fiat money
g. fractional-reserve system
h. liquidity
i. money supply
j. multiplier effect
k. primary reserves
l. prime rate
m. secondary reserves

____ 1. Liquid assets held by banks and individuals
____ 2. Interest rate that the Fed charges for loans to member banks
____ 3. Currency based on some item of value, such as gold or precious stones
____ 4. Tools used to estimate the size of the money supply
____ 5. Interest rate banks charge their best and most reliable customers
____ 6. Cash on hand, deposits due from banks, and the percentage required by the Federal Reserve System
____ 7. Phenomenon that creates new deposits from lending
____ 8. Interest charged for short-term, interbank loans
____ 9. Practice of reserving only part of a deposited quantity
____ 10. Money deemed legal tender by the government, but not based on or convertible into a commodity
____ 11. Measure of how quickly things may be converted to something of value like cash

Review Concepts

12. What are the components of the money supply?

_____

_____

13. Identify and define two types of money.

_____

_____

14. List three measures of the money supply and describe them.

_____

_____

_____

15. List and define three types of bank reserves.

_____

_____

_____

_____

16. How does the multiplier effect create new deposits?

_____

_____

_____

17. Why might Federal Reserve notes be thought of as IOUs?

_____

_____

18. What actually backs the currency of the United States?

_____

_____

19. What is the difference between the discount rate and the prime rate?

_____

_____

_____

20. What factors determine interest rates?

_____

_____

_____

21. How do interest rates influence the quantity of money available in the economy?

_____

_____

_____

Apply What You Learned

22. Why is an expanding money supply generally a good thing?

_____

_____

23. What are the dangers of a money supply that expands too rapidly?

_____

_____

24. Under what circumstances is it a good idea to contract the money supply?

_____

_____

25. What are the dangers of contracting the money supply too much?

_____

_____

26. How does adjusting the reserve requirements cause the money supply to expand or contract?

_____

_____

_____

27. Why would a booming economy affect the demand for money?

28. Why do banks want interest rates to remain low?

Make Academic Connections

29. **BANKING MATH** Calculate the total amount of money "created" from a deposit of $10,000 as it moves through three further cycles of deposit. Assume a reserve rate of 8 percent.

30. **HISTORY** Many people objected strongly when the United States adopted a fiat money system (and some still object today). Learn more about the gold standard and how it established currency values. Write a one-page summary of what you learn.

31. **COMMUNICATION** If economics is a science, and economic data are measurable, why is there so much disagreement about the best way to handle the economy? Collect statements from ten people about the best thing that could be done to help the economy and why their ideas would help. Which of them seem to make the most sense to you and why?

32. **ECONOMICS** Find current information about the money supply at www.federalreserve.gov/releases/H6/Current/. Examine this data and draw conclusions about the growth of the money supply. Do your conclusions seem to match the current state of the economy?

5 Deposits in Banks

5.1	Deposit Accounts
5.2	Interest-Bearing Accounts
5.3	Flow of Deposits
5.4	Deposit Regulations

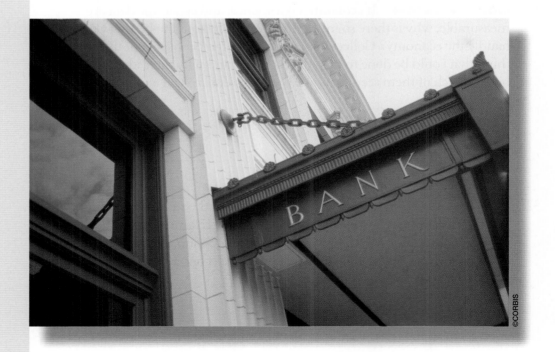

©CORBIS

climbing the ladder

From Trust Associate to Trust Department Director

Kisho, the trust department director for a large bank, is reviewing the presentation he plans to give to a group of employees who are either new hires or recent transfers into the trust department. Preparing an overview of trust department job functions has caused Kisho to reflect upon his own career.

When he began his career as a trust associate, he was responsible for maintaining designated trust liquidity levels for trust clients. Using clients' standard letters of direction, Kisho determined the appropriate trade actions that were needed to maintain daily authorized liquidity levels. He was also responsible for identifying any type of recurring activities in daily processing that could lead to corporate liability. Sometimes he recommended processing changes to reduce liability.

Kisho's curiosity regarding the most effective way to invest to maximize trust performance led him to his next position as an investment analyst in the institutional trust department. By working on investment modeling, performance analysis, and risk analysis across all asset classes, Kisho gained a deeper understanding of trust performance.

Software selection and management was a critical part of Kisho's job. He kept current on new software developments in risk management, returns-based analysis for marketable securities, and holdings-based analysis.

After learning the nuts and bolts of how trust asset decisions were made and managed, Kisho decided to learn more about compliance. Working in his next position as a trust auditor, Kisho participated in the bank's trust audit programs to identify regulatory requirements, assist in the establishment of internal controls, and help other departments with periodic compliance reviews. The position helped Kisho increase his personal network by maintaining relationships with external auditors and bank examiners.

Kisho spent three years earning a chartered financial analyst (CFA) designation through evening coursework. This helped Kisho land his next position as a portfolio manager. In this role, he was responsible for managing trust account assets to maximize investment return relative to an acceptable amount of risk. He also assisted with developing short- and long-term investment strategies that satisfied management needs and met customer investment objectives.

Currently, as trust department director, Kisho manages a high volume of complex trust accounts and achieves aggressive sales goals. He is responsible for the execution of the terms of any complex plan servicing the trusts of high-net-worth individuals. As some of these trusts are multigenerational trusts, managing the relationships among all involved parties requires tact and discretion.

Upper Rungs to Consider

One facet of his current position that Kisho particularly enjoys is being involved with the community and with professional organizations to keep current on relevant events. As he always enjoys interacting with a wide variety of people, he is going to monitor job postings to look for a position as a marketing director or as a relationship development director.

Preparing for the Climb

Maintaining a strong and diverse personal network is important for career advancement. What steps can you take to expand your personal network?

5.1

goals

+ Define transaction accounts and identify major types of checking accounts.

+ Define time deposits and identify major types of savings accounts.

terms

+ transaction account

+ demand deposit

+ Check 21

+ time deposit

+ statement savings account

+ money market deposit account (MMDA)

+ certificate of deposit (CD)

Deposit Accounts

Banking Scene

Rosa Lopez is preparing to open a checking account at a local bank. She knows that there is a wide variety of checking accounts, and that similar accounts may have different names at different banks. She has decided to collect information from various banks in an effort to find an account that will best suit her needs. To do so, she plans to make a list of questions about how she expects to use the account. Using answers to her questions, Rosa hopes to be able to match her requirements to account features offered by banks. What kind of questions about her own needs should Rosa include in her list?

MAKING YOUR DEPOSIT •

You have studied the big picture of how the national banking system works to keep money circulating. Now you will walk through the local bank doors and look more closely at various types of accounts available to individual consumers. You may see a bewildering array of accounts, but things are not as complicated as they seem. Although each bank may use different names for the various accounts offered, most banks offer similar accounts. A bank may assign "marketing names" to accounts as a way of distinguishing itself from its competitors. Features and fees may vary, but the essential services are the same with a few exceptions. Federal and state regulations require banks to provide explanations of their fees and policies.

Transaction Accounts

Deposit accounts fall generally into one of two categories: *transaction accounts* and *time deposits*. A **transaction account** is an account that allows transactions to occur without restrictions on the frequency or the volume of transactions. Many transaction accounts are **demand deposit** accounts and are payable on demand whenever the depositor chooses. The total funds in transaction accounts affect the money supply because of their high liquidity. Transaction accounts are a large component of M1. These demand deposits require banks to hold reserve funds, because the money could be transferred immediately at the direction of the account holder.

The most common form of a transaction account is a *checking account*. You withdraw money from the account by means of a check, which is a written notice to the bank to pay a named person a specified amount from your account. Checking accounts offer customers quick access to their money, provide a convenient way to pay bills, and facilitate transferring funds to other institutions. Prior to writing a check, customers need to have sufficient funds in the bank to cover checks written and any fees to be deducted. Because there are many kinds of checking accounts from which to choose, consumers can find accounts that best meet their needs.

Historically, checks were paper documents. During the 1970s, direct deposit and auto debit, two forms of electronic funds transfer (EFT), began replacing checks. More recently, advances in Internet sophistication, as well as increased Internet experience among consumers and businesses, have prompted a shift to electronic checking. Online banking, which incorporates electronic checking, provides an assortment of streamlined account management services. These services range from accounts summary information through electronic bill pay.

Checking Accounts

Checking accounts have various characteristics. All are generally classified according to their ownership—single or joint. An *individual account*, sometimes called a *single account*, is owned by one person. A *joint account* has two or more owners, each of whom has equal and independent access to it. There are two different types of joint accounts. One, held by *tenants in common*, is frequently used by business partners. The approval of all owners is required to make withdrawals. The *joint tenancy* account, used by two or more persons wishing to have co-owner accounts with others, allows each co-owner to make deposits and withdrawals independently. Joint tenancy accounts may be used by siblings, roommates, spouses, domestic partners, or any individuals who have a consumer partnership. A joint tenancy account provides the *right of survivorship*, which gives a surviving owner the right to the account's assets upon the other owner's death.

Check 21, federal legislation that became effective in October 2004, created a new category of negotiable instrument. This *substitute check* allows banks to electronically process check information. Consequently, photographic replications of the front and back sides of checks are commonly returned to customers who have check return included in their checking account services.

The names of checking accounts can differ from one bank to another. Regardless of the name, checking accounts can be categorized by their characteristics.

Basic Basic checking accounts offer a few simple services for minimal cost. These accounts may vary considerably in set fees and services, and most do not pay interest. Some may have no charges as long as a minimum balance is maintained, but most have a basic fee and price extra services per item. For example, you may have a set number of checks or deposits allowed per month, and all transactions beyond these incur an extra charge. Extra charges may also be incurred for automated teller machine (ATM) and debit card transactions. The return of canceled checks may cost you, or may not be an option at all.

There are numerous forms of basic checking accounts with many names, but the same fee-for-service principle applies. Generally, a basic checking account is ideal for those who don't plan to keep a high balance.

"Free" This checking account usually requires a minimum balance but waives certain fees, such as ATM and per-check fees. Fees are charged to consumers who fail to maintain the minimum balance.

"No Service Charge" This account, which may charge for ATM withdrawals, has no other service fees and no minimum balance. Minimum balance requirements for free checking accounts should be compared for brick-and-mortar banks and online banks. Some online banks have lower minimum account requirements than brick-and-mortar banks.

Interest-Bearing These checking accounts also vary widely. They do pay interest on the balance deposited in the account, but usually only if the deposited balance is maintained at or above a required level. Generally, the higher the interest offered, the higher the minimum balance required. Minimum balance may be calculated based upon the average balance in the account each day of the month, or it may be a preset level. If the balance falls below the level on any day of the month, higher service charges apply.

Express Designed for people who prefer to bank by ATM, telephone, or online, this account usually offers unlimited check writing, low minimum balance requirements, and low or no monthly fees. However, teller fees as

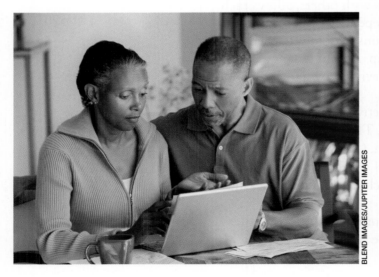

BLEND IMAGES/JUPITER IMAGES

high as $6 a visit, or a flat monthly fee of $8 or more for teller visits, are charged. These accounts are popular with students and younger customers on the go who don't want to spend a lot of time on banking.

Lifeline This account's low minimum deposit and balance requirements as well as monthly fees—from zero to $3, depending on the bank—are attractive to low-income bank customers. It limits the number of checks per month that you can write. Some states require banks to offer such accounts.

"No-Frills" Many banks offer special checking deals if you are age 55 or over or are a student. The benefits may include the following.

- Free personal checks

- Free cashier's or traveler's checks

- Increased use of ATMs

- Better rates on loans and credit cards

- Discounts on a variety of items such as travel

Asset Management   Many banks offer this advanced type of checking account that offers the convenience of one account to take care of typical banking and investment needs. The account typically provides unlimited check-writing privileges and a comprehensive end-of-year statement that documents the year's transactions. Requirements include a higher minimum balance to open and an annual fee.

Online Banking   Online banking services are available as either independent accounts or as an additional service to standard brick-and-mortar accounts. Due to their lower cost structure, online banking accounts may offer lower minimum balances and fewer fees than traditional banks. Online banking services, either through an online bank or as part of a brick-and-mortar bank's package of services, offer a variety of services ranging from consolidated management of multiple accounts through automated bill payments.

Mobile Banking   Although other countries have achieved higher utilization of mobile banking, some American banks have begun offering mobile banking services to customers. Transactions that consumers can perform from a mobile phone include balance inquiries and payment requests. Information that banks can automatically send to customers includes paycheck deposit alerts and bounced check notification. These mobile services can be linked to a variety of checking accounts.

ATM Fees   Fees for using an ATM should be carefully assessed. Depending on the type of checking account, consumers have the potential to incur two fees when using an ATM that is not affiliated with their own bank. A single transaction may prompt the non-member bank to charge one fee and the member bank to charge another fee.

Consumers should look closely at the services included with their checking account as well as the fee structure for the account. A basic account may actually cost more money to operate than another type of account if there are transaction-based fees. In the same way, the interest earned on an interest-bearing account may not be enough to offset the higher cost of fees if the balance maintained is fairly low, especially if it falls below the minimum balance requirement. Account regulations for each account as well as account usage patterns should be carefully considered. Finding a good match between the two can result in cost savings.

Other Demand Deposit Transactions

Certain other transactions are also categorized as demand deposit transactions, such as traveler's checks, money orders, ATS (automatic transfer service) transactions, and EFT (electronic funds transfer) that make automatic withdrawals or transfers to pay bills without writing checks. Most checking

The government wants to educate consumers to make sure that online banking transactions occur legally and safely. Access www.cengage.com/school/pfinance/banking and click on the link for Chapter 5. Visit the FDIC site and review the article on *Safe Internet Banking*. What risks do you incur by using a bank that is chartered overseas? What should you do if you are not certain that an online bank is legitimate?

www.cengage.com/school/pfinance/banking

accounts also allow access to deposits via ATMs, electronic banking, and debit cards. Some banks allow account access through mobile phones. Debit card transactions function like check transactions, except that no check is written. All deposits to cover these transactions are called *checkable deposits*, as are the funds deposited in checking accounts.

checkpoint

What is a transaction account and why is it a demand deposit?

_____

_____

TIME DEPOSITS •••••••••••••••••••••••••••

Time deposits, as the name implies, are deposits that are held for or mature at a specified time. Generally, time deposits include savings accounts, money market deposit accounts, certificates of deposit (CDs), and various bonds. Time deposits are less liquid than checkable deposits. There are no reserve requirements imposed by the Federal Reserve on time deposits.

Savings Accounts

The most common time deposit account is the savings account. For time deposits, banks may require up to a seven-day notice from a depositor who wants to withdraw money. In contrast, demand deposits require no notice. As a practical matter, most banks don't impose the prior notice requirement for savings accounts, but they reserve the right to do so. Savings accounts valued at less than $100,000 are part of the M2 money supply.

Passbook savings accounts, which helped build the banking industry, provided a ledger of activity that the teller updated when the customer made deposits or withdrawals. This traditional type of savings account has all but disappeared, replaced by statement savings accounts. Both types of accounts allow you to make deposits in person, by mail, electronically, or by direct deposit.

Statement savings accounts, now the industry standard, provide a monthly or quarterly computerized statement detailing all account activity, including interest credited and fees charged. Often, statements are combined with those of other accounts held at the bank, providing a complete and clear picture of all banking activity.

Savings accounts are among the safest places to put money. Accounts are insured by the Federal Deposit Insurance Corporation (FDIC) up to $100,000 per depositor per bank. For high net worth individuals with more than $100,000 to keep in a bank account, any deposit amounts exceeding a combined total of $100,000 at a single banking company should be transferred to a bank owned by a different company. The Emergency Economic Stabilization Act of 2008 temporarily increased the FDIC cap to $250,000 per depositor through the end of 2009. As interest income on savings accounts is relatively low, high net worth individuals would probably invest their money in products providing a higher yield than savings accounts. If liquidity is needed, then savings accounts are a good option.

Money Market Deposit Accounts

Money market deposit accounts (MMDAs) offer a higher rate of interest than savings accounts, but they usually require a higher initial deposit to open an account. In addition, minimum balance requirements to avoid the imposition of fees are also higher. The FDIC insures MMDAs for amounts up to $100,000 per depositor. The bank invests money market deposits in a variety of savings instruments. Similar accounts, called *money market mutual fund accounts*, invest the money in mutual funds. Although they are not insured, banks make most of these investments in safe, short-term savings instruments with high credit ratings.

Liquidity of these accounts is not as high as savings accounts. You may be restricted to six transactions per month. Only three of them may be checks, and you may have to wait up to three days to get your money.

Certificates of Deposit

Certificates of deposit (CDs) are certificates issued by banks that guarantee the payment of a fixed interest rate until the *maturity date*, which is a specified date in the future. Banks offer CDs with maturity dates from seven days to ten years. Generally, the larger the amount of the CD and the longer the term, the greater the interest rate.

Some CDs offer fluctuating rates. Variable rate CDs are often linked to the prime rate and may offer an interest rate at a predefined percentage rate less than the prime rate. For example, a variable rate CD might offer interest at 2.25 percent less than the prime rate. Some CDs offer *bump-ups* that provide the opportunity to increase the interest rate on the CD when interest rates rise. A *callable* CD is one that can be called in at the discretion of the issuing institution. Be sure not to confuse the callable date with the maturity date.

Usually, the rate for CDs is higher than the rates offered by money market or savings accounts. For the vast majority of CDs the maturity date is fewer than eighteen months. You can get your money before the maturity date if you need to, but you will pay an interest penalty, anywhere from three to six months' worth of interest, if you withdrawal the money early.

branching out

Wal-Mart

Realizing that a substantial number of its customers do not have traditional bank accounts, Wal-Mart developed creative ways of providing financial services to consumers. Wal-Mart partnered with a variety of third parties to provide bank-like services to its customers. By developing these partnerships, Wal-Mart was not required to go through the regulatory processes and approvals required of banks. The Wal-Mart MoneyCard is one example of a product developed as a result of a partnership. The MoneyCard, issued by GE Money Bank, allows customers to set up direct deposit of their payroll checks onto their Wal-Mart MoneyCard. When the MoneyCard is used for a transaction, the stored value of the money on the card is used. The Money-Card is not a credit card. No credit check or bank account is required. There can be fees for reloading the card, for monthly card maintenance, and for assorted administrative costs that a customer may elect to use. Under certain circumstances, specific fees may be waived.

Think Critically
How does the entry of a retail outlet with the consumer reach of Wal-Mart affect competition within the banking industry?

Certificates of deposit are quite safe, as the FDIC insures them for amounts up to $100,000 per depositor, but they are not very liquid. Consumers should consider the maturity date when investing in CDs, because the interest rate remains the same on fixed rate CDs. If interest rates rise, the CD rate will not earn as much as other forms of time deposits. But if interest rates fall, locked-in CD rates can be an advantage. Depositors must also decide how long they are willing and able to tie up their money.

Sometimes *brokers* sell callable CDs. You should understand which bank issued the callable CD. The FDIC insurance rates of $100,000 apply to each depositor at each lending institution. Knowing which institution issued a CD will help you or your bank's customers avoid exceeding the $100,000 limit at an institution.

Credit Union Products   Credit unions offer both transaction accounts and time deposits. These holdings usually represent shares in the credit union rather than deposits. A *share-draft account* is much like a checking account, a *share account* is essentially like a savings account, and a *share certificate* is equivalent to a certificate of deposit.

✔ checkpoint

List three types of time deposits. Which of these are exempt from reserve requirements?

_____

_____

_____

assessment 5.1

Think Critically

1. Why does the Federal Reserve require reserves for demand deposits but not for time deposits?

2. How might competitive pressures have led to different types of checking accounts?

3. Why do you think passbook savings accounts have disappeared?

4. What factors should be considered when contemplating a certificate of deposit?

Make Academic Connections

5. **COMMUNICATION** With a partner, make a list of questions you need to ask to help determine your checking account needs. Compare various types of checking accounts and focus your questions on what you now know about differences in checking accounts. Come up with at least four questions, and then compare lists with those of other pairs.

6. **BANKING MATH** According to a Federal Reserve study, Americans wrote about 31 billion checks and made about 63 billion electronic payments in 2006. This reflects a steady trend to shift away from checks in favor of electronic payments. At that time, the population of the United States was about 300 million. Using those figures, how many checks and how many electronic payments were written per capita in a year in the United States?

5.2

Interest-Bearing Accounts

goals

+ Explain how interest is calculated.

+ Discuss why compound interest is such a powerful savings tool.

+ Describe how interest rate variations can impact consumer behavior.

terms

+ interest

+ compound interest

+ annual percentage rate (APR)

+ annual percentage yield (APY)

Banking Scene

As she considered what type of checking account to open, Rosa Lopez felt it would be a good idea to open a savings account as well. She looked for advertised interest rates for accounts and certificates of deposit, and began to consider how those rates would affect her savings over time. She wanted to design a chart or table to compare rates and intervals at which interest would be paid, and then fill it with some example numbers. How would Rosa design such a chart?

IN YOUR INTEREST •

It might not always be good to be called a "calculating person," but when it comes to your finances, you had better be. Banks offer interest on many deposit accounts, and they charge interest on loans they make. Understanding these calculations is absolutely necessary to analyzing your own finances. Whether it's money coming to you or money you're paying to borrow, interest will likely determine how well you fare.

Interest is the price paid for the use of money. The bank is using your money when you deposit funds. In some cases, the bank pays you for the use of your money. If you borrow from a bank or other financial institution, you pay to use that money, and interest is the amount you pay. Interest is almost always expressed as a rate or percentage of the total amount of money in use, and it is calculated over time.

Calculating Interest

To calculate simple interest, you must know the amount of money that is being used. This beginning amount is called the *principal*. The basic formula for calculating interest is $P \times R \times T = I$, where P is principal, R is rate, T is time, and I is interest. Rate is expressed as a percentage. Time is expressed in years or parts of years. Portions of a year are expressed as a decimal value. For example:

$$P \times R \times T = I$$

six months is 0.5 years
nine months is 0.75 years
a year and a half is 1.5 years

Banking Math *Connection*

Calculate the simple interest earned on a savings account in nine months that begins with a deposit of $2,200 and pays 4½ percent interest.

Solution

The formula for calculating interest is

Principal × Rate × Time = Interest
$2,200 × 0.045 × 0.75   = $74.25

If you had such an account, you would have earned $74.25 in interest, giving you a balance of $2,274.25. This example assumes no compounding and that the interest is paid at the end of the nine months, which might not reflect conditions of an actual account.

Interest in the Real World

Calculating simple interest provides an idea of the process, but in the real world there are some complexities. Banks calculate the interest they pay on some fixed interval. Interest may be paid once a year (annually), every six months (semiannually), every three months (quarterly), or any other interval as defined in the account regulations. If the bank paid 4½ percent interest on a $2,200 account semiannually, at the end of six months $49.50 would be added to the account. For the next six-month interval, the beginning principal would not be $2,200 but would be $2,249.50. Interest would now be earned on the higher amount.

©KAREN ROACH/SHUTTERSTOCK

Adding interest to the principal and paying interest on the new total is called paying **compound interest**. It is the most powerful savings tool.

✔ checkpoint

What do the terms in the formula P × R × T = I stand for?

For the purposes of computing
interest compounded daily, a
year is generally considered to
be 360 days or twelve 30-day
months. Using this figure
actually increases the effective
rate of interest compared to
a 365-day year. ■

THE POWER OF COMPOUNDING ••••••••••••••••••

Compound interest "starts over" with a new principal every time interest is paid, adding the paid interest to create a higher principal on which interest is paid in the next interval. For example, assume you loaned $10,000 to your cousin for three years at a simple interest rate of 5 percent per year. You'd make $500 in interest the first year, $500 in interest the second, and $500 in the third, for a total of $11,500.

Assume you put the same $10,000 in a bank account paying 5 percent interest compounded semiannually. You'd get back $11,597.10. In effect, that's a rate of 5.3 percent per year.

Time	Simple Interest 5%		Compound Interest 5%	
	Interest	Principal	Interest	Principal
6 months	$250	$10,000	$250.00	$10,250.00
1 year	250	10,000	256.30	10,506.30
1½ years	250	10,000	262.70	10,769.00
2 years	250	10,000	269.20	11,038.20
2½ years	250	10,000	276.00	11,314.20
3 years	250	10,000	282.90	11,597.10
Total	**$1,500**		**$1,597.10**	

The algebraic formula for calculating compound interest is $F = P(1 + R)^n$, where F stands for future value, P is principal, R is rate, and n is the number of intervals. There are many online calculators that will compute compound interest for you. Memorizing the formula is less important than understanding the idea behind compound interest.

Larger principals and longer terms have a more dramatic effect, especially if regular additions are made to the principal, as on a regular savings plan. For example, if you put $20 a week in a savings account earning 5 percent interest compounded annually, at the end of five years you would have deposited $5,200, but your balance would be $6033.99.

APR and APY

Two terms you may encounter when evaluating interest are APR and APY. Both allow you to compare interest. **Annual percentage rate (APR)** is the nominal rate on which interest is calculated per year. In the example above, both investments have an APR of 5 percent. Another measure gives a better comparison. The **annual percentage yield (APY)** represents the effect of compounding. In the example above, the APY of the simple interest is 5 percent and of the compounded interest is 5.3 percent. APY varies according to the APR and the frequency of compounding. APY is mandated as the required quotation by the Truth in Savings Act. Although banks may elect to present an APR, they must present the APY.

checkpoint

Why is compound interest such a powerful savings tool?

_____

_____

INTEREST RATES IMPACT CONSUMER BEHAVIOR • • • • • • •

Savvy consumers, who want to make money in a fairly low-risk environment, have focused their energy on earning personal income by exploiting the spread of interest points in the marketplace. The spread is the variation in value of two competing interest rates.

By using sophisticated online software that analyzes and summarizes the highest interest levels offered by assorted savings institutions, these consumers are perpetually moving their funds among various accounts to obtain the highest interest available at any point in time. In some cases, these consumers will borrow money on a credit card, at either low or no interest introductory rates, and use those borrowed funds to gain interest in a high-yield online account.

Some financial institutions, who offer the high rates in hopes of obtaining long-term customers, have tried to combat these customers by increasing the minimum deposit required to participate in the high-yield accounts.

Consumers who use these tactics are often referred to as *rate chasers*. A variety of websites are available that offer comparative interest rates.

 checkpoint

Why do financial institutions try to thwart the efforts of rate chasers?

_____

_____

_____

assessment 5.2

Think Critically

1. Why is it important for consumers to compare interest rates on bank accounts and other interest-bearing instruments?

2. How does the frequency that interest is compounded change the effect of compounded interest rates?

3. Why is APY a more useful measure for comparing interest rates than APR?

Make Academic Connections

4. **BANKING MATH** Marie Broussard puts $10 a week in a savings account. At the end of two years, how much more would Marie have in savings if she found an account that paid interest of 5½ percent instead of 4½ percent per year, assuming both accounts compound annually?

5. **HISTORY** The practice of paying and charging interest has been around a long time. Do research on interest, and write a one-page report on the earliest beginnings of the practice.

6. **TECHNOLOGY** Online financial calculators are becoming increasingly useful tools, performing complex calculations quickly. Find three such calculators on the Internet, and describe the particular features, advantages, and disadvantages of each.

Flow of Deposits

5.3

Banking Scene

Rosa Lopez has made her decisions about what services she needs in checking and savings accounts. Now her task is to choose accounts that match her needs. With so many banks, so many accounts, and so many similar but not identical names, collecting information on specific offerings could be complicated and time consuming. How would you recommend Rosa pursue this task most efficiently?

goals

+ Explain the complexity of forces that influence the flow of deposits.
+ Identify limitations of the Federal Reserve's influence of the flow of deposits.

terms

+ interbank transactions

A COMPLEX PATTERN •

You go to work, get your check, and deposit it in the bank. Of course, your employer wrote that check against funds deposited in the company's bank, and the money for those deposits came from somewhere too. The next time you are in a bank or waiting in a drive-through, look around and multiply the process by everyone you see. Then multiply the process by the millions of people at work in the United States, using thousands of banks. If you are starting to get a picture of a complex flow of deposits rocketing around the nation, you are getting the idea.

The Federal Reserve, or Fed, came into being to serve as the nation's central bank. The money supply is sometimes adjusted by the actions of the Fed. Because banking is so important, it may be easy to assume that the government is running everything, but that is not really how it works. In addition to new money and the easing or tightening of credit, the flow of deposits also includes all the money already circulating in the day-to-day business of economic life. Money doesn't just mean currency, but includes checks, ledger transfers, and even credit.

The Economic Engine

The engine that drives the flow of deposits is the economy itself. Basic economic principals of supply and demand for goods and services push money through banks. In a way, the movement of money is like the movement of communication through phone lines and cellular phones. Individual transmissions may not be very complicated, but there are a lot going on at once, and they may be going in many different directions. At the same moment you deposit your check at the teller window, someone else cashes his or hers at the drive-through. In addition to these small transactions,

tech talk

Cup of Java?

Many banks offer interactive tools on the Internet, such as interest calculators of various types. Have you ever wondered how they work? Many of them run by means of Java, a programming language specially designed to run small applications, called "applets," over the Internet. Advantages of Java are that it works with any operating system, such as Windows, Macintosh, or OS/2, and that it allows for distributed processing, so the software need not all be resident on your computer.

Think Critically   Why do you think interactive tools on bank Internet sites have become so popular? Search the Internet for bank sites that offer interactive tools. List at least five useful tools you find.

banks themselves, just like you, may have changes in cash-flow needs. Maybe revenues are down, or expenses are up, or maybe business is so good they need more money to support it. The transactions that occur when banks make or receive deposits from each other or from the Fed are called **interbank transactions**.

It is not always easy to predict the results of these transactions, but the best predictor is the past. That is why economists, banks, and the Federal Reserve pay close attention to recording and analyzing economic statistics.

In fact, the economy at large plays a far greater role in determining how money is moving than does the government. Market forces are a primary determinant of interest rates. Fluctuations in interest rates are caused by variations of capital needs, individual tendencies toward saving or spending, and on inflation-related effects.

Disintermediation of funds also affects the economy. *Disintermediation of funds* occurs when depositors take their money out of bank accounts and invest those funds directly into capital markets. The term also captures the activity that occurs when companies, seeking financing, go directly to capital markets to secure the financing. In both instances the traditional role of a bank, of accepting deposits from one group and providing loans to another group, is diminished. This financing method increased during the 1980s and 1990s. However, during the credit squeeze that began in 2007, the trend began to reverse. At that time, mutual funds began to seek financing directly from banks in an effort to maintain the required liquidity of their funds.

✔ checkpoint

What is the greatest factor in the flow of deposits? Why do economists track and analyze so much data?

"communicate"

Conduct a survey among 20 friends, family members, and classmates to examine consumer attitudes. Ask these questions:

1. How much do you consider the economy at large when making purchase and loan decisions?

2. What do you think is the state of the economy at large at present, and what are its prospects for the next year?

Based on responses to your survey, write a two-page report describing the economic mood of the country.

DEPOSITS AND THE FED •••••••••••••••••••••

Whether the money supply is expanding through the creation of new money or contracting as credit tightens, supply and demand for money affects deposits. The Federal Reserve also has an effect on deposits. For example, the Federal Reserve sets reserve requirements. If reserve requirements are high, banks must keep back more money and consequently have less to lend. If reserve requirements are low, more money may be available for loans. Still, there are reasons not to overestimate the power of this capability.

- Reserve requirements do not change that often and are not as much a factor in bank lending as general economic conditions.

- Reserve requirements only apply to the M1 money supply (the checkable deposits that are already moving freely). Other parts of the money supply are operating entirely by means of market forces, and though less volatile, are not under the Fed's control.

- The Fed does not control other forms of commerce. Much wealth today is generated by nonbank financial institutions, such as stockbrokers and the securities and other instruments they trade, which are a form of money themselves. These instruments, the institutions that sell them, and the policies they have are not controlled by the Federal Reserve, though they affect the economy at large.

In general, the money supply is determined by the supply and demand for credit, and although the Federal Reserve responds to these conditions, it does not necessarily create them.

Adjusting the Money Supply

It is true that the Fed does have an influence on the money supply and the flow of deposits, most frequently through its *open market operations*.

- **The Federal Reserve can put more money in the economy.** To do so, it buys U.S. government securities on the open market. The Fed buys these securities by using money that is part of the Fed's balance sheet. The sellers of the securities deposit money from the Fed in financial institutions. Thus, deposits flow from money on the Fed's balance sheet into bank accounts. By generating funds from the sale of government securities, banks then have more money to lend, and the money supply expands as a consequence of the multiplier effect.

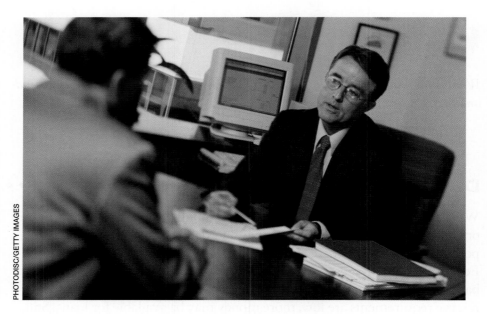

- **The Federal Reserve can effectively take money out of the economy.** If the Fed feels it needs to slow the economy, it sells the Treasury securities it holds. There is a market for them because of their security. When it sells the securities, the money comes from bank deposits, thus leaving less in the system at large. The money the Fed receives for the securities is removed from the economy, as it does not go into a bank account of any kind. It effectively disappears.

In addition, the Fed can adjust the discount rate, which is the rate it charges banks for loans. If the discount rate is low, banks are more likely to borrow money to use to make money. If the discount rate is high, just like consumers, banks are less likely to borrow.

The Banking Business

Governmental measures influence but do not entirely control the flow of deposits. Banks are businesses and do what they can to make a profit. Deposit flow is determined by the needs of all businesses, bank and non-bank, moving money around in the banking system. Banks move money from themselves to consumers, back and forth among themselves as a function of normal business or borrowing funds from each other, and back and forth from the Federal Reserve, in a constant flow of deposits. They function just as you do but on a larger scale, moving and using or even borrowing money to acquire things they need.

How does the Federal Reserve influence the flow of deposits?

assessment 5.3

Think Critically

1. Why is it sometimes hard to predict the flow of deposits in the banking system?

2. How might political or national events affect the flow of deposits in the banking system?

3. Do you think the government should have more direct control of the economy and thus the flow of deposits? Why or why not?

4. Give examples of daily economic activities that are more likely to have predictable effects on the flow of deposits.

Make Academic Connections

5. **GRAPHICS** Make a graphical representation or flow chart of how money is added to or removed from the economy by the Federal Reserve. What activities should be included in the representation?

6. **SOCIAL STUDIES** How do current economic conditions affect social conditions in our country? Explore the effect of the economy on daily life in the United States. Write a one-page personal essay about ways that you think the state of the economy affects how we live, the values we hold, the ways we spend our time, our political opinions, our career choices, and any other aspects of our lives that you find interesting. Incorporate information about how the credit collapse of 2008 affected your life. These ideas may be personal opinions, but try to express them clearly and be sure to give reasons for your thinking.

5.4

goals

+ Describe several deposit account documents.

+ Identify basic deposit account rules and what they cover.

terms

+ governing documents

+ stale check

+ post-dated check

Banking Scene

When Rosa Lopez opens her checking and savings accounts, she is given a variety of brochures explaining the features and benefits of the accounts. She is also given sheets that list rules and regulations pertaining to each of her deposit accounts. They are detailed documents that include legal language and are printed in small type without graphics. Why should Rosa read these documents carefully, even though she has a clear picture of account features, charges, and interest rates?

DEPOSIT ACCOUNT DOCUMENTS ● ● ● ● ● ● ● ● ● ● ● ● ● ● ● ● ●

The relationship between a financial institution and its customers is more than a business relationship. It is also a legal relationship that offers rights and imposes responsibilities on each party. Banks document these rights and responsibilities. When an account is opened, customers receive documentation outlining the rights and responsibilities associated with the account.

State and federal governments require banks to provide this documentation to customers so that questions about account policies and procedures have clear answers. These documents protect both the consumer and the bank from misunderstanding and loss.

The Federal Reserve, in its regulatory capacity, along with state and sometimes local governments, performs reviews to ensure that deposit account documents are specific, complete, clear, and used appropriately. Banks, including online banks, must comply with various state and federal consumer laws, including laws about fairness and full disclosure. Several documents are typically included in this document package.

- **Account rules** explain characteristics of each type of account. They include definitions, requirements, restrictions, and other information associated with each account.

- **Deposit rate schedules** list interest rates in effect at the time for various types of accounts.

- **Fee schedules** show all charges that apply to each specific type of deposit account.

- **Check hold policies** explain when deposited funds will be available for use by the consumer. Usually, deposited funds are credited provisionally, until full and final payment is received. In most cases, funds are available for use immediately, but the bank may charge back to the account any amount that is uncollectible.

- **Disclosure statements** provide full information about bank policies, such as electronic funds transfer policies, lending policies, interest crediting, and compliance with banking regulations. These statements are required by law.

- **Opting out options** allow you to notify your bank that you do not authorize the bank to share your personal financial information, like average account balance, with any other businesses. Using this option can also keep the bank from sharing information with other divisions within the bank. For example, you may prohibit the bank from sharing your personal information with the financial planning division of the bank.

Deposit account documents are sometimes collectively called **governing documents**. Banks are free to change them, but they must give customers written notice of changes.

Why are governing documents necessary?

ACCOUNT RULES ••••••••••••••••••••••••••

The statement of account rules supplied for each account provides a detailed explanation of the policies, procedures, requirements, and agreements applying to that account. It is usually very specific, spelling out what is expected of both the customer and the bank.

Reference to Governing Documents   The bank notes that account holders agree to abide by the rules as set forth in the rest of the governing documents. The bank also states that it may change the rules from time to time and acknowledges its responsibility to provide updated documents to account holders.

Signature Policies   Banks keep a card on file with the signature of all parties to an account, whether it is held solely or jointly. Signature policies spell out who may do what, both in terms of the account as it exists when it is opened and in the event of inconsistencies, disputes, or the death of parties. Usually, in the event of disputes among parties, the bank refuses to pay items on the account until the parties resolve the dispute. The bank notes that it has no responsibility for a dispute, its resolution, or its choice to freeze the account. Orders to freeze accounts may originate due to the death of an account holder, lawsuits filed against account holders, or bankruptcy proceedings.

Ethics in Action

Some consumer advocates believe that many governing documents are made deliberately hard to read so that consumers won't read them. Banks argue that precise legal language is necessary to protect both themselves and consumers.

Think Critically

Would you support legislation that required account rules to be written in "plain English"? Why or why not?

Opening and Closing Accounts Policies governing opening accounts may include a specified minimum opening deposit, the presence of the person opening the account with proper identification, and the right not to open an account for a person if the bank so chooses. The bank also reserves the right to close an account at its discretion.

Resolution Form When opening an account for a business that is set up as a limited liability company (LLC), a corporation, or a partnership, the business may need to provide the bank with a *resolution* form. This form grants authority for specified individuals to manage account transactions on behalf of the business.

Deposit Collection This provision is similar to federal regulations concerning funds availability except that it goes further in explaining the effect of uncollected deposits on the account. The bank notes that it is not responsible for collecting deposits beyond using reasonable care in their processing. This statement often notes exactly when deposits are credited. For example, deposits made after 3:00 P.M. may be credited during the next business day.

Overdraft Policies When an account has insufficient funds to meet its obligations, it is *overdrawn*. Depending on the account type, the bank may pay the obligation or return the check to whoever presented it. If an account holder has multiple accounts within a bank, the bank might transfer funds between accounts to cover overdrafts. An *overdraft* occurs when withdrawals are greater than deposits. Fees are charged for overdrafts. A reference to the fee schedule usually appears in the statement of account rules.

Minimum Balance/Service Charges The bank specifies the exact fee schedule for service charges when an account fails to maintain a minimum balance.

Withdrawal Policies Requirements for withdrawing funds from the bank vary by account type. They include maturity dates and penalties for early withdrawal of time deposits, making withdrawals in person, identification needed at withdrawal, and various other requirements for withdrawing funds.

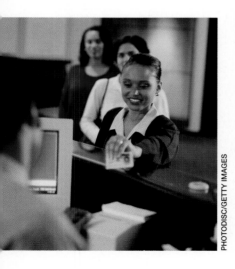

PHOTODISC/GETTY IMAGES

Check Policies   These policies relate to the accurate dating of checks and their timely deposit or presentation. A **stale check** is dated six months or more before it is presented for payment or deposit. A **post-dated check** is dated later than when it was written. A bank may refuse to honor either.

Account Statement Policies   These policies deal with the bank statement. They state what is and is not included with each statement, the account holder's obligation to review the statement in a timely manner, and the discrepancy handling process.

Other Policies   Account rules usually include assorted bank policies. Stopping payment of a check, handling inactive or dormant accounts, and reimbursement of expenses incurred by the bank on the account holder's behalf are a few examples of policies covered in this section.

Waivers   Account rules may also contain notices about various waivers, such as the customer's agreement to waive protest of dishonored items and the bank's willingness to waive certain fees. The bank's waiver does not prevent it from enforcing the same provision(s) that it had waived previously.

Governing documents and account rules serve as the legal basis for the relationship between you and your bank. If you do not like a provision or some of the account rules, you are free to choose another bank. Most account and deposit regulations are fairly similar from bank to bank. In their precision and specificity, they protect the bank and the consumer.

Federal Reserve Regulations

Just as banks enforce account rules on consumers, the Federal Reserve imposes a number of requirements on banks or depository institutions. These may apply to transaction accounts as well as time deposits.

Regulation DD   This policy implements the Truth in Savings Act of 1991. It requires banks to disclose the interest rate paid and the fees charged on deposit accounts to enable consumers to make informed decisions. The purpose of providing this information is to allow consumers to make comparisons among depository institutions.

In May 2005, Regulation DD was amended to require that banks provide explicit disclosure regarding the details of overdraft protection. Under this amendment, banks must clearly list all fees associated with overdraft protection services on banking statements. Final amendments to this rule, which became effective in July 2006, discuss which disclosures must be included in marketing materials related to overdraft protection.

Regulation D   This regulation requires banks to maintain adequate reserves for the funds they have on deposit. Regulation D defines the types and number of transactions that the bank may allow on time deposits, such as savings accounts and money market accounts. Check or debit overdraft, preauthorized automated transfers, preauthorized electronic debit, and automatic or assisted phone transfers are limited to six per month. Balance inquiries, loan payments, and all transactions from a checking account do not count as part of these transactions.

"communicate"

Multiple federal agencies use a similar naming structure for regulations. For example, "Regulation D" is used by both the SEC and the Federal Reserve. For the SEC, Regulation D covers exemptions from registration requirements. For the Fed, Regulation D defines bank account reserve requirements. Use the Internet to find another overlap. Prepare a PowerPoint chart that clearly explains the difference in regulations with the same name. Be sure to include an easy-to-understand reference to the agency listing the regulation.

Regulation CC   This is known as the Availability of Funds and Collection of Checks regulation. Regulation CC sets the schedules under which banks must make funds deposited into transaction accounts available for customer withdrawal. Usually, the maximum time to clear a check deposited into a checking account is two to five business days. Business days are defined as Mondays through Fridays, except most federal holidays. Some types of deposits require a next-day availability. To meet the requirements of Regulation CC, a bank must:

- Provide consumers who have transaction accounts, such as a checking account, with disclosures stating when their funds will be available for withdrawal.

- Post a notice of the bank's availability policy pertaining to consumer accounts. The posting is required in the bank as well as at all ATMs.

- Include a notice of funds availability on the front of all *preprinted* deposit slips. It does not have to appear on blank counter deposit slips.

Many financial institutions have been cited for violating various parts of Regulation CC. Thus, it is important for a bank to ensure it is in compliance with the requirements of Regulation CC.

In October 2004, Regulation CC was amended to include the Check 21 Act. As noted in lesson 4.1, Check 21 authorized the use of electronic checks as a viable negotiable instrument.

Regulation E   EFTs are regulated under Regulation E. EFT is commonly used for direct deposit of paychecks or preauthorizing repetitive monthly payments of a consistent amount (like authorizing automatic payment of monthly health club fees from your checking account). Regulation E is designed to protect the rights of consumers who use EFT and to outline the responsibilities of financial institutions providing EFT. Consumers must receive EFT disclosures prior to making their first EFT transaction. Information to include in the disclosures includes:

- Limits of a consumer's liability and of an institution's liability if unauthorized EFT transactions occur

- Descriptions of the type and number of transactions that can be made

- ATM fees that can be incurred when using the bank's ATMs as well as the ATMs of other banks

- Contact information for reporting unauthorized EFTs

 checkpoint

How do governing documents and account rules differ?

assessment 5.4

Think Critically

1. Why do banks supply a separate set of account rules as part of the governing documents for each account?

2. Do you think most people carefully read the documents associated with their bank accounts? Why or why not?

3. Why does the government feel it is necessary to require that written copies of documents related to bank accounts be provided to customers?

4. In what circumstances might a bank waive a fee it had charged?

Make Academic Connections

5. **SOCIAL SCIENCE** Learn more about consumer protection and the banking industry. Using research materials of your choice, make a timeline showing key events in the growth of fair and reasonable banking practices.

6. **PROBLEM SOLVING** If you had a dispute with a bank, how would you resolve it? What approaches would you take, and what further actions would you pursue if you could not come to an agreement? List steps that you would take to resolve a disagreement over an uncredited deposit, for example.

chapter 5 **assessment**

Chapter Summary

5.1 Deposit Accounts

A. Transaction accounts, like checking accounts, are demand deposit accounts that allow unlimited transactions.

B. Time deposits include savings accounts, money market deposit accounts, and certificates of deposit.

5.2 Interest-Bearing Accounts

A. Interest is the price paid for the use of money. Simple interest is calculated with the formula $P \times R \times T = I$.

B. Compounding greatly expands the power of interest. The formula for calculating compound interest is $F = P(1 + R)^n$. APR represents the annual percentage rate, and APY represents the annual percentage yield.

5.3 Flow of Deposits

A. The flow of deposits includes all economic transactions, not just those between banks and the Federal Reserve.

B. The Federal Reserve influences the flow of deposits, but supply and demand have a greater influence on deposit flows.

5.4 Deposit Regulations

A. For each account, banks provide a package of governing documents that include account rules, deposit rate schedules, fee schedules, check hold policies, and disclosure statements.

B. Account rules list detailed policies. The Federal Reserve imposes requirements on banks through various regulations.

Vocabulary Builder

a. annual percentage rate (APR)
b. annual percentage yield (APY)
c. certificate of deposit (CD)
d. Check 21
e. compound interest
f. demand deposit
g. governing documents
h. interbank transaction
i. interest
j. money market deposit account (MMDA)
k. post-dated check
l. stale check
m. statement savings account
n. time deposit
o. transaction account

Choose the term that best fits the definition. Write the letter of the answer in the space provided. Some terms may not be used.

____ 1. Price paid for the use of money

____ 2. Effective rate of interest when compounding is factored in

____ 3. Savings account earning a competitive interest rate from invested deposits

____ 4. Deposit held for or maturing at a specified time

____ 5. Account that allows transactions to occur at any time and in any number

____ 6. Deposit payable on demand whenever the depositor chooses

____ 7. Savings instrument with fixed interest rate and fixed maturity date

____ 8. Return calculated by adding interest to principal for next interval

____ 9. Nominal rate on which interest is calculated per year

____ 10. A transaction made between banks

____ 11. Account-specific documents outlining the legal rights and responsibilities of both the bank and the account holder

____ 12. A check that is dated six months or before it is presented for payment or deposit

Review Concepts

13. What is a demand deposit?

_____

_____

_____

14. Name three forms of demand deposits.

_____

_____

15. What is a minimum balance?

_____

_____

16. Name three types of time deposits.

_____

_____

17. Why are savings accounts not subject to the Fed's reserve requirements?

_____

_____

18. Describe a certificate of deposit and its maturity date.

_____

_____

19. What do the letters in the formula $P \times R \times T = I$ represent?

_____

_____

20. Explain the basic idea of compound interest.

_____

_____

_____

_____

21. What is the difference between APR and APY?

_____

_____

_____

22. What is the most significant factor influencing the flow of deposits in the United States?

_____

_____

_____

23. Name five main types of documents typically supplied with new accounts.

_____

_____

_____

Apply What You Learned

24. Why are transaction accounts the most liquid of all funds?

_____

_____

_____

25. What factors should a person consider when choosing an account?

_____

_____

_____

_____

26. Why is the annual percentage rate an ineffective measure for comparing accounts?

_____

_____

_____

_____

27. Why won't the Federal Reserve's monetary policies completely control the flow of deposits in the U.S. banking system?

_____

_____

_____

_____

28. Why must banks provide customers with documents such as account rules, and how do account rules protect both banks and consumers?

_____

_____

_____

_____

29. How do Federal Reserve regulations protect consumers?

_____

_____

_____

Make Academic Connections

30. **ADVERTISING**   Collect advertisements for checking and savings accounts that appear in print media. Evaluate the ads in terms of attractiveness, clarity, quality of product, and overall effectiveness. What makes a fair and good advertisement?

_____

_____

31. **BANKING MATH**   Calculate the interest earned on a three-year certificate of deposit (CD) with an initial value of $12,500 earning 5½ percent, compounded annually. What will be the final account balance? Then calculate the interest earned on a one-year CD with an initial value of $5,000 earning 7 percent compounded semiannually. What will be the final balance?

_____

_____

_____

32. **DESIGN**   Create a marketing brochure for a checking account. Select what features your account will offer, choose what type of customer you would like to attract, decide on a name, and design a brochure that will effectively and fairly present the features. You may wish to gather real brochures to use as models.

_____

_____

Negotiable Instruments

6.1	Types of Negotiable Instruments
6.2	Presenting Checks for Payment
6.3	Processing Checks
6.4	Changing Forms of Payments

STOCK ILLUSTRATION/GETTY IMAGES

skills that pay dividends

Public Speaking and Persuasion

When speaking to a group of people, it is important to have a clear idea of your topic and the purpose of your presentation. You should know your audience and what actions you are trying to motivate your audience to take.

If giving a prepared presentation to a specific group of people, research the composition of the audience prior to developing the presentation. Anticipate the concerns of audience members and proactively plan to address those concerns. For example, are you speaking to a company's employees at their place of work to introduce your bank to the employees? If so, where are the employees in their careers? Are they new college graduates just getting accustomed to managing a large salary who need advice on checking, savings, and investment accounts? Are they employees who are mid-career who are interested in starting a savings plan for their children's college educations? Knowing who the audience members are will allow you to customize your presentation to address their specific needs. It will enable you to bring the appropriate product literature for distribution.

Proactively addressing their concerns enables the audience to know their concerns are being addressed. It frees up their thoughts to focus fully on new material that you present.

You should show the audience that you are a credible source of information. You should have a thorough understanding of the material you present. Your knowledge of the topic should extend beyond what you present. Then, when questions or discussions occur, you will have additional knowledge that you can share with the audience. When the audience knows that you are fully aware of the implications of what you are recommending, they can be sure you have the skills to protect their interests.

Make sure any presentation tools you use, whether PowerPoint slides, flip charts, or handouts, are easy to understand. All visual tools should be concise with clearly identified titles.

Engage your audience by using humor or personal experiences that evoke a positive emotional response.

Be sure to be direct in your closing. Ask the audience if they have questions, concerns, or issues that need clarification. Ask the audience to take the action you intended. In the workplace example, you could ask audience members to open new accounts at the close of the presentation.

These same techniques can be adapted for addressing an individual. If you need to give an impromptu presentation to an individual client who enters the bank, have a brief list of screening questions available. These questions can help you direct the customer to clearly define his or her thoughts, needs, and preferences. After the client states his or her needs, you can tailor the discussion to meet those needs and you can suggest the appropriate products.

Develop Your Skill

Select a product you will need to explain to customers. Prepare a persuasive presentation to describe the product to a customer. Give your presentation to classmates and solicit feedback on the strengths and weaknesses of the presentation.

PHOTODISC

6.1

goals

+ Define the term negotiable instrument.

+ Identify different types of negotiable instruments.

terms

+ negotiable instrument

+ bearer instrument

+ draft

+ bill of exchange

+ promissory note

Types of Negotiable Instruments

Banking Scene

Midori Akita is finishing her career as a postal worker and moving from her home in New York to a small town in Florida. She will receive a monthly pension check from the government. The government wants her to use direct deposit to receive these payments. As she prepares for her new life in Florida, Midori must consider many options about the best ways to receive, transfer, and handle her money. When moving, how does someone learn about the financial choices they need to make in their new location? How can they research them before they move?

NEGOTIABLE INSTRUMENTS •

Money is zipping around the banking system every day, 24 hours a day, seven days a week. The flow of deposits that carries both national and international economies moves constantly. In what forms does that money move?

When most people think of money, they think of cash, but only a small part of the money that moves in this country is cash. Increasingly, ledger entries add to one account and subtract from another without actual currency changing hands. Today, electronic transfers of one kind or another create these entries. Most large transfers within the banking industry have taken place this way for years. The electronic world is increasingly apparent to consumers, as electronic payment systems are becoming a routine part of retail businesses as well. But, for many people, money moves both to them and from them in the form of *negotiable instruments*, such as checks, drafts, and other written documents of value.

A **negotiable instrument** is a written order or promise to pay a sum of money, either to a specified party or to the person who holds it. Negotiable instruments include drafts, bills of exchange, and some promissory notes, but the most common form of negotiable instrument is a check.

What is Negotiable?

Don't let the word *negotiable* in *negotiable instrument* confuse you. The word means transferable. Consider that a check, like money, is a medium of exchange. The "negotiation" that goes on refers to the transfer of the instrument from one party to another. That transfer may mean passing the instrument between two people, or from one bank to another, or even from one country to another. The recipient or holder of the instrument negotiates the instrument in order to obtain its value. For example, your company gives you your paycheck. By signing your name on the back of the check, or *endorsing* the check, you are transferring the title of the check. Endorsing the check has made it negotiable and it can be deposited in your bank. Then you have use of its value.

Unless you and the bank agree that the instrument is negotiable, you won't be able to use it. The negotiation, however, may be restricted by one party or another in the transfer. As you might imagine, banks have a great interest in seeing that the negotiable instruments they receive for deposit are genuine and worth their assigned value. Most of the terms of negotiation relate to making certain an instrument does indeed possess real value, so that the bank in which you deposit it can negotiate the instrument to get the value from it just as you did.

What is an Instrument?

In the broadest sense, almost any agreed-upon medium of exchange could be considered a negotiable instrument. A Federal Reserve note is a written promise to pay on demand a certain value to the person who owns it. Certificates of deposit, bonds, treasury bills and other securities, and even a winning lottery ticket may also meet that definition. In day-to-day banking, a negotiable instrument usually refers more narrowly to checks, drafts, bills of exchange, and some types of promissory notes.

✔ checkpoint

What is a negotiable instrument? What is the most common form of negotiable instrument?

_____

_____

_____

FORMS OF NEGOTIABLE INSTRUMENTS • • • • • • • • • • • • •

A negotiable instrument is a written order promising to pay a sum of money. It may be a **bearer instrument**, which is payable to the *bearer* (whoever holds it), or it may be an instrument with highly specified terms, including the date of maturity and the intended recipient. What makes it negotiable is that it can be used for value and is a medium of exchange.

Checks

Checks are the most common form of negotiable instrument and are the preferred method of payment for many debts. They offer convenience for both writer and recipient, a relatively high degree of safety, and a record of transactions. They are accepted for most transactions when supported by appropriate identification, and their common and recognizable form makes them a part of normal life for most people. There is a huge industry devoted to the printing, transporting, safeguarding, and processing of checks around the country. The Federal Reserve provides some of these services, but there are many private companies involved as well.

The standard features of personal checks are the following:

- **Check number** is the number of the check being written.

- **Date** is the date the check is written. Checks are payable on demand and cannot legally be predated or postdated.

- **Payee** is the receiver of the funds. This line directs the bank to "pay to the order of" a specified party.

- **Amount** spaces allow for the amount of the check to be entered in both numbers and words, to minimize errors. In the event the words and numbers don't match, the amount written in words takes precedence.

- **Signature** is a valid signature of the maker of the check. Banks will not negotiate checks without a signature.

- **Memo** is an optional entry to note the check's purpose or other information.

- **Identification numbers** give the check number, the bank number, and the account number. They are printed with magnetic ink in machine-readable characters, called magnetic ink character recognition (MICR) numbers.

- **Drawee** identifies the bank that maintains the account and holds the funds of the person or business that is writing the check.

- **Drawer** is the person who is writing the check.

When you write a check, you may issue it to the person whose name is on the payee line, but you are really writing it to your bank. You are giving the bank instructions to pay the sum "to the order of" the recipient.

As a percentage, check use per person declined in the United States by about 6.4 percent between 2003 and 2006. In 2007 the Fed processed more than 10 billion checks. In 2003, the Fed processed about 37 billion checks. Increased use of electronic payments has reduced the number of checks written.

©JASON STITT/SHUTTERSTOCK

Drafts

A draft is similar to a check. In fact, a check is one form of a draft, but there are other forms. A **draft** is an order signed by one party (the *drawer*, or drafter) that is addressed to another party (the *drawee*) directing the drawee to pay to someone (the *payee*) the amount indicated on the draft. The payment may be at sight or at some defined time. If you (the drawer) were writing a draft, you would be directing your bank or other institution (the drawee) to pay the payee of the order the sum shown on the draft. The process is similar when you write a check. The terms for writers and receivers of drafts are the same as those used for checks. In fact, some credit unions provide "share drafts" instead of checks for their members. Most drafts are used for the purchase of goods and services when the transaction goes beyond the bounds of U.S. banking law.

Bills of Exchange

A **bill of exchange** is a negotiable and unconditional written order, such as a check, draft, or trade agreement, addressed by one party to another. The receiver of the bill must pay the specified sum or deliver specified goods on demand or at a specified time. Bills of exchange are a common form of internationally negotiable instruments.

Promissory Notes

A **promissory note** is a written promise to pay at a fixed or determinable future time a sum of money to a specified individual. You might not regard promissory notes as negotiable instruments, but it is easy to see why they are. Suppose you wrote an IOU to LaTasha for ten dollars. LaTasha, as it happens, owes Jamal ten dollars. Why couldn't LaTasha just give Jamal your IOU? You pay Jamal the ten dollars, and everyone comes out even. That is

Banking Math *Connection*

Do you balance your checkbook? Undetected errors can cause problems. Your bank statement of October 15 says you have $1,114.72 in your account. Your checkbook register shows $1,146.57. You have made one deposit, written two checks, and visited the ATM once since the statement was printed.

Solution

Begin with ending balance from the Oct. 15 statement.		$1,114.72
Add deposit made since the date of the bank statement.		
Oct. 22	$954.00	954.00
		$2,068.72

Subtract checks and debits in your check register not shown on the bank statement.

Oct. 15 Check 1114	$125.00	
Oct. 21 ATM	90.00	
Oct. 26 Check 1115	707.15	
	$922.15	922.15
		$1,146.57

Your calculation agrees with your checkbook register. If the account doesn't balance, recheck your math, compare deposit slips and checks for entry errors, check for outstanding checks that haven't cleared, and check automatic withdrawals or fees that you may not have recorded.

exactly what happens when certain promissory notes are used as negotiable instruments. These two-party documents are legally binding documents with many specified terms that may vary widely. For example, you might obtain a mortgage loan from ABC Mortgage Company, which might then sell the mortgage note to DEF Finance, which now owns your obligation.

Such trading practices on short-term notes make up a large part of a rapidly moving investment economy. *Commercial paper*, a short-term (270 days or fewer) note or draft issued by a corporation or government, is a common investment instrument. Remember that fast-moving overnight loans between banks make up a segment of the money supply.

 checkpoint

List the standard features of a personal check.

assessment 6.1

Think Critically

1. How is a negotiable instrument different from cash?

2. Before electronic payments became widely used and accepted, why did people like to use checks?

3. Why can a promissory note be considered a negotiable instrument?

4. What risks might be associated with negotiable instruments?

Make Academic Connections

5. **BANKING MATH**   According to a study released by the Federal Reserve in 2007, there were 62.7 billion electronic payments in 2006. The total value of electronic payments was $34.1 trillion. Debit card payments were 25.3 billion with a value of $1 trillion, ACH transactions were 14.6 billion with a value of $31 trillion, credit cards were 21.7 billion with a value of $2.1 trillion, and electronic benefits transfers were 1.1 billion with a value of $29.6 billion. Calculate the percentage of each type of electronic payment and calculate the average payment per transaction.

6. **TECHNOLOGY**   In groups, list every company or group you can think of that might be involved in the business of preparing or processing checks. Which of these groups might successfully adapt if electronic payment systems displaced checks? Which might go out of business? What effects might these changes have on the economy and the banking system?

6.2

goals

+ Identify bank requirements for honoring checks.

+ List common forms of check endorsements.

terms

+ elements of negotiability

+ holder in due course

+ blank endorsement

+ restrictive endorsement

+ full endorsement

+ qualified endorsement

Presenting Checks for Payment

Banking Scene

After moving to her new neighborhood in South Florida, Midori Akita opened a checking account at a nearby bank. She used her final paycheck from the Postal Service to open the account. Her account representative politely requested two separate forms of identification, including one with a photograph. Midori knew that the bank needed to be certain of both the check and its depositor. What was the bank trying to determine?

ELEMENTS OF NEGOTIABILITY

A check is a negotiable instrument. When you present a check to a bank for payment, the bank must assure that the check meets certain legal requirements. These conditions are commonly called **elements of negotiability**. The Uniform Commercial Code, Articles 3 and 4, covers notes, drafts, and checks. Every state has adopted these legal guidelines. They require a written, signed, unconditional promise or order to pay a fixed amount on demand or at a defined time to the **holder in due course**. This is the person or financial institution that acquires a check or promissory note received in good faith as payment and who is entitled to payment by the drawer of the check or note.

When you bring a check to a bank to cash or deposit, the elements of negotiability directly affect how the bank looks at the check, the maker of the check, and you. After all, if the check you deposit turns out to not be a legal negotiable instrument, the bank is not going to get paid and neither are you.

Written

The first requirement for a negotiable instrument is that it must be written. Remember that the law surrounding negotiable instruments grew up long before electronic payment systems. In addition, written documents are easily transferable and universally recognized as legally binding. If a document conforms to the law, it is a negotiable instrument.

You might be surprised to note that there is no legally prescribed form for a check. A check is a written order to pay someone. There is not even a necessity that the "document" be written on paper. If all proper information were present, the check would be honored. There are old stories of checks written on various materials, tax payments made with "the shirt off one's back," or even written on a person's actual back. Whether these tales are true is hard to prove, but they illustrate that the information on the document is what matters, not the medium on which it is written.

Of course, checks written on shirts would wreak havoc in the automated check-processing system. Standards created by the American Bankers Association and the American National Standards Institute (ANSI) govern the size and placement of information on checks, as well as paper thickness, colors, and security features. Most checks are in one of three sizes—the standard, personal-check size and two larger sizes of checks common for payroll. These standards are for the industry's benefit, but they do not determine negotiability.

Signature

A document must be signed by a person capable of making the order or promise for it to be a negotiable instrument. Legally, a check is not payable if it does not bear the drawer's genuine signature. The bank that paid such a check would be liable, not the drawer. Like any legal document the signature must be valid, but it does not necessarily need to be human. Machine signatures are perfectly acceptable if the bank obtains a resolution or agreement that liability for forgery resides with the customer using the machine.

Unconditional Promise or Order

To be negotiable, an instrument must make an unconditional promise or order to pay. First, the promise or order must be explicit. Authorizing a payment or acknowledging a debt is not enough. Second, the promise or order must be unconditional. Reasoning for this rule has to do with transfer. If the order to pay is conditional, a third party, who has no control or relation to any conditions set, may not be able to obtain the instrument's value. If its value cannot be transferred or obtained, an instrument is not negotiable.

Sum Certain

A negotiable instrument must state clearly on its face the principal amount to be paid, and it must be a monetary value. Although interest may be referenced, as may other documents regarding fees and charges, the principal sum in a note or order must be defined.

Payable on Demand or at a Defined Time

If a negotiable instrument bears no instruction as to when it is due, it is payable on demand, that is, immediately. It may show a time when it is payable, such as a promissory note does, but that must be a defined time. Checks are commonly payable on demand.

Words of Negotiation

Remember that *negotiation* applies to the ability of the holder to obtain its value, not to conditions or terms. Words of negotiation are instructions about how the instrument's value may be obtained. *Pay to the order of Keshia Smith* lets the instrument be negotiated by Keshia Smith with her endorsement, or to whomever she may later assign it. *Pay to the order of Cash* makes the instrument a bearer instrument, valuable to anyone who has it regardless of endorsement.

When you hand a check across the counter, the bank's representative will quickly check for all six elements of negotiability. Banks spend considerable time and effort training employees to understand and identify these elements. Recognizing them not only protects against fraud, but also allows the bank or other institution to know exactly how to handle a negotiable instrument.

 checkpoint

What is meant by "elements of negotiability"?

ENDORSEMENT AND IDENTIFICATION • • • • • • • • • • • • • • • •

When you present a check to the bank for payment or deposit, the banker will assure that the check has been endorsed. Although the maker of a check may have created a perfectly negotiable instrument, the actual negotiation of it involves the transfer of both the instrument and its value. *Endorsement* of the instrument allows it to be negotiated, not only by you but by other parties later. After all, if the instrument cannot be used by others, it is not really negotiable. After you have endorsed the check, the teller may ask to see identification, especially if you seek cash or are depositing only a small part in your account (known as a *cash back transaction*).

Types of Endorsement

There are four primary types of endorsement, and each affects the degree of negotiability of the instrument. Some of these endorsement types have varying names, but they mean essentially the same thing.

Blank Endorsement   A blank endorsement, sometimes called an *open endorsement*, is the least secure of the four main types of endorsement, but it is also the most negotiable. It is simply the signature of the holder.

For example, assume a check has been written to Maria Mills. Maria simply writes her name in the endorsement area on the back of the check and does what she wants with the check thereafter. Maria must take care of this check, however. Once she signs it, it could be cashed by anyone. A check with a signed blank endorsement is a bearer instrument and is as good as cash to anyone who can find someone to accept it. It is a good idea not to endorse a check with a blank endorsement until the very moment you intend to cash or deposit it. Your signature implies that you have negotiated the check, and if you sign it and lose it, anyone who finds it may cash it.

Perhaps Maria intends to pass the check to someone else. Assume the check is for $100.00, and Maria happens to owe her cousin Martina exactly $100.00. Maria could use a blank endorsement and simply give the check to her cousin. Martina could then endorse it again and deposit or negotiate the check as she pleases. Martina's endorsement is called a *secondary endorsement*. In fact, checks may receive multiple secondary endorsements as they work their way back to their originating banks.

The blank endorsement is the most common type of endorsement, and millions of people negotiate checks on a daily basis with it. Blank endorsements call for care, though, just as you would care for cash.

Restrictive Endorsement   The holder of a check may wish to prescribe a little more carefully how the check is negotiated. A **restrictive endorsement** limits the use of the instrument to a means specified by the endorser. In theory, a restrictive endorsement ends further negotiation of the check. The most common restriction is "For Deposit Only," which limits the negotiation of the endorsed check to deposit in an account. By ending the instrument's transferability, a restrictive endorsement renders the instrument no longer negotiable.

Restrictive endorsements do not necessarily guarantee the end of negotiation, though. Perhaps an inattentive teller may not respond to the restriction properly, or perhaps the check might be deposited into another account other than that of the intended payee. Such cases are more common when business accounts are involved, or when the payee has many accounts. More restrictive endorsements such as "For Deposit Only, Hobbit Corporation" provide greater protection. Specifying the name of a particular account if a company has multiple accounts restricts negotiation more effectively. A *split deposit* occurs when a depositor designates that a single check should be divided to have portions of it deposited in different accounts.

Full Endorsement   A **full endorsement** transfers the check to another specified party. From there, its negotiability depends on what that party does with it. Sometimes called a *special endorsement*, a full endorsement limits neither the transferability nor the further negotiability of the check. Suppose again that Maria Mills owes her cousin Martina $100.00. She could just endorse the check with a blank endorsement. She could just cash the check and hand Martina the cash. She could also use a full endorsement to transfer the check completely to Martina. In effect, it is just the same as if Martina had been the original recipient of the check. Martina must endorse the check whenever she wishes to negotiate it further, and she has the same range of options that Maria did. What the full endorsement provides is protection for the endorsed check. No one but Martina can use the check next.

Of course, negotiability is also determined by the next holder. Martina has to find a bank that will accept Maria's check, and she must identify herself and endorse the check to the satisfaction of the bank. If it is a different bank from Maria's, Martina's endorsement also acts as an *accommodation endorsement*, guaranteeing that the bank will eventually collect the money from Maria's account, wherever it may be.

Qualified Endorsement Another endorsement, the **qualified endorsement,** is an attempt to limit the liability of the endorser without limiting an instrument's further negotiability. The words "without recourse" appear in the endorsement, intending to move the instrument along without incurring liability if the check is no good. A qualified endorsement often guarantees payment if the person of primary liability does not pay.

Although qualified endorsements are not common, persons acting as representative for others may use them. If, for example, a lawyer representing Martina Mills received a check for funds owed to her, the lawyer might simply transfer the check to her by endorsing it as with a full endorsement but adding the words "without recourse." If the check were no good, assuming the lawyer had met other legal requirements for endorsement, neither Martina Mills nor any later holder of the check could require the lawyer to make good on the check.

The deposit agreements in the governing documents cover in detail when deposits are accepted, when funds are available from them, and what happens in cases in which the funds cannot be collected. Every account holder, especially those who receive checks from many sources, should be thoroughly familiar with the rules of his or her own bank.

PHOTODISC/GETTY IMAGES

You are walking down the street and notice a $20 bill. No one is around, and there is no way you can discern who might have dropped the bill. You congratulate yourself on your good fortune, think sympathetic thoughts about the person who lost it, pick up the bill, and go on your way. The next day, as you walk to your bank to deposit your paycheck, you notice a blue piece of paper on the curb. It's a check, in good shape, made out to John Dolan, whom you don't know. The check is drawn on your bank, and Dolan has placed a blank endorsement on it.

Think Critically

How is the check different from the $20 bill? How is it the same? Knowing this check is a bearer instrument, what will you do with it? Discuss the issue with classmates.

Identification and Check Acceptance

Does the bank really care who you are if you present a check made out to Maria Mills and want to cash it? It sure does. Check fraud is a serious issue for banks, and there are ways that banks and companies work to prevent it. One of the ways banks protect themselves is to require adequate identification.

Banks may require as much or as little identification to cash or deposit a check as they wish. Some banks even require fingerprinting. The greatest risk to banks comes from personal checks cashed by new customers or noncustomers. A bank may charge fees for noncustomers, even for checks drawn on that same bank. It may make different rules for customers and noncustomers, and it may refuse to cash a check about which it is doubtful. Sometimes these policies make people feel they are being treated poorly, but a bank

PHOTODISC/GETTY IMAGES

must balance customer service and risk management. When a bank cashes your check, it is essentially giving you money it has yet to recover, so it has a great interest in seeing that you are who you say you are and that the check is genuine.

✔ checkpoint

Name the four main types of check endorsement.

assessment 6.2

Think Critically

1. How do elements of negotiability provide for the transfer and use of a negotiable instrument?

2. Why do the words "pay to the order of" play such an important part in negotiability?

3. What role does endorsement play in the negotiability of checks?

4. If you were cashing a check at a bank and were asked to supply a fingerprint, would you be offended? Why or why not?

Make Academic Connections

5. **COMMUNICATION** Create a flip chart or PowerPoint presentation on types of endorsements for checks. In your presentation, indicate the advantages and risks of each type as they apply to both safety and negotiability.

6. **SOCIAL STUDIES** Being able to open and maintain a checking account is a basic skill critical to participation in American economic life. Should such business skills be a required part of public education? What basic business skills should be taught? Write a one-page paper in which you clearly identify your opinion on these issues and provide logical reasons to support it.

Processing Checks

6.3

goals

+ Identify key laws that make today's check-clearing process possible.
+ Explain the sequence of events as a check is processed for payment.

terms

+ float
+ transit number
+ returned check

Banking Scene

As Midori Akita adjusted to her new life in Florida, she received a check in the mail from a brother-in-law in upstate New York as a retirement gift. She considered cashing it, but then remembered the account rules for her new account and thought it might be smoother to deposit the check. Still, her account rules noted that there might be a "hold" on the funds until the check cleared. Why might banks have such policies? What do you think is a reasonable time for a hold to occur?

A NATIONAL SYSTEM OF PAYMENT • • • • • • • • • • • • • •

Electronic payments and checks are not only common forms of negotiable instruments, they are a way of life in the United States. As of 2006, more than twice as many payments were made electronically relative to checks. Electronic payments and checks are far safer and more convenient than cash for bill payment. The legal status of electronic payments and checks makes them a dominant force in the economic life of the nation. Both can provide proof of payment. Enhanced technology and communications have made the processing of checks more efficient and accurate. Although electronic payments have surpassed check payments, check payments remain a fact of economic life and the banking system.

The Legal Structure of the Check Payment System

For a massive system of check processing to work, there must be clear and coordinated cooperation among banks. In the United States, with its unique blend of private and public institutions in the banking system, check payment depends upon the legal foundations that set up and maintain the banking system itself. Although many state and federal regulations govern the banking industry, five key legislative acts most critically affect the check processing system.

Federal Reserve Act of 1913 In establishing the structure of our banking system, the Federal Reserve Act of 1913 also established the fundamental relationship between the Federal Reserve and banks, as well as among banks. The Act created a national check collection system and other rules for payments. Today, the Fed is deeply involved in check collection and plays a leading role in the industry. It has fostered technological advance, beginning with automatic sorters more than 40 years ago and continuing through the latest state-of-the-art technology. The Fed has also used its regulatory authority to influence applicable legislative acts by Congress. In addition, the Federal Reserve has helped set and apply standards for checks and the technology that processes them. Not only the backbone of the banking system, the Federal Reserve is an up-to-the-minute participant in the check processing and collection system.

Uniform Commercial Code of 1958   The Uniform Commercial Code (UCC) of 1958 established a consistent code for commercial law transactions. Adopted eventually by all 50 states, the UCC largely eliminated the wide variation of legal regulation that could hamper the national payments system. Articles 3, 4, 5, and 9 of the UCC pertain to banking and negotiable instruments and contain terms, definitions, and regulations, many of which form the foundation of account agreements.

Expedited Funds Availability Act of 1987   The Expedited Funds Availability Act (EFAA) of 1987 was passed to combat an abuse of the check payment system practiced by a few banks. When checks were deposited, these banks did not credit the accounts until long after the checks had been paid by the banks on which they were drawn. Although the banks had credit for the checks in their funds, they would not make payments on them, creating in effect a "float" fund for their use at the expense of their customers. The EFAA directed the Federal Reserve to set rules that balanced the needs of consumers with the need for banks to protect themselves from uncollectible checks. Federal Reserve Regulation CC established these rules and procedures.

Check 21   In October 2004, a federal law was passed to enact Check 21. To streamline check processing, banks can take a picture of the front and back of a check and transmit images of the check to other banks. This image allows pertinent financial data to be exchanged so the value of the check can be obtained. The image also enables a bank receiving a check image to produce a substitute check, or paper copy, of the check. Copies of the image can also be included on monthly account statements which are sent to account holders. Check 21 eliminates the need for the processing of paper checks. Like a paper check, a substitute check or a digital image of a check can be used for proof of payment.

Electronic Check Conversion   Electronic check conversion is distinct from Check 21. Electronic check conversion allows a billing party, whether a utility, a retail outlet, or any other business, to use the information on a check to initiate an electronic fund transfer from your account. Your check, which may be returned to you (if you are at a retail business) or destroyed, is not the payment form. The electronic fund transfer is the method of payment. Businesses are required to inform consumers when an electronic check conversion will occur.

Consumer rights vary according to the method of payment. Checks, substitute checks, and electronic check conversion have distinct rights associated with them.

✔ checkpoint

Why does the check processing and collection system depend on the Federal Reserve?

CHECK PAYMENT AND PROCESSING • • • • • • • • • • • • • • • • •

What happens to your check after you write it and give it to the payee? The process of adjusting various accounts and returning checks involves several steps.

1. Suppose you write a check for $95.50 for this month's electric bill. You are the drawer or maker of the check. The electric company is the payee. Your bank, A National Bank, is the drawee.

2. The electric company deposits your check in B National Bank. If the drawer and the payee of a check have the same bank, that bank handles the processing in-house. About 30 percent of all check-clearing ends here. If the banks are different, the processing continues.

3. B National Bank puts a magnetic code on your check showing the dollar total and sends it on to the Federal Reserve or other intermediary. Note that B National Bank has *not* credited the electric company's account for $95.50 yet, because the check has not cleared.

4. The Federal Reserve clears about one-third of the nation's checks. There are several large private banks, called *correspondent banks*, that also clear checks, and some have created check-clearing corporations. The check is sorted, and the bank ID and the dollar amount are read from the magnetic codes.

5. The Federal Reserve or intermediary credits B National Bank $95.50 in its account at the Federal Reserve. All financial institutions using the Fed to clear checks have an account at the Federal Reserve. Correspondent banks also have accounts at the Fed. Your check is then sent on your bank, A National Bank. At this point B National Bank has been credited with the $95.50, but A National Bank has not paid out anything. Thus, for this brief period, both banks count the same funds. These funds are called **float**, and they distort the money supply and reserve figures.

6. A National Bank pays the Federal Reserve $95.50 and debits your account $95.50. If your

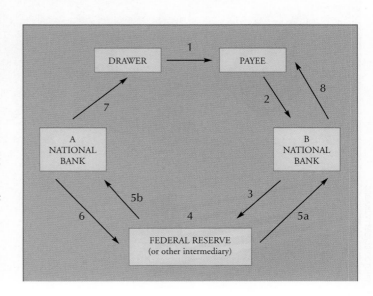

account doesn't have $95.50 in it, the check is returned unpaid to B National Bank, and ultimately, to the electric company. Penalties may be applied by the bank as well as the electric company.

7. In the past, the canceled check, which is your original check that was processed by both the check cashing location and your own bank, was returned to you. Today you are likely to receive an image of the check or a transaction summary with your bank statement. Actual return of physical paper checks is nearly obsolete because it is more costly than the digital-imaging systems banks use.

8. Finally, B National Bank credits the electric company's account for $95.50. This may have happened earlier in the process, depending on B National Bank's policies for deposits. The entire process usually takes two to five days, and banks are required to make a depositor's funds available within five days.

These steps may vary somewhat if a correspondent bank or other intermediary is used, or if along the line the check is converted into an electronic transaction rather than moving physically through the system.

The millions of checks written daily create a lot of float. Float has several causes, and each has a separate name. *Malfunction float* is caused by machine breakdown. *Transportation float* refers to delays in moving checks from one place to another. It occurs most often in winter. *Holdover float* occurs when banks are slow in processing transactions. Some banks have been accused of deliberately holding checks to create float to earn short-term interest. Electronic check processing has greatly reduced float.

Transit Number

To aid in the check processing procedure, a transit number is printed at the bottom left-hand corner of a check (see page 154). The **transit number** is a 9-digit number that identifies the bank that holds the checking account and is responsible for payment. It was created in 1910 by the American Bankers Association (ABA) and is also known as the *routing number*, *transit/routing number*, and *ABA number*. Transit numbers are issued to only federal or state chartered financial institutions that are eligible to hold an account at a Federal Reserve Bank. The transit number system also now identifies participants in automated clearinghouses, electronic funds transfer, and online banking.

EDI Implementation

Computers "talk" to each other by means of conventions, called protocols, for information exchange. EDI is an acronym for electronic data interchange, a set of standards for business-to-business exchange of information. As technology improves and extends further into the banking business, implementation of EDI becomes more critical to run such applications as online banking, smart card applications, and other forms of electronic commerce.

Think Critically Research EDI systems. What sort of challenges do you think might be involved with implementing EDI?

Other Types of Check Processing

Banks may encounter checks that require special handling and processing. One example is the *postdated check*, which is a check that is dated later than the date on which it is actually written. The rules on processing postdated checks vary by state, depending on whether the state follows the Uniform Commercial Code (UCC). According to the UCC, a postdated check is allowable as long as the bank customer gives the bank advance "notice" of the check, including the check number, account number, amount, date, and to whom the check is payable. If proper notice is given, the bank, not the customer, would be liable for damages if the check is cashed before the date on the check. States not following the UCC may consider these checks illegal.

Another kind of check that requires special handling is a returned check. A check written on an account that does not have adequate funds to cover it and which is returned unpaid to the person who deposited it is a **returned check**. It is also known as a *bounced check* or an *NSF* (nonsufficient funds) *check*. Policies for processing returned checks vary, but overdraft fees usually apply. If a check does not clear the bank the first time it is processed, some banks will automatically process it a second time. Other banks offer an overdraft protection program. For a fee, which can range from $17 to $35, the bank will cover the amount of the returned check. The bank stipulates that the overdrawn account must return to a positive balance within 30 days.

✔ checkpoint

What is float? What causes it?

assessment 6.3

Think Critically

1. Could banks in the same city create an independent check-clearing network that didn't use any intermediaries? Why or why not?

_____

_____

_____

2. How does the foundation of the Federal Reserve make a national check-clearing system work more smoothly?

_____

_____

_____

3. Why does the Federal Reserve work to limit float?

_____

_____

_____

4. Why does advanced technology minimize float?

_____

_____

Make Academic Connections

5. **BANKING MATH**   According to the Federal Reserve, float averaged about $133 million in 2005, down from $774 million in 2000. What percentage decrease does this drop represent?

_____

_____

6. **PROBLEM SOLVING**   You have a roommate who routinely writes checks before receiving a paycheck. Your roommate claims the money will be deposited by the time the checks clear. Make a list of practical reasons why this idea is not a good one and the consequences it could bring.

_____

_____

_____

Changing Forms of Payment

6.4

goals

+ List modern forms of payment systems.

+ Explain how banks and other financial institutions use automated forms of payment.

terms

+ charge cards

+ credit cards

+ cash cards

+ debit cards

+ smart cards

+ person-to-person payments (P2P)

+ radio frequency identification (RFID)

Banking Scene

Although Midori Akita had long had the option of having her paycheck deposited electronically, she had never used it, preferring to have the check in her hands. Now living in Florida, she is considering having her retirement checks go to her new bank through direct deposit. What questions might she ask about electronic funds transfer (EFT)?

CONSUMER PAYMENTS

Although checks still make up the largest volume of payments in the United States, change is on the horizon. Other forms of payment now exceed the use of cash in dollar volume for transactions. With more rapid and more secure electronic capabilities, growth in electronic forms of payment is likely to alter forever the way payments are made and processed. The banking system already is adapting to these changes, but some of the newest possibilities also pose challenges for the existing system.

The growth of varied forms of payment is a product of two phenomena. One is the entrepreneurial spirit. Merchants and banks have always looked for ways to increase revenue. Providing alternative payment methods increases business by making purchasing easier. Revenue is further increased when fees, including credit card fees, are charged for the use of the new methods. Along with this opportunistic spirit, advancing technology is supporting creative, convenient, rapid, and efficient forms of payment. Banks and the banking system are adapting to meet this evolution.

Charge Cards

Today's credit card industry grew from the use of charge cards. Because of the similarities, it may be easy to confuse the two. With **charge cards**, a consumer purchases but must pay the account in full at the end of the month. Most of the monthly bills are paid by check, with the card issuer doing the record-keeping. Charge cards, in effect, lend the amount of purchases for a month. Originally charge cards were store cards, but eventually third-party companies formed networks of participating businesses to expand the market.

Credit Cards

Credit cards allow consumers to pay all or part of their bills each month and finance the unpaid balance. Because of limits on interstate banking, credit cards did not become big business until banks devised a system using two banks (the card issuer's and the retailer's) that met regulations. Then the business exploded to become the competitive and powerful economic force it is today. To make the system work, the credit slips (or records of them) function more or less like checks. The retailer sends the slips to its own bank, which pays the retailer, records the transactions, and sends the slips to a clearing system. The clearing system routes them to the issuing bank, which pays the retailer's bank and collects from the consumer. In 2007, Visa held the largest market share of credit cards.

Cash Cards

Cash cards are commonly used at an automated teller machine (ATM). Consumers can get cash, make transfers and deposits, or perform almost any other banking function at the machine by inserting the card and entering a *personal identification number* (PIN). Banks encourage the use of cash cards, as they are less expensive than human tellers and are usually available 24 hours a day. Some banks even charge for the use of a human teller in an effort to encourage ATM or online banking to hold down costs. Internetworking of different bank computers has made cash cards a way of life in the last 20 years, but the simple cash card is beginning to disappear. The same functions are often combined on a card that is also acceptable to retailers for payment. These cards are, in effect, debit cards.

Debit Cards

Taking advantage of current computer networking technology, **debit cards** transfer money from a person's designated account to the account of the retailer. A debit card allows an immediate *point-of-sale* (POS) transaction. The

consumer swipes the card through a magnetic reader, enters a PIN, and authorizes the transfer. A record of the transaction appears on the consumer's bank statement, and the bank usually charges a monthly fee for use. Debit cards are rapidly growing in popularity as consumers become more comfortable with them. Checks still travel nicely by mail, but debit cards may replace them for point-of-sale transactions.

©ILKER CANIKLIGIL/SHUTTERSTOCK

Smart Cards

Smart cards are credit, debit, or other types of cards with embedded microchips. The microchips store values and, unlike magnetic strips, use the embedded logic to change values and record transactions. Smart cards enable a wide variety of "electronic purse" programs. The use of smart cards has grown rapidly in Europe, but is just beginning to take off in the United States. Retail, security, and customer loyalty programs frequently use smart cards. Eventually, smart cards could combine all plastic-card functions on a single card.

Bill Payment Services

There are multiple ways for consumers to streamline the way they pay businesses. Bill payment services vary in the methods used and fees assessed. Many consumers who have bank accounts use the bill pay option offered as a free service by their bank. After a consumer authorizes a payment, the bank transfers the funds electronically, if the business is set up to receive electronic payments. For businesses not equipment to receive electronic payments, banks will print out and mail a check to the business.

Some third party services allow consumers the opportunity to direct all bills to the service—whether a paper bill or an electronic bill. The service then pays all bills after receiving authorization from the consumer. This eliminates the need for the consumer to receive, sort, and manually pay bills. Charges for this type of service vary. Sometimes a monthly fee is charged in addition to a fee for each transaction.

Some credit card services allow consumers to preauthorize repetitive monthly payments to third parties, like cell phone or Internet providers. This service is often provided free of charge. It is best to use this service for bills that have the same value each month.

Person-to-Person Payments (P2P)

Online systems have been developed to allow consumers to pay each other directly for a product. The businesses that facilitate these **person-to-person (P2P)** payments provide an Internet platform for payment transfers. The businesses generate revenue by charging a fee for serving as the payment intermediary. The service fee may be either a flat rate, be based on a percentage of the value of the sale, or be a combination of both. Prominent P2P systems facilitate international payments that include currency conversions.

Highly developed P2P systems may compete with services historically provided by banks. Offering branded credit cards, money market investment accounts for balances held in their system, and tracking deposits and payments are services that may be offered by P2P providers. There

BLEND IMAGES/JUPITER IMAGES

are significant differences involved when dealing with a P2P provider versus a bank. For example, the money market account offered by a P2P provider is not protected by FDIC insurance, whereas a money market deposit account at a bank with FDIC insurance is protected.

Contactless Payments

There are multiple technologies available that enable consumers to make a payment without having their credit or debit cards make physical contact with the credit card reader. The technology used most frequently in the U.S. for contactless payments is **radio frequency identification (RFID)**. RFID, which is also known as *automatic identification and data capture (AIDC)*, uses a transponder to convey identifying information including the account holder's account or balance information and the fees being assessed to the account by the business for products or services.

RFID is appealing to consumers and businesses alike. The chips that carry account information can be embedded in a variety of products including key chains, credit cards, and cell phones. Without having to fiddle with the proper orientation of a credit or debit card to insert it in the reading device, transactions can occur more quickly. As RFID technology is commonly used instead of cash for low-value transactions, the need to make change is eliminated. Commuters who encounter tollbooths or mass transit payment turnstiles also appreciate the convenience provided by RFID.

Deferred Payments Processed by an Intermediary

A number of companies are available to serve online consumers who either don't want to use their credit cards online or who do not have either a traditional credit card or bank account. Sometimes the services provided by these intermediaries are called either *electronic wallets* or *online wallets*. Methods used by intermediaries include allowing a consumer to preload a card that is later activated online to pay for merchandise, letting a consumer make a purchase that the intermediary bills for later, or helping a consumer make a direct payment for an online purchase by using the funds in their online banking account. Similar to P2P remuneration, the intermediary may charge either a flat rate, a rate based on the percentage of the sale, or a combination of both.

Biometrics

Biometrics refers to using a distinct individual characteristic to uniquely identify a specific person. Fingerprints, retina scans, and voice recognition are some of the more common sources of biometric data. Fingerprint data was in use for a number of years at various grocery food chains. It was also being tested at gas stations. After initially linking credit account data to a fingerprint, consumers were able to pay their grocery checkout bill or their fuel bill by placing their fingerprint on a fingerprint reading scanner. Although a major provider of this service filed for bankruptcy during the first quarter of 2008, the technology behind this product is viable and may come into popular use again.

flat world...

Global Biometrics

Internationally, biometrics have become widely accepted as a method for safeguarding financial security. In Japan, cell phones are widely used for mundane through sophisticated financial transactions—from ordering fast food through accessing bank accounts. Fingerprint sensors are used in lieu of passwords to safeguard the financial information stored on cell phones. In Australia and Indonesia, banks use employees' fingerprints to provide access to secure areas. The U.K. is developing a national identity program called the U.K. National Identity Scheme. The program will combine biographical information and biometric data to provide an extremely secure way to uniquely determine the identity of citizens. This identifying information will be linked with businesses to secure the financial safety of British citizens. In the U.S., however, biometric firms are struggling. In early 2008, Pay By Touch, a firm that facilitated using fingerprints to identify customers buying groceries, filed for bankruptcy. Two new U.S biometric firms that were set to go public in 2008 have decided to wait to go public.

Think Critically Why does the U.S. lag other countries in adopting biometric technology? How would U.S. citizens react to a system similar to the U.K. National Identity Scheme?

Banks are in the process of adopting biometrics. In the U.S., current applications focus on employee verification. For example, a retina scan may be performed to confirm the identity of an employee who is servicing an ATM.

Other countries have adopted biometrics for customer service measures. For example, in Japan, a retina scan may be performed on ATM users to confirm their identity.

©TYLER OLSON/SHUTTERSTOCK

The Need for Caution

Experts recommend using a credit card as the source for online payments. Credit cards usually offer limited liability for false or disputed charges. Resolving disputed charges that are paid for from a bank account or a prepaid card can be more difficult than resolving erroneous bills paid for from cash or bank accounts. Consumers should also be careful that any networks used to authorize online bill payment are secure.

 checkpoint

Name ten payment systems other than cash or check.

BANK PAYMENTS

Innovations that are changing payment methods for consumers are also changing bank processes. Not only have banks implemented systems for recording and processing new forms of consumer payments, they have also developed innovative systems for conducting their bank-to-bank transactions and internal operations as well.

EFT

EFT is an acronym for *electronic funds transfer*. Funds transfers occur between banks, between banks and the Federal Reserve, between banks and the government, and between banks and consumers.

Direct Deposit One common form of EFT is direct deposit. A law was passed by Congress in 1996 that required most federal payments be made by EFT. To encourage compliance with this law, the government established Electronic Transfer Accounts (ETAs). For recipients of federal accounts who do not have or cannot qualify for a typical bank account, these low-cost accounts allow recipients to receive their payments electronically. These accounts also help ensure recipients can receive their payments in the event of a natural disaster that requires recipients to evacuate their homes. For EFT recipients, a statement arrives instead of a check, and the overhead cost of processing checks is eliminated. Safety, accuracy, and immediate use of the funds are reasons that many people prefer direct deposits.

The Financial Management Service (FMS), which is a bureau of the United States Department of the Treasury, distributes more than $1.6 trillion in annual payments to more than 100 million people. In 2007, FMS made more than 78 percent of its disbursements by EFT. FMS data indicates that each paper check payment costs $0.88 more than each EFT payment.

GoDirect In April, 2005, FMS began a marketing campaign called GoDirect to encourage recipients of federal funds to receive payments by EFT. If all FMS disbursements were made by EFT, $131.5 million annual savings could be achieved. A related program, launched in April, 2008, called Direct Express, offers federal fund recipients who choose not to open a bank or ETA account the chance to receive their payments on a Direct Express debit card. The card has no fees associated with it and the funds on the card have FDIC insurance.

As the government is such a large distributor of funds, these programs help drive EFT further into the psyche of American consumers. This makes consumers more receptive to efforts by private employers to encourage direct deposit as well.

NETBookmark

British citizens are scheduled to begin receiving their national identity cards, including biometric information, in 2009. Access www.cengage.com/school/pfinance/banking and click on the link for Chapter 6. According to Britain's Home Secretary, Jacqui Smith, "improved protection and greater convenience" are two important benefits of the National Identity Scheme. How are British citizens adapting to the new program? What are the benefits they are enjoying?

www.cengage.com/school/pfinance/banking

Automated Clearing Houses

Many transactions are handled by *automated clearing houses* (ACHs). The Federal Reserve led the development of ACHs in the 1970s and still operates most of them. Magnetic tapes exchanged among banks read streams of data into computers, ideal for large volumes of smaller payments such as payrolls or recurring payments. Although ACH technology is older and slower than online transfer, the cost per transaction is considerably less.

Online Transfers

For instant movement of high-volume amounts, banks and the Fed use interbank online transfers. These online transfers take place via dedicated networks not for public use. The transfers are usually time sensitive, so the instant and final transfer of these funds is critical. *Fedwire*, the funds transfer system run by the Federal Reserve, handles transfers for federal funds, interbank dealings, and securities transactions. In 2007, for example, Fedwire handled about 537,000 transactions per day, with a combined daily average value of $2.7 trillion. Another online system for private-sector transactions is the *Clearing House Interbank Payment System (CHIPS)*, which specializes in large-dollar transactions for international business. A central computer keeps constant track of all interbank business. In 2007, CHIPS processed over 40 million daily payments that had a combined total value of $2.1 trillion. At the end of each day, banks settle their accounts by transferring money to accounts at the Federal Reserve.

Check 21

Digital-imaging technology is the technology that enabled Check 21 legislation. Significant cost savings have been achieved by eliminating storage, recordkeeping, postage, and labor costs associated with paper checks. Instead of saving the actual processed check, a digital photo of the check becomes the document of record. A bank may send a customer reduced images of checks or merely a record of checks processed. If a customer needs a canceled check, the image can be retrieved from digital storage.

As of the third quarter of 2006, the Fed processed about 17 percent of their checks with Check 21 technology. On a daily basis, that represented more than six million checks with a combined value of around $20 billion. Check 21 has enabled the Fed to consolodate regional check processing centers. In 2003, there were forty-five check processing offices. In 2008, there were eighteen check processing offices. It is anticipated that during 2010 there will be only four check processing offices.

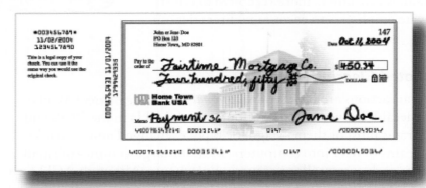

Front view of a substitute check

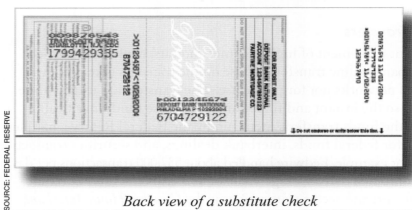

SOURCE: FEDERAL RESERVE

Back view of a substitute check

 checkpoint

Name three systems banks use for funds transfers.

assessment 6.4

Think Critically

1. Why do you think banks are interested in new payment systems?

_____

_____

2. Why might banks choose not to use up-to-the-minute technology for funds transfers or internal operations?

_____

_____

_____

3. Why is the government transitioning to electronic deposits?

_____

_____

4. How do digital-imaging techniques eliminate float?

_____

_____

_____

_____

5. How do P2P systems help stimulate the economy?

_____

_____

_____

Make Academic Connections

6. **ECONOMICS** The technological innovations that have enabled new payment methods, ranging from bill payment services through biometrics, have created many new business opportunities for the intermediaries who develop the platforms that provide the services. There are, however, some industries that will experience a decline in the demand for their services as a result of the new technologies. Select two new technologies and one old technology and research how businesses providing the technologies are performing. Provide a brief description.

7. **COMMUNICATION** Interview someone who works in the banking industry. Learn that person's thoughts about the future of payment systems. Summarize your findings in a brief report to the class.

chapter 6 **assessment**

Chapter Summary

6.1 Types of Negotiable Instruments

A. A negotiable instrument is a written order or promise to pay a sum of money to a specified party or to the person who holds it.

B. Checks are the most common form of negotiable instrument. Other forms include drafts, bills of exchange, and promissory notes.

6.2 Presenting Checks for Payment

A. Elements of negotiability call for a signed, unconditional promise or order to pay a defined sum on demand or at a defined time.

B. Types of endorsement include blank, restrictive, full, and qualified.

6.3 Processing Checks

A. The Federal Reserve Act of 1913, the Uniform Commercial Code of 1958, the Expedited Funds Availability Act of 1987, and Check 21 provide the legal framework for today's check payment system.

B. Checks travel a circuit among drawer, payee, banks, and the Federal Reserve or other clearing house. Postdated and returned checks require special processing.

6.4 Changing Forms of Payment

A. Technological developments have fueled innovations in payment options.

B. ACHs, Fedwire, and CHIPS are computer systems that transfer high volumes of transactions between banking entities.

Vocabulary Builder

a. bearer instrument
b. bill of exchange
c. blank endorsement
d. cash cards
e. charge cards
f. credit cards
g. debit cards
h. draft
i. elements of negotiability
j. float
k. full endorsement
l. holder in due course
m. negotiable instrument
n. person-to-person payment (P2P)
o. promissory note
p. qualified endorsement
q. radio frequency identification (RFID)
r. restrictive endorsement
s. returned check
t. smart cards
u. transit number

Choose the term that best fits the definition. Write the letter of the answer in the space provided. Some terms may not be used.

____ 1. A negotiable and unconditional written order
____ 2. Certain legal requirements that a check must meet
____ 3. Negotiable instrument payable to whoever holds it
____ 4. Endorsement that limits further negotiability
____ 5. Commonly used at an ATM
____ 6. Endorsement that transfers the check to another party
____ 7. Least secure type of endorsement
____ 8. Transfers money directly from buyer's bank account to merchant's account
____ 9. A written order or promise to pay a sum of money to a specified party or the person who holds it
____ 10. Card with embedded microchips
____ 11. A card that requires consumers to pay off purchases each month
____ 12. The technology that enables contactless payment
____ 13. When consumers pay each other directly for a product
____ 14. A check that is returned due to insufficient funds

Review Concepts

15. What is a negotiable instrument?

_____

_____

_____

16. What does *negotiable* mean as it applies to negotiable instruments?

_____

_____

_____

17. List the six elements of negotiability for a legal negotiable instrument.

_____

_____

_____

_____

_____

18. Identify four types of endorsement and what effects they have on a negotiable instrument.

_____

_____

_____

_____

_____

_____

19. Briefly explain the check-clearing process. Clarify differences between paper checks and electronic checks.

_____

_____

_____

_____

20. Why might you want to use a postdated check?

_____

_____

_____

_____

21. What is a transit number? What is its purpose on a check?

_____

_____

_____

22. List ten types of consumer payments other than cash.

_____

_____

_____

23. Give five examples of electronic funds transfer (EFT).

_____

_____

_____

24. What are automated clearing houses?

_____

_____

_____

25. Why would banks choose to use digital imaging technology?

_____

_____

_____

Apply What You Learned

26. How are negotiable instruments similar to money?

_____

_____

_____

27. Why are there specific legal requirements for an instrument to be negotiable?

_____

_____

_____

28. When you cash a check, why does the bank care whether or not you are the actual payee?

_____

_____

_____

29. What personal factors might cause someone to use a bill payment service?

_____

_____

_____

30. Why is float harmful?

_____

_____

31. How has technology affected the forms of payment used by consumers?

_____

_____

_____

Make Academic Connections

32. **BANKING MATH** Alan's bank statement shows a balance of $674.32. Since the statement date, Alan had deposits of $800.00 and $50.00. He has visited the ATM for withdrawals of $20.00, $50.00, and $20.00, and he has written checks for $42.11, $79.80, $600.00, $81.50, and $174.00. His checkbook register shows a balance of $556.91. Is his account properly balanced?

_____

_____

33. **COMMUNICATION** Why do government programs, like GoDirect, that utilize advanced technology, have a significant impact on the behavior of businesses and consumers? Explain your thoughts in a two-page persuasive paper that gives clear reasons for your findings. Distinguish between direct business impact and the more subtle impact of increased familiarity leading to increased adaptation.

34. **ART/DESIGN** Develop a brief PowerPoint presentation to explain to someone unfamiliar with the Internet their online payment choices.

35. **TECHNOLOGY** Learn more about encryption, one of the ways in which computer networks protect their data. What are the main methods, advantages, and issues surrounding secure data transmission today?

36. **SOCIAL STUDIES** The growing availability of personal and financial information troubles many people. In groups, research privacy issues as they apply to banking and the Internet. Present a report on current problems, possible solutions, and potential legislation about protecting consumers' privacy.

7 Bank Loans

7.1	Consumer Loan Theory
7.2	Consumer Loans
7.3	Granting and Analyzing Credit
7.4	Cost of Credit
7.5	Bank Loans and Policy

PHOTODISC/GETTY IMAGES

From Loan Service Clerk to Credit Card Risk Specialist

As he packed up the mementos in his office to move to the bank's new downtown headquarters, Vladimir was flooded with memories of prior positions he held at the bank.

By working his way through his first years of college as a loan services clerk, Vladimir obtained an initial understanding of how a bank processes loans. For new loans, he was responsible for processing research requests and for preparing participation sold certificates. He also made sure that customer loans stayed in balance by managing the general ledgers. If necessary, he corresponded with customers.

During his first few college cooperative education assignments, Vladimir worked as a commercial loan documentation specialist. He prepared all loan documentation and booked loans into the loan system. Coordinating loan details with title companies, tax service companies, and government filing agencies was another duty. He also carefully reviewed all loan-related documents for errors or fraud.

For his final two cooperative education assignments, Vladimir had worked as a collections associate. This position gave him early exposure to the importance of learning to live within a budget. Dealing with clients who were financially overextended, because they bought more than they could afford, showed Vladimir how tough it could be to get out of debt.

As a collections associate, Vladimir had been responsible for making outbound phone calls to delinquent card holders. He had also handled incoming phone calls from the same account holders. Vladimir used various software tools, including skip trace software, to locate delinquent cardholders. As the bank had provided training on the legalities associated with tracking down debtors, Vladimir conducted his searches within the appropriate legal constraints.

When talking with delinquent card holders on the phone, Vladimir often encouraged them to make an immediate payment over the phone. He communicated with bank personnel and debt counselors regarding delinquent accounts.

After graduation, Vladimir began working as a credit card risk specialist. He helped analyze loan product mix, losses, and whole loan sale performance. He performed statistical analyses to help guide underwriting practices. He also made recommendations regarding how to optimize profit and minimize credit loss exposure. Updating the credit risk software, including the credit scorecard module, was another duty. An important part of his job was to develop strong relationships with sales and product managers so they would appreciate the value of his risk-based analyses.

Upper Rungs to Consider

Vladimir wanted to apply his skills and knowledge on a broader level. He was researching a position as a collections and loan servicing manager. If he took that role, he would be responsible for managing the entire loan servicing department. Primary responsibilities would include ensuring loan losses were minimized and meeting regulatory requirements.

Preparing for the Climb

Managing personal credit prudently is critical to financial stability. Many employers check credit scores during the hiring process. What steps can you take to proactively manage your credit and your credit score?

7.1

goals

+ Explain asset transformation and modern portfolio theory.

+ Describe components of consumer lending.

+ Explain nonloan sources of bank revenue.

terms

+ asset transformation

+ modern portfolio theory (MPT)

+ adverse selection

+ captive borrower

+ moral hazard

+ credit rationing

Consumer Loan Theory

Banking Scene

Jamar Brown wants to buy some equipment for a house painting business he is starting this summer. He has put together a basic business plan regarding how much he will spend on equipment and how much he will charge for each job. He has lined up his first three customers. He applied for a $5,000 loan at the bank, but they have only approved a $2,500 loan. Jamar wondered why the bank would not approve his entire loan amount. What do you think?

MANAGING A BANK'S PORTFOLIO

Loans make up a large percentage of bank revenues. Three general categories of loans are consumer loans, mortgage loans, and commercial loans. According to the FDIC, in March 2008 there was about $1 billion in outstanding loans to individuals in FDIC-insured institutions. About $387 million of that amount was credit card loans.

The pie chart from the March 31, 2008 edition of the FDIC's Quarterly Banking Profile shows how loan portfolios are diversified across the banking industry. Together, credit card and consumer loans comprise 13 percent of the industry's loan portfolio. Residential mortgages comprise 28 percent and commercial and industrial loans comprise 19 percent. Assorted other categories of a diversified portfolio are also included in the data.

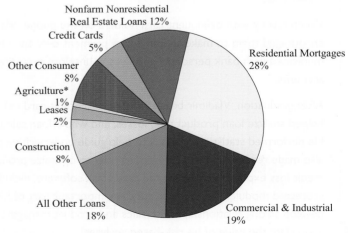

Loan Portfolio Composition
March 31, 2008

Nonfarm Nonresidential Real Estate Loans 12%
Credit Cards 5%
Other Consumer 8%
Agriculture* 1%
Leases 2%
Construction 8%
All Other Loans 18%
Commercial & Industrial 19%
Residential Mortgages 28%

* OTS—Supervised Savings Associations do not identify agricultural loans.
SOURCE: FEDERAL DEPOSIT INSURANCE CORPORATION

Asset Management

Banks are financial intermediaries. They attract money in the form of deposits. Money leaves banks through loans. Bank income is generated through interest and fees.

Asset transformation refers to using deposits to generate revenue by putting deposits to work via loans. The largest component of bank revenue comes from loans. Some revenue is generated by securities investments.

Deposits are bank liabilities because they could be withdrawn by a customer at any point in time. Loans are bank assets because they represent money that the bank will receive back, in the form of principal and interest payments. When banks transform liabilities (deposits) into assets (loans), asset transformation has occurred.

For a bank to be profitable, it must astutely engage in asset transformation. Returns need to be generated with minimal risk. There should be a staggered process of making loans, the expiration of loan payments, and investment maturity dates.

Modern Portfolio Theory

In 1952, Harry Markowitz developed the concept of **modern portfolio theory (MPT)**. This theory states that within any portfolio of investments, diversification should be used to spread out risk. Diversification should include variation by industry and variation in maturity dates. Maintaining a diversified portfolio shields investors from downturns in a particular industry. Ideally, a downturn in one industry, which leads to reduced profits in that industry, would be offset by increased profits in a different industry. In this way, a relatively stable level of return can be achieved within a diversified portfolio.

Another type of diversification that occurs within a portfolio is the staggering of maturity dates of securities within a portfolio. This allows portfolio managers to assess, on a rotating basis, whether to reinvest in a particularly security. This ongoing reassessment of the value of particular securities encourages adaptability. As market conditions change, portfolio managers can adjust the particular mix of assets included in a given portfolio. Variations in maturity dates trigger a perpetual review, on a rotating basis, of the securities within a portfolio.

The loans held by a bank are essentially a portfolio of assets. How those assets are selected, managed, and maintained affects the stability and profitability of the bank. Loan diversification, both by type and by maturity date, helps stabilize the performance of the bank's loan portfolio.

 checkpoint

What is asset transformation?

_____

_____

CONSUMER LENDING THEORY

Consumer loans comprise a specific portion of a bank's loan portfolio. Consumers represent a specific market segment for bank loans. Consumer loan theory has evolved as part of the methodology for developing profitable consumer loan portfolios.

Loan Selection

Revenue from loans is the primary income source for banks. Therefore, banks are very selective in deciding the type of customer with whom they will do business. Years of experience have taught bankers some key lessons regarding which type of lending situations are desirable and which are not.

If a bank has the opportunity to lend $25,000 to two customers and can charge one customer an 8 percent interest rate and can charge another customer a 12 percent interest rate, which customer would it want to secure? Remember that loan interest rates are determined by overall economic conditions, the prime rate, and the amount of risk associated with the loan. **Adverse selection** is the concept that the borrowers who are most willing to accept a high interest rate are the same borrowers who are most likely to default on their loans. So if the first customer is offered a $25,000 loan at an 8 percent rate because they have a strong credit history with good collateral, it is because they are very likely to repay their loan on time.

If an 8 percent interest rate is available on a $25,000 loan, why would a borrower consider paying 12 percent interest for the same amount of principal? Suppose this borrower wants to start a side business out of their home and they need $25,000 to buy equipment. This borrower has a weak credit history. Because they are just starting their side business, it is unknown how much revenue will be generated by the business. But because they are very passionate about their business idea, they really want to start the business. They think the business will grow and lead to financial independence. Without an initial loan, they cannot start their business. They believe so strongly in their idea that they are willing to risk other assets to get the start-up capital. They will gladly pay 12 percent interest, even though they know similar loans are available for 8 percent interest. The bank is unsure about the profitability of the business because the business is new. As many new businesses fail, there is a relatively high risk of loan default. To help offset the financial exposure of default, the bank charges a higher interest rate on the loan. Adverse selection led the high-risk borrower to accept a loan with less favorable terms.

Some segments of borrowers are more likely to prefer one type of lender to another. For example, if a car company has a lower loan qualification standard than a bank, then a consumer with a relatively weak credit history might opt for auto financing from a car company. Because it is easier for a consumer with a weak credit history to obtain a loan from the car company, then that consumer is a **captive borrower** relative to the car financing company. On the flip side, when higher-risk customers migrate to the auto company for a loan, then the auto loan company will have a higher default rate. This is another example of adverse selection.

Moral hazard occurs when a borrower takes greater risks if they think the harm they will incur from those risks will somehow be minimalized. In the case of a high-risk individual borrower willing to accept a high loan rate, if they have assets they are willing to surrender to the lender because of loan default, then they may accept the high-rate loan. Moral hazard, as applied to industries, has a similar connotation. In early 2008, when the government intervened to rescue Bear Stearns, there was a great deal of concern whether other financial companies would continue to engage in high-risk behavior because they knew the government would provide a safety net if they got into trouble. Many would argue, to decrease moral hazard, the government should not intervene to rescue firms that engaged in high-risk behavior.

Banks can decide on an appropriate customer base. Not everyone who applies for a loan receives a loan. Sometimes banks will loan someone a portion of the requested amount. When banks refuse to provide a loan, or when they lend less than the customer requested, they are engaging in **credit rationing**. By carefully allocating how their deposit funds will be used, banks are maintaining the stability of their portfolios.

Downstream Loan Profit

Banks do not always keep loans. They often sell loans on the secondary market. *Securitization* of loans occurs when individual loans are pooled together. These combined loans can then be sold as securities. The individual return rate for each loan and the individual risk associated with each loan is combined into a collective return rate and a collective risk rate for the pool of loans. Sometimes banks issue these securities directly. Sometimes banks sell individual loans to an intermediary who pools the loans and issues securities based on the pooled loans. When sold to an intermediary, banks achieve profits from the loans in two ways. The first method is by charging loan origination fees to the borrower. The second method is by selling the loan for a slightly higher principal than the original loan. The buyer of the loan gets, in effect, a slightly lower interest rate than the original loan. The securitized loans are then sold to investors. Securitization can occur for any type of consumer loan including vehicle loans, education loans, and miscellaneous loans.

✔ checkpoint

What is adverse selection?

_____

_____

ADDITIONAL SOURCES OF BANK REVENUE • • • • • • • • • • •

In addition to generating revenue from astutely managing loan portfolios, banks also generate revenue from charging a variety of fees. For instance, according to the FDIC, during the first quarter of 2008, banks earned $9.9 billion from service charges on deposit accounts.

Off-Balance Sheet Activities

There are a number of services banks offer that generate revenue but that are not included on their *balance sheets*. A balance sheet is a brief summary that lists the net profit, owner's equity, assets, and liabilities for a company. Balance sheets are prepared at least annually and, for public companies, are public documents. As public documents, they are seen not only by company management, but also by investors. In contrast, off-balance sheet activities are not seen by investors.

Off-balance sheet activities include overdraft protection and assorted letters of credit. Consumer lending can generate fees from overdraft

branching out

Credit Card Kiosks

Credit cards are a form of consumer loans. Private-label credit cards are for a particular retailer and can only be used in the stores of the retailer issuing the card. Although a retailer may promote its own credit card, the company that issues the credit card bears responsibility of owning the loans associated with the cards. Following market trends of providing consumers with easy access to credit, numerous retailers installed kiosks in their stores so that customers could sign themselves up for a new instant credit card. The kiosks can provide either a temporary credit card or a permanent plastic card to use right away. When customers have a higher amount of credit available to them, they often spend more money while shopping.

Think Critically Why do stores want to increase the number of private-label credit card holders? Why do the private-label issuers want to enroll more credit card holders?

protection. Fee-based letters of credit are used both domestically and internationally to facilitate obtaining a loan or transacting business. There are a variety of forms of overdraft protection. A checking account can be linked to either a savings account or a credit card. If an overdraft occurs from the checking account, funds are transferred from the linked account. Although charges for this fund transfer vary, some banks charge $9 each day that a fund transfer is required. To discourage use of overdraft protection, some banks increase the daily charge for overdraft protection if it occurs too often.

Overdraft protection can also be linked to a home equity line of credit, which is also referred to as a *flex line*. Charges for flex lines vary but may include no application fee or charges in the first year. Additional years may require a fee to maintain the flex line. Although fees vary, a $65 annual fee to maintain a flex line is typical. Some institutions may charge a fee if the flex line is closed down too quickly. Although these fees vary, some institutions will charge $300 if a flex line is closed within the first three years. Interest rate on flex lines vary. As of July 2008, some flex lines of credit were charging between 3.49 percent and 3.99 percent interest.

Other Revenue Sources

There are other fees a bank may charge. Account service charges, safe deposit box rental, ATM charges, insurance sales fees, and trading fees are examples of additional fees. Account service fees vary by account, but may include charges for a certified check, researching past transactions, verbal funds transfer, counter checks, and returned checks.

The pie chart from the FDIC's Quarterly Banking Profile provides an overview of noninterest income throughout the banking industry. Service charges on deposit accounts represent about 18 percent of noninterest income and net servicing fees represent nearly 7 percent of noninterest income.

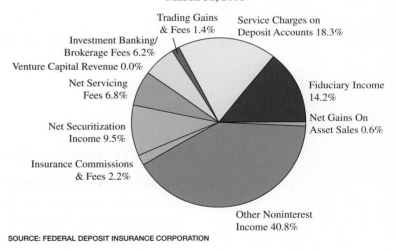

Composition of Commercial Banks' Noninterest Income
March 31, 2008

Trading Gains & Fees 1.4%
Investment Banking/ Brokerage Fees 6.2%
Venture Capital Revenue 0.0%
Net Servicing Fees 6.8%
Net Securitization Income 9.5%
Insurance Commissions & Fees 2.2%
Service Charges on Deposit Accounts 18.3%
Fiduciary Income 14.2%
Net Gains On Asset Sales 0.6%
Other Noninterest Income 40.8%

SOURCE: FEDERAL DEPOSIT INSURANCE CORPORATION

checkpoint

What are three methods of providing overdraft protection?

_____

_____

_____

assessment 7.1

Think Critically

1. What are the two key ideas of modern portfolio theory?

2. Explain why people raised concerns about moral hazard when the government intervened to help out Bear Stearns. What are the long-term concerns with moral hazard?

3. How do banks earn revenue by selling loans?

4. What is the advantage of off-balance sheet activities?

Make Academic Connections

5. **MARKETPLACE COMPETITION** Look up various account fees at three local banks. Compare the charges assessed to accounts. Summarize your findings and be prepared to share them with the class. Also be prepared to discuss which accounts provide the best value for your particular needs and why.

6. **RESEARCH** Go to the FDIC website www4.fdic.gov/QBP/qbpSelect.asp?menuItem=QBP and download the Complete Quarterly Banking Profile (QBP) for the most recent quarter. Refer to Table II-A, Aggregate Condition and Income Data. What is the total amount of consumer loans? Compare the current amount to recent quarters. Is the trend increasing, decreasing, or staying constant? Provide reasons for the trend.

Consumer Loans

Banking Scene

Jamar Brown needs a better truck for his house painting business. He has saved $2,000 for a down payment and has researched the kind of truck he wants. In addition to his business loan, he now needs to consider a truck loan. He wants to find the best loan with terms that are right for his situation, but he is not sure where to start. What questions should Jamar ask himself as he prepares to seek a loan?

INSTALLMENT LOANS •

Since the earliest days of human activity that could be considered banking, loans have been at the center of the business. Lending is the foundation of the banking industry, a mainstay of all business, and critical to the working of our economic system. When you consider that lending supports the banking industry and that banks, in turn, help stabilize the economy, then the lending process is key to our nation's soundness. Loans, when responsibly used and administered, are a powerful financial tool. Like any powerful tool, they can also be dangerous when used without proper knowledge.

With increasing competition among banks and financial institutions, a wide array of loan products is available from which to choose. Most consumer lending falls under two categories: installment loans and open-end loans.

Installment loans are perhaps the most familiar of banks' consumer lending products. An **installment loan** is a loan for which the amount of the payments, the rate of interest, and the number of payments (or length of term) are fixed. Installment loans are repaid on a periodic basis. Monthly payments are typical. An installment loan contract is a legal document obligating both parties to the written terms, so it is important for consumers to read and understand every word carefully.

Personal Loans Personal loans do not require that a specific purpose be stated. You might take out a personal loan for a vacation, optional medical procedures such as cosmetic surgery or dental work, or almost anything you choose. There is an almost unending variety of terms and schedules for personal loans, based on the consumer's credit rating and the specific type of loan he or she seeks. There are many types of installment loans available, usually marketed according to purpose.

Vehicle Loans Automobile loans may be the most common type of installment loan. After the automobile price is settled, the trade-in value and down payment negotiated, and the deal established, consumers can finance the remaining balance with an installment loan. Although manufacturers have financing available through their own corporations, banks often offer competitive rates and establish relationships with dealers to provide the service. With installment loans, the term and payments are fixed and scheduled, based on the principal and the interest rate calculated on the balance. A better credit rating typically results in a lower interest rate. The *Truth in Lending Statement*, required to be given at the time of signing, should be carefully read by buyers to help protect their rights.

Home Equity Loans Home equity loans are an increasingly popular form of lending. These loans, based upon the difference between what a home is worth and how much the homeowner owes on a first mortgage, are in effect second mortgages. This type of loan generally carries a low interest rate, and interest charges may be tax deductible.

When home values drop, as they did in the aftermath of the mortgage crisis, many homeowners have mortgages that exceed the market value of their homes. In these cases, home equity loans are not an option.

Education Loans Education loans help many students achieve an education they might not otherwise be able to afford. In many cases, loans are backed or subsidized by the government. Stafford loans for students and

PHOTODISC/GETTY IMAGES

PLUS loans for parents are examples of government-backed programs. If the borrower for some reason defaults, the government may pay these loans. Because of government backing, there is less risk to the lending bank, so interest rates are often lower than those available for other loans. Students are not required to make payments while they are in school. Payments begin once a student is out of school. If the student meets certain need-based requirements, the government will pay the interest that accumulates on the loan until student payments begin. Employers may also help arrange loans through credit unions or the employer's bank for continuing education programs for employees.

Secured and Unsecured Loans

Although there are many types of consumer loans, they all fall into one of two categories. A **secured loan** is one in which some item of value backs the loan in case the borrower defaults on the loan. The item that secures the loan is called **collateral**. The bank could use the collateral, if necessary, to recover the financial loss of an uncollected loan. For example, if you take out an auto loan, the lender typically has a **lien** on the car, a legal claim to the property to secure the debt. The car will go to the lender if you fail to make the payments, and the lien is noted on the car's title.

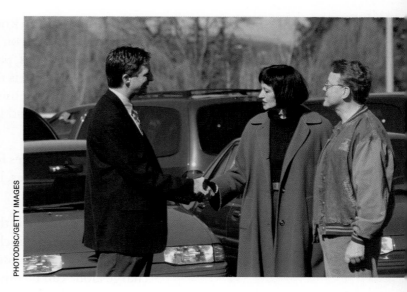

Collateral offers the bank a degree of safety for its loan. In theory almost anything agreed to between borrower and bank could be collateral, but for most loans used to make a large purchase, the purchased item is the collateral. A banker might accept other things of value to secure a personal loan, such as a savings account, CDs, stocks or other securities, a personal possession of value, or any other financial asset. Be certain that banks don't want an inventory of used cars and diamond rings, though. They examine creditworthiness carefully before granting any loan, secured or otherwise.

An **unsecured loan** is a loan backed only by the reputation and creditworthiness of the borrower. Sometimes called a *signature loan*, these loans are typically for smaller amounts than secured loans. There may be exceptions for customers who do large volumes of business with the bank or have a great track record and credit rating. Commercial lending often blends secured and unsecured loans.

Lending Terminology

Loans are legal contracts between lender and borrower, and so they include precise language. With the many types of loans and many varieties of plans within those types, there may be a great deal of variation in details and numerous terms. Although banks are required to disclose the truth about their loans, it is still in the consumer's best interest to read carefully and understand everything in the loan agreement. Reputable bankers explain and answer questions about loan terms. It is in their interest to do so not only for good customer relations, but also to help ensure a smooth and steady income for their business.

Some fundamental terminology applies to nearly every loan.

- **Principal is the amount borrowed.** If you need to borrow $12,000 after your trade-in and down payment on a car, the $12,000 is the principal.

- **Interest is the amount you pay to use the principal.** The interest rate is the amount of interest, usually expressed per year as a percentage of the principal, such as 9.9 percent. The annual percentage rate (APR) is one of the most important figures to compare when considering loans. Rates for most installment loans are *fixed rates* for the life of the loan, but in some loans they may be *variable rates*, changing over time. *Indexed rates* are linked to some other rate, such as the Federal Reserve's prime rate (usually plus some other figure) to allow for changes in the economy.

It is important to know how interest is calculated. In some loans, interest is calculated on the declining principal balance as payments are made. In other loans, payments go toward the interest first, then toward the balance, so there is no advantage in paying off the loan early. In such a case, you may owe more on the principal at the time of payoff than you would have if you had financed with a loan that charged interest on a declining balance.

- **Fees are other charges for the loan.** Examples are application fees, document preparation fees, late charges, and so forth. The loan agreement must specify all fees.

- **The finance charge is the total dollar amount to be paid for the loan.** The finance charge includes all interest calculations, fees, and other costs. It must be disclosed to the consumer. Sometimes the finance charge alone can be misleading. For example, if you borrowed $1,000 for a year with a loan fee of $10 and interest totaling $100, your finance charge would be $110. The APR would be 10 percent if you kept the whole $1,000 the full year, but you probably wouldn't. Assuming that you began to pay the loan back immediately in 12 equal payments of $92.50, you don't have the use of the full $1,000 for the year. The math gets a little tricky, but the actual APR would be 18 percent.

- **Total payments are the total amount a consumer must repay.** They include the principal and the total finance charge. This figure must be disclosed at the time a loan is signed. The total payments figure reveals the effect of an interest rate over time. The APR, the finance charge, and the total payments are the three key figures to evaluate.

- **Payment is the amount the borrower repays each specified period.** The schedule of payments specifies exactly when payments are due and what penalties are assessed if payments are not made on time. Sometimes an *acceleration clause* brings the entire loan due if payments are missed. A missed payment may also be cause for a variable interest rate to increase. Payments are usually monthly and fixed for the life of the loan. Some loans may include a balloon payment (a single large payment) at the end of the loan. Although the balloon payment reduces the payments before it, paying the final large amount may be difficult.

 checkpoint

What is the difference between a secured loan and an unsecured loan?

_____

_____

_____

Ethics in Action

Some credit card issuers offer teaser rates, extremely low rates for balance transfers or for a brief period of time. Later, the rates may change to normal or even high levels. Credit analysts note that moving your credit accounts too often can hurt your credit rating.

Think Critically

Do you think that offering teaser rates is a misleading policy? Why or why not? Should credit lenders hold it against consumers who take advantage of such offers?

OPEN-END LOANS

Open-end loans are another type of loan with an almost endless variety of applications. The amount owed on an **open-end loan** is flexible, as is the term. The longer you use the money, the more you pay.

Credit Cards

You may not think of credit cards as forms of consumer loans, but that is exactly what they are. The issuer is lending you the money for a period of time and charging interest for its use. The principal changes as your balance goes up and down, but you are still borrowing and paying interest. Because the balance changes, finance charges vary as well. One variable is the method used to calculate the balance. Some cards offer a **grace period**, which is an amount of time you have to pay the bill in full and avoid any finance charges. Most cards have an annual fee that is added to the balance. Transaction fees for cash advances or charges for exceeding your credit limit may apply. Some issuers charge a monthly maintenance fee even if you do use the card. Late penalties for bills paid after the due date raise the cost of credit cards, and delinquency rates may raise the APR significantly.

Lines of Credit

Other forms of open-end loans are the various line-of-credit plans that banks may offer. These may include a home equity reserve or an overdraft protection plan. Essentially, these plans allow consumers to establish a line of credit that they may draw on as needs arise. Borrowings may be for any amount up to an agreed-upon limit. As the balance is paid down, more money may be borrowed. Terms of agreement are similar to those of credit cards.

 checkpoint

What is an open-end loan?

assessment 7.2

Think Critically

1. Why do you think consumer loans have so many names and forms?

_____

_____

2. What is the difference between the interest and the finance charge of a loan?

_____

_____

3. Why might it be important for consumers to understand their credit card agreements?

_____

_____

_____

4. In your opinion, how many credit cards are too many? Explain your reasoning.

_____

_____

_____

Make Academic Connections

5. **COMMUNICATION**   With a partner, make a list of questions persons should ask themselves to decide whether taking on debt makes sense for them. Include questions about needs, budgets, and possible changes in lifestyle. Convert the questions into a checklist for consumers that offers guidance for responsible borrowing.

6. **CURRENT CONDITIONS**   According to the FDIC, a Net Charge-Off is the total of loans and leases removed from a balance sheet because they are uncollectible (minus any funds from prior charge-offs that were collected). Go to www2.fdic.gov/QBP/toc.asp?rptdate=/ qbp/2008mar&htmfile=alltoc.html#AIS and, in the Credit Quality section, click on the chart for the Composition of FDIC-insured Institutions' Loan Charge-Offs. At the end of first quarter 2008, 25 percent of all charge-offs were for credit cards. Does the current percentage reflect an increase or decrease? Be prepared to provide reasons for the changes.

Granting and Analyzing Credit

7.3

Banking Scene

Jamar's business is booming. He wants his friend Larry to buy a truck, and to work with him painting houses. Larry, who has a poor record of paying off his credit cards, is having trouble getting financing for a new truck. What might Jamar and Larry need to know about the credit-granting process?

goals

+ List steps in the credit-approval process.

+ Identify major criteria in a person's credit rating.

terms

+ underwriting

+ subprime rates

+ consumer reporting agency (CRA)

+ FICO score

GRANTING CREDIT

Every borrower represents a potential risk to the lender. If you can't or don't pay off any loan you have, you not only ruin your credit rating, but you hurt the bank as well. In fact, bad loans of various types are the number one reason banks get into financial trouble. Banks have to make sound decisions when it comes to loans, and they need defined methods of doing so. According to the FDIC, a Net Charge-Off is the total of loans and leases removed from a balance sheet because they are uncollectible minus any funds from prior charge-offs that were collected At the end of 2007, net charge-offs were about $16 billion. This represents a substantial increase from a year earlier when net charge-offs were $8.5 billion. Banks need to lend wisely to avoid risk exposure that can lead to large losses.

Before a bank is willing to advance its money (or more accurately, its customers' money) to you, it takes a number of steps to minimize the likelihood of a bad decision. Most of these steps are part of a well-defined policy of risk management.

Risk Management

Risk management for bankers is the practice of minimizing financial loss through effective policies. Banks face risks in operations, credit, liquidity, legal and regulatory compliance, and even marketing matters. Regarding credit granting, risk management policies include consideration of the bank's overall financial position, reserve requirements, cash flow, and ratio analyses of liabilities and assets. These factors all influence the credit-granting process, determining how flexible a bank can afford to be in granting credit. In addition, a bank's risk management policies are carefully scrutinized by bank examiners during an audit. Sometimes legal requirements complicate these issues. Banks must document that they comply with the law in such areas as extending credit fairly and equally throughout the community.

Credit-Approval Process

To ensure credit granting decisions are made in an accurate, efficient, and fair manner (and to be able to document them as such), well-run banks have written credit-approval procedures. Procedures and the specific standards for them may vary depending upon the type of loan. Variations from bank to bank also occur. Some of these steps may be combined, or for large loans may have several cycles of processing and underwriting for approval. Some of the procedures may be automated, such as with an online application, but the essential credit-approval process follows some basic steps.

- **Application**   The first step in the credit-approval process is obtaining a complete and accurate application. This may seem self-evident, but it is critical, for much of the later processing of the loan depends upon the information provided here. It is not unusual for a credit application to fail because it lacked an important detail or gave inconsistent information. Even something as basic as a name can cause confusion. Is it George Walker Bush, George H. Bush, George Bush, Sr., or George Bush, Jr.? A Social Security number may clear up such problems, but an incorrect digit could ruin everything. A loan officer or other representative often works with the customer, guiding him or her through the application and clarifying exactly what information and what degree of detail is necessary. Often bank representatives help consumers with this step as part of a loan analysis or a needs analysis. This process helps consumers decide what kind of loan may best meet their needs.

- **Documentation**   The next step for the bank is gathering the necessary documentation for the loan. Some of this information may come from the application itself, depending upon how detailed it is. Other information includes such items as a credit report, employment verification, bank account information, appraisal of properties for secured loans, and so forth. Sometimes preliminary approval is granted based on these documents.

- **Processing**   The bank builds a loan file, as the loan officer verifies statements on the application and checks information on all documentation the bank receives. The processing time depends upon the type and amount of the loan and the credit history of the applicant. The loan officer may ask for explanations or seek further information during this step.

- **Underwriting**   When all required information has been gathered and verified, the loan officer forwards the loan file for **underwriting**, or reviewing the loan for soundness. The underwriter's job is to make sure the loan is a prudent use of bank funds. The underwriter reviews the application package to make sure it is complete and makes an evaluation of the loan based on the assembled documentation. Underwriters evaluate the three Cs: *collateral, capacity,* and *credit reputation*. Collateral refers to the security (if any) required for the loan. Capacity refers to the ability to repay, based on income, job history, and amount currently owed. Credit reputation, or credit history, is a record of how well the applicant has repaid debt in the past. Based on these factors, the underwriter approves or disapproves the loan.

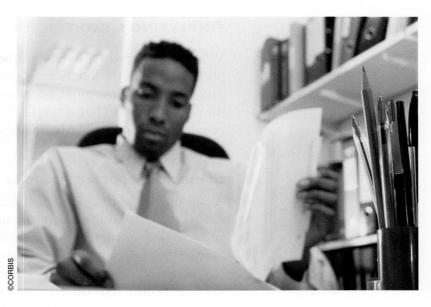
©CORBIS

Today, underwriting is increasingly automated. Sophisticated software programs provide statistical analyses and models based on vast quantities of data. Banks may sometimes grant a loan to applicants who don't meet standards, grant a loan with certain conditions, or offer a loan at subprime rates. **Subprime rates** are those higher than normal to offset the increased risk represented by a less-than-perfect borrower. The days when a banker might offer a loan based on acquaintance are disappearing. Many banks have less flexibility in underwriting than they once did, although they may offer more programs to meet varying needs.

- **Closing**   At the closing, a bank representative discusses and explains the terms of the loan, and the borrower signs the documentation that has been prepared. Included with the documentation are disclosure statements required by law.

- **Funding**   When the documents are signed, the bank either adds the funds to the borrower's account or issues a check.

Not all of these steps are followed for every type of loan nor in this exact order. However, some form of credit-approval process takes place for every loan, whether it is a credit card application through the mail or a loan officer working face to face with the consumer.

 checkpoint

What is underwriting?

ANALYZING CREDIT •

When an underwriter (whether human or electronic) looks at your loan application, one of the key factors considered is your credit history. It is fairly easy to verify your income, how long you have had your job, and how much the car you want to buy is worth. It is not so easy, however, to predict how people will pay bills. The best way to predict the future is to see how a person has done in the past.

Consumer Reporting Agencies

A **consumer reporting agency (CRA)** is a company that compiles and keeps records on consumer payment habits and sells these reports to banks and other companies to use for evaluating creditworthiness. Sometimes called credit bureaus, CRAs include information about whether a person has been sued, arrested, or has had financial judgments issued against them by a court. The three largest consumer reporting agencies are Equifax, Experian (formerly TRW), and TransUnion, but there are many such agencies. Among the three largest, records on almost every conceivable use of credit by every American exist. These comprehensive records form the foundation of credit analysis. Most credit reports contain the following types of information.

- **Personal data** includes names (including former ones), Social Security number, addresses, and employment history. Similar information for a spouse may also appear.

- **Accounts history** includes detailed history of active credit accounts, such as names and addresses of creditors, when an account was opened, co-signers, accounts status, whether the manner of payments (MOP) is timely, and whether the account is in default or a judgment has been issued. These records for active accounts typically show 24–36 months of history, and creditors keep reporting as long as the account remains open. Banks and credit unions, credit card companies, mortgage companies, finance companies, and department stores report this information regularly.

- **Delinquent accounts** are sometimes the only accounts reported to a consumer reporting agency. In these cases, the same sort of information as described above appears, as well as the current status of the delinquent account. Utilities, insurance companies, doctors, and landlords are typical reporters of this data.

- **Public records** include bankruptcies, judgments, liens, divorces, child-support arrearages, and criminal records. Private companies track and sell this data to credit bureaus.

- **Inquiries** are records of all who have requested a copy of the credit report within the last year. Although consumers have little control over these records, too many inquiries in a year can appear as if a consumer is having trouble obtaining credit.

With the enormous volume of credit records, errors inevitably enter into some records, and sometimes they are the first evidence of identity theft. Credit investigations have been criticized as not always being reliable. One study cited on CNNMoney.com in 2004 indicated that seventy-nine percent of credit reports had some type of error, with twenty-five percent of reports having errors serious enough to affect a consumer's ability to rent an apartment or get a job.

Although credit bureaus are private organizations, consumers are entitled to a free credit report each year from each of the three major credit agencies. As TransUnion, Equifax, and Experian each issue their own report, it is a good idea to review a report from each agency annually. By checking reports annually, consumers can learn whether anyone has tried to open an account in their name. This is one way to detect identity theft.

The Fair Credit Reporting Act guarantees consumers the right to review and dispute information in the reports. Consumers should be persistent in resolving errors and they should keep good records of all communication regarding error resolution efforts. In some instances, it can take more than five years to resolve errors.

tech talk

Online Identity Verification

With identity fraud on the increase, lenders and businesses are looking for ways to be certain customers are who they say they are, especially in online applications. Some applications use networking technology to link credit applications directly to consumer reporting agencies to aid in verification.

Equifax's eIDverifier™, for example, was among the earliest software programs that asks for verification information beyond Social Security number, driver's license number, and address. The program asks consumers to answer a multiple-choice questionnaire that is created from their own credit histories, answers to which only genuine consumers would know. These answers are compared to the Equifax data, and only if they match can the consumer move forward with the transaction.

In 2006, Recombo, a company that provides electronic signatures for electronic contracts, formed a partnership with Equifax. By using the eIDverifier, Recombo can improve the safety of their web-signing documents.

Think Critically
Search the Internet for more information about online identity verification systems, and write a short report on your findings. Does the use of such systems increase your confidence regarding online security? Why or why not?

"communicate"

Go to the Internet and search for a free credit report. Get your credit report from several agencies. When reports are received, compare the results. Share with the class the nature of any discrepancies you find in the reports and actions you plan to take to resolve the discrepancies.

Credit-Scoring Systems

A credit-scoring system can provide an efficient and unbiased method of evaluating credit. For many years, banks have used credit-scoring systems to evaluate the potential creditworthiness of loan applicants. These scores place a numerical value on the performance or status of an applicant in various categories. Income, debt, age (as long as it is not used to discriminate), years on the job, and even whether one has a telephone are the kinds of factors a credit-scoring system evaluates. The points in each category are added for a total score. There are many such systems in use, typically requiring a minimum score to qualify an applicant for a loan.

FICO

The FICO credit-scoring system developed by Fair, Isaac and Company, Inc. has come to dominate the dozens of credit-scoring systems in use. The **FICO score** is a three-digit number that credit granters can use in making a loan approval decision. Using a sophisticated model, the FICO system weighs all categories of information, with the importance of factors depending on the amount and type of information available on the person being evaluated. The FICO system excludes income and the type of credit for which the applicant has applied. Also excluded are race, ethnic background, religion, gender, and marital status, all of which are prohibited by law from being factors used to make a credit decision. FICO uses the following criteria in its ratings. Percentages are approximate.

- **Payment history (35 percent)** includes a consumer's track record on many types of accounts, including credit cards, installment loans, mortgages, and other types of borrowing, as well as public records on collections, bankruptcies, judgments, and wage attachments. Details on late payments and how many accounts have no late payments appear.

- **Amounts owed (30 percent)** include the total amounts owed on all accounts, the types of accounts that are open, how many of those accounts have balances, whether certain types of accounts have balances, how much of a credit line is in use, and how much is still owed on installment loans compared to the original loan value.

- **Length of credit history (15 percent)** considers how long accounts have been established and how long it has been since each was in use. In general, a long, solid credit history increases the FICO score.

- **New credit (10 percent)** is often sought by people in financial trouble. Although shopping for the best rate is a good idea, too much new credit is a sign of overextension. FICO considers how many new accounts exist, how long since a new account was opened, how many recent requests for credit have been made, and what recent credit history shows.

- **Types of credit (10 percent)** are evaluated, including what types of accounts exist and how many there are of each. A "healthy mix" of credit yields a higher score than a dependence on a single type of credit account.

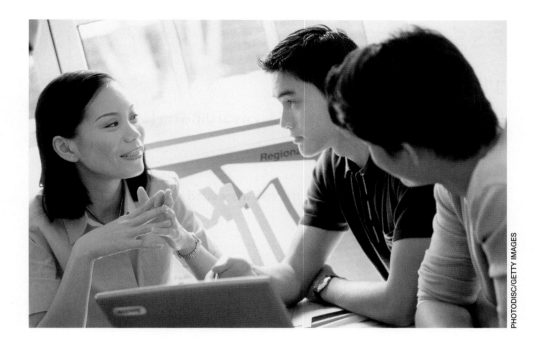

FICO scores range between 300 and 900, with about 620 being the point below which consumers may be regarded as high-risk. The sophisticated (and secret) FICO scoring system is not without critics. Some analysts say that potential creditors depend too much on it, rather than carefully weighing all factors. FICO is not responsible for errors in content.

Consumers can obtain their FICO scores online, but they may need to pay for them. Just as each credit agency generates its own credit report on each consumer, each credit agency generates a separate FICO score on each consumer. FICO scores can vary by as much as 50 points between the three credit agencies. As FICO scores are generated based on information in credit reports, consumers need to be sure that their credit reports are accurate at each of the three agencies. As consumers' interest rates are impacted by their FICO scores, ideally they should know what their FICO scores are well in advance of applying for loans. With advance knowledge of a negative FICO rating based on erroneous information in a credit report, consumers can try to correct the information in the credit report prior to applying for a loan.

 checkpoint

What is a consumer reporting agency?

_____

_____

_____

assessment 7.3

Think Critically

1. Why might underwriting standards vary at different banks?

2. How do subprime rates offset the risk associated with borrowers who have less-than-perfect credit?

3. How might a stranger having your Social Security number ruin your credit rating?

4. Do any of the categories of personal information on a credit report strike you as being a violation of privacy? Discuss.

Make Academic Connections

5. **PROBLEM SOLVING** Critique the methods and concepts of credit investigation described in this lesson. Then, working in groups, design a credit-scoring system that produces a maximum score of 100. Assign point values to at least six types of information. State the weight of each type of information and how relevant you believe each is in predicting likelihood of payment.

6. **CONSUMER AFFAIRS** Visit at least three noncommercial websites that provide information about how you can correct errors on your credit report. Summarize your findings.

Cost of Credit

Banking Scene

Jamar has established a strong credit record through timely payments on his business and truck loans. While at the bank, his loan officer asks whether he would also like to apply for a business credit card. He doesn't know if this is a good idea. She offers him several possibilities and options. Jamar has also seen many such offers in the mail. What should Jamar consider before he applies for a business credit card?

goals

+ Identify key factors in the cost of credit.

+ Explain the impact of negative credit ratings on consumers.

terms

+ revolving credit

+ sum-of-digits method

+ previous balance method

+ adjusted balance method

+ average daily balance method

+ predatory lending

WHAT CREDIT COSTS •

More than ever, the nation's economy runs on credit. Not only is it the foundation of banking income, it is also the engine that makes possible growth and development throughout the economy, bringing into being the standard of living you know today. Credit is a convenient tool for consumers to use to enhance their lives. At the start of 2008, consumer credit was growing about 7 percent annually.

Like any tool, credit can be dangerous if misused. In April 2008, total U.S. consumer credit was $2.56 trillion. The portion of the total that could be attributed to revolving credit was $956 billion. **Revolving credit** is a line of credit that has a maximum limit. It can be used on an ongoing basis until the limit is reached. When the balance (or a portion of the balance) is paid off, the credit can be used again until the next time the maximum is met. Credit cards are an example of revolving credit.

The easy availability of credit that results from fierce competition among lenders has allowed some consumers to accumulate more debt than they can manage. Instead of cutting back in a financial pinch, they simply add more debt to cover the shortfall. Eventually this can lead to disaster. Understanding the cost of credit and knowing how it is calculated helps consumers use it wisely. Banks want and need to make money on loans, but they have no interest in struggling to collect debt or losing what they lend in default. For this reason, banks have an interest in promoting consumer education. Many banks offer information on the best use of credit, and they are required by law to make full disclosure of the costs.

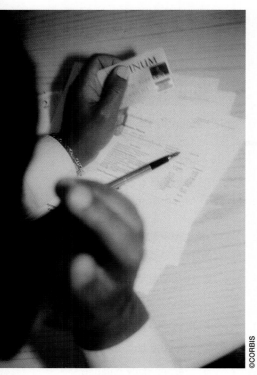
©CORBIS

Reviewing APR and Finance Charge

The annual percentage rate (APR) is the amount of interest charged on the loan principal expressed as a yearly figure. APR does not include annual fees, transaction fees, penalties, loan origination fees, or other such costs.

The APR is a key aspect of comparing credit costs. Understanding the total finance charge depends on how interest charges are applied. How does the principal change? Lenders can calculate interest in many different ways, as long as they explain clearly what they are. Some of the methods are more advantageous to consumers than others. Finance charges may be very different, depending on which method is used. In many cases, the interest is charged on the declining principal balance.

Sum-of-Digits Method Sometimes the interest gets paid first, so paying ahead saves the consumer no money. This payment structure has essentially built in prepayment penalties, which may be fixed charges or may be based on the **sum-of-digits method**. This method takes the total finance charge, divides it by the number of months in the loan term, and assigns a higher ratio of interest to the early payments. For example, consider a 12-month loan. By adding $12 + 11 + 10... + 1$, calculate that the sum of the digits 1 through 12 is 78. In the first month, 12/78ths of the total payment goes to interest. In the second month, 11/78ths, the third month, 10/78ths, and so on. Although the total cost to the consumer is the same, there is no advantage to paying early, because the interest is front-loaded.

Below is a chart showing the sum-of-digits method for a $1,000 loan that has a 6 percent interest rate and a $30 loan processing fee. For this loan, the total financing charges are $90 ($60 for interest and $30 for loan processing). The total loan cost, comprised of principal, interest, and the loan processing fee, is $1,090. Monthly loan payments are $1,090 ÷ 12 = $90.83.

Month of Loan Payment	Numerator for Month	Denominator for Month	Ratio of Payment Applied toward Interest	Monthly Loan Payment	Amount of Payment Applied to Interest	Amount of Payment Applied to Principal
1	12	78	0.15	$90.83	$13.97	$76.86
2	11	78	0.14	$90.83	$12.81	$78.02
3	10	78	0.13	$90.83	$11.64	$79.19
4	9	78	0.12	$90.83	$10.48	$80.35
5	8	78	0.10	$90.83	$9.32	$81.51
6	7	78	0.09	$90.83	$8.15	$82.68
7	6	78	0.08	$90.83	$6.99	$83.84
8	5	78	0.06	$90.83	$5.82	$85.01
9	4	78	0.05	$90.83	$4.66	$86.17
10	3	78	0.04	$90.83	$3.49	$87.34
11	2	78	0.03	$90.83	$2.33	$88.50
12	1	78	0.02	$90.83	$1.16	$89.67

If the loan repayment were calculated as a simple combination of principal and interest, then each loan payment of $90.83 would be comprised of $7.50 interest and $83.33 of principal. Therefore, if a consumer paid off a loan in eight months, he or she would expect to achieve a savings of $30 in interest and finance charges ($7.50 multiplied by four months). However, with the sum-of-digits method, the interest payment is front-loaded. Therefore, a consumer who pays the debt off after eight months only achieves a savings of $11.64. Summing the amount of payment applied to interest for months nine through twelve provides a total of $11.64.

This method of calculating payment is sometimes referred to as the *Rule of 78*. The name derives from how the denominator sums for a one-year period. The same method of interest calculation can be used on loans of any duration. The denominator used in the calculations would be the sum of the total months. For example, a fifteen-month loan would have a denominator of 120.

Previous and Adjusted Balance Methods   For open-ended credit, the finance charge is based on the rate multiplied by the balance. How the lender computes the balance matters in terms of the total finance charge. Some creditors take the amount owed at the beginning of the billing cycle and calculate interest on that figure, regardless of payments or charges. This method is called the **previous balance method**. Others subtract payments made during the billing cycle, but usually don't count purchases. This method is called the **adjusted balance method**.

Banking Math *Connection*

What portion of a credit card payment goes toward the principal? Suppose you have a balance of $1,500 on a credit card. Your minimum payment is 4 percent, or $60, on a card with an APR of 18 percent. How much of that payment will go toward paying the interest?

Solution
The formula for finding the interest is

$$\text{Rate} \div 360 \times 30 \times \text{Balance} = \text{Interest}$$

Rate is the APR, in this case 0.18. Dividing it by 360 gives the rate per day, or 0.0005. Multiplying this figure by 30 provides the rate per month, and multiplying that product by the balance gives the interest.

$$\text{Rate} \div 360 \times 30 \times \text{Balance} = \text{Interest}$$
$$0.18 \div 360 \times 30 \times \$1,500 \quad = \$22.50$$

In this example, $22.50 goes toward interest, and only $60.00 − 22.50 = $37.50 goes toward reducing your balance. It is going to take a long time to pay off the balance. Consumers should always pay as much beyond the minimum payment required as they can afford.

Average Daily Balance Method Probably the most common method is the **average daily balance method**. The balances for each day of the billing cycle are added and then divided by the number of days in the billing cycle to yield an average figure on which the finance charge is calculated.

Minimum Payments

Most credit cards require a minimum payment of about 4 percent of the unpaid balance every month. The minimum payment was increased from 2 percent because of guidelines issued by federal legislators at the end of 2005. To help consumers avoid a perpetual cycle of debt and to save on interest payments over the long term, consumers are now required to pay at least 1 percent of the principal amount. The other 3 percent of the minimum payment is applied to interest and fees. Prior to this legislation, consumers could make a minimum payment of just 2 percent. A 2 percent payment only covered interest and fees and did not contribute to the reduction of principal. Lower minimum payments increase bank profits, but contribute to greater consumer debt. Although paying the minimum payment keeps the account in good standing, it doesn't reduce the principal much.

Term

For installment loans, length of term also affects the total finance charge. Lenders must disclose the total payments. This figure along with the APR and the finance charge helps consumers evaluate the cost of a loan accurately. The following chart from the Federal Reserve shows loan costs for three possible $6,000 loans.

	APR	Length of Loan	Monthly Payment	Total Finance Charge	Total Payments
Creditor A	14%	3 years	$205.07	$1,382.52	$7,382.52
Creditor B	14%	4 years	$163.96	$1,870.08	$7,870.08
Creditor C	15%	4 years	$166.98	$2,015.04	$8,015.04

Repaying the loan over a longer period reduces the monthly payment considerably. It also increases the total payments for this installment loan. So which loan is the best deal? The answer depends upon the individual consumer's needs and abilities. The least expensive loan is the shortest one with the highest payments. Perhaps a larger payment won't fit your budget, so paying a little more to use the money longer is a wiser decision than saddling yourself with a payment that is difficult to make. The consumer's credit rating may dictate which interest rate is available. Knowing and understanding the details of the cost of credit is critical for consumers.

 checkpoint

What is it a good idea for consumers to pay more than their minimum balances on open-ended credit accounts?

THE IMPACT OF CREDIT

Could you imagine our society without the availability of credit? Our economic system would collapse almost overnight. Yet too much debt is not good for the economy at large, either. The more in debt consumers become, the less they can buy. The less they can buy, the slower the economy. If the economy slows, jobs may be lost, and the spiral of recession deepens. Healthy economic growth depends upon healthy use of credit.

Overextension

Consumers become overextended when they take on more debt than they can really afford. Some consumers mistakenly believe that just because someone approves them for credit, that must mean they can afford it. They take on two, three, four, five, or more new credit cards, thinking that they will have only a small balance on each without really totaling up the costs. They may be able to make minimum payments, but their overall debt load increases.

The effect of overextension on personal finances can be disastrous. If an emergency arises or a situation changes, such as a job loss, some consumers are suddenly in real trouble. A snowball effect may occur as late charges, penalty interest rates, and other fees apply.

One consequence of overextension is a ruined credit rating. Documentation of most credit problems stays in a consumer's file for at least seven years. During that time, new opportunities such as a great deal on the perfect house, an auto loan at an advantageous rate, or needed orthodontia may be inaccessible. In addition, with disposable income going to service debt, day-to-day life becomes more difficult. If you are barely making minimum payments and energy prices rise dramatically, your entire budget may collapse. Consumers have a responsibility to inform themselves about credit costs and use credit wisely.

THE ROLE OF BANKS ●

Predatory lending occurs when lenders create problems for consumers by making credit too easily available without regard to the borrower's ability to pay. Fierce competition and the growth of subprime lending rates have led some banks to relax their underwriting standards. Regulations aimed at reducing predatory lending have been revised. These regulations will be discussed in Chapter 8.

In the long run, excessive consumer debt is not in banks' interest. Banks need creditworthy customers, and practices that ruin the credit ratings of people serve no one. Collecting debt is expensive, if not impossible, on loans that are in default. Responsible lenders not only evaluate credit carefully and disclose costs as required by law, but they help consumers make the best choices for their own particular situations. Customer service representatives will take the time to explain terms and answer questions fully. Still, the lending business is increasingly market driven, and consumers must understand and choose carefully the best use of financial resources.

PHOTODISC/GETTY IMAGES

Credit Counseling

Numerous agencies for credit counseling, both profit and nonprofit, exist to help overextended consumers. Most of their plans involve reorganizing debts and sometimes renegotiating terms. Banks and other creditors will often accept such arrangements rather than lose their money altogether. Consumers should look carefully, though, because some credit-counseling companies are simply looking for ways to offer more subprime loans or to make a profit from doing what the informed consumer could do alone. In extreme cases, a consumer may seek protection from creditors by declaring bankruptcy. Because doing so may have long-term consequences, professional legal advice is a worthwhile investment.

Why do consumers become overextended?

assessment 7.4

Think Critically

1. How can a consumer find the best deals on credit?

_____

_____

_____

2. What factors should consumers consider when choosing a loan?

_____

_____

_____

3. In your opinion, why has there been rapid growth in subprime lending?

_____

_____

_____

4. What danger signals might indicate to a consumer that he or she is becoming overextended?

_____

_____

_____

_____

Make Academic Connections

5. **ART/GRAPHICS**   Design a chart that a person could use to compare loan products. Include spaces for all relevant information and factors.

6. **BANKING MATH**   Assume a $3,000 balance, a 16 percent APR, and a 2 percent minimum payment requirement. How much is the minimum payment? How much of the minimum payment will go toward reducing the balance?

_____

_____

_____

7. **CONSUMER AFFAIRS**   Investigate credit-counseling agencies on the Internet. Summarize your findings of at least three types.

_____

7.5

goals

+ Explain how loans affect a bank's income.
+ Describe the purpose of a bank's loan policy committee.

terms

+ liquidity risk
+ credit risk
+ market risk

Bank Loans and Policy

Banking Scene

As a new borrower, Jamar Brown has become interested in bank loans. Jamar has gotten partial approval for his house painting business loan and complete approval for his truck loan. Larry's parents had agreed to co-sign a loan so Larry could buy a truck to help out with Jamar's business. Jamar now wonders about the risks that banks take in making loans and the guidelines banks follow in determining whether to approve an application. What risks do banks face? Who sets the policy affecting loan decisions?

LOANS, THE "BOTTOM LINE," AND LIQUIDITY

A bank's main business is lending money, which is the source of its profits. Loans represent the largest portion of a bank's interest-earning assets. A bank earns profits by obtaining funds from savers at a cost to the bank (interest paid) and by lending those funds at a cost to consumers (interest received). To be profitable, a bank must carefully manage the loans it makes to ensure that more interest comes in than goes out and that its loans are repaid in a timely manner. A bank's loan customers range from individuals to families, individually owned and other small businesses to giant international corporations, and small to large governments—even foreign ones. A bank frequently has more requests for loans than it can finance using depositor funds. To be able to make these loans, the bank itself raises additional funds by borrowing. If the bank can charge higher interest rates on the loans it makes than the rates it pays on the loans it obtains, it can still profit from lending in this way.

Loans and Income

Loans have a direct impact on a bank's income, because the interest charged on them is its major income source. Therefore, managing its loan programs is crucial to a bank's "bottom line." Interest rates on loans must be set carefully. The loan policies a bank sets must protect its income. Approving questionable loans could lead to *default*, or failure to repay a loan as called for in the loan contract, and, in turn, to lower income. Policy that is too strict can also result in lower income if it prevents the bank from using its funds to make loans and subsequent interest income. Therefore, a bank's income depends on how well it manages its loans. While attempting to increase income, however, banks can never ignore liquidity.

Loans and Liquidity

For a bank, *liquidity* means having the funds to meet its obligations when required. Its liquidity requirement is tied to both the deposit function and the credit function. Customers expect their bank to meet their legitimate needs for credit and to make funds available to them. Several loan factors affect the lending bank's liquidity.

- **Loan term** *Term* refers to the length of time until the borrower pays off the loan. Short-term loans produce profit more quickly than long-term loans.

- **Interest rate** Higher interest rates result in more profit than lower ones.

- **Loan type** Interest on consumer installment loans is generally paid monthly, but some business loans are paid only once a year.

- **Collateral** Specific property that secures the loan is called *collateral*. If the borrower defaults, the bank has the right to sell the collateral to liquidate the loan.

Overemphasizing liquidity by keeping large amounts of currency on hand as protection against possible increases in customers' demand for withdrawals reduces a bank's ability to make profits from loans. This would impair its credit function and decrease its profit. In making decisions on loan applications, banks consider the impact that their loan mix—individual versus business, short-term versus long-term, and so on—will have on their liquidity.

PHOTODISC/GETTY IMAGES

Liquidity Risk **Liquidity risk** refers to the risk that a bank will have to sell its assets at a loss to meet its cash demands. A sluggish market can prevent the sale or limit the funds bank assets can generate. Some assets are highly liquid and have low liquidity risk (stock of a publicly traded company), but others are highly illiquid and have high liquidity risk (a house).

Credit and Market Risk

By its very nature, lending money is risky. A bank is never certain that it will get back the money it has loaned out. A bank faces two types of risk when it puts its funds to profitable use through lending: credit risk and market risk.

Credit Risk A primary risk in bank lending is **credit risk**, the bank's estimate of the probability that the borrower can and will repay a loan with interest as scheduled. To limit credit risk, banks must carefully screen loan applicants, set and apply loan policies, and monitor outstanding loans.

Market Risk The risk that an investment will decrease in price as market conditions change is called **market risk**. General changes in economic conditions can increase or decrease an asset's value. An example of market risk is the fluctuation in interest rates and in the stock markets. To avoid market risk, a bank must invest its assets wisely. Liquidity risk and market risk are highly correlated.

DIGITAL VISION/GETTY IMAGES

Loan Decisions and Trade-Offs

Making loan decisions is a difficult process that generally requires weighing one factor against another. For example, a short-term loan generally has low risk and represents relatively quick liquidity, but it is likely to have a low interest rate and thus produce a relatively low profit. A long-term loan has a higher interest rate and thus increases profit but involves more risk and liquidity concerns. High interest rates could increase income but could also decrease it if the rate causes borrowers to take their loan needs elsewhere. Knowing how to analyze these and other factors helps determine the profit a bank can make from its loans.

checkpoint

How do credit risk and market risk differ?

LOAN POLICY COMMITTEE

All banks must have a *lending policy*, which is a written statement of the guidelines and standards to follow in making credit decisions. A bank's board of directors through membership on its *loan policy committee* sets its lending policy. The loan policy committee is actively involved in the credit function in the following ways:

- Ensures that the bank's outstanding loan portfolio meets the needs of its customers and its community and that it complies with the Community Reinvestment Act

- Sets the maximum amount that an individual loan officer can approve and the combinations of higher authority needed for larger amounts

- Determines the types of loans that the bank will or will not consider

- Periodically reviews or audits the bank's loan portfolio to ensure that proper procedures are being followed and no undue risks are being taken

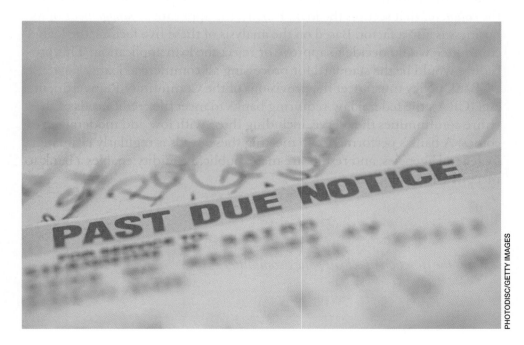

PHOTODISC/GETTY IMAGES

- Tightens credit standards when conditions dictate

- Implements policies that set loan collateral, loan maturities, maximum lending to various business types, and standards for down payments according to type of loan

- Authorizes all loans for which the amount exceeds the authority of any combination of loan officers to make

The lending policy is generally reviewed annually or as the need arises. It establishes rules such as minimum credit standards for new loans, the process used to check applicants' credit history, the documents required as part of the application, the interest rate for various loan types and risk types, the bank's loan mix, and the treatment of past-due and delinquent loans. Note that the *loan policy committee* sets the guidelines that the *loan committee* follows in evaluating, approving, or rejecting loan applications. They are usually two separate committees.

The lending policies must be fairly administered and standardized for all applicants in a category. For example, when administering commercial loans, lending policies often dictate that banks first evaluate five factors to help measure the risk of such loans. First, *cash flow* is considered to determine whether the business will generate sufficient cash flow to service the loan. *Liquidity* is as important for a borrower as it is for the bank. *Leverage* denotes the amount of debt the business already has. Policy also considers the *collateral* that secures the loan. Finally, the applicant's *management* of its business is also a factor. Based on the analysis of these five factors, the loan committee would decide to approve or reject the loan application. This procedure would be the standard for processing all commercial loans.

Bank policy must meet the provisions of the Community Reinvestment Act (CRA), the federal law requiring banks to meet the credit needs of the entire communities they serve, including those with low and moderate incomes. A bank's performance in meeting these needs is regularly evaluated by federal agencies, and results are made public. Liquidity enables a bank to meet its CRA obligations.

 checkpoint

What is the function of a loan policy committee?

assessment 7.5

Think Critically

1. How do loans affect a bank's income?

_____

_____

2. Why is liquidity risk of considerable importance to a bank's loan policy?

_____

_____

_____

3. How does market risk affect a bank?

_____

_____

_____

4. What role do liquidity, credit, and market risk play when a loan policy committee sets the bank's lending guidelines?

_____

_____

_____

Make Academic Connections

5. **RESEARCH**   Liquidity is a crucial factor for banks. Use the Internet to research liquidity management for a bank, and write a one-page report explaining this process.

_____

_____

6. **COMMUNICATIONS**   Interview someone in a local bank's loan department. Find out what types of educational loans are available and the bank's policy requirements for them and the typical interest rates involved. Present your findings here.

_____

_____

_____

_____

chapter 7 assessment

Chapter Summary

7.1 Consumer Loan Theory
A. MPT is used to help banks diversify their loan portfolios. Asset transformation enables a bank to generate revenue from deposits.
B. Borrowers who are most willing to accept nonfavorable loan terms are the borrowers that are least attractive as customers. Banks can earn revenues by charging fees that are not reflected on their balance sheets.

7.2 Consumer Loans
A. Installment loans are the most common form of consumer lending. Banks are legally required to explain loan terms.
B. The amount owed on an open-end loan is flexible, as is the term. Open-end loans include credit cards and lines of credit.

7.3 Granting and Analyzing Credit
A. Creditworthiness must be assessed before loans are granted. Application, documentation, and underwriting are steps in this process.
B. CRAs and lenders often use credit-scoring systems such as FICO.

7.4 Cost of Credit
A. The cost of credit varies with annual percentage rate and term, and depends on the method of calculation.
B. Consumers should pay close attention to their credit standing, because poor credit can result in numerous long-term financial problems.

7.5 Bank Loans and Policy
A. Lending allows a bank to make a profit, but it must carefully monitor its policies to avoid liquidity, credit, and market risk.
B. A bank's loan policy committee sets guidelines used to make loans.

Vocabulary Builder

a. adjusted balance method
b. adverse selection
c. asset transformation
d. average daily balance method
e. captive borrower
f. collateral
g. consumer reporting agency (CRA)
h. credit rationing
i. credit risk
j. FICO score
k. grace period
l. installment loan
m. lien
n. liquidity risk
o. market risk
p. modern portfolio theory (MPT)
q. moral hazard
r. open-end loan
s. predatory lending
t. previous balance method
u. revolving credit
v. secured loan
w. subprime rate
x. sum-of-digits method
y. underwriting
z. unsecured loan

Choose the term that best fits the definition. Write the letter of the answer in the space provided. Some terms may not be used.

____ 1. Period for which no interest charges accrue if balance is paid in full by due date

____ 2. Providing borrowers with downside risk protection increases their risk-taking behavior

____ 3. Loan with fixed amount of payments, rate of interest, and length of term

____ 4. Loan backed by some item of value in case the borrower defaults

____ 5. Dominant credit-scoring system

____ 6. Loan backed by reputation and creditworthiness of the borrower

____ 7. Company that compiles and sells credit records

____ 8. Item used to secure a loan

____ 9. Reviewing a loan for soundness

____ 10. Loan with flexible principal and term

Review Concepts

11. Give three examples of installment loans.

_____

_____

_____

12. What is a secured loan?

_____

_____

_____

13. What is moral hazard?

_____

_____

_____

14. What is the difference between the interest rate and the finance charge?

_____

_____

_____

15. Why are credit cards a form of consumer lending?

_____

_____

_____

16. What is a line of credit?

_____

_____

_____

17. List six steps in the credit-granting process.

_____

_____

_____

_____

18. What are the three Cs?

_____

_____

_____

19. What is a credit-scoring system?

_____

_____

_____

_____

_____

20. Why are credit investigations sometimes criticized?

_____

_____

21. What five items appear in most credit reports?

_____

_____

22. How does liquidity affect a bank's income?

_____

_____

23. Compare and contrast liquidity, credit, and market risk.

_____

_____

_____

24. Explain the functions of a loan policy committee.

_____

_____

_____

Apply What You Learned

25. Should FICO scores be released to consumers? Why or why not?

_____

_____

_____

26. Why do banks engage in credit rationing?

_____

_____

27. What factors should a person consider before obtaining a loan?

_____

_____

_____

28. Why is it important to pay every bill on time?

29. Why is having many credit card accounts a risky practice?

30. Why do banks offer overdraft protection?

31. Why are banks required to have loan policies?

Make Academic Connections

32. **CURRENT CONDITIONS**   The FDIC's Quarterly Banking Profile provides a wealth of current information on the banking industry. Go to http://www4.fdic.gov/QBP/toc.asp?rptdate=/qbp/2008mar&htmfile=alltoc.html#AG and find the Asset and Liabilities section. Within that section, click on "Loan Portfolio Composition." Examine the resulting pie chart. How has the composition of bank loan portfolios changed? What may have caused these changes?

33. **BANKING MATH**   Calculate how much of the minimum payment goes toward reducing the principal on a credit card with a 2 percent minimum payment policy, a $4,000 balance, and an 18 percent APR.

34. **ART/DESIGN**   Prepare a brochure for consumer education that highlights effective ways to choose and use credit. Outline the true costs of credit. Reference government agencies that consumers can contact for more information.

35. **COMMUNICATION**   Interview an executive of a local bank about consumer lending. Ask how portfolio diversification is managed and how regulatory changes and the credit crisis have affected business. Present your findings to the class in an oral report.

CHAPTER 8

Mortgages

8.1	Mortgage Lending
8.2	Mortgage Loan Processing
8.3	Mortgages and the Law
8.4	Government-Backed Loans
8.5	The Mortgage Crisis

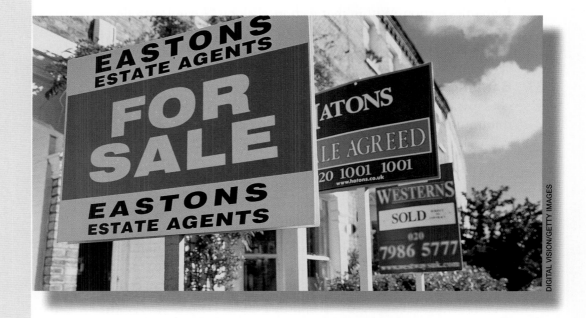

DIGITAL VISION/GETTY IMAGES

Ethics at Work

Specific definitions of ethics vary. Most definitions include a sense of what is right or wrong. Cultural and social context affect the definition of what is right or wrong. What one society may deem acceptable may be taboo in another society.

Each individual has a distinct sense of right or wrong. The old adage "Do onto others as you would have them do onto you" captures part of the spirit of ethical behavior. Certainly you should treat people with the same kindness and respect that you would hope to receive. This includes kindness that comes even when your knowledge of a topic is superior to someone else's knowledge. By treating people fairly, including helping to educate them about the impact of decisions they are making, you will behave ethically with them. Treating people ethically has the added benefit of fostering long-term relationships. Repeat business is the result of long-term relationships.

Corporations are managed and staffed by individual people working toward the common goal of profitability. Corporations are not societies, but they do have corporate cultures. A corporation can formulate a code of conduct to set the direction and tone for how employees are expected to behave. A code of conduct can delineate how individuals should act relative to each other and how they should perform their duties. It can also address the framework for making decisions and developing solutions in a manner that is consistent with a company's code of conduct.

American society has formalized the collective belief of what is right or wrong by passing laws supporting these beliefs. For example, it is illegal to steal someone else's property.

By providing thorough employee training regarding a company's code of conduct, a company can ensure that all employees understand the code and can apply the concepts implicit in the code into their decision-making. When a code of conduct incorporates the requirements of legal behavior, then employees can behave in a manner that is consistent with legal requirements.

Financial incentives and performance standards need to be constructed in a way that reinforces the code of conduct.

During the mortgage crisis of 2008, each player in the chain had superior, thorough knowledge that the subprime loans were too steep for many homeowners to manage. The loan originators, the underwriters, and the dealers who bought and sold loans in the subprime loan market were motivated by profit. Each participant wanted to obtain a share of this profit even if providing the loan meant that some homeowners would be left with an overwhelming financial burden.

Develop Your Skill

Make a list of five thoughts that would have been on your mind if you were qualifying a customer for a subprime loan. In small groups, share the list with group members. Assign half the group to provide reasons that would allay your concerns. Have the other half provide reasons that would support your concerns. Reflect together on how easy it can be to justify either side of a situation.

PHOTODISC

8.1

goals

+ Define a mortgage.
+ Identify several types of mortgages.

terms

+ mortgage origination
+ mortgage
+ foreclosure
+ fixed rate mortgage
+ balloon mortgage
+ adjustable rate mortgage
+ buy-down mortgage
+ point
+ shared appreciation mortgage (SAM)

Mortgage Lending

Banking Scene

When Katrina Harris finished college, she found a good job in her career field of web design. After a few years, she paid off her student loans and began to feel more financially secure. She was tired of living in an apartment and began to consider buying her own home. She didn't know anything about mortgages. What kinds of information might she want to research?

WHAT IS A MORTGAGE?

Banks have grown in the nineteenth and twentieth centuries from banks that did business only with other businesses to banks that sought to serve the needs of individuals. Nowhere in the twentieth century has this growth been more evident than in the growth of mortgage lending. Tax breaks, growing equity, rising property value, and a sense of security provide an incentive to undertake long-term debt in the form of a mortgage. The idea of getting a mortgage to buy one's own home is the essence of the American dream, and in good times or bad, owning real estate is one goal that remains constant.

Mortgage lending is a good business for banks, too, although by percentage, it's not as great as it once was. The crush of competition, not only between banks but also from companies who specialize in mortgage lending, has reduced banks' dominance in this field. Mortgage lending is now the third source of revenue in banking, behind wholesale banking and services. Total mortgage lending continues to rise. In 2000, new mortgages, called **mortgage origination**, exceeded $1 trillion. Of that $1 trillion, more than half consisted of refinancing existing debt, while the rest was entirely composed of new business. As interest rates dropped in 2001, only a slowing economy kept the business from expanding even further. The mortgage business is linked to numerous other segments of the economy, such as construction and durable goods, and often provides a good idea of how the economy as a whole is doing.

The term *mortgage* comes from Old French language and Anglo-Saxon law. It literally means "dead pledge," and it was the most serious obligation one could undertake. At that time, property was conveyed to the creditor, who held it until a debt was repaid and then conveyed it back. If the debt wasn't paid on time, the creditor kept the property. Over time, the idea of the property as security remained, but restrictions eased, and now in almost all cases the borrower has full use and title to the property. Today, a **mortgage** is a note, usually long-term, secured by real property. Essentially, the mortgage places a lien on the property that is not released until the debt is paid. If the mortgage is not paid, the creditor seeks a court-ordered sale of the property called a **foreclosure**, and the debt is paid from those funds.

The obligation of a mortgage today is no less serious than it was hundreds of years ago. For most people, the largest and longest debt they will ever incur is a mortgage. It's a serious investment, usually ten or more times the cost of a new car. Because it usually involves land, a mortgage is tied to the government by deeds and title records in ways that are unique. It's also a serious obligation for the lender. Prior to the prevalence of subprime loans that precipitated the mortgage crisis, obtaining a mortgage involved a careful review of a borrower's capability and record.

 checkpoint

What is a mortgage?

"communicate"

Home ownership is often referred to as the American dream. Take an informal poll of as many homeowners as you can to learn about their experiences with home ownership and mortgages.

TYPES OF MORTGAGES

There are many names and variations in loan products, and such is the case in the mortgage business as well. Whatever a mortgage is called, though, it essentially falls into one of three general categories: fixed rate mortgages, adjustable rate mortgages, and other forms of financing.

Fixed Rate Mortgages

Fixed rate mortgages, also called *conventional mortgages*, are loans with a fixed interest rate for the life of the loan. Payments on the loan itself (not including insurance and taxes, which may be included in payments) are set for the life of the loan. Terms are set, too. The most common terms are 30- and 15-year terms, but other terms are available.

Consumers are comfortable with fixed rate mortgages because there are few surprises. Once the interest rate is set, it remains the same, and the consumer has a pretty good idea of ongoing housing costs. If interest rates rise, the consumer is still paying that original rate, which will look better and better as years pass. If interest rates fall, the consumer might lose money, but he or she has the option to refinance which involves getting a new mortgage, at a lower rate. Interest rates are usually highest for fixed rate mortgages.

For banks, a fixed rate mortgage offers a reliable source of income, or more often, a negotiable instrument to resell. There is some risk for the bank, however. If interest rates do rise, the holder of the note is making money on less than a market rate. This risk is the reason why interest rates

PHOTODISC/GETTY IMAGES

are usually higher for fixed rate mortgages and why those mortgages are sold and resold, as holders try to maximize revenue.

One type of fixed rate mortgage that is sometimes confusing is called a **balloon mortgage**. In a balloon mortgage, the interest rate and payment stay fixed, but at some specified point, perhaps five years, the entire remaining balance of the loan is due in one single "balloon" payment. Although balloon mortgages allow some people to get mortgages who would not otherwise qualify, they are risky. Few people can pay off a house in five years, so as that balloon payment approaches, they must refinance. If they can't, they are likely to lose their houses and ruin their credit ratings.

Adjustable Rate Mortgages

Adjustable rate mortgages (ARMs), as the name implies, are those with rates that change over the course of the loan. Usually the interest rate and payments are fixed for some period of time at the outset but then change according to some index value. Initial rates and payments may be extremely low but are adjusted later to a rate closer to the normal rate, including some addition to make up for an artificially low start. Such *teaser rates* bring in business, but the borrower must make up for it and takes a risk that rates won't rise beyond what is affordable. There are lots of variables with ARMs, so it's extremely important for borrowers to understand their loans thoroughly. The chart on the following page summarizes some of the varying components.

The many possibilities of ARMs offer both opportunity and potential confusion for borrowers. When overall interest rates are low, ARM rates usually don't vary much from conventional rates. In times of rising interest, ARMs may offer a good starting point for those hoping rates will later fall. If a homeowner plans to be in a house only a few years, an ARM might

ARM Variables

Variable	Definition	Explanation
Interest Rate	The rate the lender charges for the loan, expressed as an annual percentage rate.	Initial rates for ARMs may be close to other rates, or they may be much lower, depending on the lender's product. Eventually, after adjustments over time, they are usually slightly lower than conventional mortgages, dependent on the index. Some ARMs offer a fixed rate for several years at the outset of the loan.
Payment	The amount, usually per month, that a borrower repays the lender. Mortgage payments often include principal, interest, taxes, and insurance.	Payment calculation typically varies with the interest rate, although some lenders may also use a formula that begins with a low payment not related directly to the interest rate. Taxes and insurance, if included, may vary over time in any mortgage.
Index	The measure to which the lender's interest rate is tied. Usually this is a U.S. Treasury security rate plus some figure or percentage.	Each lender may choose any index it wants, and some are better than others for the buyer. Fully understanding the index and its past performance and comparison shopping for ARMs are keys to consumer success.
Formula	The means by which the payment's relationship to index and to principal is calculated.	Each lender may use its own formula, so long as it is clearly specified in documentation. Comparing products side by side and seeing actual payment numbers helps the evaluation process.
Adjustment Interval	The length of time that a given rate and payment are in effect.	Adjustment intervals also vary with each lender's loan product. Some may be as short as three to six months. One year is typical. Whether a long adjustment interval is advantageous to lender or borrower depends upon the formula used and how stable the index has been over time.
Periodic Cap	The maximum amount, usually a percentage, by which an ARM can increase or decrease on an adjustment date.	This feature can protect both lender and borrower from rapid changes in interest rates. For example, a flex limit of one-half percent on any adjustment date keeps change from being too dramatic.
Lifetime Cap	The specified overall maximum or minimum rate of an ARM, regardless of index.	The cap sets a top and bottom interest rate, also called a floor, between which the rate and payment vary. If the floor is 5 percent, and the cap is 12 percent, for example, the rate may not vary outside that range regardless of the index.

be an excellent way to get the most house for the least money. A majority of consumers are most comfortable with conventional mortgages. This explains why, historically, they were the most common type of mortgage.

Other Forms of Financing

Other forms of financing involve various ways that lenders calculate or adjust interest or other values. Most often these vary to suit particular circumstances that are not well adaptable to conventional financing.

Buy-Down   In a **buy-down mortgage**, the borrower buys down, or prepays, part of the interest in order to get a lower rate. The borrower pays *points* to the lender at the outset, and the lender agrees to lower the rate so much per point. How much the interest drops is agreed to by the lender and the borrower as part of the deal. It's important to understand that a point is *not* an APR percentage point. A **point** is a value equal to 1 percent of the loan. For example, 2 points on a $200,000 home would be 2 percent of $200,000, or $4,000. The principal on the loan remains $200,000, but the interest for the life of the loan would be lowered by some rate agreed to by the lender and the borrower. For its part, the lender usually foregoes some long-term income for the sake of more cash up front. If the lender is planning to sell the note, this may earn the lender more money. The borrower, by paying more up front, may save far more in the long run.

Shared Appreciation Mortgage (SAM)   Although this form of mortgage is not new, it is having something of a comeback in the competitive lending business. A **shared appreciation mortgage** can lower interest rates for borrowers who agree to share profits with the lender when the house is sold. *Appreciation* is the amount that a house increases in value. With a SAM, the lender receives a part of the appreciation, often 50 percent. Say a borrower buys a house worth $150,000, and when the borrower sells it five years later, it's worth $200,000. The lender would receive a lump sum payment of $25,000 at payoff in addition to the remaining principal. In housing markets with little appreciation, a SAM can let a borrower get a low-rate loan without costing a lot at payoff. But SAMs also limit profit on the house for the borrower, who must share the appreciation. Sharing housing profits may make it hard for the seller to have a new down payment on another house after paying the lender. In markets that appreciate rapidly, SAMs can be very profitable for banks. SAMs allow borrowers to have a house they might not otherwise be able to afford, as long as they are willing to sacrifice a portion of future profits.

Refinancing   Essentially, refinancing is starting over with an entirely new loan, using part or all of the loan funds to pay off the old mortgage. If interest rates are low, consumers save money by getting new mortgages at lower rates. Banks and other lenders earn money on fees, points, and closing costs of the new loan and add business (usually at the expense of other lenders) at the new rates. Prepayment penalties for the old mortgage may also raise the cost of refinancing, although some states do not allow prepayment penalties on mortgages. Generally, the lower the refinancing rates, the higher the fees and points. Borrowers need to understand and consider all costs carefully.

The process for refinancing is the same as obtaining the original mortgage in most cases, and all steps and underwriting conditions apply. It used to be said that the new interest rate had to be at least two percentage points lower than the old one to make the cost of refinancing pay off, but competition in the business has led to low-cost, zero-point, low-fee offerings from some lenders. Refinancing is also a good time for consumers to consider another type of mortgage if they are unsatisfied or struggling with the one they have.

Home Equity Loans   Home equity loans can be another active area in the lending industry. *Equity* is the difference between the market value of an item and what is owed on it. Depending on the geographical area and the economy, homes historically appreciated in value 3 to 6 percent or more per year. A home worth $160,000 at purchase might have been worth $185,000 in five years' time.

When home values are appreciating, homeowners can use the difference between what they owe and what their homes are worth to secure a loan. Let's say a borrower purchases a $160,000 house with $20,000 down and after five years has a remaining principal of $135,000. The house appreciates during that time and is now worth $185,000. The homeowner has equity of $50,000. That home equity may be used to secure a loan up to or even beyond the value of the equity.

Home equity loans take one of two forms. One type is a simple loan, a single disbursement of money for the borrowed amount. Another type is a line of credit, sometimes with paper checks or accompanying credit cards. Borrowers have a credit line up to the equity limit. As they pay down the balance, they can add new expenses to the line if they choose.

The recent mortgage crisis and subsequent tightening of credit changed the outlook on home equity loans. According to Fannie Mae, median home prices declined by about 5.5 percent in a three-year period. In 2006, the median home price was $221,900; in 2008 it was $209,600. When housing prices are falling, it is harder and less wise for homeowners to obtain home equity loans.

In many respects, a home equity loan is just another consumer loan, but there is a big exception. It's a second mortgage. It is secured by the home. If borrowers are unable to repay the loan, they may lose their homes. In recent years, the easy availability of home equity loans has led some borrowers into trouble. Some irresponsible lenders have also extended credit to people who are not really in a position to repay, a predatory lending practice that can lead to disaster. Responsible lenders underwrite home equity loans carefully, but consumers should be very cautious about borrowing against their largest and most important asset.

PHOTODISC/GETTY IMAGES

Reverse Mortgages   A reverse mortgage is not a mortgage used to purchase a home. It is really another form of consumer loan tied to the appreciated value of a property. In most cases, reverse mortgages are limited to homeowners 62 years or older. With a *reverse mortgage*, a homeowner receives a sum from the lender secured by the value of a home and does not pay the loan back as long as he or she lives there. Typically, a senior homeowner owes less on a mortgage because he or she has been paying on it for many years. Also, the house may well have appreciated considerably since purchase. The lender is repaid, including fees and interest, when the borrower sells or dies. Borrowers may receive their funds in lump sums, a credit line, or a monthly payment direct from the lender, or some combination of the three.

The advantage of a reverse mortgage is that it allows homeowners the opportunity to get cash from the value of their homes without selling and moving. Although loan advances are not typically considered income by the

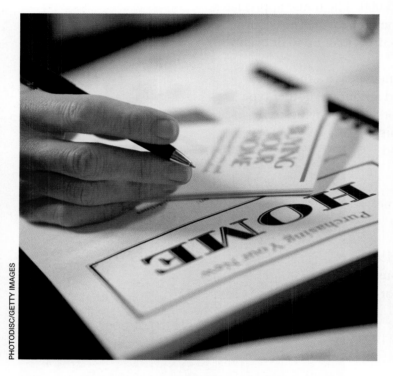

Internal Revenue Service, obtaining a reverse mortgage may affect eligibility in some other government-benefits programs and can affect taxes and estate planning considerably. Equity in the home declines throughout the life of a reverse mortgage, and the homeowner is still responsible for taxes, insurance, and maintenance. As with any loan, there are many variations in features, terms, and lenders, and it's wise to shop for the best terms. Those considering a reverse mortgage should thoroughly understand all terms of the mortgage, as well as all other aspects of their retirement, financial, and estate planning. This type of loan is usually very expensive in terms of the interest rate.

That advice holds true for any type of mortgage from any type of lender. For most people, mortgages represent the largest debt for the largest financial transaction they will ever undertake.

✔ checkpoint

What is the basic difference between conventional and adjustable rate mortgages?

assessment 8.1

Think Critically

1. What incentives make home ownership and the undertaking of long-term debt attractive to consumers?

_____

_____

2. Explain the advantages and disadvantages to the consumer of balloon mortgages.

_____

_____

_____

3. Why might a consumer choose an adjustable rate mortgage over a fixed rate mortgage?

_____

_____

_____

4. What is a *point* and why do some consumers choose to pay points on their mortgages?

_____

_____

_____

Make Academic Connections

5. **HISTORY**   Though it changes, land lasts forever. Pick an area, a neighborhood, a small town, a subdivision, or even an individual property and trace the history of its owners. You may need to do some initial research to learn how to conduct a search of county records.

_____

_____

6. **RESEARCH**   Refinancing is a big portion of the lending business. Learn more about refinancing using resources such as the Internet, newspapers, and magazines. Write a brief report on your findings.

_____

_____

8.2

Mortgage Loan Processing

goals

+ Describe what is involved in obtaining a mortgage.

+ Explain the mortgage approval process.

terms

+ PITI

+ escrow

+ loan-to-value (LTV)

Banking Scene

Katrina Harris has done some research on mortgages and now has a better understanding of the loan process. She has been looking at some real estate properties and is now ready to obtain a loan. Where should she start?

OBTAINING A MORTGAGE

Because of the typical size of the loan, lenders scrutinize mortgage applications closely. The potential risk involved is greater for the bank both in terms of the amount of the loan and the liquidity of the collateral. Banks don't want to own houses.

Lenders typically require a down payment of 5, 10, or 20 percent for a mortgage. (FHA and other government-sponsored loans, which you'll learn about in a later section, may require less, as do some other programs.) A larger down payment not only lowers the cost of the monthly payment, it affects how the lender views the borrower. Lenders may make the loan if a down payment is high, even if the borrower's credit rating is not ideal.

In addition, a higher down payment allows a borrower to have more house for the same money. In a healthy lending environment, most lenders don't want a person's housing costs to exceed 25 to 28 percent of gross monthly income. Total debt should not exceed 36 percent, including housing costs. For the same monthly payment, a borrower could get a house worth about $170,000 with a 20 percent down payment, as opposed to one worth $135,000 with 5 percent down. A higher down payment may also avoid a requirement of private mortgage insurance.

PITI

Monthly payments to the lender usually consist of **PITI** or principal, interest, taxes, and insurance. These are the housing costs that the lender considers in the loan analysis and are itemized on the monthly mortgage statement.

Principal is the remaining unpaid balance of the mortgage. The figure shown on the statement may not be the payoff amount but merely the remaining principal calculated currently. The payoff figure may differ based on the type and terms of the loan.

Banking Math *Connection*

Private mortgage insurance (PMI) rates may vary, but a typical PMI rate is ½ of 1 percent of the borrowed principal. The formula for calculating the monthly PMI cost is

$$\text{Rate} \times \text{Principal} \div 12 = \text{PMI}$$

Calculate the monthly PMI cost for a principal balance of $140,000.

Solution

If PMI were required for a principal of $140,000, the calculation would be

$$\text{Rate} \times \text{Principal} \div 12 = \text{PMI}$$
$$0.005 \times \$140,000 \div 12 = \$58.34$$

Interest is the amount of the monthly payment that goes toward interest. In the early years of a mortgage, this is by far the largest figure. Because interest is usually deductible, the tax advantages of a mortgage make homeownership doubly attractive.

Taxes include local real estate taxes. Most lenders require an amount to be paid to them in advance, called **escrow**, from which they pay the real estate taxes. Many loans also require an additional amount for an escrow buffer so that the escrow fund never falls below a set level.

Insurance refers to property insurance and sometimes private mortgage insurance. To protect the lender against potential loss, almost all mortgages require the homeowner to maintain adequate property insurance against fire, storms, and other calamities. The lender collects the insurance premium as part of the payment to make sure its security is covered. *Private mortgage insurance* (PMI) protects the lender against loan default. PMI is not typically required for those whose down payment is 20 percent or greater. It can be eliminated once the principal balance reaches 20 percent of the original loan value.

As with all loans, specific terms, methods of calculation, and costs may vary, and it is a good idea for borrowers to have legal counsel about the details of mortgages.

 checkpoint

What is private mortgage insurance?

THE APPROVAL PROCESS

Few things in financial life are as nerve-wracking for many consumers as the mortgage approval process. The many details, close examination of finances, and legal language intimidate many borrowers, producing considerable anxiety. Although the process is detailed, it is getting simpler and certainly faster.

Application, documentation, underwriting based on credit reputation and capacity, and closing are all part of the credit analysis and credit-granting process and are common across loan categories. The process is more detailed for mortgages, largely because the transfer of real property brings into play more legal issues than a simple contract. Here are the basic steps.

- **Application** for a mortgage may be more involved than for other forms of loans, and accuracy and completeness are essential. Unlike many small consumer loans, for which a quick credit check is sufficient, every detail of a mortgage application will be evaluated carefully. Missing, incomplete, or wrong information will delay the process at the very least and may result in denial of the loan.

- **Documentation** for a mortgage loan must also be complete and accurate. Often, it takes some time to assemble full documentation, which usually includes a professional appraisal of the property. Lenders pay attention to the **loan-to-value (LTV)** relationship, which is the value of the loan compared to the value of the asset. Most reputable lenders prefer to lend no more than 95 percent of the appraised value of a house so that their risk is supported. It's not merely a question of what you're willing to pay the seller, but also what the house is really worth that may determine whether you get a mortgage. Other documents include complete credit reports, employment and/or income verification, and verification of existence and source of the down payment. If you borrow the down payment, that debt must be considered as well, and most lenders like to have the down payment deposited for some period of time before the application (60 days is best).

- **Underwriting** is the critical step, as documents arrive and are verified and reviewed. Some lenders have loan processors who verify completeness and accuracy separate from the underwriters,

PHOTODISC/GETTY IMAGES

and some combine both functions. As with any loan, *collateral, capacity,* and *credit reputation* determine whether a mortgage is a good investment for the bank. Mortgage underwriters look hard at a borrower's ability to repay as measured by a debt-to-income ratio and the track record of a borrower over a long period of time. Often, underwriters may want more information or a letter of explanation about some circumstance or item in the credit record. Applicants can't hide much from a thorough underwriter, and completeness and fullness on applications is the best approach. Sometimes underwriters may modify the terms of a mortgage one way or another to fit the circumstances. Although mortgage underwriting is becoming automated by software, the underwriting process for mortgages is still the most careful and painstaking part of obtaining a mortgage.

- **Drawing documents** is another carefully considered step in the process. The sale of a home involves many documents between lender and borrower. As you'll recall, many promissory notes are negotiable, and mortgages are often sold for servicing many times. It is essential that all documents be accurate and all terms and requirements met so that the note remains negotiable no matter where it eventually goes. Once the note is signed, the bank prepares the funding.

- **Closing** requires the signing of all documents involving the transfer of the property from one party to another. These documents go beyond the scope of just the mortgage. Closing costs, including fees for application, origination, title search, surveys, appraisal costs, inspections, taxes, attorneys, escrow, and recording are paid, as well as any points and applicable realtor fees. Frequently, a title company, which specializes in researching and transferring property between owners, will handle the closing.

- **Recording** the Mortgage/Deed of Trust at the county recorder's office makes the mortgage public record. Records may be available online, either from a recorder or from another company that compiles such records.

Although the process of obtaining a mortgage is often longer and more involved than obtaining other types of loans, the lending business, like all of the financial industries, is changing. Lenders need to lend money. Prior to the recent mortgage and credit crises, competition among lenders made it easier than ever before for borrowers to apply and be approved. The risk to both lender and borrower is greater for a mortgage than it is for other types of loans. It's best for consumers to understand as much as they can about the process and their own payment capabilities before undertaking a transaction that will have lifelong implications.

 checkpoint

What are the basic steps of the mortgage approval process?

_____

_____

assessment 8.2

Think Critically

1. Why is the mortgage loan application process longer and more involved than that for other consumer loans?

2. Why do you think a lender might overlook less-than-perfect credit for a borrower with a large down payment?

3. Why do lenders (or the holders of a mortgage) usually want taxes and insurance included as part of the payment?

4. What types of information do you think are requested on a mortgage loan application?

Make Academic Connections

5. **RESEARCH** Online mortgage sales are now a big business. Find a mortgage financing website and write a short description of the mortgage loan process used by the financier.

6. **BANKING MATH** Most lenders prefer that a mortgage not exceed 28 percent of your gross monthly income. Assuming that you make $40,000 per year, what is the maximum PITI that the bank would deem acceptable?

Mortgages and the Law

8.3

Banking Scene

When Katrina Harris conducted her research on mortgages, she learned about many laws related to mortgage lending. Katrina wondered if any of these laws really applied to her. In what ways do these laws affect Katrina?

CONSUMER PROTECTION LEGISLATION • • • • • • • • • • • • •

Numerous laws affect mortgage lending. Parts of consumer protection legislation apply to mortgage lending as well. Most of these laws are designed to protect consumers from unfair practices relating to lending, collecting, or maintaining privacy as described below.

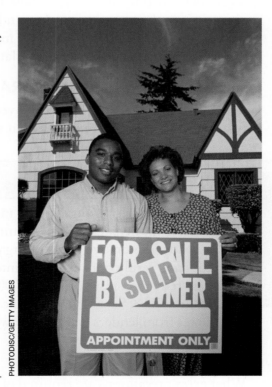

• The Truth in Lending Act (TILA) promotes informed use of consumer credit by requiring disclosures about its terms and costs.

• The Equal Credit Opportunity Act (ECOA) prohibits creditors from discriminating against applicants on the basis of race, color, religion, national origin, sex, marital status, and age.

• The Fair Credit Reporting Act (FCRA) is designed to promote accuracy, fairness, and privacy of information in the files of consumer reporting agencies (credit bureaus).

• The Fair Debt Collection Practices Act (FDCPA) prohibits abusive practices by debt collectors.

- The Gramm-Leach-Bliley Act requires that financial institutions protect the privacy of consumers.

Many of the provisions of these laws apply specifically to the mortgage lending industry. Targeted sections and enforcement specifications for various laws rests within various agencies such as the Federal Trade Commission (FTC), the Federal Deposit Insurance Corporation (FDIC), and the Federal Reserve.

 checkpoint

How do consumer protection laws apply to mortgage lending?

MORTAGE LEGISLATION

Other laws exist that relate directly to mortgage lending. Complying with this legislation and documenting compliance requires considerable effort and expense on the part of financial institutions. A few of these laws are described below. Most of these laws have been amended numerous times since their passage, and amendments on many of them are pending. Most states also have similar measures, although they may not always be consistent with federal legislation.

Community Reinvestment Act (CRA)

Congress passed the Community Reinvestment Act (CRA) of 1977 in response to widespread complaints that some banks refused to lend to

Ethics in Action

According to reports throughout the media, Senator Chris Dodd, Chairman of the Senate Banking Committee in 2008, received interest rate reductions on two of his mortgages held by Countrywide. One rate reduction resulted in an annual interest savings of $2000. The other rate reduction resulted in a $17,000 reduction over the life of the loan. In June 2008, Senator Dodd indicated he had solicited multiple rate quotes from lenders and was unaware of any special treatment.

Think Critically

What extra precautions are required of a politician during financial transactions? What probing questions would be wise to ask to avoid the appearance of favoritism?

residents of certain neighbor-hoods, a practice called **redlining**. The law requires that banks document their lending decisions and demonstrate an effort to serve their local communities. CRA investments increase home ownership and help stabilize neighborhoods, which is good for the local economy. Periodic government examinations monitor compliance with the law.

Some critics of the law note that the statute is enforced only when banks merge or expand. They point out that the Gramm-Leach-Bliley Act, though imposing new requirements on privacy, weakened the CRA by slowing the cycle of examination for many banks.

Many lenders, however, struggle with the CRA, both in terms of the burden of compliance and their need to follow sound banking practices. It's not always easy to balance the desire to lend liberally in local communities with the need to meet strict (and increasingly inflexible) conditions for making good loans, which are subject to government examination.

Home Mortgage Disclosure Act (HMDA)

The Home Mortgage Disclosure Act (HMDA) of 1974 was a forerunner of the CRA. It requires banks and other financial institutions to record and report data on home lending in order to identify possible discriminatory patterns. As a practical matter, it set into motion the huge recordkeeping responsibilities of compliance regarding home mortgages. In 2000, for example, there were about 19 million loan records reported by 7,713 financial institutions. These data become the basis for statistical analysis and compliance monitoring by various agencies.

Home Ownership and Equity Protection Act (HOEPA)

Congress passed the Home Ownership and Equity Protection Act in 1994 to protect consumers against predatory lending. Provisions of this act also apply to second mortgages and refinancing. If a loan's annual percentage rate (APR) is 10 points higher than a rate on a Treasury Bill for the same length of time (for example, fifteen years on a fifteen-year note), the loan is a high-interest-rate loan, also called a HOEPA loan. Loans with noninterest fees of more than $465 or 8 percent of the loan value are also HOEPA loans. For HOEPA loans, lenders must make disclosures three days before closing, may not pay a contractor directly, may not require balloon

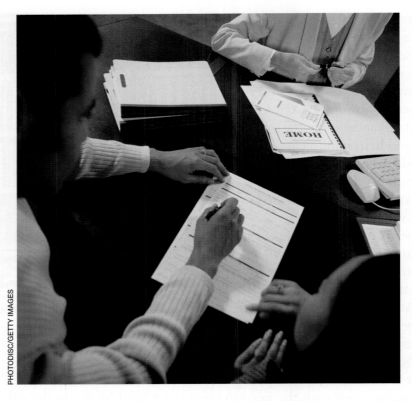

PHOTODISC/GETTY IMAGES

payments due in less than five years on most loans, and are limited in the type of prepayment penalties allowed. In some cases, a few lenders deliberately engage in deceptive practices to obtain properties they then resell. HOEPA is intended to discourage such equity stripping and educate those consumers who may not be fully informed.

During July 2008, to address some of the root causes of the mortgage crisis, the Federal Reserve Board announced some new rules under HOEPA. These new rules amend Regulation Z, which is the Truth in Lending Regulation. These updates govern all mortgage lenders, including lenders not directly supervised by the Federal Reserve. Highlights of these proposed rules include:

- Lenders are prohibited from routinely making loans that exceed a borrower's reasonable ability to pay off the loan. The lender must make sure the borrower can make loan payments based on the highest payment expected in the first seven years of the loan.

- "Stated-income" and/or "stated-asset" loans are prohibited. Lenders are required to verify income and assets prior to making loans.

- Escrow accounts need to be established for real estate taxes and homeowner's insurance for all first-lien mortgage loans. It is the lender's responsibility to establish the account.

- If a payment can change within the first four years, prepayment penalties are prohibited. A prepayment penalty period cannot exceed more than two years for higher-priced loans.

Other revisions include the requirement that good faith estimates of all payments be provided within three days of applying for a loan, that lenders are prohibited from pressuring a real estate appraiser to provide a false estimate of the value of a home, and that *pyramiding* late fees are not allowed. When a loan servicing company continues to charge late fees until all late fees have been paid (even if payments made after the late payments were made in full and on time), late fee pyramiding occurs.

Advertising requirements have also been revised. Loan features, including rates and monthly payments, must be clearly stated. Seven particularly deceptive practices are prohibited. Lenders are not allowed to state that a payment is "fixed" when the payment can change.

Real Estate Settlement Procedures Act (RESPA)

Congress enacted the Real Estate Settlement Procedures Act (RESPA) of 1974 to protect consumers from hidden costs or expensive surprises at closing time. The law requires disclosures to be provided to the borrower at various times during the transaction. At the time of application, the borrower must receive a booklet explaining various real estate settlement services, a good faith estimate of what closing costs are likely to be, and a mortgaging service disclosure statement, which indicates whether the lender will service the loan or sell it to another lender. Before closing, the lender must also disclose any business relationships with other service providers in the transaction. The lender may not require the borrower to use such parties, such as titling companies or attorneys, affiliated with the lender. At the time of closing, the borrower is entitled to an itemized list of actual closing costs and an initial escrow statement showing anticipated principal, interest, taxes, and insurance (PITI), including the amount collected beforehand (escrow) for taxes and insurance. An escrow analysis must be done once a year, and any surplus more than $50 must be returned to the borrower.

RESPA also prohibits giving or accepting fees in exchange for referrals of settlement service business. The law bans kickbacks and fee splitting for settlement businesses and outlaws fees for services not actually performed.

The Homeowners' Protection Act of 1998 requires that lenders drop private mortgage insurance (PMI) when equity reaches 22 percent in loans closed after July 29, 1999.

 checkpoint

What is redlining and what legislation was enacted to address it?

_____

_____

_____

assessment 8.3

Think Critically

1. Why is there a need for consumer protection legislation related specifically to mortgages?

2. What is the purpose of escrow in a mortgage?

3. Why might financial institutions look at mortgage legislation as being burdensome?

4. Which of the laws related to mortgage lending discussed in this section do you believe is most important? What are your reasons?

Make Academic Connections

5. **HISTORY**   Select one of the laws that apply to mortgages and use the Internet to research the history of the law. Present your report to the class.

6. **RESEARCH**   Using the library or Internet, find out what path someone should take if he or she encounters discrimination while trying to obtain a home mortgage loan.

7. **COMMUNICATE**   Talk with a loan officer at your local bank about how mortgage laws affect the officer's job responsibilities. Summarize your discussion below.

Government-Backed Loans

goals

+ Explain the concept of government-backed loans.
+ Identify government-backed programs to encourage home lending.

terms

+ Fannie Mae
+ Freddie Mac
+ Ginnie Mae

Banking Scene

Katrina Harris learned quickly that she didn't have the resources or the credit history to obtain conventional funding for a home loan. She turned to the government. She had gone to college on government-backed loans, and it occurred to her that there might be similar programs to help new homeowners. What might be a good way for Katrina to start searching the vast amount of information available from the U.S. government?

WHAT IS A GOVERNMENT-BACKED LOAN?

The government sometimes acts as a partner to the banking industry, as well as to people and businesses. Numerous government programs help banks help people get loans they need.

With these programs, the Federal government offers a number of ways to help people obtain financing for worthwhile purposes. In most of these

EQUAL·JUSTICE·UNDER·LAW·

PHOTODISC/GETTY IMAGES

programs, the banks provide funding and the government absorbs some of the risk. The government backs the loans by promising to repay them should the borrower default. In order to minimize its own risk, the government also examines the borrower's finances and has eligibility requirements for participation. Some states even operate such programs, and consumers can get more information on these and federal programs from prospective lenders. Lenders want to make loans, and they are happy to work with the consumer and government agencies to find financing solutions.

 checkpoint

How do banks and the government work together to provide loans?

FEDERAL MORTGAGE PROGRAMS

The Federal government has been interested in housing programs since the Great Depression of the 1930s. At that time, many new programs came into being to help people who had lost everything in the crisis. Social Security is probably the most prominent program introduced by President Roosevelt and Congress during that time. Many other programs to help the unemployed, farmers, and others, including those who were struggling with housing, arose as well. The Federal Housing Administration, established in 1934, supported both homebuyers and banks by replenishing funds available for home lending. Today, there are many such programs with varying missions, services, and operations, but the twin benefits of supporting homeowners and backing the banking industry continue.

Federal Housing Administration (FHA)

The Federal Housing Administration is the oldest of the many government agencies working to help homeowners. The banking industry was in trouble during the Great Depression, but it was not the only industry in trouble. Two million construction workers were out of work, as well as millions of others, and all the businesses they supported with their incomes were faltering. The FHA was an attempt to get the housing industry back on its feet. By guaranteeing loans and providing mortgage insurance, the FHA helped to reverse the tough climate for borrowers. Before the FHA was established, mortgages were typically limited to half of a property's value and had to be repaid in three to five years, typically with a balloon payment. Few people could afford such terms, even fewer in an economic disaster. The FHA made it possible for banks to offer better terms without shouldering all the risk. Helping to pioneer the long-term loans that make homeownership possible, the FHA changed the face of lending.

Today, what was once the FHA is now the Office of Housing, and it is part of the Department of Housing and Urban Development (HUD). It still performs the same services, guaranteeing loans with low down payments—often as little as 3 percent—to help people obtain housing who perhaps could not otherwise afford it. These loans, still called FHA loans, are not direct loans from the program, but they guarantee the lender that the mortgage will be paid. If it isn't, the agency repays the lender. The loans are arranged through lenders and may be fixed or adjustable rate mortgages. The FHA 203(b) loan program for conventional loans is most common, but there are many variations and resources for getting help with the down payment. The mortgage insurance premium is charged up front (usually 2 to 2.25 percent of the loan, with another 0.5 percent per year) and goes to defray the costs of administering the program. Almost anyone can qualify for an FHA loan, subject to some credit and residency restrictions, and there are limits to the size of the loan. The FHA program pioneered the government's entry into the mortgage business and has backed over 30 million mortgages.

FHASecure

In an effort to help homeowners impacted by the subprime mortgage crisis and resulting ARMs, FHASecure was developed in 2007. Homeowners who are struggling to meet their ARM payments can participate in FHASecure to refinance their homes with a government-insured mortgage. To participate, homeowners must have enough income to make regular mortgage payments on the refinanced loan.

Fannie Mae

The Federal National Mortgage Association (FNMA) was so often referred to by its acronym that the corporation came to be referred to as **Fannie Mae**, which is now its registered trademark. Fannie Mae was also born of the Depression. It was created in 1938 to help lenders find funds to make available for mortgages. If the FHA was a source of help for consumers, Fannie Mae was a source of help for lenders. Fannie Mae is a government-chartered corporation that buys mortgages from the originating institutions and either keeps them or exchanges them for securities that it guarantees. The effect is that there is a pool of money available

PHOTODISC/GETTY IMAGES

to lenders for mortgage loans. In the Depression, this made money available quickly to lenders to expand the available funds, as it still works today.

To participate, lenders must be licensed to originate mortgages, have a net worth of at least $250,000, be bonded and insured, and have written policies for underwriting and loan servicing, among other requirements. Although once a part of the FHA, Fannie Mae is now an independent corporation.

Freddie Mac

The Federal Home Loan Mortgage Corporation, nicknamed **Freddie Mac**, operates a similar program. Freddie Mac also buys home mortgages from banks and other lending institutions and combines them into large groups, selling interest in the groups to investors. Expanding the market for mortgages as negotiable instruments in this way expands the amount of funds invested in the lending and housing businesses. Created in 1970 as a fully independent corporation, Freddie Mac has financed a significant number of mortgages in the United States since its beginning. Like Fannie Mae, Freddie Mac also lends for multifamily dwellings and rehabilitation projects. Freddie Mac also invites lenders to participate, with eligibility requirements similar to those of Fannie Mae.

tech talk

Fannie Mae DU and Freddie Mac LP

As underwriting of mortgage loans becomes increasingly automated, government-chartered agencies that work with private lenders have developed tools for their lending clients. Fannie Mae's Desktop Underwriter (DU) and Freddie Mac's Loan Prospector (LP) are two automated systems that are helping streamline the underwriting communications between agencies and the client lenders.

The desktop programs are based on statistical models of FHA underwriting data to create an automated scoring system specifically designed with FHA criteria in mind. As a result, these customized automated underwriting systems streamline the often cumbersome process of working through the agencies and the FHA. The systems are FHA approved and can return a routine underwriting decision and conditions within an hour. Lenders enter data from their own sites, using a standard Residential Loan Application. Although they are not the only ways to get FHA approval for Fannie Mae and Freddie Mac funds, these two software programs are the wave of an interconnected future in underwriting.

Think Critically   What type of information had to be factored into the DU and LP programs in order for them to be reliable? What are some elements of the underwriting process that make it difficult to automate?

The Combined Impact of Fannie Mae and Freddie Mac

A *government-sponsored enterprise* (GSE) is a business that receives some legal exemptions and privileges from the federal government, which, in effect, lowers its operating costs. Due to a lower cost structure, a GSE can charge lower interest rates. GSEs also have an implicit guarantee of the government as a backer. This implicit guarantee fosters greater confidence within the business community. Both Fannie Mae and Freddie Mac are GSEs.

As of July 2008, Fannie Mae and Freddie Mac either owned or guaranteed about $5 trillion of mortgages. This represents almost half of all outstanding U.S. home mortgages. According to *The Wall Street Journal*, in a nine-month period that concluded at the end of March 2008, Fannie Mae and Freddie Mac lost a combined total of $11 billion.

Although not stated outright, investors have historically relied on an implicit guarantee from the government of loans from these companies. Given that together they represent such a large portion of the U.S. mortgage market, steps are underway to stabilize these companies.

Ginnie Mae

A third government initiative, unlike the other two, remains part of the federal government. The Government National Mortgage Association, called **Ginnie Mae**, is part of the Department of Housing and Urban Development (HUD). Originally an arm of the FHA, it split. It neither buys nor sells mortgages, but it backs securities issued by holders of pools of mortgages. By guaranteeing the worth of the securities, Ginnie Mae attracts investors, and the pool of funds for mortgages remains high. Ginnie Mae encourages funding for FHA, Veterans Administration (VA), and other low-income housing, assuring that there will be funds available for these programs.

Veterans Administration (VA)

Loans from the Department of Veterans Affairs (DVA) have helped millions of servicemen and -women get government-backed loans with low down payments. Veterans may get loans with no down payment, no prepayment penalties, and negotiable interest rates. Similar to the FHA loan program, VA loans allow qualified veterans to buy, build, remodel, or refinance a home. In general, to qualify for a VA loan, a person must meet one of the following criteria.

- Have served 181 days of active duty between 1940 and 1981 or 24 months for those who served after 1981, or discharged with a service-related disability in less time (certain exceptions apply for Gulf War veterans)

- Have served six years in the National Guard or Selected Reserves, completing all weekend and active duty time

- Be an unremarried spouse of a service person killed in action or who died of a service-connected disability

- Be a spouse of a prisoner of war or a service person missing in action

In some cases, the VA may declare other persons eligible, such as Public Health Service officers, merchant seamen with WWII service, members of service academies, and others.

NCSHA

At the state level, many programs also exist that help families buy homes. The National Council of State Housing Agencies (NCSHA) is a national organization of Housing Finance Agencies (HFAs) throughout the states that provide and administer programs for lower-income and other people who seek help at the state level to buy or renovate a home. There is an HFA in every state. There are also 350 affiliated profit and nonprofit agencies that work in this field. These agencies and firms have a variety of programs for affordable housing.

Other Government-Backed Loans

There are many other government-backed loan programs as well. For example, the U.S. Department of Agriculture's (USDA) Rural Housing Service offers both direct loans and grants from the government as well as guaranteed loans. Designed for low- and moderate-income rural residents, the program also offers opportunities for lenders and developers by making doing business in rural areas a safer investment. The Farm Service Agency, formerly the Farmers Home Administration (FmHA), is an agency of the U.S. Department of Agriculture that provides credit assistance to farmers, both by guaranteeing and sometimes making loans. Borrowers are offered 30- to 40-year loans at fixed interest rates as low as 1 percent.

It's not easy to find every government loan program that's out there. The *Catalog of Federal Domestic Assistance* is available in government depository libraries or online from the General Services Administration at www.cfda.gov. It provides information on agencies and programs with which individuals may be able to work.

 checkpoint

How do the FHA and VA make more loans available?

assessment 8.4

Think Critically

1. How do government-backed loan programs help the economy?

_____

_____

2. What benefits do government-backed loans provide to lenders?

_____

_____

_____

3. Why do you think there are limits to the size of FHA loans?

_____

_____

4. How do Fannie Mae, Freddie Mac, and Ginnie Mae make more mortgage funds available?

_____

_____

_____

Make Academic Connections

5. **HISTORY**   Visit the Fannie Mae foundation website at www. fanniemaefoundation.org. List some of the information available.

_____

_____

_____

6. **COMMUNICATION**   Using the Internet or the library, gather information about FHA, Fannie Mae, and VA loans. List some of the requirements and restrictions that must be adhered to when applying for these loans.

_____

_____

_____

_____

_____

_____

8.5

The Mortgage Crisis

goals

+ Describe why mortgages are a sound investment.

+ Explain the causes and consequences of the mortgage crisis.

terms

+ mortgage-backed securities

+ negative equity

Banking Scene

Katrina Harris has enjoyed being a homeowner for a few years. Unfortunately, due to a recently diagnosed medical illness, which kept her out of work frequently, she was earning less income. As her bills started to pile up, she thought about refinancing her mortgage to lower her monthly payments. There were many loans available that could help her out—but they seemed almost too good to be true. What should Katrina consider as she investigates these new loan products?

MORTGAGES AS AN ATTRACTIVE INVESTMENT

Historically, mortgages represented a secure, steady investment for lenders. Interest rates, or in the case of a variable rate loan, the range of interest rates, are predetermined. The payment schedule, typically spread out in monthly installments over a 15- or 30-year period, is predetermined. Lenders could count on a steady flow of revenue from mortgages.

By carefully prequalifying buyers and making sure they purchased a home within their budget, lenders could be fairly certain that loans would be repaid in a timely fashion. As housing prices typically appreciated, if there was a loan default, the house the lender would take possession of would have a higher value than the defaulted mortgage. Therefore, if the lender needed to sell the house because of a default, they could recoup some, if not all, of their loss due to the appreciated house value.

Many lenders who stuck with the traditional methods of maintaining stringent loan qualifying standards and matching income to house payments managed to remain in strong financial condition during the mortgage crisis. By taking a long-term view of the mortgages they qualified and by focusing

©ROB MARMION/SHUTTERSTOCK

on the overall health of the loan, they made sound, safe lending decisions. Foregoing higher profits associated with higher-risk loans kept these lenders in good condition.

checkpoint

Historically, why have lenders considered mortgages a good investment?

_____

_____

_____

THE MORTGAGE CRISIS

Multiple factors contributed to the mortgage crisis. A number of countries, including China and India, which had traditionally been less developed with fewer financial resources than highly industrialized countries, were becoming more advanced. Other countries, including Saudi Arabia, increased their revenues by selling oil. As the productivity of these countries increased, more national income was generated. The individuals and businesses within these countries wanted to invest their newfound wealth and receive a high return on their investments. There was also shift in how banks financed home mortgages. Traditionally, mortgages had been made with money from local deposits. Over time, mortgage financing transitioned from local deposits to money from the bond markets.

At about the same time, the Federal Reserve announced that to stimulate the economy, the Federal Funds rate would be maintained at about 1%. As U.S. Treasury bonds had traditionally been a safe, steady investment with a satisfactory rate of return, they became a less attractive investment due to their lower interest rate. Other investments, with return rates that moved relative to this rate, also became less attractive.

The lower interest rates made it easy for consumers to obtain many forms of credit, including mortgage loans. Easy access to mortgage loans drove up the demand for houses. Increased housing demand caused housing prices to continue to escalate.

Mortgage-Backed Securities

Lenders do not always hold on to loans. Sometimes loans are sold to other investors. The originating lender sells the loan with a higher principal than the original loan. The buyer receives the interest income on the loan. As the principal amount is slightly higher than it was on the original loan, the effective interest rate is slightly lower than it was on the original loan. However, even with a slightly lower interest rate, it is still an attractive investment.

There are businesses that pool these individual loans and sell them as a group to other investors. Any risk associated with a specific loan becomes

interesting *facts*

Ignoring FICO can hurt Fido. The Humane Society has experienced an increase in abandoned pets, which they attribute to people leaving behind pets when they are forced to leave their homes. ■

©BRIAN A. JACKSON/SHUTTERSTOCK

part of the collective risk of the pool of loans. These pooled loans are called **mortgage-backed securities**. These securities became an attractive investment for investors from countries that had newly found wealth. Dealers who packaged mortgage-backed securities were trying to generate enough securities to meet the increasing demand.

Prior to the mortgage crisis, investors were eager to buy mortgage-backed securities. These investors believed there was a predictable, safe income stream that would be realized from these securities. The monthly mortgage payments made from the groups of homeowners whose mortgage loans were in the pool generated this steady income. What some investors did not realize, however, was that in an effort to meet the increased demand for mortgage-backed securities, many firms had begun to lower loan qualification standards.

As the firms originating these loans planned on selling them very quickly into the mortgage-backed securities market, they became less concerned with the long-term risks associated with loans made to unqualified buyers. The firms that pooled the mortgages were of the mindset that in a pool of mortgages, if some were very stable mortgages and some were subprime mortgages, the risk would even out.

Lowering Lending Criteria

Traditionally, collateral, capacity, and credit reputation were all considered before a loan was approved. All information on a loan application was verified. LTV ratios were maintained at a maximum value of 95%.

These qualifying criteria changed as loan qualification standards were loosened. A variety of new loans became available that shared the same goal—allowing more people to qualify for mortgages. Some of these loans allowed 100% financing and did not require PMI. The long-term welfare of the borrower and the long-term risk of default were disregarded.

Interest-only loans allow a homeowner to pay only the interest on their loans for the first 3–10 years. After the initial interest-only period, the loan payments will be recalculated to include principal and interest. This recalculation substantially increases monthly mortgage payments. No home equity is built during the interest-only phase of the mortgage.

Stated Income Verified Assets loans (SIVA) enable a borrower to obtain a loan based on stated income, credit history, and verified assets. Claimed income levels do not need to be verified with a W2, tax return, or pay stub.

Stated Income State Assets loans (SISA) allow a customer to merely claim their income level and asset level. No verification is necessary.

No Income No Asset loans (NINA) do not require a borrower to provide either income or asset information. Loan approval is based on property value, credit history, and down payment. Verification of employment history of the prior two years is required. One hundred percent of a mortgage can be financed with a NINA loan.

No Income, No Asset, No Employment loans require no verification of employment, assets, or income. These loans are also referred to as No Documentation Mortgage Loans (No Doc).

Rating Mortgage-Backed Securities

The Securities and Exchange Commission (SEC) began regulating underwriting firms in September 2007. In July 2008, the SEC released a report citing a failure to adhere to ethical underwriting standards by a number of prominent ratings firms.

NET Bookmark

All across America, families are being touched by the mortgage crisis. Access www.cengage.com/school/pfinance/banking and click on the link for Chapter 8. The Hope Now Alliance is an alliance of mortgage-related industries and service providers that is focused on keeping homeowners in their homes. The Treasury Department and HUD supported the formation of this alliance to help stabilize the mortgage market. Use the site to learn more about FHASecure and Project Lifeline. How can these programs help troubled homeowners?

www.cengage.com/school/pfinance/banking

The rise in demand for mortgage-backed securities generated an increase in the number of annual ratings. Firms were often either understaffed or had insufficient time to perform a full risk analysis of the securities. Sometimes analysts needed to issue ratings even though they did not have time to complete their analysis. Analysts are expected to assess the risk of a security without knowing who is issuing or selling the security. In some instances, this process of shielding an analyst from the corporate ownership of securities they were analyzing was violated. When analysts knew that the firm's profits could be impacted by a nonfavorable rating, that impacted the rating assigned to the security.

A number of investments received an AAA bond rating even though they were backed by subprime mortgages. An AAA bond rating is the highest rating a security can receive and means that the repayment of interest and principal is expected to be stable and reliable. Many of the mortgage-backed securities that received AAA bond ratings lost a substantial amount of their value.

Who Owns My Loan?

Distressed homeowners who seek out credit counseling may be able to develop a plan that could enable them to make monthly mortgage payments. Sometimes this plan hinges on renegotiating the interest rate that is in effect on their mortgage. Homeowners who have loans that have been sold multiple times and whose loans are now part of some large pool of mortgage-backed securities often have a difficult time determining who owns their mortgage. If they cannot determine who is holding their mortgage, they cannot negotiate new interest rates.

flat world...

The International Impact of the Mortgage Crisis

Just as a stone thrown in a pond makes a ripple effect throughout the water, the U.S. mortgage crisis has sent shockwaves through financial systems across the globe. In April 2008, the International Monetary Fund (IMF) estimated that the U.S. subprime mortgage crisis could cause global losses of about $1 trillion. The euro zone is the second largest economy in the world. In June 2008, the euro zone experienced an inflation rate of 4 percent. The central bank of the euro zone had targeted inflation to be about 2 percent. By July 2008, European banks with investments in securities backed by U.S. mortgages suffered losses.

There was a tightening of European lending and a rise in European interest rates as a result of these losses. Countries that exported products to the U.S. received fewer orders because U.S. consumers had less money available to spend on nonessential items.

Think Critically
Investigate current ramifications of the mortgage crisis online. In this age of global financial interdependence, what steps can individual economies take to shield themselves from financial exposure due to investments in other countries?

The Fallout

Just as investors hungry for a large profit drove up demand for mortgage-backed securities, which caused housing prices to escalate, now the opposite has happened. With mortgage-backed securities failing, investors are no longer seeking them out as investments. The credit market is tightening up. It is harder for consumers to obtain credit or mortgages. People are buying fewer houses. Housing prices are declining.

During the first half of 2008, some sobering estimates were made. One estimate was that by the time the crisis concludes, 25 percent of U.S. homes will have **negative equity**. When the amount owed on a home is more than the current value of the home, then negative equity occurs. If a homeowner with negative equity faces foreclosure, it might make financial sense to not fight the foreclosure.

A second estimate was that 3 million to 4 million homeowners are expected to experience foreclosure. An inability to make monthly payments on high-interest subprime loans will cause these homeowners to lose their homes.

 checkpoint

List five loan products that were developed to support loosened loan qualification standards.

assessment 8.5

Think Critically

1. What motivated lenders to shift from funding mortgage loans from locally held deposits to funding mortgages with Wall Street financing?

2. Strong relationships within a community help bankers increase their customer base. How would ongoing, personal relationships with customers impact a bank's decision regarding qualifying customers for appropriate loans?

3. Review the description of a AAA bond rating online. What do you think is an appropriate rating for a subprime mortgage-backed security?

4. Look for SIVA, SISA, NINA, or No Income, No Asset, No Employment loans online. Are they still available? List reasons explaining their current level of availability.

Make Academic Connections

5. **COMMUNICATION**   The Humane Society, recognizing that the mortgage crisis is preventing people from keeping their pets, has instituted a grant program to help agencies reach out to pet owners with ideas for keeping their pets. These pets are suffering downstream effects of the mortgage crisis. What other parts of society, either living entities or businesses, are being affected by the crisis? Prepare a chart describing the affected entities and how they are affected. Share the chart with the class.

6. **THE RIGHT DECISION**   During July 2008, the *Cleveland Plain Dealer* featured three local lending institutions that were in solid financial condition despite the mortgage lending crisis. They shared a common trait of maintaining conservative lending standards. The names of these banks are Valley Savings, First Federal of Lakewood, and Third Federal Savings. Research these banks online to see how they are doing today. How do you think their conservative approaches affected their longevity?

chapter 8 **assessment**

Chapter Summary

8.1 Mortgage Lending
A. A mortgage is a note secured by real property.
B. Mortgage lenders provide many types of loan products for buying a home.

8.2 Mortgage Loan Processing
A. Monthly mortgage payments to lenders usually consist of principal, interest, taxes, and insurance (PITI).
B. Six steps in the mortgage approval process are application, documentation, underwriting, drawing documents, closing, and recording.

8.3 Mortgages and the Law
A. Consumer protection legislation applies to mortgage lending as well as other loans.
B. Lenders must comply with numerous housing-specific laws.

8.4 Government-Backed Loans
A. The government backs some loans by guaranteeing to repay the lender if the borrower defaults.
B. Mortgage programs like FHA loans, VA loans, and others make loans possible to people who might not otherwise qualify.

8.5 The Mortgage Crisis
A. Historically, mortgages were a sound, safe investment because they provided a reliable, steady income stream.
B. The mortgage crisis was caused by a combination of factors including an increased demand for mortgage-backed securities, lowered lending criteria, and bond ratings that were issued without due diligence.

Vocabulary Builder

a. adjustable rate mortgage
b. balloon mortgage
c. buy-down mortgage
d. escrow
e. Fannie Mae
f. fixed rate mortgage
g. foreclosure
h. Freddie Mac
i. Ginnie Mae
j. loan-to-value (LTV)
k. mortgage
l. mortgage-backed securities
m. mortgage origination
n. negative equity
o. PITI
p. point
q. redlining
r. shared appreciation mortgage (SAM)

Choose the term that best fits the definition. Write the letter of the answer in the space provided. Some terms may not be used.
___ 1. Value of loan compared to value of asset
___ 2. Prepaying part of the interest to get a lower mortgage rate
___ 3. When banks refuse to lend in certain neighborhoods
___ 4. Mortgage with changing interest rate
___ 5. A note secured by real property
___ 6. A value equal to 1 percent of loan principal
___ 7. A mortgage in which the entire remaining balance of the loan is due in one single payment
___ 8. Principal, interest, taxes, and insurance
___ 9. Conventional mortgage
___ 10. When the amount owed on a home is more than the current value of the home

Review Concepts

11. What is a mortgage?

_____

_____

12. What is a foreclosure?

_____

_____

13. List four types of traditional mortgages and five types of mortgages associated with the mortgage crisis.

_____

_____

_____

14. What distinguishes the mortgage crisis mortgages from the traditional mortgages?

_____

_____

_____

_____

15. Define equity and negative equity.

_____

_____

_____

16. Why is it significant that Fannie Mae and Freddie Mac are GSEs?

_____

_____

17. What is the LTV ratio and why is it important to lenders?

_____

_____

_____

18. What role did bond ratings play in the mortgage crisis?

_____

_____

19. List three consumer protection laws that apply to mortgage lending.

_____

_____

_____

20. What are the consumer and business implications of the Community Reinvestment Act (CRA)?

_____

_____

_____

21. To comply with RESPA, what must lenders disclose to borrowers?

_____

_____

_____

_____

22. How do government-backed loans differ from conventional loans?

_____

_____

_____

23. According to _Inside Mortgage Finance_, subprime mortgages were 20% of all mortgages in 2005 and 2006. In the last quarter of 2007, subprime mortgages were 14% of all mortgages; by the second quarter of 2007, they were only about 8% of the total. What does the drop in the percent of subprime mortgages mean? How will the drop impact the economy?

_____

_____

_____

24. Explain how a buy-down mortgage works.

_____

_____

Apply What You Learned

25. Under traditional circumstances, why does obtaining a mortgage initiate the most thorough credit review most consumers will ever undergo?

_____

_____

_____

26. What factors does a lender judge in order to assess consumer capability?

_____

_____

27. How will the HOEPA revisions announced during July 2008 help restore stability to the mortgage loan market?

28. Why does the government have an interest in guaranteeing loans for private purposes?

Make Academic Connections

29. **BANKING MATH**   Calculate the PMI (private mortgage insurance) for a principal balance of $125,500. Assume the PMI rate is ½ of 1 percent of the borrowed principal.

30. **TECHNOLOGY**   Use the Internet to learn more about the impact of technology on the real estate and mortgage industries. Prepare an oral report on what you learn.

31. **HISTORY**   Learn more about past discriminatory practices, such as redlining, that led to various consumer protection laws in the mortgage lending industry. Write a one-page report on the topic.

32. **COMMUNICATION**   Interview a mortgage lender in your community. Find out what lenders like to see from an applicant, and make a top-ten list of things homebuyers can do to increase their chances of getting mortgages for their dream homes.

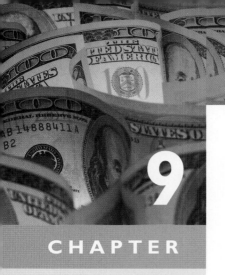

CHAPTER 9

Commercial Lending

9.1	Commercial Loans
9.2	Commercial Credit Analysis
9.3	Small Business Loan Programs
9.4	The 2008 Financial Crisis

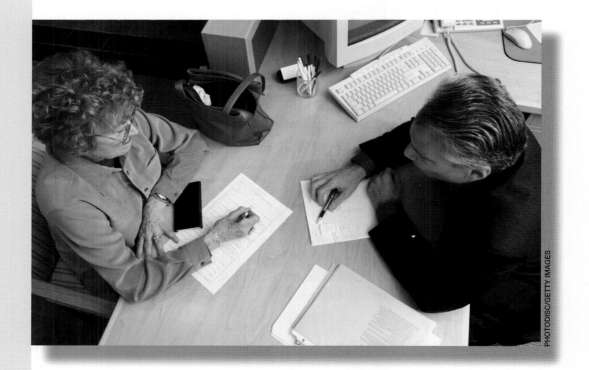

PHOTODISC/GETTY IMAGES

climbing the ladder

From Commercial Banking Associate to Portfolio Manager

After Hillary sent her youngest child to college, she began to consider how much longer she needed to work and what positions she would like to have before she retired.

Hillary reflected on her past experience. To establish a college fund, Hillary had spent a few years after high school working as a commercial business banking associate. Providing administrative support to commercial lenders, Hillary helped prepare credit memos so loan authorities could make decisions on requests for new credit and renewals. She worked with the bank's small business administration department to prepare loans for closing. She made sure that post-closing requirements were met. If a loan request was denied or modified, Hillary helped prepare a denial letter that complied with government regulations.

The experience Hillary gained in commercial lending helped her obtain summer internships during college as an assistant commercial loan underwriter for the financial services subsidiary of an auto manufacturer. With supervisory oversight, Hillary performed credit analyses for dealer financing products. She evaluated loan requests that included floorplan lines of credit, revolving credit lines, and wholesale lease lines of credit. She helped review existing wholesale relationships to determine if any risk factors had changed.

Hillary's first full-time job after college utilized her prior commercial lending experience. Working as a commercial lending officer, Hillary developed and maintained profitable account relationships. She also managed a small commercial loan portfolio.

Hillary's skill at managing the small commercial loan portfolio led to her current position as a commercial portfolio manager. Working with large loan customers, Hillary formulated credit strategies to enhance business service. Focusing on industry constraints, credit exposure, and the specific needs of each borrower enabled Hillary to develop customized loan products. Hillary worked with customers to develop performance metrics for their businesses. She helped customers measure actual performance to planned performance. Hillary made on-site visits to customer locations to assess the on-going health of the business. Her close working relationship with individual customers helped her proactively identify and manage any potential changes to credit risk. She had developed a strong reputation within the community, which helped her bring new clients to the bank.

Upper Rungs to Consider

Hillary has decided she likes her current job. She excels at it. She is comfortable staying in the job until she retires. However, to help the bank remain competitive in future years, Hillary is going to seek out mentoring and training opportunities to help develop the skills of the next generation of employees.

Preparing for the Climb

To successfully manage commercial loans, it is critically important to have a thorough understanding of the industries and geographical areas in which you approve loans. What is the best way to develop specialized knowledge for a particular industry or geographical area?

PHOTODISC

9.1

Commercial Loans

goals

+ List purposes for commercial loans.

+ Identify types of commercial loans.

+ Identify types of businesses.

terms

+ commercial lending

+ term loan

+ short-term loan

+ factoring

+ merchandiser

+ manufacturer

Banking Scene

Gloria Velez successfully obtained a house mortgage and was happy with the way that transaction went. Her job sometimes frustrated her, and she began to toy with the idea of starting her own business. To do this, she realized she would need to obtain a loan. Before going very far with the idea, she knew she would have to write some sort of a business plan. What are the components of a good business plan?

THE NATURE OF COMMERCIAL LENDING ● ● ● ● ● ● ● ● ● ● ● ● ●

Just as consumer loans allow you to have things you could not otherwise readily afford, commercial lending makes it possible for businesses to accomplish what they might otherwise never achieve. **Commercial lending**, as its name makes clear, is lending to business enterprises. Commercial lending is for businesses, but commercial lending practices may apply to individuals as well, such as a person who is buying rental property. Although perhaps less visible to the everyday citizen, commercial lending is actually a larger dollar market than consumer and mortgage lending. If you're trying to finance a $200,000 house, imagine financing a $2 million building. If you're concerned about paying utilities and taxes on a house, multiply that by the needs of a typical business and its employees.

Banks and other financial institutions are keenly interested in this market and usually maintain specialists dedicated to commercial lending. Large banks dominate this field, although some small banks establish niches in their own communities. Although the underlying principles of sound lending apply to commercial as well as consumer lending, some of the products and analyses differ in their complexity. The best commercial loan officers understand thoroughly the business their customers are in and look for effective and efficient ways to structure financing. Business needs may be variable as well as complex, and creative financial solutions can make the difference between success and failure. A private citizen can probably live without financing debt (although not easily in today's world). Almost no business can. One key to success in commercial enterprises is growth, and the careful acquisition and use of debt makes growth possible. Commercial loans are good business for lenders, businesses, and the people they serve.

Commercial Loan Purposes

Commercial lending markets and customers may vary widely in size and scope. Whether it's a small one-person printing franchise in your neighborhood or a multinational hotel empire, businesses face many of the same challenges in terms of remaining adequately capitalized. Some of the purposes for commercial lending include the following.

PHOTODISC/GETTY IMAGES

- **Real Estate** Commercial real estate requirements differ from private residential mortgages, although many of the analyses are similar. Because facilities often need to be developed or redeveloped, and there may be local government issues involved, acquiring commercial real estate is a large and complex process. Even for investment real estate for residential purposes, the lending analysis is not quite so simple as for buying a home and requires a close look at the property as a business asset.

- **Construction** Closely linked, and often part of the same financing package as real estate loans, construction loans are a significant part of the commercial lending business. The size of construction loans often makes them subject to careful analysis of the value, purpose, and even design of the construction, as well as the overall financial position of the borrowing business. In order to assess whether the construction supports the loan value, underwriters must judge the worth of the building within it business function and its potential market value beyond the business.

- **Equipment** Most businesses need equipment to operate, and equipment is often the greatest start-up cost of new businesses. Because the value of equipment over time changes, equipment loans are often tied to the overall cash flow, business plan, and financial position of the borrower as well as to the equipment itself. This change in value, called *depreciation*, requires that the loan officer understand fully the function, use, and effective lifetime of the equipment for the business.

- **Operations** Cash flow is an unending concern of business. Whether funding is needed to purchase inventory or supplies, meet unexpected expenses, or even hold the company over through a difficult time, operations expenses are often part of a commercial lending package. Here, perhaps, is where a loan officer may need the most in-depth understanding of a business to assess the risk adequately. Operations expenses are sometimes seasonal or cyclical, as in agriculture and textile industries, and ongoing patterns of lending and repayment are part of the day-to-day life of these businesses. Many financial institutions involve themselves deeply with client businesses on a daily basis, managing cash flow, lines of credit, debt servicing, and operations costs as part of a total business relationship with the customer.

✔ checkpoint

Name four purposes for commercial loans.

TYPES OF COMMERCIAL LOANS • • • • • • • • • • • • • • • • • • •

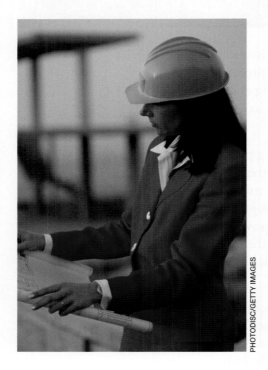

PHOTODISC/GETTY IMAGES

There is a wide range of commercial loan products available, and they offer considerable flexibility. Like consumer loans, commercial loans are secured or unsecured, depending on the type of loan, and vary widely in terms and rates. Just like individuals, businesses have credit ratings too, and the type and availability of funds depends on their track record and income prospects.

Term Loans

Most **term loans** finance permanent working capital, equipment, real estate, business expansion, or acquisition of another business. Terms and rates vary with the asset securing the loan or the expected life of the asset. Many varieties of commercial loans are available, such as fixed rate, adjustable rate, and balloon loans. Adjustable rate loans operate just as they do in the consumer sector, with rates tied to indexes as outlined in the loan contract, usually including caps and floors. Balloon loans, although somewhat risky for the individual, are more common in commercial lending because they often offer more advantageous rates. As the loan matures, the borrower may sell the property to meet the balloon or may refinance the note. Still, careful analysis is necessary, because business conditions at maturity may be hard to estimate and refinancing can become difficult or expensive.

Short-Term Loans

Most **short-term loans** are for a year or less, and a business may have many of them in sequence or even concurrently to finance expenses. Most short-term loans are used for seasonal or cyclical business costs, such as increasing inventory or maintaining the business until predictable receivables arrive. Short-term does not necessarily mean small. Short-term financing is a regular part of big business, and large short-term loans are common. Depending on the credit rating of the business, short-term loans are frequently unsecured, leading to trouble for lenders and borrowers if business goes poorly. Monitoring business conditions and performance is an important part of the loan analyst's job. Most short-term loans require lump-sum payment at maturity. However, businesses often refinance short-term debt as well, rolling debt servicing into part of their ongoing operations costs.

Lines of Credit

Lines of credit for businesses work just as they do for individuals. The lender provides cash in the form of regular amounts, single disbursements, or a credit account to a business to cover routinely occurring expenses. Credit lines often finance contract work (which may not be paid until complete), inventory, or receivable intervals. They may also be used for day-to-day expenses, depending upon the lender's relationship with the borrower. Essentially, a line of credit is an open-ended loan, and though it has no specific term, its rates and conditions vary with the particular lending agreement.

Real Estate and Equipment Loans

Particular commercial mortgage loans for real estate and equipment are tied to and secured by the asset being purchased. These loans may also vary in terms and rates, but, depending on the equipment or real estate, they are typically long-term notes with 10- to 20-year repayment periods. Usually, the loan-to-value relationship (LTV) is limited to around 75 percent for real estate and anywhere from 60 to 80 percent for equipment. Second and third mortgages are also available for commercial real estate in amounts dependent on the first mortgage principal and the property value. However, second and third mortgages affect the overall debt structure of the business.

Contract Financing

Contract financing is secured by the value of a specific contract and allows for an orderly flow of funds to a company or organization performing services under contract. Funds are advanced as the work is performed, and contract payments often go directly to the lender until the obligation is satisfied.

Bridge Loans

Bridge loans are a particular form of short-term loan used to cover expenses until long-term financing is in place. Bridge loans are especially important in start-up enterprises or in complex transactions where many separate purchases, developments, or sales depend upon each other. Timing may be difficult to coordinate in such deals, and bridge loans offer a way to keep the business rolling.

Leasing

Many lenders finance leases for businesses, usually with lease terms of three to five years. The advantage of leasing is that it can allow businesses to possess needed equipment for less total cost than they would be obligated for if they bought the equipment. Lenders review the business and the equipment just as they would any other type of loan. At the end of the lease period, the business might return the equipment, buy the equipment, or renew the lease.

Asset-Based Loans

Another type of financing is called *asset-based lending*. Banks analyze profit and loss (P&L) statements, tax returns, and business plans to make lending decisions based on business income. Lenders of asset-based loans secure the loans with the overall assets of the business, including equipment, inventory, and accounts receivable, rather than just business income or a specific piece of equipment. A form of asset-based lending called **factoring** advances cash to a business in exchange for its receivables. The amount advanced is usually some percentage of the accounts. The factor then collects the invoices, forwarding the money to the borrower less fees and interest kept by the factor. Most businesses seeking asset-based lending are those that do not easily qualify for other types of loans, such as new businesses without a track record or businesses with high potential that has not yet been realized.

✔ checkpoint

What is a bridge loan?

TYPES OF BUSINESSES ●

Businesses can be categorized in a number of ways. Business ownership can be classified as sole proprietorship (one person as the owner), partnerships (two or more persons), or corporations (entities that have the legal authority to their own rights, privileges, and liabilities distinct from those of their members). Another way is to categorize businesses as to whether they are *merchandisers* (they sell goods or services) or *manufacturers* (they build items to sell to merchandisers). Merchandisers and manufacturers have similar yet somewhat specialized needs for commercial loans.

Merchandisers

You do business with **merchandisers** on a daily business. Think of the local independent shops that sell groceries, repair appliances, sell T-shirts, prepare your income taxes, sell ice cream, as well as the services you receive from the plumber, the dentist, the veterinarian, and the hairdresser or barber. These businesses must generate income to support themselves. Income can vary from month to month for some businesses. Consider a small local nursery. Its business is typically seasonal: in the spring and summer, its busiest seasons, it sells trees, shrubs, flowers, lawn equipment, fertilizer, and so on. In the early fall, sales include end-of-season

flowers and trees, and perhaps pumpkins, Indian corn, and cornstalks. In the winter, its sales are limited primarily to Christmas trees, greenery, and other seasonal items. Can its income from the spring and summer support the business from fall to spring? Even if the nursery were to close during the winter, it will still have most, if not all, of the following obligations:

- Mortgage or rent payments

- Utilities

- Insurance—property (and health for owners and/or employees if offered)

- Auto loan payments

- Payments for inventory purchased earlier

- Salaries or incentives to keep employees during the downtime

- Income and sales taxes and any employee-related taxes

In addition to these expenses, the company must order inventory for the new spring season.

Managing cash flow is one of the most difficult aspects of running a business, and loans may need to be acquired to help with cash flow.

PHOTODISC/GETTY IMAGES

The time to obtain the best terms for any loan or credit arrangement is to anticipate needs rather than waiting until a crisis arises before seeking out money. In addition to offering loans, bankers have expertise to help business owners plan to meet all of their financial needs and have cash when they need it.

A specific problem for some businesses is extremely costly inventory. The auto industry, for example, maintains expensive inventory. Even a small auto dealer may need 10 versions of a new model (with different features and colors), each of which has a dealer cost of $18,000, or $180,000. Add to this the various other models it must keep on hand to be competitive, with all their versions, and the costs can quickly skyrocket. Banks offer floorplan loans to meet the inventory financing needs of such small and mid-sized businesses. These plans include competitive features such as flexible credit limits to accommodate seasonal needs and market fluctuations as well as model-year buildups, plus Internet access to their inventory.

Manufacturers

Although their focus is making or building items for others to sell, **manufacturers,** whether large or small, have the same basic needs that merchandisers have. They cannot meet orders to make their products unless they have the cash or other arrangements to purchase raw materials that compose their products, support research and development, maintain buildings and equipment, and pay employees.

Manufacturers are impacted by industry conditions. Between 2007 and 2008, the price of crude oil doubled from about $60 per barrel to about $120 per barrel. As oil is used both as a raw material in manufactured products and as an energy source to manufacture products, the rapid increase in price drove up manufacturing costs across industries. Increased manufacturing costs can drive up demand for working capital loans.

Many banks have loan officers who are extremely knowledgeable about various industries and can help these companies plan their financial needs. These bankers can, for example, suggest ways to make arrangements with suppliers for ordering and managing inventory items.

 checkpoint

What is the difference between merchandisers and manufacturers?

assessment 9.1

Think Critically

1. Identify three major differences between consumer lending and commercial lending.

2. Why is it essential that loan analysts understand the nature of a business, not just the balance sheets, to determine the soundness of a loan?

3. How is it possible that a bank might make poor loans to a long-time commercial customer?

Make Academic Connections

4. **COMMUNICATION** Interview a realtor to determine the differences between selling commercial real estate and residential real estate. Uncover differences in the lending analysis process for both types of real estate.

5. **SOCIAL STUDIES** Small and new businesses are a vital part of our economy. These businesses could not survive, however, without financial backing. How do you think commercial loans help the economy?

6. **COMMUNICATION** Interview a commercial loan officer. Ask the loan officer to explain the job to you, including required education, experience, and training. Present a brief oral report to the class.

7. **RESEARCH** Identify a merchandising company or a manufacturing company with which you are familiar. Research and describe the type of inventory this company is likely to stock.

9.2

goals

+ Identify basic ratios used in commercial underwriting.

+ List other items used to evaluate commercial loans.

+ Explain the importance of disclosure in commercial loans.

+ Explain the mortgage crisis ripple effect.

terms

+ debt ratio

+ debt service coverage ratio (DSCR)

Commercial Credit Analysis

Banking Scene

To prepare for starting her own business, Gloria Velez has developed a business plan. She intends to share this plan with the lender when applying for a loan to finance her new business. Besides the business plan, what other things do you think Gloria will need to provide the lender to help her obtain a loan?

COMMERCIAL CREDIT ANALYSIS TOOLS

Commercial credit analysis is not in principle a great deal different from the process used for consumer loans. The same general steps and ideas apply, but with some modifications. Assessing an individual's employment, income, and current amount of debt is necessary to determine an individual's ability to repay a loan. Analyzing a business can be far more complicated. Past financial statements are studied. Underwriters estimate the likelihood of the business' future success. The relationship between the bank and the company is also significant.

In the case of large corporations, evaluating those prospects can be an extremely complex process. Lenders hire or employ professional financial analysts to carefully study as much as can be determined about a company's financial position. Whether a company is large or small, the financial analysis for a particular loan often comes down to the results of three measurements. Though making the measurements may be complicated, the results determine whether the loan makes sense.

Debt Ratio

Debt ratio for businesses is not much different from the debt ratio of consumers. **Debt ratio** is the total obligations compared to the total income.

The formula for calculating debt ratio is simple. Debt ratio equals the debt obligation divided by income for some period of time.

Debt ratio = Debt ÷ Income

For example, in a given month, if your income is $3,000 and your monthly debt is $1,500, you have a debt ratio of $3,000 ÷ $1,500 = 0.5, or 50 percent. If you have a debt ratio of 200 percent, in which your debt is twice your income, you have a problem. Lenders usually will not consider a candidate with a debt ratio above 40 percent.

Assessing the debt ratio may be a major task in the case of a corporation, for merely compiling all the numbers can be a large job. Most of the processing of a commercial loan application is an attempt to verify the numbers that the prospective borrower provides.

Loan-to-Value (LTV) Ratio

Another critical ratio is loan-to-value. The loan-to-value ratio is the principal amount of the loan divided by the value of the securing property, just as it is in residential mortgages.

Loan-to-value ratio = Principal ÷ Market value

Lenders for commercial mortgages tend to be more conservative than for residential ones. Lenders look for a loan-to-value ratio of 80 percent maximum and often will not lend more than 60 percent of the appraised value.

The principle of loan-to-value gets complicated when you consider other types of business property such as equipment. Unlike real estate, which usually appreciates, or becomes more valuable, most business property depreciates, or loses value. Although depreciation offers tax breaks, it complicates securing a loan. Information technology equipment, for example, which becomes obsolete quickly, depreciates so rapidly that it's virtually worthless in a few years. How much can you get for a used computer? Lenders analyze those types of loans by carefully considering the overall health of company finances.

Debt Service Coverage Ratio

A more sophisticated tool for assessing a company's overall debt structure is the debt service coverage ratio. Used extensively for commercial real estate, it also provides a look at a company's overall position. The **debt service coverage ratio (DSCR)** compares net operating income to the total cost of debt. Net operating income is gross income minus expenses, taxes, insurance, utilities, and so on. Note that net operating income does not include the cost of debt for mortgages or other debts for equipment, services, and other such things. Compiling these numbers may not be a simple task because there may be many items from many sources to be considered and verified. When net operating income is divided by the total cost of debt service, it yields the debt service coverage ratio.

Debt service coverage ratio = Net operating income ÷ Total debt service

Consider a small business with a $650,000 net operating income on a gross income of $1 million. Assume that the total cost of servicing the debt of the business, including all principal and interest but not counting taxes or insurance, which were taken out already to derive net operating income, is $520,000. Dividing $650,000 by $520,000 yields a DSCR of 1.25.

A lender wants to see the highest DSCR possible, for the higher the DSCR, the more net operating income is available for debt service. The higher the total debt service cost rises, the lower the DSCR falls. A ratio of less than 1.0 indicates a negative cash flow. Different lenders may require different levels of DSCR. Conservative lenders might seek 1.25 or higher, while other lenders would accept 1.20 or 1.10. Only rarely will a lender accept a DSCR near or below 1.0, and then only when there are strong mitigating reasons, such as other sources of potential income or a clear indication of a future upsurge of net operating income.

 checkpoint

List three analytical tools used to evaluate commercial lending.

OTHER EVALUATION

In order to perform ratio and other analyses of a company's finances, lenders want full access to company financial records. Remember that verification of capability is far more complex and difficult in the case of a business than in the case of an individual. In addition, changing business conditions may alter a company's profitability rapidly. Only by understanding the true nature of a company's financial position can a lender hope to make a sound decision. Typically, lenders want to examine the following:

- Federal and state income tax returns for three years

- Company financial statements for three years (all assets and liabilities and pro-forma profit and loss statements)

- Year-to-date profit and loss and balance statements

- Projected cash flow estimates for at least the coming year

- Valuations and appraisals for collateral used to secure the loan

- Written business plan (for small businesses)

- Personal financial statements of owners (for new or small businesses)

Only by knowing the complete picture can a lender make an informed decision about a loan. As in all of the lending industry, competition has sometimes led lenders to less strict underwriting, which can lead to defaulted loans. Bank examiners review commercial lending policies just as they do consumer loans, and in times when larger numbers of bad loans are being made, examiners conduct more stringent examinations.

checkpoint

Why does a lender need access to a company's financial records?

DISCLOSURES

Unlike consumer lending, most commercial lending is regulated only by the terms of the loan agreement and some state laws. The assumption is that both parties to the loan are business professionals and can comprehend and negotiate the loan agreement with terms to which all parties agree. Still, it is in the interest of the business relationship to make sure that all terms are explained and understood, as both parties seek to prosper from the loan.

Although it is fraud to falsify records for the purposes of acquiring a loan, desperate businesses hoping to refinance large amounts or forestall collapse sometimes provide inaccurate or incomplete information. Sometimes close relationships between lenders and businesses themselves lead to poorly underwritten loans. A financial collapse can doom not only the company that

Banking Math *Connection*

Banks typically use the debt ratio, the loan-to-value ratio, and the debt service coverage ratio to determine if a commercial loan is viable. Using the following data, calculate each ratio.

Monthly income	$4,500
Monthly debt	$1,250
Loan principal	$30,000
Market value	$45,000
Gross income	$160,000
Net operating income	$100,000
Total cost of debt	$85,000

Solution

Debt	÷ Income	= Debt ratio
$1,250	÷ $4,500	= 0.28 or 28 percent

Principal	÷ Market value	= Loan-to-value ratio
$30,000	÷ $45,000	= 0.67 or 67 percent

Net operating income	÷ Total debt service	= Debt service coverage ratio
$100,000	÷ $85,000	= 1.18

undertook the loan, and sometimes the lender, but also the personal finances and even the pensions of employees who had no part in the fraud. It is the ethical and professional responsibility of all parties involved with commercial lending to see that loans are honestly and soundly underwritten.

✔ checkpoint

Why isn't commercial lending as heavily regulated as consumer lending?

THE MORTGAGE CRISIS RIPPLE EFFECT • • • • • • • • • • •

The Office of the Comptroller of the Currency (OCC) conducts an annual survey of national banks to determine trends in lending standards and credit risks as reflected in underwriting practices. The survey that was released in June 2008 reflected trends for about 83 percent of total loans in national banks. These loans had a value of $3.7 trillion.

Tightened Underwriting Standards

In response to the economic uncertainty caused by either nonperforming or under-performing mortgage loans, banks tightened their underwriting

Ethics in Action

You work as the accountant for a large manufacturing company. The company has fallen on hard times recently due to increased competition throughout the industry. The company is seeking a loan to buy new, state-of-the-art equipment to improve its operations, in turn making it more competitive in the market. After reviewing the company's finances, the president of the company is concerned that it cannot obtain a loan in its current financial state. She asks you to "rework" the financial statements and inflate earnings by reducing some of the recent debt taken on by the company. She thinks this will help secure the loan. The president feels that no harm is done because the company will increase profits in the long run with the new business it will acquire after the acquisition of the new equipment.

Think Critically

Do you agree or disagree with the president? Explain why. If the loan is obtained and financial disaster ensues, whom will this ultimately affect?

standards for both commercial and retail loans. The poorly performing mortgage loans affected not just the mortgage loan portfolios directly, but also the investment products that were backed by the mortgage loans.

Reasons banks cited in the OCC study for tightening underwriting standards included a shift in appetite for risk, less market liquidity, the slowing in the residential real estate market, and the overall state of the economy. Specific ways that underwriting standards were tightened include increasing the credit spread for hightened credit risk, increasing the number of conditions written into the loans, lowering LTV ratios, and increasing collateral requirements.

The Federal Reserve conducts a quarterly survey of bank lending practices by soliciting input from senior loan officers. The results of this survey are consistent with the OCC findings. The chart below summarizes the trend for tightening lending standards.

The OCC's annual report on bank lending trends provides a wealth of current information on lending trends. Access www.cengage.com/school/pfinance/banking and click on the link for Chapter 9. Go to the OCC site. Glance at the 2008 report. Search the site for the most current report. How have lending trends changed? What are the reasons for the changes?

www.cengage.com/school/pfinance/banking

Measures of Supply and Demand for C&I Loans, by Size of Firm Seeking Loan

Net Percentage of Domestic Respondents Tightening Standards for C&I Loans

SOURCE: APRIL 2008 SENIOR LOAN OFFICER OPINION SURVEY ON BANK LENDING PRACTICES BY THE FEDERAL RESERVE BOARD.

✔ checkpoint

What caused banks to increase underwriting standards for commercial loans?

assessment 9.2

Think Critically

1. Why is the credit analysis process so much more detailed for commercial loans versus consumer loans?

_____

_____

2. What does a company's debt ratio reveal to the lender?

_____

_____

_____

3. What things can a lender learn from reviewing a company's financial statements?

_____

_____

_____

Make Academic Connections

4. **BANKING MATH** Assume that a small business owner has come to you with a loan request. Your careful analysis of the records shows a net operating income of $875,000 and total debt of $798,000, including the new loan. According to the debt service coverage ratio, is this a good candidate for a loan? Why or why not?

_____

_____

5. **RESEARCH** Locate the website of a commercial lender. Gather some background information on the lender and list some of its services and the various types of loans it offers.

6. **PROBLEM SOLVING** Assume you just obtained a loan to finance new equipment for your business. You later discover that the lender did not disclose all terms of the loan and that your interest rate will not remain fixed throughout the life of the loan as you had discussed. What recourse can you take?

_____

_____

_____

Small Business Loan Programs

goals

+ Describe the purpose of the SBA.

+ Explain SBA loan eligibility requirements.

+ Identify SBA loan options.

terms

+ Small Business Administration (SBA)

Banking Scene

Gloria Velez learned quickly that she didn't have the resources or the track record to obtain conventional funding for a business loan. She kept her job, but began to work hard on her own time to learn more about running her own business. She turned to the government. She had gone to college on government-backed loans, and it occurred to her that there might be similar programs to help new businesses. What might be a good way for Gloria to start searching the vast amount of information available from the U.S. government?

THE SMALL BUSINESS ADMINISTRATION

The **Small Business Administration (SBA)** offers a number of financial, technical, and management programs to help businesses. The SBA grew out of a Depression-era agency, the Reconstruction Finance Corporation (RFC), a lending program for businesses of any size hurt by the Depression. The Department of Commerce's Office of Small Business, primarily an advisory agency, and RFC functions were combined in 1952 into the Small Business Administration.

The definition of a small business varies. The SBA correlates business size to industry codes that are defined in the North American Industry Classification System (NAICS). A comprehensive table of these codes is available on the SBA website. Classification as a small business is based either on the number of employees or the average annual revenue of a firm. As an example, in wholesale or trade businesses, a small business is one that has 100 or fewer employees, and in manufacturing businesses, a small business has 500 or fewer employees.

Of course, small businesses can and do seek financing through many avenues. Commercial lending is available from many sources. Many small or new firms, however, don't easily qualify for standard commercial loans. As in consumer lending, credit scoring is critical in commercial lending. Things may not be easy for those small firms that don't have cash flow or collateral to qualify.

The SBA has an ongoing mission of education and assistance for small businesses. There's nothing small about the project, though. A report commissioned by the SBA Office of Advocacy stated that there were $685 billion in small business loans outstanding for the years 2006–2007. For purposes of the study, loans under $1 million were considered small business loans. About twenty five million loans from about 8,600 lending institutions contributed to this total.

The financial assistance the SBA provides to small businesses comes in the form of loan guaranties. The loan guaranty program guarantees a lender that if the borrower defaults, the SBA will repay most of the loan. The SBA guarantees between 50 percent and 100 percent of the loan funds depending on the size of the loan and terms.

Borrowers apply to and receive funds from lenders, who must approve the loans. The SBA reviews the loans as well and provides the lender a written authorization of the guaranty. The basic interest rate of the loan is the Wall Street Journal Prime Rate (WSJ Prime). Lenders establish their own interest rates based on WSJ Prime plus a few percentage points. The SBA does set interest rate maximums for lenders. Payments go to the lender. Although there is more paperwork involved for both borrower and lender, the added trouble allows the lender to make loans it probably couldn't make without the assurance of SBA backing, and borrowers get funding they probably couldn't get on their own.

Lenders are familiar with SBA loans, and many have SBA application forms either on site or posted on their websites. SBA certified lenders are those that work frequently and well with the SBA, and they have some authority to make their own decisions within the program. They also get faster SBA service. The SBA also maintains a preferred lender program for its best and most reliable lenders. In exchange for a lower rate of guaranty, preferred lenders have full authority to approve SBA loans on their own.

Still, an SBA loan is no free lunch. Borrowers must meet standards set by both the SBA and the lender. Although these standards may be more relaxed than those for other commercial loans, applications are still examined for soundness. Neither the SBA nor the lender wants to get stuck with a bad loan.

How do SBA loans differ from standard commercial loans?

SBA Eligibility ●

Most businesses are eligible for SBA loan guaranties, but the SBA makes a decision on a case-by-case basis, based on the type of program. In general, eligibility is determined by the following.

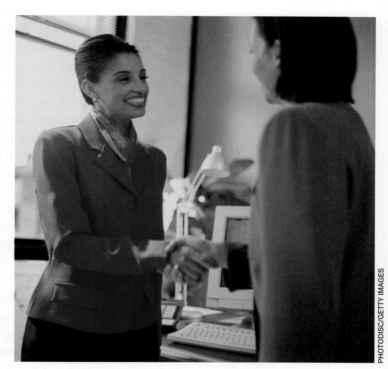

- **Type of Business** Businesses must be operating for profit in the United States or its possessions, have reasonable owner equity, and use other financial alternatives, including personal assets of owners. Some types of businesses are ineligible. Charitable or religious groups, real estate investment, lending, pyramid sales plans, gambling businesses, and businesses engaged in illegal activities may not participate.

- **Size of Business** The SBA has precise definitions of a small business. It must be independently owned and not dominant in its field. When businesses are affiliated, all affiliated parties must meet the size standard for its field of operation, which varies from industry to industry. For example, the miscellaneous store retail size standard is $7 million in revenue, while for agricultural farming businesses, $750,000 is the upper limit.

- **Use of Loan Funds** Although SBA-backed loans may be used for most business purposes, funds cannot be used to finance floor plan needs, to purchase real estate when a commitment has already been made to a developer or for investment, to pay delinquent taxes or to make payments to owners, or to pay existing debt unless it can be shown that refinancing will benefit the business and is not the result of poor management.

Certain other conditions apply in special circumstances, based on the particular field in which the business is engaged.

 checkpoint

What three factors determine SBA loan eligibility?

SBA Loan Terms and Conditions

A borrower seeking an SBA loan must expect to meet all the criteria for a commercial loan. In general, the borrower needs a down payment, which can range from a minimum of 20 percent to as much as 35 percent. Most importantly, the borrower needs to demonstrate that he or she has the experience and knowledge required to run the business successfully. The SBA expects that the loan will be repaid from the normal business cash flow and, therefore, joins the lender in seeking full documentation of the operation of the business. As you saw earlier in this chapter, lenders require federal and state income tax returns, company financial statements, up-to-date P&L statements, projected cash flow estimates, personal financial statements of the owners, and a well-written business plan. Like the lender, the SBA wants to see as much collateral for a loan as possible, but it treats collateral as one part of the overall credit picture.

Maximum loan amounts and the size of the guaranty vary with the particular loan program, as do terms and other conditions. Loan terms may vary from 1 to 20 years, depending on the purpose of the loan. Interest rates are set by the lender but are subject to SBA maximums. Whether the interest rate is fixed or variable is also between the lender and borrower.

7(a) Loan Guaranty

The 7(a) Loan Guaranty program is the SBA's most popular loan program and the foundation of the agency. In 2008, the agency had a loan portfolio of more than $84 billion. Businesses can use the funds to expand or repair facilities, purchase equipment or make improvements, finance receivables, or in some cases, refinance existing debt or purchase land or buildings. Although 7(a) loans are not fully guaranteed by the SBA, lenders can apply to the SBA to have a portion of a loan guaranteed against default. Even with a guarantee, borrowers are still responsible for

loan repayment. The legal maximum for a 7(a) loan is $2 million, but in practice, the SBA says it can generally issue a guaranty up to $1.5 million.

SBA Express Loans

The three types of express loans offered by the SBA are SBA Express, SBA Patriot Express, and Community Express. These loan programs offer quick turnaround time on loans, often within 36 hours. Loan maximums vary

PHOTODISC/GETTY IMAGES

between $250,000 and $500,000 depending on the loan program. Express programs generally follow the 7(a) guidelines.

CAPLines

The CAPLines loan program supports short-term lending for seasonal, contract, or other cyclical capital needs with either short-term loans or revolving lines of credit. Generally, 7(a) guidelines apply.

Microloans

The SBA Microloan program makes funds available to nonprofit intermediary lenders to help small, newly established businesses. A microloan has a maximum value of $100,000. The lending intermediary agrees to provide technical assistance and advice, and the borrower may be required to undergo training or meet planning requirements.

Special-Purpose Programs

There are several special-purpose programs targeted to particular needs or businesses. The U.S. Community Adjustment and Investment Program (CAIP) helps businesses hurt by the North American Free Trade Agreement (NAFTA). The DELTA program helps small businesses affected by defense contract reductions, and there are Economic Injury Disaster loans available in special circumstances.

In addition, the SBA also operates a Small Business Investment Company (SBIC) program, consisting of about 40 for-profit corporations that raise and distribute venture capital to promising businesses. The program has been around since the 1950s but expanded greatly in the 1990s. The SBICs have

"communicate"

Talk to several small business owners about their experiences as entrepreneurs. Compile a list of pros and cons of owning your own business.

branching out

Financial Matchmaking with CDARS

The Certificate of Deposit Account Registry Service (CDARS) offers individuals and businesses an easy way to insure their bank deposits. To provide FDIC insurance coverage for deposits over $100,000, CDARS redistributes the money in an individual's or business's account to other banks. The redistributed money is invested into CDs valued under $100,000. CDARS has a network of banks involved in the program. Essentially, banks trade CDs with one another, so that each bank can make sure their depositors' money, up to $50 million, receives full FDIC insurance coverage. The trading process allows each bank to also receive back the full value of any deposits that they've entered into the system (by accepting CDs from other network banks). In addition to receiving complete FDIC insurance coverage, depositors also achieve streamlined administration of their deposits—one account statement summarizes the locations of all their deposits.

Think Critically
Why is CDARS an appealing idea for businesses? How does this type of financial innovation benefit the economy?

SBA guidelines about how and with whom they invest but operate independently of the SBA on a day-to-day basis. Federal Express and America Online are examples of companies that received funding from SBICs.

Fraud Prevention

The SBA is very serious about making sure that SBA loans go only to businesses that truly meet the small business qualifying criteria. In April 2008, the U.S. Small Business Administration Office of the Inspector General (OIG) reported that they had made 43 indictments and 29 convictions for fraud. The office was continuing to investigate a large fraud case involving at least 76 fraudulent loans totaling over $76 billion involving a variety of businesses that were illegally trying to qualify noneligible loan applicants for SBA guaranteed loans. It is crucially important that all individuals and businesses involved in the loan application and approval process use due diligence to ensure that parties applying for SBA guaranteed loans actually meet the eligibility criteria.

What general criteria must a borrower meet to obtain an SBA loan?

_____

_____

assessment 9.3

Think Critically

1. Why does our society support small businesses?

_____

_____

_____

2. Compare an SBA loan to a standard commercial loan. Why would someone choose one loan over the other?

_____

_____

_____

3. Why do you think most charitable and religious groups are not eligible for SBA help?

_____

_____

_____

4. Why is a well-written business plan an important factor in getting an SBA loan?

_____

_____

_____

Make Academic Connections

5. **COMMUNICATION**   Interview a person in your community who runs a small business. Find out how he or she obtained start-up capital, what the greatest challenges are in running a small business, and what advice or assistance this person has obtained and from what sources. Summarize your interview in a one-page report.

6. **HISTORY**   Learn more about the history of the Small Business Administration. Find out how it changed from an organization intended to support business in general to one dedicated to small businesses. Write a one-page report on the history of the agency.

7. **SOCIAL STUDIES**   Visit the Small Business Administration's website at www.sba.gov. Learn more about emergency relief funds for businesses affected by the September 11, 2001, attacks. Outline the details here.

9.4

The 2008 Financial Crisis

goals

+ Identify the root causes of the 2008 financial crisis.

+ Discuss self-regulation and its effects.

terms

+ risk averse

+ risk preferrer

+ credit default swap (CDS)

+ speculation

+ synthetic financial product

Banking Scene

Gloria Velez has had a successful few years running her own business. She has some extra money she'd like to invest. Although traditional investments, like CDs, are comforting to consider because of the low risk and guaranteed interest rate, she'd prefer to make more money faster. Gloria's heard about a great way to make money with credit default swaps. Although they sound lucrative, she's a little concerned about the uncertainty associated with them. What factors should she consider before making this investment?

THE PROFIT MOTIVE

Most people are interested in making money. Some people rely on traditional ways to produce income, which include working for a corporation, directly selling products or services to individuals or companies, or through making investments. If someone is **risk averse**, he or she would prefer to invest in a product that has very little risk of failure. In exchange for the certainty of the investment, he or she is willing to accept a comparatively low rate of return on the investment. Government bonds and CDs are a few examples of investments that a risk averse investor might select. A **risk preferrer** is an investor who seeks a high level of return on investments. To achieve those high returns, the risk preferrer is willing to invest in assets whose soundness or long term performance is not predictable.

Relying on Each Other

As discussed in Chapter 4, money is a fiat system. Money works as a medium of exchange because everyone agrees on the common definition of the underlying value of the money. Swapping services can also work, as it did on page 102, when friends traded services. Refer to the figure on the next page for a summary of traded services. For the service swapping system to work, each participant must hold up his or her end of the bargain. The services swap has value because everyone has agreed upon the underlying value of the services offered. Imagine what would happen if someone in the system allowed someone else to buy something on credit. And what

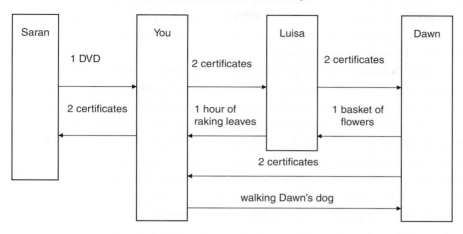

A Fiat System that Functions as an Interdependent Economy

if the person buying on credit could not pay for the product because they did not receive payment for work they did for someone else?

Suppose Dawn allowed Luisa to buy one basket of flowers on credit. Luisa raked leaves for you to earn the money to pay for the flower basket. But you decided, for whatever reason, not to pay Luisa. Income would be lost by Luisa that she could have made by providing a service for someone else. Luisa would be unable to pay Dawn because no wages were received from you. Now Dawn would be unable to pay you for walking her dog. Now multiply this scenario a million times, with payments being continually exchanged among millions of people for millions of products and services. If anyone in the chain fails to receive compensation for their service or product, then he or she will hesitate to participate in the system. The uncompensated participant may withdraw from the trading system and either hold onto his or her product and service or find a new system to participate in.

Revenue Generation from Assets of Dubious Value

A number of products were developed despite having an underlying poor asset value.

Mortgage-Backed Securities A large volume of mortgage-backed securities, which pooled mortgages of various risk values, were sold. These securities did not receive bond ratings that accurately reflected their level of risk. Highly rated securities lost money. Investors were shocked by these losses.

Credit Default Swaps Traditional insurance is based on the idea that a person or business that owns a specific asset, like a home or a manufacturing plant, buys an insurance policy to protect against the risk of damage.

The value of the asset is clearly known. Policy owners can only be an entity with a direct stake in the asset—like a homeowner or corporation insuring their own home or business. The policy holder pays a premium to the insurance company. The insurance company can count on premium payments as a reliable income source.

A **credit default swap (CDS)** is like an insurance product gone awry. If a corporation wants to generate funds without getting a bank loan, then the corporation may issue bonds on the open market. These bonds are for a fixed amount of time and pay investors a fixed rate of return. Bond investors may want to protect themselves from two possible scenarios. First, they want protection from the issuing company defaulting on bond payments. Second, they want protection from tying up their money at a fixed return rate when that return rate could end up being less than return rates in the market. To protect against losses, the buyer of a bond may want to buy a CDS, which is an insurance policy to protect against losses. A third party who is neither the company issuing the bond or the buyer of the bond agrees to provide a CDS for the bond. In exchange for a regular premium, which may be based on a percentage of bond value, the CDS provides insurance against downside risks to the bond holder. In essence, the CDS seller is willing to "bet" that they understand both the financial stability of the company issuing the bond and whether market interest rates will move up or down relative to the bond. The CDS seller is happy to accept a steady income stream from the CDS investor's premium because the CDS seller does not expect to have to pay the CDS investor.

CDS Complicating Factors

There are a number of factors making CDSs more complicated than traditional insurance. Perhaps the most astounding complicating factor is that, unlike a traditional insurance policy where the person or business taking out the policy has a direct ownership stake in the asset being insured, anyone can take out a CDS on anything. For example, say you live in Arizona. Say that, due to growing concerns that global warming will wreak havoc on traditional weather patterns, you predict that hurricane-force winds will damage homes in Ohio. You decide to take out an insurance policy on a friend's home in Ohio. You have absolutely no ownership stake in the home, but you've got a feeling that your friend's home will incur damage from hurricane-force winds. With a CDS, you can, in essence, place a bet on your feelings. **Speculation** occurs when people make investments based on anticipated or hoped-for outcomes, without having an ownership stake in the asset being insured. High risk is associated with speculation.

CDSs are financial products that have a value. To maintain that value, buyers of CDSs need to be financially stable enough to pay their premiums in a timely fashion. Sellers of CDSs need to be stable and have sufficient reserves to pay any claims that arise from their buyers' losses.

Initially developed to insure against downside interest rate risks on a tangible asset, CDSs eventually began to be used to insure against default on securitized investments. For example, once subprime mortgages were pooled into securities, portions of the securitized mortgages were sold off. The portions that had the least risk of default were sold off with the highest ratings. In exchange for the high ratings, a lower rate of return was offered for them. Likewise, portions with a higher risk rate were sold off. A higher return rate was offered on the lower-rated portions to offset the risk. CDSs were developed to insure against default on the securitized mortgages.

There were multiple layers involved. First there were the mortgages, many of which were subprime. Then there were the mortgage-backed securities. Then there were the slices of mortgage-backed securities, all sold with different ratings and returns. Then there were the CDSs. This was a pyramiding financial structure. The structure collapsed because each level of the pyramid was unsound. Each additional level that was added to the pyramid exerted more pressure on the levels beneath it. Each level added to the pyramid was more diluted in actual assets then the level below it. Companies were buying each other's investments. So when one level of the pyramid collapsed, they all came tumbling down.

Another complicating factor is that CDSs are unregulated. There is no limit to the number of people allowed to bet on the trend of someone else's assets. Unlike banks that are required to hold a certain percentage of funds in reserve to cover deposits, CDSs are not subjected to reserve requirements. Because CDSs represent a private deal between two private parties, it is hard to assign a value to the total global CDS market. Likewise, it is also difficult to assess the value of the underlying CDS assets.

Something for Nothing

Because of the potential to earn great sums of money, there are many risk preferring people attracted to certain investment products. With an above-average understanding of financial markets and with a great drive to generate a profit, these individuals are motivated to develop profit producing products. Sometimes, however, the hunger to develop high-yield investments clouds judgments. Sometimes people try to make a profit on **synthetic financial products**, which are products that lack an underlying value in their assets (like a CDS written on a subprime mortgage-backed security).

✔ checkpoint

What is a credit default swap?

_____

_____

_____

_____

THE INEFFECTIVENESS OF SELF-REGULATION ● ● ● ● ● ● ● ● ● ●

During the tenure of Alan Greenspan, there was an ideological belief that protecting the long-term self-interest of the companies and the industries participating in the CDS market was sufficient to keep the companies acting in a fiscally responsible way. With the realization that the CDS market players were sophisticated market participants accustomed to managing huge quantities of money, it was believed that participants had the intellectual capability to understand the long-term impact of the products they were selling and the investments they were making. Unfortunately, this ideological belief in the power of the industry to self-regulate was flawed. The sheer volume of CDSs written on pyramiding assets of dubious value, the ability of private parties to conduct CDS transactions without regulation, the increased global demand for more investment products, and the lack of a reserve requirement for CDS products proved to be overwhelming for the industry to effectively self-regulate. In addition, the complexity of the CDS process may have proven somewhat overwhelming to regulators contemplating the potential need for regulation. Failing to proactively appreciate the catastrophe looming in the future, decision makers allowed the CDS market (and related products) to grow exponentially without regulation.

The Aftermath

The cumulative effects of the financial crisis of 2008 are staggering. It is generally agreed that it is the worst financial crisis since the Great Depression. According to statistics reported in late November 2008 by *The New York Times*, the U.S. government had already assumed about $7.8 trillion in both direct and indirect financial obligations. This amount is about half the size of the U.S.'s entire economy. In December 2008, *The New York Times* reported that a recession had actually begun in December 2007. As the recession was already 12 months long at the time it was reported, it was anticipated that the recession might be one of the longest on record.

According to *The New York Times*, the purpose of the government's financial interventions is to resuscitate the economy and avoid a depression. The nation's unemployment was at 6.5 percent in October 2008. Unemployment was expected to rise to 7.5 or 8 percent in 2009. As a rule of thumb, economists consider unemployment rates of 9 to 10 percent to signal a depression. At the time of this writing, it was uncertain whether the assorted government interventions would have the desired impact.

 checkpoint

Why did industry self-regulation of the financial markets fail?

_____

_____

_____

assessment 9.4

Think Critically

1. What is a risk preferrer and how does his or her risk preference impact financial markets?

_____

_____

2. What is a synthetic financial product?

_____

_____

3. As a CDS investor, do you need to own the asset that the CDS insures?

_____

_____

4. What is speculation?

_____

_____

Make Academic Connections

5. **GOVERNMENT INTERVENTION**   The Term Asset-backed Securities Loan Facility (TALF) provided $200 billion in government financing to lend money to private investors who purchased securities backed by small-business loans, student loans, credit card debt, and auto loans. TALF was an unprecedented government program in that the government became involved in directly helping with consumer debt financing. By purchasing consumer debt-backed securities, the intent of the TALF was to get credit in consumer markets flowing. Government purchases of debt from these markets provided lenders with revenue to make loans in these markets. Research the current status of the TALF program. How much government money has been spent on this program so far? Did the program have the intended effect? Summarize your findings in a one-page report.

6. **CURRENT EVENTS**   In November 2008, former Vice President Al Gore, wrote an editorial in *The New York Times* promoting the concept that the nation could free itself from energy dependence on foreign nations and develop millions of new jobs that cannot be outsourced by focusing on developing 100 percent of the U.S.'s electricity from carbon-free sources within 10 years. Proposed initiatives include offering investment incentives for solar thermal plants, developing smart electricity grids, transitioning the auto fleet to plug-in hybrids, and making buildings more energy efficient. Research the current status of these initiatives. Prepare a chart summarizing the jobs created and the impact the jobs have had on the economy.

chapter 9 assessment

Chapter Summary

9.1 Commercial Loans
A. Commercial lending is defined as lending to business enterprises.
B. There are numerous types of commercial loans.

9.2 Commercial Credit Analysis
A. Debt ratio, loan-to-value, and debt service coverage ratio are used in the credit analysis process.
B. To complete a credit analysis, the lender will require full access to a company's financial records.
C. Commercial lending is regulated only by the terms of the loan and some state laws.
D. The mortgage crisis affected not just the mortgage loan portfolios directly, but also the investment products that were backed by the mortgage loans.

9.3 Small Business Loan Programs
A. The SBA guarantees a lender that the loan will be paid if the borrower defaults.
B. Eligibility for an SBA loan is determined by the type of business, the size of the business, and the use of loan funds.
C. There are several SBA loan options for small businesses.

9.4 The 2008 Financial Crisis
A. Mortgage backed securities, CDSs, and a lack of regulation combined to help cause the 2008 financial crisis.
B. As self-regulation failed, the government is trying multiple ways to rescue the economy.

Vocabulary Builder

a. commercial lending
b. credit default swap (CDS)
c. debt ratio
d. debt service coverage ratio (DSCR)
e. factoring
f. merchandiser
g. manufacturer
h. risk averse
i. risk preferrer
j. short-term loan
k. Small Business Administration (SBA)
l. speculation
m. synthetic financial product
n. term loan

Choose the term that best fits the definition. Write the letter of the answer in the space provided. Some terms may not be used.

____ 1. Making an investment based on a hoped-for outcome
____ 2. Loans to business enterprises
____ 3. Preferring to make investments with very little risk of failure
____ 4. Comparison of net operating income to the total cost of debt
____ 5. Financing for permanent working capital, equipment, and real estate
____ 6. Financial products that lack an underlying value in their assets
____ 7. Financing for a year or less
____ 8. Agency that offers financial, technical, and management programs to help businesses
____ 9. A form of lending that advances cash in exchange for a business's receivables
____ 10. Total obligations compared to total income

Review Concepts

11. What is commercial lending?

_____

_____

_____

12. List one purpose for commercial lending and describe how the loan might be used.

_____

_____

13. What is depreciation and how might it affect a loan?

_____

_____

_____

14. What is a risk averse investor and how would he or she participate in the financial markets?

_____

_____

_____

15. What is a line of credit and how would a business use it?

_____

_____

_____

16. What are the costs and benefits of factoring to a business?

_____

_____

17. Explain the loan-to-value ratio. What do lenders consider an acceptable loan-to-value ratio?

_____

_____

_____

18. What is the debt service coverage ratio (DSCR) and why does a lender prefer to see the highest possible DSCR?

_____

_____

_____

_____

19. List five things a lender will need to get from the borrower when considering a commercial loan.

_____

_____

_____

_____

_____

20. How does the Small Business Administration define a small business?

_____

_____

_____

21. Explain how the Small Business Administration helps businesses obtain loans.

_____

_____

22. List distinct roles the government took while trying to rescue the economy.

_____

_____

23. Describe the SBA 7(a) loan program.

_____

_____

_____

_____

Apply What You Learned

24. What is a CDS and what role did CDSs play in the 2008 financial crisis?

_____

_____

_____

_____

25. Why do many businesses choose to lease equipment rather than buy it?

_____

_____

_____

26. Why might a business choose to misrepresent itself as a small business?

_____

_____

_____

27. Why does the government have an interest in guaranteeing loans for small businesses?

_____

_____

_____

_____

Make Academic Connections

28. **BANKING MATH**   Calculate the debt service coverage ratio for a small business that has a gross income of $1,400,000, a net operating income of $800,000, and total debt service of $650,000.

_____

_____

_____

29. **TECHNOLOGY**   Learn more about venture capital that is used to fund many high-tech enterprises. Visit the Small Business Investment Company (SBIC) website at www.sba.gov/aboutsba/sbaprograms/inv/index.html and prepare an oral report on how the program works.

_____

_____

_____

30. **COMMUNICATION**   Small or new businesses may need to submit a business plan to obtain financing. What is a business plan? What makes a good one? Visit the Small Business Administration website at www.sba.gov/smallbusinessplanner/index.html and find information about starting a business. Study the information about the contents of a business plan. List the three major elements here.

_____

_____

_____

_____

Specialized Bank Services

10.1	International Banking
10.2	Insurance and Brokerage
10.3	Cash Management
10.4	Trusts

From Associate Team Leader to Product Manager

Ike had spent the majority of his career in banking working with nondeposit products. He had joined his current employer, a regional bank, after earning a number of insurance licenses. As an associate team leader for insurance products at a regional bank, Ike's responsibilities included investment sales, business development, and customer service. To develop new business, he followed up on leads from bank branches. He sold investment products and services to banking customers. Sometimes he would cross-sell banking services to customers by recommending products that would be of interest to them but went beyond their original focus. He advised customers regarding investment choices. He trained personnel at the branches by teaching them about products, coaching them on their sales efforts, and providing support when they had questions.

Next Ike worked as a product development specialist. He was part of a team that developed product-specific strategy and pricing policies. For product maintenance or product distribution that would be outsourced, he worked on vendor agreements and information sharing plans. When existing products were modified, he helped plan and coordinate the changes, including communicating the changes to bank personnel. Contributing to the writing and revising of product-specific marketing was another of his duties. He developed procedures to make sure that all product changes were reflected in product literature.

Ike took the knowledge he obtained developing products and applied it to his next position as a request for proposal (RFP) writer. When businesses had a need for banking services, they would formalize those needs by writing an RFP that outlined the required products and services. As an RFP writer for the bank, Ike prepared detailed responses to a perspective client's RFP. His response described the products his bank offered, the costs associated with those products, and the benefits of working with his bank. Ike helped the bank increase its business by writing accurate and intriguing RFPs. In some instances, like when a city was looking for a bank to provide CDs each month, successful completion of the RFP process allowed Ike's bank to participate in the monthly bidding process that occurred for the CDs.

Leveraging his in-depth product and marketplace knowledge helped Ike obtain his current position as a product manger. He performed competitor and market research, developed new products, and created marketing and sales plans for new products.

Upper Rungs to Consider

Ike was thriving in his current position. Each day he came to work with many new ideas. He enjoyed keeping current on the banking industry, anticipating what his competitors would do, and proactively developing products to grow his bank's business. Although he wanted to stay on this career path, he hoped to earn a promotion to a new product director. In that role, he would provide direction to the entire department and manage other product managers.

Preparing for the Climb

Banks sell a variety of financial services. Why is product development important? Why is it necessary to conduct research about industry changes and competitive products?

PHOTODISC

10.1

International Banking

goals

+ Identify financial entities involved in international banking.

+ Describe international services offered by banks.

terms

+ sovereign wealth fund
+ edge corporations
+ correspondent bank
+ currency risk
+ country risk
+ money laundering
+ letter of credit
+ foreign exchange rate

Banking Scene

Amelia Lopez owns a small business. The market for the firm's major product is growing rapidly in South America, and she wants to investigate the advantages and disadvantages of selling her product there. What issues should Amelia consider? Where can she get sound advice about this possible venture?

STRUCTURE OF INTERNATIONAL SERVICES

You don't need a textbook to tell you that the world of finance is increasingly an international one. The changing economy in the 1970s introduced waves of new imports to American life, and the computer and telecommunications revolution of the 1980s and 1990s eliminated national boundaries in many ways. Companies looking for new markets sought to sell to developing nations, and expanding economies in the Pacific Rim altered the balance of economic power. Changes in geopolitics, such as the end of the Soviet Union and the emergence of the People's Republic of China, realigned trading partnerships. New trade agreements and economic alliances such as the North American Free Trade Agreement and the European Union shifted the way the world does business, as did the growth of multinational corporations with branches in many countries. Middle Eastern countries flush with cash from oil revenues and newly industrialized countries generating revenues from manufacturing contributed to an increase in global cash flow.

Behind all this trade is money, and international banking is a huge and growing segment of the banking industry. According to the Bureau of Economic Analysis, in 2007 foreign acquisition of U.S. financial assets by businesses in other countries was about $2.1 billion. Likewise, U.S. acquisition of foreign financial assets was about $1.3 billion. With more and more U.S. companies operating abroad and involved in international trade, banks are expanding their services to provide the expertise that is needed. International banking can be a complicated business, with traders needing to understand the differences among currencies, governments, languages, laws, customs, and even computer systems that affect funds transfers. It is a vital business for the future of banking, because in the global economy, more business will have an international component. Banks that can help provide smooth, efficient, and trouble-free flow of funds and credit around the world may find a profitable and growing business.

International Lending   Relatively few banks specialize in international lending. Only about 750 of more than 14,000 U.S. commercial banks have international lending departments, with a smaller number having foreign branches or subsidiary corporations abroad. Although the number of these banks is small, both the scope and the size of their international business are expanding rapidly, and more banks are likely to expand into this area.

World Bank   The *World Bank* is a partner in strengthening economies and expanding markets to improve the quality of life for people everywhere, especially the poorest. Unlike aid programs, the World Bank doesn't make grants but lends money to developing countries and expects the loans to be repaid. A member of the World Bank Group, the International Finance Corporation (IFC) promotes sustainable private sector investment in developing countries to reduce poverty and improve people's lives. The functions of the IFC include the following:

- Financing private sector projects located in the developing world.

- Helping private companies in the developing world mobilize financing in international financial markets.

- Providing advice and technical assistance to businesses and governments.

Single Euro Payments Area (SEPA)   The *European Payments Council (EPC)* was formed in 2002 to streamline and coordinate payments for the European banking industry. The EPC developed the Single Euro Payments Area (SEPA), which provides an area for standardized euro payments either within a country's borders or across countries' borders. Common legal rights apply to these transactions. Although SEPA currently includes the 27 EU member states, as well as Iceland, Liechtenstein, Norway, and Switzerland, other nations are expected to become involved with the payment system. According to the EPC website, in January 2008, more than 4,300 banks in 31 countries began using the SEPA Credit Transfer Scheme (SCT). Allowing a standardized, predictable, no-cost transfer of funds between businesses participating in SCT is a benefit of SCT. The banks using SCT represent 95 percent of the payment volume in Europe. The European Payments Council is developing other initiatives to streamline euro payments.

PHOTODISC/GETTY IMAGES

Other Services   Lending is not the only international service. The number of banks that are helping companies conduct business overseas is growing. Other international services offered range from foreign exchange to collection of payments from overseas customers. Banks with

interesting *facts*

According to the FDIC, as of June 2008, U.S. banks held $1.6 trillion in total assets in their foreign offices. ◼

knowledge of international business offer help in a complex world with which a firm may have little experience. It makes good business sense for companies to buy expertise they may not possess.

Foreign Banks

Many types of foreign-based banks, branches, agencies, subsidiaries, and holding corporations share features with U.S.-based banks doing international business, and they are supervised accordingly. Foreign bank branches and agencies may be chartered either by federal or state governments. They may offer a full range of banking services, but most of their business involves short- and long-term commercial loans. Although foreign branches can accept deposits of any size from foreigners, they can accept deposits only greater than $100,000 from U.S. citizens and residents (in order not to harm domestic banks), and deposits made after 1991 are not insured by the FDIC.

Since 1991, the responsibility for supervising the branches and agencies of foreign banks operating within the United States has belonged primarily to the Federal Reserve. It annually examines the banks' policies of risk management, operations, compliance, and asset quality (ROCA). If an examination reveals problems with a foreign bank, the Fed has a range of actions it can take. Usually, a letter of commitment from the bank to the Fed explaining how a problem will be corrected is required. Occasionally, further legal action occurs, and in extreme cases, the activities of a foreign bank in the United States will be terminated.

U.S-Based International Banking

The *Office of the Comptroller of the Currency* (OCC) charters and supervises U.S. national banks that do international business. The OCC has the power to remove bank officers and directors, negotiate agreements to change banking practices, issue orders to stop certain practices, and levy financial penalties for unsound practices. The Federal Deposit Insurance Corporation, whose director is the Comptroller, reviews the safety of international banking operations.

Sovereign Wealth Funds

When the government of a country has excess cash to manage, the government may create a **sovereign wealth fund**. These funds are segregated from the country's official currency reserves. Sovereign wealth funds can be used to generate profit for a country by making investments. In September 2007, the IMF estimated that sovereign wealth funds controlled about $3 trillion globally. The IMF estimated that by 2012, $12 trillion could be managed by sovereign wealth funds.

Other Types of International Operations

Edge corporations or *agreement corporations* are financial corporations that are federally chartered and allowed to engage only in international banking or other financial transactions related to international business. Edge corporations must verify that every transaction is related to international business.

Correspondent banks act as points of contact for other banks that do not have a branch, agency, subsidiary, or corporation in the host country. Correspondent banking is unique as highly competitive banks competing for the same businesses share services with one another for a fee. These banks are subject to the banking regulations of the host country. The Federal Reserve, as well as other international banking organizations, works to communicate and standardize international banking policies to ensure a more stable flow of funds.

Special Considerations

Think of the potential hazards of doing business globally. Different economic conditions, different currencies, different political systems, and different cultural practices add uncertainty. For bankers involved in underwriting such business, these other elements of risk must be considered.

- **Financial Risk** Financial risk may not seem all that different compared to domestic banking, and the evaluation of credit risk is similar. However, acquiring reliable information about a creditor's financial position may be considerably more difficult. The format, quality, and relative detail of financial statements around the world vary considerably. Many of these statements are unaudited, and in some cases, they are unreliable. Although international banks do share information, there are sometimes political barriers to the free flow of accurate information, especially when the potential borrower is a government itself. The task of assessing risk is considerably harder.

- **Currency Risk** The risk posed by variations in exchange rates between countries is called **currency risk.** In every transaction, the lender or borrower is at some degree of risk because of currency risk, as relative values fluctuate with economic and political conditions. The value of currencies compared to each other at the outset of the term may not be at all the same later in the term. Although many lenders minimize their risk by dealing only in U.S. dollars, some countries must convert those dollars into local currency to use them. If the exchange rate changes, more local currency may be required to repay the loan than was expected at the outset. Banks need to be able to assess this risk as accurately as possible, which is not always an easy task.

- **Country Risk** The term for the entire range of political, legal, social, and economic conditions that may put international business at risk is **country risk**. International bankers spend a lot of time trying to assess

PHOTODISC/GETTY IMAGES

country risk. Analysts consider the likelihood of political or social changes or unrest, the economic condition and prospects of the country, whether a government might seize private assets or renounce foreign debts, and whether the government is able to ensure the stability of its currency. These analyses produce varied classifications of risk for international business. A bank's activities in a foreign country in light of the country's risk classification are part of the Fed's regulatory examination of a bank.

The political and cultural environment is not the same in other parts of the world as it is in the United States. Bankers must be vigilant not only to protect their own interests, but also to avoid being unwitting allies of people who have illegal or harmful intent. The Bank Secrecy Act of 1970, updated again in 2000, intended to create a "paper trail" for currency so that people could not deposit, invest, or exchange money in such a way as to conceal its illegal source, called **money laundering**. The Foreign Corrupt Practices Act of 1977 requires banks to follow strict accounting procedures in their international dealings and prohibits offering or accepting bribes. Commerce Department regulations prohibit exporters and banks from complying with boycotts that discriminate against U.S. citizens or companies on the basis of race, color, religion, sex, or national origin, and require reporting of them.

The financing of illegal activities came into sharp focus after the terrorist attacks of September 2001. Among its many provisions, the USA Patriot Act of 2001 attempted to make money laundering more difficult. The law prohibits establishing correspondent relations with foreign "shell" banks, banks that had no physical presence in their host country. It also requires due diligence on the part of banks to know the identity and source of transactions as well as to report suspicious transactions. Some privacy advocates whose fierce objections had led to the withdrawal of expanded "Know Your Customer" provisions in 1999, worried that the Patriot Act gave banks and government too much power. Even so, the law passed quickly and went into effect October 26, 2001, with most of its provisions in place by summer 2002.

✔ checkpoint

What is an edge corporation? Name three types of risk for international banking.

INTERNATIONAL SERVICES •

Banks offering international services help their customers negotiate, finance, ship, transfer, and collect their international accounts. Specialists in international finance and the export-import business help clients make their way through the sea of documents that are part of doing business across national boundaries.

Trade Financing

There are numerous forms of trade financing for international business. Some may take the form of simple domestic loans to be used for capital in an import or other international venture. Some may be direct loans to foreign governments through government-run banks or industries. Funds may go to foreign banks in the form of deposits or other loans as a means of making an indirect loan to a foreign business. Sometimes a direct loan may be made to a foreign business or individual. Loans for complex syndications of businesses may be very complicated but are not uncommon. In all cases, banks must review international financial statements, the borrowers themselves, and any other parties involved, such as parent companies, banks, and government institutions. Bank management must estimate if it can safely extend credit based on its own financial position; the financial condition of the borrowers and other parties; the bank's own marketing objectives; and the financial risk, currency risk, and country risk involved.

Letters of Credit   The most common type of trade financing involves a letter of credit. A **letter of credit** is an instrument given by a bank on behalf of a buyer (applicant) to pay the bank of the seller (beneficiary) a given sum in a given time provided that documents required by the letter are

flat world...

Export-Import Bank of India

In some foreign countries, governments run banks rather than merely supervise them. Such is the case of the Export-Import (Ex-Im) Bank of India. Founded in 1982, Ex-Im Bank was created by an act of the Indian Parliament, and the government of India wholly owns it. Its purpose is to finance, facilitate, and promote India's foreign trade. EXIM Bank has nine offices in India and overseas offices in Singapore, Durban, London, Dubai, Dakar, and Washington, DC. It has expanded services to include financing at competitive rates to buyers of Indian goods in foreign countries.

Think Critically   Of what potential benefit is the Indian government's involvement in export-import banking? Why might a foreign buyer benefit by financing through a bank of the seller's home country?

presented to the issuing bank. The required documents usually consist of an invoice, transportation documents (listing the cargo), insurance, and other verification that the goods have been delivered. Until those documents have been accepted by the issuing bank, the letter of credit is of no value. When the documents are accepted, the bank debits the buyer's (applicant's) account, wires the specified amount to the correspondent bank of the seller (beneficiary), and the buyer can collect the shipment. In this way, both buyer and seller have some guarantee of the performance of the other, and the bank's funds are secured by the documentation for the goods. A *standby letter of credit* assures the seller of the buyer's creditworthiness by guaranteeing the bank to pay the seller in the event of nonperformance by the buyer. Standby letters of credit are charged an origination fee, which varies based on the size of the letter and the security pledged. Typically the fees range from one to three percent of the size of the letter of credit.

Drafts and Wires   Similar to a check, a draft is an order signed by one party (the *drawer*, or drafter) that is addressed to another party (the *drawee*) directing the drawee to pay someone (the *payee*) the amount indicated on the draft at sight or some specified time. Banks dealing in international banking can provide drafts in the specified currencies of many nations if necessary, so that the draft can be negotiated within that country. Banks can also provide international wire transfer. Messaging is not necessarily limited to ledger entries of funds but may also include letters of credit or any other communication or documentation necessary for international business.

International Collections   Banks perform international collections services based on their relationships with correspondent banks and their knowledge of international commerce.

Foreign Currency Exchange   Foreign currency exchanges are essential for international transactions. For example, before a U.S. importer can purchase commodities from Japan, it must first obtain Japanese yen to pay for them. Banks can provide this service. Banks may exchange currency through foreign exchange markets or may have correspondent relationships with banks in other countries for the trading of currency. A **foreign exchange rate** is the value of one currency in terms of another. Current foreign exchange quotations must be used to calculate the exchange. For example, the table on the next page shows the exchange rates for select countries as of May 1, 2004.

To calculate what $1,000 U.S. dollars would be worth in euros, use the exchange rate from the table for U.S.$ to euros: $1,000 × 1.157 = $1,157.

To calculate what 1,157 euros would be worth in U.S. dollars, use the exchange rate for euros to U.S.$: $1,157 × 0.8642 = $1,000 (rounded).

Factors affecting exchange rates for the currency of a given country are interest rates, rate of inflation, trade balance (if a country's

PHOTODISC/GETTY IMAGES

Currency	U.S. $	Yen	Euro	Can $	U.K. £	Aust $	SFranc	DMark
Last Trade	N/A	May 1	May 1	May 1	May 1	May 1	May 1	May 1
U.S. $	1	0.00910332	1.1861	0.735835	1.76839	0.7303	0.761267	0.604383
Yen	109.85	1	130.293	80.8315	194.259	80.2235	83.6252	66.0068
Euro	0.843099	0.007675	1	0.620381	1.49093	0.615715	0.641823	0.511292
Can $	1.359	0.0123714	1.61191	1	2.40325	0.992477	1.03456	0.823665
U.K. £	0.565483	0.00514777	0.670719	0.416103	1	0.412972	0.430483	0.342029
Aust $	1.3693	0.0124652	1.62412	1.00757	2.42146	1	1.0424	0.827569
SFranc	1.3136	0.0119581	1.55806	0.966593	2.32297	0.959322	1	0.796475
DMark	1.65440	0.0151517	1.95583	1.21414	2.92373	1.20833	1.25553	1

exports exceed its imports), and economic forecasts for that country. The demand for a given currency will be strong if the country is experiencing relatively high interest rates, low inflation, a positive trade balance, and a strong economic forecast.

Trade Consulting

Using their expertise, banks can help companies assess both their prospects and risks in international commerce and help companies with the paperwork associated with international transactions. The international banking consultant may also work with and/or recommend other agencies that can be of help to a business wanting to branch into international markets.

U.S. Export-Import (Ex-Im) Bank   Some banks work with the U.S. Export-Import (Ex-Im) Bank to help raise capital for companies that have the potential to produce goods or services for export but need funds to do so. Ex-Im offers a number of financing programs, as well as credit insurance programs, that cover the risks of nonpayment by foreign buyers. Ex-Im does not compete with commercial banks, but assumes higher risks than commercial banks can normally accept. Its goal is to increase U.S. exports.

Overseas Private Investment Corporation (OPIC)   Overseas Private Investment Corporation's (OPIC's) goal is to assist U.S. companies in building their business in developing nations. OPIC's programs are beneficial for both the developing nations and U.S. exports. OPIC will provide loans, loan guarantees, and political risk insurance to qualifying companies. OPIC will provide this assistance for ventures seen as too risky for commercial banks. In spite of the assumed risks, OPIC has made money every year since it was created in 1971.

 checkpoint

What is a letter of credit?

assessment 10.1

Think Critically

1. What factors do you think contribute to the increasing globalization of economies?

2. Name two organizations that specialize in helping U.S. firms engage in foreign trade.

3. Give two specific instances of events that might be part of country risk.

4. Why might banks dealing in international services be in a good position to offer trade consulting?

Make Academic Connections

5. **SOCIAL STUDIES**   Although English is the language of business around the globe, it helps traders immensely to know the language of their business partners. Find out the top five languages in the world, as ranked by number of speakers. List them and the number of speakers for each below.

6. **BANKING MATH**   In January 2002, eurodollars, or euros, became the currency of member nations of the European Union, a group of Western European nations banding together for economic purposes. Using the Internet, find the current value of a euro as compared to the U.S. dollar and convert the cost of U.S. goods valued at $40,000 to euros.

7. **POLITICAL SCIENCE**   Locate information on countries with fluctuating currency exchange rates and analyze the causes for inflation.

Insurance and Brokerage

Banking Scene

As a small business owner, Amelia Lopez is considering offering a health insurance plan for her employees, but she is undecided as to which type is the best. She is surprised to learn that her bank now offers insurance policies. What types of plans are available to her? What are some of the choices she must make in addition to the type of plan to offer?

A NEW ERA

Banks are offering more products and services than ever before. The competitive nature of today's banking business, along with the mergers and acquisitions many banks have undertaken, have placed them in a position to diversify even further. As a result of ongoing changes in financial services industries and new legislation, banks may now offer financial services that they once were prohibited from selling. This "one stop shopping" approach can offer customers a way to combine their financial planning into a single package, with products and expertise available from a single source. In addition, the door swings two ways: insurance companies can acquire banks just as banks can enter the insurance business. The new rules do more than open the door to unsupervised market chaos in the financial services industry. One sure result of the new era is that competition for consumers' financial business, whether in banking, insurance, or securities, will become even more keen.

The Old World: Glass-Steagall Act

The Glass-Steagall Act of 1933 was a response to the Great Depression. Bank failures and investment losses nearly destroyed the banking system and the national economy. Among other provisions, the law prohibited banks from owning brokerage firms and selling stock and from affiliating or sharing offices with businesses that did. The intention of the law was to create a "firewall" between speculative businesses and banking institutions. Enacted during our nation's darkest economic period, it was part of a set of legislative actions that stabilized the banking system.

The Glass-Steagall Act kept banks from competing with other financial service providers. As the economy modernized, banks and other financial institutions suffered and occasionally were at risk because they couldn't compete. Gradually, laws such as the Bank Holding Company Acts of 1956 and 1970 allowed some side roads into other financial businesses, but they still prohibited direct affiliation and limited the regions in which banks could do business. Even as banks became deregulated in the 1980s, the prohibition of direct securities trading and insurance underwriting remained.

The New World: Gramm-Leach-Bliley Act (GLBA)

The Gramm-Leach-Bliley Act of 1999 was the most dramatic change in banking regulation since the Great Depression. After years of involving themselves in insurance and securities businesses only tangentially, banks were at last free to pursue those businesses directly. The law also required financial services companies to have and provide to customers a written privacy policy. Furthermore, the law allowed the sharing of consumers' financial information among affiliated firms so long as the consumer was notified. The responsibility to prohibit sharing of information with third parties, called an "opt-out," rests with the consumer. Some proponents of the law oppose the privacy-policy portion of it. They feel that requiring companies to seek permission of every consumer to share information creates an unnecessary burden of compliance. They also believe that free sharing of information among affiliates allows for quicker, more efficient, and less costly service to customers with less duplication of effort. Some privacy advocates strongly oppose this view, feeling that the law was structured to make it easier for companies to trade in private data with little restriction, and note that many of the uses of data in affiliated companies fall outside the third-party opt-out provisions.

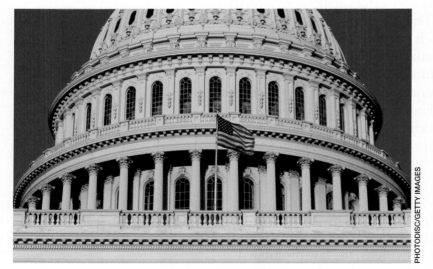

PHOTODISC/GETTY IMAGES

In June 2008, HR 6312 was passed to remove the requirement that debt buyers provide an annual privacy notice to consumers. *Debt buyers* are companies that buy delinquent accounts from other companies. Debt buyers were concerned about the administrative costs of not only the initial mailing of the notices but also about the subsequent phone calls made by consumers who were confused by the notices.

Limits and Regulation

The Gramm-Leach-Bliley Act effectively supersedes state law, although it acknowledges the interest of states in "reasonable" regulation of the financial service industries. State commissions on banking, insurance, and securities still have jurisdiction on some practices, but may not discriminate in licensing against affiliated firms. Other controls come from agencies directly involved in the businesses themselves, such as the Securities and Exchange Commission and the Federal Trade Commission.

✔ checkpoint

Why did the Glass-Steagall Act limit the participation of banks in a wide range of financial businesses? What was the major result of the Gramm-Leach-Bliley Act?

INSURANCE PRODUCTS •

The GLBA essentially repealed the Glass-Steagall Act, sweeping away legal barriers that had separated the securities, insurance, and banking industries. Modernizing the financial services industry, the law allows for a new corporate structure, called the financial holding company (FHC), and allows banks, securities firms, and insurance companies to diversify and/or merge their businesses if they so choose. The stated purpose of the GLBA is to promote competition. Banks, therefore, can offer a complete range of insurance products for individuals and businesses.

The Workings of Insurance

The primary goal of insurance is to allocate the risks of loss from the individual to a great number of people, or to protect holders against financial disaster. Each individual pays a *premium* into a pool from which losses are paid. Whether the particular individual suffers the loss or not, the premium is not returnable. Thus, when a home is destroyed by fire, the loss is spread to the people contributing to the pool. In general, insurance companies are the safekeepers of the premiums. The government and the courts use a heavy hand in ensuring these companies are regulated and fair to the consumer.

Personal Insurance Products

Operating as full-service financial institutions, banks offer a full spectrum of insurance products.

- **Auto Insurance** Auto insurance protects the owner from the risk of injury to people and damage to vehicles or other property in the event of an accident. It can also protect the owner against loss or damage through theft, vandalism, or natural disasters.

- **Credit Insurance** This insurance, sometimes called *credit life,* is designed to repay the balance of a loan in the event the borrower dies before the insured loan is repaid.

- **Disability Insurance** Disability insurance pays benefits when the holder is unable to earn a living because of illness or injury. Most disability policies pay a benefit that replaces part of the disabled holder's earned income.

- **Life Insurance** Various types are available, as shown in the following table.

TYPES OF LIFE INSURANCE POLICIES		
Policy Type	*Characteristics*	*Suitable For*
Decreasing Term	Level premium, decreasing coverage, no cash value	Financial obligations that reduce with time, such as mortgages or other amortized loans
Annual Renewable Term	Increasing premium, level coverage, no cash value	Financial obligations that remain constant for a short or intermediate period, such as income during a minor's dependency
Whole Life	Level premium, level coverage, cash value that typically increases based on insurance company's general asset account portfolio performance	Long-term obligations, such as surviving spouse lifetime income needs, estate liquidity, death taxes, funding retirement needs
Universal Life	Level or adjustable premium, level or adjustable coverage, cash value that increases based on the performance of certain assets held in the company's general account	Long-term obligations, such as estate growth, estate liquidity, death taxes, funding retirement needs, and so forth
Variable Life and Variable Universal Life	Level or adjustable premium, level coverage (can be increased by positive investment performance), cash values that are directed to a choice of investment accounts (bond, stock, money market, and so forth) by the policy owner	Long-term obligations, such as estate growth, estate liquidity, and death taxes, and so forth for the more active investor
Single-Premium Whole Life	Entire premium is paid at purchase, level coverage, cash values	Asset accumulation vehicle for long-term obligations, such as surviving spouse lifetime income needs, estate liquidity, death taxes, funding retirement needs

- **Health Insurance** The need for a comprehensive, high-quality health care program, equitably accessible to all residents of the United States, has been the topic of national debate for years, but no national policy has been legislated. Various health policies include the following.

   Traditional This type of policy allows holders to visit any doctor or hospital they want and receive coverage for any treatment covered under the policy. Premiums for traditional insurance tend to be higher than those for other plans.

   HMO A health maintenance organization (HMO) is a health-care system that organizes doctors and hospitals in a network. An HMO's two basic features are that members must choose a primary care network physician who performs basic health checkups and approves visits to other specialized physicians, and members pay a set per-person fee that gives them access to the HMO's services.

   PPO A preferred provider organization (PPO) is a collection of physicians and hospitals that agree to provide health care at reduced cost to PPO members. PPOs limit health care costs without the restrictions of an HMO.

- **Homeowner's Insurance** Homeowner's insurance is designed to protect against a wide range of potential disasters, such as fire, vandalism, and theft of property, as well as against lawsuits if someone is injured while on the owner's property.

- **Mortgage Disability Insurance** Generally, if an illness or accidental injury renders an insured borrower disabled, mortgage disability insurance pays monthly home loan payments up to a specific amount.

- **Title Insurance** This policy type compensates the owner of real estate if his or her clear ownership of property is challenged.

PHOTODISC/GETTY IMAGES

Business Insurance

Whether for-profit or nonprofit, businesses need certain types of insurance, such as liability insurance, which is highly recommended for property and automobiles. Workers' compensation is state-required insurance for any business with employees. The following briefly describes several types of business insurance.

- **Commercial Liability** Commercial liability insurance pays part or all of the damages for liability that the law applies to a business as well as the cost of defending the firm when a claim is made against it. Unprotected liability could cause financial hardship or bankruptcy.

- **Disability—Short-Term**   Regular employees working 30 hours or more a week who become disabled are provided with a level of income protection for a short period of time, such as 90 days. Coverage is generally for a percentage of normal income, often as much as 90 percent.

- **Disability—Long-Term**   This insurance is available to regular employees meeting short-term requirements but who have been disabled beyond the time limits of short-term disability benefits. Coverage is for a percentage of income less than that normally covered by short-term disability, often 60 to 70 percent.

- **Health Insurance**   Many firms allow employees to participate in group health insurance plans covering basic health care, sometimes including vision and dental care. The employer determines the plan's coverage and the portion of the cost, if any, that employees must pay for it.

- **Officers' Liability Insurance**   This insurance protects the company from losses due to the company's directors' and officers' alleged or actual breach of duty, neglect, error, misstatement, misleading statement, omission, or act.

tech talk

First Internet Bank of Indiana

Based in Indianapolis, Indiana, First Internet Bank of Indiana (or First IB) is the first state-chartered Internet bank with accounts insured by the FDIC. It is the first "extended value online bank" to deliver a full range of real-time Internet banking products with personalized interactive services as well as offering competitive rates. "Real-time" means that transactions are reflected in the customer's accounts immediately. First IB's business model enables customers to facilitate Internet banking in a real-time environment and to empower users to better manage their own finances.

First Internet Bank was one of the earliest banks to allow customers to conduct bank-related business from their web-enabled cell phones. First IB customers can now check their account balances, transfer funds from one First IB account to another, view their last ten transactions, set up new electronic bill payments, change due dates, and alter amounts or cancel planned payments for the first time from their mobile phone or hand-held computer.

Think Critically   How does the success of this bank reflect on changes in our society? Why might some people be hesitant to use a bank without an advertised address for a walk-in lobby? Would you use this bank? Why or why not?

- **Property Insurance**   Like individual policies, business insurance protects the policyholder against risk. Policies can be customized to meet the special risks the specific firm faces.

- **Workers' Compensation**   This insurance pays for medical care and physical rehabilitation of workers injured in the performance of their job, and it helps to replace lost wages while they are unable to work.

✔ checkpoint

What is an HMO?

_____

_____

_____

BROKERAGE SERVICES ●

Brokerage refers to bringing together parties interested in making a transaction, such as buying and selling shares of stock. A broker charges a fee to execute such a transaction. Banks now offer full investment services. To enhance the liquidity offered by brokers, the Securities and Exchange Commission strictly regulates them to ensure accurate disclosure of information, to prevent fraud, and to restrict trades based on insider information. A topic of interest recently, insider information refers to facts known by people inside an organization or to parties to a transaction but not known by the general public.

Stocks

Stock is the capital raised by a corporation through the issuance of shares entitling holders to an ownership interest, or equity, in the corporation. Stocks represent the largest single category of assets in the capital market, which is the financial market where stocks, bonds, and other types of securities are sold. *Common stock* entitles owners to regular dividends (payments of money) when they are declared. It also provides a voice, through voting rights, in how the corporation operates. *Preferred stock* owners usually receive a limited but set dividend amount and have no voting right, but their claim to the corporation's earnings and assets upon liquidation takes precedence over claims of common stock owners.

Bonds

A **bond** is a debt instrument issued for a period of more than one year with the purpose of raising capital through borrowing. The federal government, states, cities, corporations, and many other types of institutions sell bonds.

Generally, a bond is a promise to repay the principal along with interest on a specified maturity date. As a buyer, you do not gain any ownership rights to the bond's issuer as you would with a stock. However, as a bond holder, your claim to the issuer's income is greater than that of a shareholder in the case of financial distress. Bonds are often divided into different categories based on tax status, credit quality, maturity, secured/unsecured, and issuer type. U.S. Treasury bonds are generally considered the safest unsecured bonds, because the possibility of the Treasury defaulting on payments is almost zero.

Mutual Funds

Mutual funds are investment companies that pool money from many savers who have small amounts to invest. With this money, the mutual fund purchases stocks, bonds, government securities, and short-term money market investments. These funds provide risk-sharing benefits by offering a diversified portfolio. *Diversification* refers to the distribution of assets in a portfolio among different types of securities and maturity dates instead of putting "all your eggs in one basket." Investing in mutual funds enables you to reduce your costs. You can buy into all shares in the funds with one transaction cost rather than incurring a cost on each instrument if you bought it separately.

Annuities

An **annuity** is a series of payments, often to a retired person, of a set amount from a capital investment. The annuity is paid at a specified frequency and for a set number of years or until the annuitant's death. Payments begin only when the annuitant reaches a certain age. All annuities are tax-deferred, meaning that the earnings from investments in these accounts grow without being taxed until withdrawal. However, withdrawal before the specified age results in penalties and taxation.

 checkpoint

What is an diversified portfolio?

assessment 10.2

Think Critically

1. How did the Glass-Steagall Act restrict banking services?

_____

_____

2. Why are banks now able to provide one-stop shopping to customers?

_____

_____

3. Explain how insurance works.

_____

_____

4. What is the difference between an HMO and a PPO?

_____

_____

_____

5. What are the advantages of investing in mutual funds?

_____

_____

_____

Make Academic Connections

6. **CONSUMER AFFAIRS**   Consumers can use the Internet to do comparison pricing. Identify four different brokerage firms that offer Internet purchases. What percentage of the sale is the company's brokerage fee?

_____

_____

7. **SOCIAL STUDIES**   The GLBA has brought dramatic changes to the banking industry. Some people contend that these changes make sharing private data among companies too easy. How did the public communicate this concern to government officials? What has the government done to prevent banks from sharing nonpublic personal information? Has this action been totally successful?

_____

_____

_____

10.3

goals

+ Explain why banks are in a good position to offer cash management services

+ List several cash management services banks perform for businesses

terms

+ outsourcing

+ factoring

Cash Management

Banking Scene

Amelia Lopez recently attended a seminar on outsourcing. Since her business recently began to sell its products in South America, the firm is growing, and its needs have changed. She thinks that outsourcing her accounting services might be a wise thing to do. How could this help Amelia manage her growing business? What advantages and disadvantages should she consider?

SYSTEMS IN PLACE FOR CASH MANAGEMENT • • • • • • • • •

Every business, no matter how large or small, needs to disburse and collect cash to complete business transactions. Banks are in a good position to provide cash management services to businesses for several reasons.

- **Experience** Banks have decades of experience in managing cash.

- **Business Knowledge** In conducting their own operations, banks have experienced the same opportunities and challenges that all businesses face, and they understand the nature and implementation of practices and policies that apply to efficient cash management for all businesses.

- **Technology** Banks have experience in applying technology to their cash management practices. Banks can afford to invest in the applicable technology and develop expertise in its use that most individual firms cannot. Banks allow other companies to tap into these efficiencies through the bank's cash management services.

- **Industry Expertise** Through their dealings with specific companies over the years, individual banks have developed expert knowledge of the practices of various industries. They can offer this expertise to other companies with similar needs.

Businesses recognize that constant changes in the financial industry and the regulatory world have increased their need to proactively manage cash, but with constant change, they find they no longer have the knowledge and experience to do so. It is not unusual for organizations that have had effective cash management systems to seek ways to improve them.

✔ checkpoint

Why is a bank in a good position to offer cash management services?

CASH MANAGEMENT •

Firms' focus on the "bottom line" has caused them to evaluate all activities they perform and to identify those that do not add value to the product or service they offer. For many reasons, one company can make a product or provide a service less expensively than other firms can.

Outsourcing refers to the practice of having an outside party supply a product or service that the firm had been producing or performing itself. For example, the firm can hire a business that specializes in human resources rather than hiring individuals knowledgeable in this field. Savings would include inside employees' salary packages, including paid vacation and sick days, benefits such as health insurance, and various payroll taxes. The firm can devote the savings obtained to the activities that differentiate it. For example, a greeting card company might hire a new artist. Outsourcing may be practical for firms with seasonal/fluctuating needs that make keeping some full-time employees impractical. The Sutter Consortium reports that firms outsource for the following reasons.

29%	Difficulty hiring skilled professionals
20%	Lack of in-house skills
14%	Budget
12%	Business changes
12%	CIO/senior management mandate
7%	Reorganization
2%	Downsizing

Frequently outsourced accounting services include the following.

- **Payroll**   All functions related to paying wages to employees. These include calculating deductions, paying employees, filing payroll taxes, and all related recordkeeping.

- **Accounts Payable**   Short-term debt from purchases on credit that must be paid to suppliers of goods or services typically within 60 days or less. These are paid for the client at the appropriate time and the client's creditor account records are kept up to date.

- **Accounts Receivable**   Money due for services performed or merchandise sold on credit. Money is collected and records maintained.

Many businesses outsource cash management services to banks. Many banks outsource services as well. For example, Fidelity National Information

interesting *facts*

Sara Lee, a well-known manufacturer and marketer of high-quality, brand-name products, has taken the practice of outsourcing to the extreme. The company now contracts with outside suppliers, bakeries, and distributors to develop, prepare, and deliver its food products. ■

Services provides information processing management and professional consulting to many financial institutions, from community banks to megabanks and mortgage lenders to consumer finance companies.

Bank collection services enable banks to collect funds and integrate information easily and cost effectively. Various products accomplish this.

- **Deposit Services**   Service that allows customers to make deposits in various ways. The bank maintains and manages deposit accounts to minimize balances in noninterest-bearing accounts and maximize balances in interest-bearing accounts.

- **Lockbox Service**   Service that allows accounts receivable payments to be sent directly to the bank, accelerating the conversion of receivables into usable cash.

- **Zero-balance Accounts (ZBAs)**   Accounts that start each business day at a zero balance and are related to a central account. Throughout the day, transactions are debited or credited as payments are made or received. At the end of the day they are reconciled with the central account and are returned once again to a zero balance. This type of program ensures that funds do not stand idle in multiple accounts and eliminates the need for the customer to monitor accounts and initiate account transfers.

- **Automated Clearing House (ACH) Network**   This is a highly reliable and efficient nationwide batch-oriented electronic funds transfer system. It is governed by rules that provide for the interbank clearing of electronic payments for participating depository financial institutions. The American Clearing House Association, Federal Reserve, Electronic Payments Network, and Visa act as central clearing facilities through which financial institutions transmit or receive ACH entries. The bank's use of this network helps it provide cash collections and transfer services efficiently.

Information Services

Electronic Data Interchange (EDI) is generically defined as the computer-to-computer exchange of business information through standard interfaces. Today, more than 50,000 U.S. companies are estimated to have implemented EDI. Banks can advise companies concerning this interchange and provide the services to the firms.

Capital Services

Businesses must often commit large sums of money (capital) to projects that will continue well into the future. Capital expenses usually involve the purchase of things that last more than a year. Examples of firms' capital purchases are large printing presses, equipment to implement environmental regulations, expansion into a new territory, and a fleet of new trucks. Many firms aren't able to perform the complex analyses necessary for making the decisions, so they turn to their bankers for help.

Banking Math *Connection*

A small business was able to make a large sale only by accepting a note of $8,075 plus a $925 service fee to be paid in 12 months rather than immediate payment. Shortly afterward, the business unexpectedly had to replace an expensive machine four years ahead of schedule. The business was short of cash and arranged for a local bank to purchase the debt for a factoring fee of 3 percent. How much will the business receive from the bank?

Solution

First calculate the factoring fee. The formula for calculating this is

(Principal + Service charge) $\times$ Factoring fee percent = Factoring fee
$$(\$8,075 + \$925) \times 0.03 = \$270$$

Then subtract the fee from the total amount owed.

Amount owed $-$ Factoring fee = Amount received from bank
$$\$9,000 - \$270 = \$8,730$$

Capital Investments Capital investments differ from investments in stocks and bonds in one significant way. Stocks and bonds can be sold on an organized market for cash. A capital investment requires a much longer time to convert to cash, during which time the firm might incur additional expenses, such as building or equipment maintenance. Making capital investment decisions requires the use of numerous analytical tools and techniques for evaluating if the investment will result in the desired profits. Banks have the expertise to use these techniques in advising their clients. Establishing capital budgets is also part of the service.

Financing Once capital investment projects are decided, banks can provide advice to their clients regarding the best ways to finance while keeping the company's debt-to-equity ratios at the desired level.

Factoring A capital service provided by banks, **factoring** is the practice of buying debt at a discount. A firm that needs cash can sell a debt. The purchasing bank provides this service for a fee, often a percentage of the amount owed. In making its decision to provide this service, the bank evaluates the ability of the firm's customer to pay the debt. The customer pays the amount owed to the bank. Factoring dramatically improves a company's cash flow so it may meet current financial obligations.

Explain how a zero-balance account works.

assessment 10.3

Think Critically

1. Many firms now outsource activities that they once performed themselves. What are the advantages of this?

_____

_____

_____

2. Name three accounting services commonly outsourced.

_____

_____

_____

3. What puts banks in a position to offer cash management services?

_____

_____

_____

4. What is the EDI service that banks offer?

_____

_____

_____

_____

Make Academic Connections

5. **TECHNOLOGY**   Many banking functions are offered over the Internet. Choose one of the services discussed in this lesson and research
its availability over the Internet. Prepare a written, oral, or computer
presentation that discusses how this service is purchased on the Internet, describes the way the service is performed, and includes the fees
involved.

6. **COMMUNICATION**   Contact several local businesses and find out
whether they outsource any of the accounting services discussed in this
lesson. Determine the reason(s) they do or do not outsource. Compile
your results as a class.

_____

_____

_____

Trusts

goals

+ Explain what trust services are.

+ Identify important types of trust services banks provide.

terms

+ trust
+ donor
+ beneficiary
+ corpus
+ IRA
+ 401(k) plan
+ variable annuity
+ estate
+ will
+ probate
+ executor
+ living trust

Banking Scene

Now that Amelia Lopez's business is successful, she thinks it's time to start planning for her family's financial future. Her two daughters plan to go to college. She also wants to make sure that she and her husband will be comfortable during retirement. Amelia realizes that she will need to plan carefully to minimize the tax consequences on her estate when she dies. What are some of the options she should consider? Could IRAs meet her needs? What should Amelia know about estate planning?

WHAT ARE TRUST SERVICES? • • • • • • • • • • • • • • • • • • •

The concept of trusts dates back some seven hundred years to Medieval England. At its simplest, a **trust** is an arrangement by which one party holds property on behalf of another party for certain defined purposes. Banks are well versed in providing trust services to their clients. Banks typically have trust departments whose members understand all types of trusts and their advantages and disadvantages and have experience in setting up and administering trusts to meet their clients' needs. Banks advise clients on the various types of trusts, which are discussed in the next section. Terminology related to trusts is somewhat specialized, and you should understand the following terms.

- **Donor** or *settlor* is the person who creates a trust.

- **Beneficiary** is the person for whose benefit the property is held.

- **Corpus** or *res* refers to the property that is held. Sometimes a distinction is made as to the *principal*, which is the property that is held in trust, and the *income* that the principal produces.

 checkpoint

What is a trust?

TRUST SERVICE PRODUCTS •

In addition to assisting a client in planning how to provide for financial needs during that person's employment years, banks offer advice regarding the client's retirement requirements and for passing assets upon death.

Retirement Planning

Various products are available to help individuals plan and save for their retirement. An **IRA** (individual retirement account) is a great way to save for retirement. There are two kinds of IRAs—traditional and Roth. Funds are invested in a traditional IRA on a before-tax basis, which allows the earnings on the investment to compound on a tax-deferred basis. This means that the money invested in a traditional IRA isn't taxed until it is withdrawn after age 59½. There are penalties for early withdrawal. You must begin withdrawals from a traditional IRA beginning at age 70½.

Beginning January 1, 1998, the Roth IRA became available. This investment is made with after-tax dollars. As long as the assets have remained inside the account for five years, all earnings and principal can be withdrawn totally tax-free after age 59½. Unlike the traditional IRA, funds do not have to be withdrawn at age 70½. The Economic Growth and Tax Relief Reconciliation Act of 2001 made changes to the amounts that an individual can invest in either a traditional or a Roth IRA. In 2008, individuals can invest up to $5,000 a year and, if over age 50, $6,000 a year.

Another retirement plan, the **401(k) plan,** allows employees to make tax-deferred contributions to a trust and direct their funds to be invested among a variety of choices, getting their money back at departure or retirement. Many companies match the employee investment, usually at between 25 and 75 cents per dollar, to a defined maximum (such as 6 percent of pay).

Many people find annuities to be a good complement to other tax-deferred retirement investments such as IRAs and 401(k)s. A **variable annuity** combines the opportunity for tax-deferral with a choice of portfolios and the flexibility to vary annual contributions according to the investors' needs or market conditions.

Estate Planning

Estate planning is the process by which an individual or family arranges the transfer of assets in anticipation of death. An **estate** is the total property, real (real estate) and personal (all other possessions, such as automobiles, jewelry, and bank accounts) that an individual owns. The cornerstone of any estate plan is a **will,** a document by which the individual gives instructions as to what is to happen upon his or her death in regard to property and remains. An estate plan seeks to preserve the maximum amount of wealth possible for the intended beneficiaries and to provide flexibility for the individual prior to death. Federal and state tax laws are major considerations in estate planning.

Probate is a court proceeding that settles an estate's final debts and formally passes legal title to property from the decedent to his or her heirs. It is initiated in the county of the decedent's legal residence at death. Wills must undergo formal probate administration, which can last two years or more, depending on the size and complexity of the estate. Court permission is needed to buy and sell assets, and beneficiaries usually must wait until the probate is concluded to receive the bulk of their inheritance. There are measures that may be taken to avoid

assets being tied up in probate, such as naming beneficiaries for retirement accounts and placing assets in a living trust.

Estate Settlement

Estate settlement generally involves the following.

- **Identifying and valuing the estate assets.** An **executor** or *fiduciary* (the person named in the will to administer the estate) must identify all assets in the estate, including securities, business interests, and retirement plans, and determine their value. The executor arranges for professional appraisals of such items as real estate, artwork, and jewelry. If there is no will, the court will appoint an executor.

- **Paying creditors, estate expenses, and taxes.** The executor must ensure that the estate has sufficient cash to pay legitimate creditors and related estate expenses, including taxes. In fulfilling this role, the executor may have to decide to sell securities or other assets.

- **Preparing and filing the necessary tax documents with Federal and/or state authorities.** Recordkeeping must be exemplary to ensure that all documents are present, accurate, and complete. The executor must file all documents with the appropriate courts and other agencies in accordance with specific requirements and deadlines.

Ethics in Action

Banks have the ethical responsibility to inform customers in a clear manner on subjects such as the customers' rights and obligations as well as any and all benefits and risks of the products and services provided to them.

Think Critically

1. What are some things you believe a banker should tell a prospective customer about the risks related to retirement planning?
2. What are some things customers should do to be sure they are making informed decisions?

- **Distributing assets to beneficiaries.**   The executor must make timely decisions concerning the distribution of estate assets in a prudent and efficient manner.

Testamentary Trusts

Testamentary trusts are established by a will and take effect at the donor's death. They receive the assets of the estate to hold and manage for the benefit of the heirs.

Charitable Remainder Trusts

A *charitable remainder trust (CRT)* is an irrevocable trust designed to convert the highly appreciated assets of a *trustor*—the person who sets up the trust—into a lifetime income stream without generating estate and capital gains taxes. CRTs have become very popular in recent years because they not only represent a valuable tax-advantaged investment, but also enable the trustor to provide a gift to one or more charities. A CRT can potentially

- Eliminate immediate capital gains taxes on the sale of appreciated assets.
- Reduce estate taxes that heirs might have to pay upon the trustor's death by as much as 55 percent.
- Reduce current income taxes with an income tax deduction.
- Increase the trustor's spendable income.
- Create a charitable gift.
- Avoid probate and maximize the assets the trustor's family will receive.

Living Trusts

In simple terms, a **living trust** is a legal document that provides an expedient way to transfer property at a person's death. Generally, living trusts are established during an individual's lifetime and can be modified or changed while that person is still alive. For this reason, a living trust is set up on a "revocable" basis. The *revocable trust provision* means that while the person lives, he or she still owns all of the property that has been transferred into the trust and can sell it, spend it, or give it away. The trust does not transfer to the beneficiary until the trustor dies. Living trusts speed up the process by which property moves to designated beneficiaries upon the trustor's death. One of the advantages of a living trust is that it avoids probate, although it may not offer the tax benefits related to CRTs.

 checkpoint

What are the responsibilities of an estate executor?

assessment 10.4

Think Critically

1. Why would a person want to set up a trust?

2. Why would a person want to avoid having his or her estate go through probate?

3. What information would you need to know if you were interested in setting up a living trust?

4. Why might people avoid deciding how to dispose of their assets at their death?

Make Academic Connections

5. **COMMUNICATION** Talk to adult family members or friends about the type of retirement plan(s) that they have. Discuss at least four different retirement plans. Prepare a one-page report. Mention any concerns that your friends and family members have about the plans.

6. **PROBLEM SOLVING** Use the Internet to find information on the topic of estate tax repeal. List the advantages and disadvantages of this legislation.

chapter 10 assessment

Chapter Summary

10.1 International Banking

A. International banking institutions include branches of foreign banks operating within the U.S., edge corporations, U.S. banks offering international services, and correspondent banks.

B. International services help customers negotiate, finance, ship, transfer, and collect their international accounts.

10.2 Insurance and Brokerage

A. The Gramm-Leach-Bliley Act allowed banks to enter a new era in which they are able to provide financial services not previously allowed.

B. Banks offer personal and business insurance, and brokerage services.

10.3 Cash Management

A. Banks possess the expertise to provide cash management services to clients.

B. Banks assist their clients in managing their cash by providing accounting, information, credit card, and capital services.

10.4 Trusts

A. Trusts are financial planning vehicles that arrange for the transfer of property from one entity to another under specific circumstances.

B. Retirement planning, estate planning and settlement, and trust establishment and supervision are services offered by banks.

Vocabulary Builder

a. 401(k) plans
b. annuity
c. beneficiary
d. bond
e. corpus
f. correspondent banks
g. country risk
h. currency risk
i. donor
j. edge corporations
k. estate
l. executor
m. factoring
n. foreign exchange rate
o. IRA
p. letter of credit
q. living trust
r. money laundering
s. mutual fund
t. probate
u. outsourcing
v. sovereign wealth fund
w. stock
x. trust
y. variable annuity
z. will

Choose the term that best fits the definition. Write the letter of the answer in the space provided. Some terms may not be used.

____ 1. Political, legal, social, and economic conditions that affect international businesses

____ 2. Practice of depositing, investing, or exchanging money in such a way as to conceal its illegal source

____ 3. Arrangement by which one party holds property on behalf of another party

____ 4. Court proceeding that settles estates

____ 5. Refers to the property held in a trust

____ 6. The value of one currency in terms of another

____ 7. Federally chartered institutions allowed to engage only in international banking

____ 8. Person who creates a trust

____ 9. Degree of risk posed by variations in exchange rates between countries

____ 10. Excess cash of a country used to invest for a profit

____ 11. Investment companies that pool money from investors with small amounts of money to invest

____ 12. A series of fixed payments from a capital investment

Review Concepts

13. List four ways that banks seek to meet their clients' international banking needs.

14. Describe the functions of the World Bank and the International Finance Corporation.

15. How does a letter of credit work?

16. What are the differences between a stock and a bond?

17. How did the Gramm-Leach-Bliley Act change banking institutions?

18. Why might firms seek to outsource products or services that they may have been previously producing or performing within their own organizations?

19. List reasons why businesses seek expert help when making capital investment decisions.

20. Give three examples of retirement planning services.

21. What is the probate process?

_____

_____

_____

_____

22. List four advantages that a charitable remainder trust provides.

_____

_____

_____

_____

Apply What You Learned

23. How does the USA Patriot Act of 2001 attempt to stop the financing of terrorist activities?

_____

_____

_____

24. How does the term "one stop shopping" apply to banks?

_____

_____

_____

25. Why are sovereign wealth funds significant?

_____

_____

_____

_____

26. Name four types of trust services.

_____

_____

_____

27. Describe factors that impact foreign exchange rates.

_____

_____

_____

_____

Make Academic Connections

28. **SOCIAL STUDIES**   Laws often result from what is happening in a society. Write a two-page report on how the Glass-Steagall Act and the Gramm-Leach-Bliley Act impacted banking. Discuss how each act was a reaction to current events of the time. Did GLBA contribute to the 2008 financial crisis?

29. **POLITICAL SCIENCE**   How did the Enron crisis affect current and former employees' retirement planning? Research on the Internet to find out how the pensions of people other than Enron employees were affected.

30. **CURRENT EVENTS**   Discuss the economic environment in the twenty-first century in terms of what makes it important for banks to advise their customers in the international arena.

31. **COMMUNICATION**   Interview an executive of a local bank on the subject of a particular insurance product. Get detailed information about how the product protects the consumer. Present your findings to the class in an oral report. Jot down ideas for interview questions here.

32. **BANKING MATH**   Find the current value of a Japanese yen (¥) as compared to a Chinese yuan. What is the cost of goods valued at 70,000 ¥ in yuan?

33. **RESEARCH**   Using the Internet, find out more about the World Bank and the International Finance Corporation. List additional functions of both institutions.

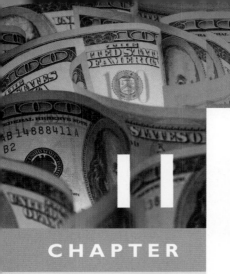

CHAPTER 11

Security, Fraud, and Ethics

11.1	Robbery Prevention and Response
11.2	Ethics in Banking
11.3	Fraud and Scams
11.4	Identity Theft

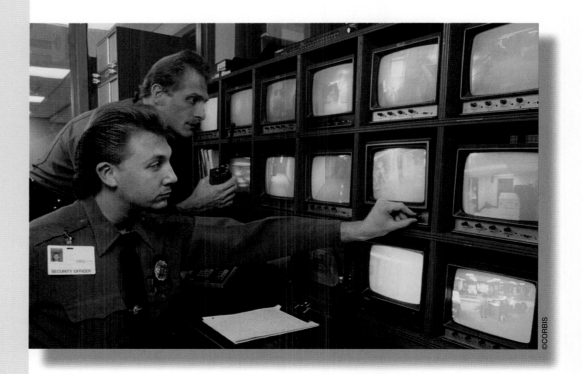

©CORBIS

skills that pay dividends

Convey a Professional Image

Strong relationships are fundamental to successful banking. Ongoing courteous, professional relationships between customers and bank representatives help maintain customer loyalty. Fair, prompt, and proactive service helps cement the relationship between businesses and banks. How do customers form their initial and ongoing impressions of a bank? What sways customers and businesses to select one bank over another? What can bankers do to put clients' minds at ease that the bank will carefully and thoughtfully handle their money?

A professional appearance of bank personnel helps influence customers' decision-making. Seeing bank staff look and act professional helps customers feel assured that their finances will be handled carefully and thoughtfully. Components of a professional appearance include personal grooming, clothing, and demeanor.

Each day you should go to work freshly showered. Hair should be neat. Fingernails should be well groomed. Remember, if you and a customer are exchanging forms or if you are counting out money to give to a customer, your hands will be quite visible. Perfume or cologne should be used moderately. Teeth should be brushed and your breath should be fresh. If you have body piercings or tattoos in nontypical, visible locations, you should consider how seeing those will influence customers' opinion of both you and your bank.

The banking industry tends to be conservative. You should select outfits that are appropriate to the industry. Trendy outfits that may make you a fashion leader in social situations may not be appropriate for the workplace. Classic, conservative styles are a better long-term wardrobe investment. Classic styles do not look dated as quickly as trendy styles. You can still inject your own personal or creative touches in a professional outfit through careful accessory selection. A well-coordinated scarf or tie can add some pizzazz to your outfit.

Match your clothing selection to the specific requirements of your job, your customer, and your agenda for the day. For example, if you are going to your customer's worksite to do a presentation on services your bank can offer to employees, a suit is probably most appropriate. If you are participating in a golf outing with the same customer on another day, then golf attire would be appropriate.

Your demeanor toward customers should be cheerful, respectful, and helpful. In most situations, sticking to the professional facts pertaining to the business situation is appropriate. Personal discussions regarding religion or politics should be avoided. You should demonstrate a knowledge of your industry and of current events that extends beyond the particular transaction you are conducting with the customer.

Develop Your Skill

Visit three workplaces in different industries. Observe the appearance of various staff members. Take notes on how the job duties of staff members affected their appearance. Reflect on how the appearance of staff members impacted your opinion of not only the employees, but of the business. Be prepared to share your observations with the class.

PHOTODISC

11.1

goals

+ Discuss how security measures can prevent bank robbery.

+ Describe what bank employees should do during a robbery.

terms

+ bandit barrier

Robbery Prevention and Response

Banking Scene

Cheyenne Rainwater has read about the recent increase in bank robberies in her city and is concerned. She knows that her money is protected, but she doesn't want to be present for one of these terrible events, which have resulted in harm to bystanders from time to time. What are some things she should look for that indicate her bank is trying to prevent robberies?

SECURITY AS PREVENTION

When asked why he robbed banks during the 1930s and 1940s, notorious bank robber Willie Sutton simply replied, "Because that's where the money is." You might think that bank robbery in today's world is merely a plot line for television and movies, but it is a reality and actually occurs all too often. Armed robbery is an inherent risk associated with financial institutions. According to the Federal Bureau of Investigation, 7,175 bank robberies—which are federal offenses—occurred in the United States during the year 2007, a 5 percent decrease over the number in the previous year. Every bank is a potential temptation to would-be robbers. Despite all of the expensive and state-of-the-art measures banks have invested in to prevent robberies, make them unprofitable, and enhance the capture and conviction of the perpetrator, robberies are a persistent problem.

Physical Security

Ensuring the security of assets, employees, and customers is a major concern for financial institutions. Physically securing the bank is an important deterrent to robbery. It's easy to picture vaults and safe-deposit boxes when you think of physical security at banks. Locking devices are certainly part of the business, but physical security includes other considerations sometimes less obvious.

- **Building design plays a role in physical security.** Everything from resistance to attack to placement of sprinklers is a consideration in facility design. Planning the facility for technology, control of physical access to the building, location and security of records, and even the types and placement of furniture are part of an integrated security plan. The bank should be well lit with the lights positioned so that they do not interfere with processing images of perpetrators captured on security video or film. The view of tellers by other employees should be unobstructed.

- **Surveillance and alarm technology continues to evolve.** Increasingly sophisticated devices with higher and higher resolution are appearing in banks. From closed-circuit television (CCTV) systems to monitoring software for all phases of processing operations, forms of surveillance are becoming increasingly complex. Surveillance cameras should be placed so they are seen by possible robbers and positioned to ensure a full front photograph of the robber.

- **Safety devices can be used. Bandit barriers,** which are bulletproof plastic shields, can be positioned in front of each teller's station. Popup security screens, which rise in a fraction of a second out of the counter to protect the teller, may also be used. Time-delay locks that require a PIN and allow access to the safe only during specific hours can be installed.

- **Transportation security is a part of physical security.** With the necessity of safeguarding cash and checks in transit, transportation security involves screening of employees involved in transportation. Companies providing this service are liable for the actions of employees.

Best Practices Recommendations

It is wise for a bank to adopt a list of "best practices" to help deter bank robberies and to aid in the apprehension of bank bandits. Some measures prevent robberies, some protect staff and customers during a robbery, some help apprehend the criminal, and some accomplish a combination of these objectives. Training is a critical factor in carrying out the best practices.

Training is the core of preventing robbery. For this reason, banks invest a lot of resources in teaching their employees how to recognize and what to do in an emergency. These procedures both lessen the risk of harm for staff and customers and minimize financial loss to the institution.

Most banks are required by law to install surveillance cameras and alarms, and properly trained staff can aid in ensuring that security devices work accurately and are used during a robbery. Security guards, customer service representatives, or others should engage customers as they enter the bank to present a plain view of the security presence and make potential robbers aware that they could be recognized later.

tech talk

Taking Technology To the Limits To Prevent Robberies

In the early 1990s in Los Angeles, as the number of bank robberies, particularly violent ones, soared, FBI and financial institutions worked together to address this problem. Subsequently, banks deemed "robbery-prone" constructed bullet-resistant "bandit barriers" or access control units (ACUs). The clear, bullet-resistant, Plexiglas partitions completely enclose the teller and adjacent cash storage areas from the top of the counter to the ceiling or from the floor to the ceiling at the entrance. The ACUs consist of an electronically controlled, double-door entrance and adjacent exit. Customers access the inside of the bank, one at a time, by entering through the entry's outer door. When the outer door closes, a device conducts an automatic magnetometer-type search for weapons. If the search proves negative, the inner door automatically unlocks, allowing entry into the facility. If the search yields a positive result, indicating a possible weapon, the bullet-resistant second door remains locked, and the person must retreat from the entry.

Think Critically How would you feel about doing your banking in a bank that uses "bandit barriers" and ACUs?

✔ checkpoint

What factors do you believe are responsible for bank robberies?

ROBBERY PREPARATION •

Just as tellers are usually the first to do business with customers, they are the first line of defense during a robbery. It is critical that teller training include what to do and *not* to do during a holdup. Training should emphasize that physical resistance is dangerous, not helpful. Tellers should do nothing that would risk their safety or that of others on the premises. Training should also include these instructions:

- Remain calm. Knowing what to do through training eliminates the need to make decisions during the crisis.

- Obey the robber's instructions. Employees should be assured that this is bank policy.

- Trigger foot-pedal or bill trap alarms and security cameras as soon as possible both to protect the safety of customers and employees and to help apprehend the robber. A *bill trap* is a device that sets off a security system when a bill or switch is pulled.

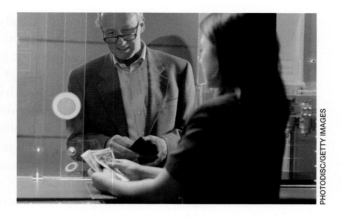

- Use decoy or marked money or specially prepared packs that contain an exploding device with a dye to mark the cash. Drop a satellite-tracking device into the bag of money.

- Call 911 as soon as reasonably possible to provide a detailed description of the perpetrator and the direction he or she seemed to be heading after fleeing the bank.

- Keep anything, such as a demand note, when possible for fingerprint identification, and minimize contamination of evidence and the crime scene. Countertops are ideal places on which bandits leave fingerprints.

- Note the robber's physical characteristics, particularly any outstanding feature. Also, if possible, note any characteristics of the get-away vehicle, such as the make, model, color, and license plate number.

- Write a description of the robber as soon as possible because memory fades quickly, especially in crisis situations. A robbery description form, such as the one below, can be used to help authorities gather information.

ROBBERY DESCRIPTION FORM (Sample)

Sex _____ Age _____ Race _____ Height _____ Weight _____

Build _____ Complexion (light, dark, etc.) _____

Hair _____ Eye Color _____ Facial Hair Beard _____ Mustache _____ Goatee, etc. ____

CLOTHING

Hat _____

Shirt _____

Coat or jacket (length and color) _____

Trousers (color and style) _____

Tie _____

Shoes _____

Other _____

MISCELLANEOUS

Weapon _____ Type _____

Speech _____

_____

Mannerisms _____

_____

Physical characteristics _____

(limp, deformities, etc.) _____

It is not uncommon for tellers to become paralyzed with fright during a robbery, leading them to forget procedures for safety and suspect identification. To avoid this situation, some banks provide training at teller schools several times per month and at high-risk banks at least annually. Individual branches reinforce the lessons through practice drills and at staff meetings. By doing so, the tellers are more likely to remember how to react during a robbery without endangering customers or employees.

Other employees at the bank play a critically important role by being sensitive to a tellers' body language and demeanor. For example, a change in a teller's voice tone or pitch could indicate that a holdup is in process. A normally relaxed teller who tenses up or a chatty one who becomes quiet could indicate trouble. In one Seattle bank, for instance, a coworker who noticed that sounds from a normally lively teller had become stiff realized that a robbery was occurring and triggered an alarm.

Types of Bank Robberies

Although bank employees can never be fully prepared for a bank robbery, it may be helpful for them to know the different types of robberies that commonly occur to help plan the appropriate actions to take.

Morning glory robberies take place prior to opening the bank for the day. The morning glory robber could break in and wait for employees to arrive, seize the employees outside the bank as they arrive, use a ruse tactic to attempt to enter the bank, or even seize an employee en route to or from work or at the employee's home. In a *takeover* bank robbery, two or more robbers carry weapons and invade the bank. This is the least common type of robbery. The most common type of bank robbery committed involves *note passing*. In this case, the robber enters the bank and passes a note to a bank employee. The note demands money. The robber may issue a verbal demand instead of passing a note. Weapons may be displayed in all types of robberies as a means of intimidating and coercing bank employees.

The FDIC as a Safety Net

When robberies occur, it is important that consumers understand that the Federal Deposit Insurance Corporation (FDIC) insures deposits in banks and thrift institutions for up to $100,000 per depositor in the event of failure. As part of the Emergency Economic Stabilization Act of 2008, FDIC insurance coverage per depositor was increased to $250,000 through 2009. Although it is unlikely that a robbery could result in bank failure, FDIC provides safety for individual accounts.

✔ checkpoint

Why is it important that bank employees not resist a robbery attempt?

assessment 11.1

Think Critically

1. How does the building facility design contribute to the physical security of a bank?

2. Closed-circuit television systems and security cameras are part of the technology that can identify suspects in bank robbery cases. What role do they play in preventing robberies?

3. Why are robbery training and preparation critical for bank employees, especially tellers?

4. In your opinion, what is the best deterrent in preventing robberies?

Make Academic Connections

5. **COMMUNICATION** Visit a local bank to find out what types of security measures it uses and employee training/preparation for robberies it offers. Present your findings in an oral report.

6. **RESEARCH** Internet banking presents new security challenges for financial institutions. Use the Internet to investigate what the most important issues are and how they are being resolved. Prepare a two-page report summarizing your findings.

7. **HISTORY** Study the bank robberies during the Great Depression. Why did the Secret Service become involved instead of leaving the crimes to local law enforcement?

11.2 Ethics in Banking

goals

+ Explain how ethics applies to financial institutions.

+ Identify ethical dilemmas that occur in banking.

terms

+ ethics

+ code of ethics

+ conflict of interest

Banking Scene

Recent scandals related to unethical and illegal activities have rocked the corporate world. Several banks have been involved. What can Cheyenne Rainwater do to determine whether her bank seeks to emphasize ethical behavior among its employees?

ETHICAL BEHAVIOR

Ethics can be defined as the process of determining standards and procedures for dealing with judgmental decisions affecting other people. Ethics refers to beliefs that distinguish right from wrong. An *ethical dilemma* involves a situation that is problematic and makes a person question what is the "right" or "wrong" thing to do. Ethical dilemmas make individuals think about their obligations, duties, or responsibilities. These dilemmas can be highly complex and difficult to resolve. Easier ones involve a right versus wrong answer. Most people will agree, for example, that it is unacceptable to pretend that someone else's work is your own. However, complex ethical dilemmas involve a decision between "right" and "right." An example might occur if you uncover a colleague's error. To whom are you obligated—your colleague or your employer? "There is only one way for a business to convince the public that it is ethical," says Gerald H. Lipkin, chairman, president, and CEO of Valley National Bancorp, "and that is to build a record of dealing fairly with its customers, communities, shareholders, and employees."

A **code of ethics** is a statement adopted by the management and board of directors of businesses to guide employees in taking appropriate actions in critical situations that could reflect on the organization. A code can help employees answer questions about a bank's policy on matters such as receiving gifts from customers and taking outside jobs. Most banks require employees to read the code regularly and certify that they are in compliance with its provisions. KPMG, the international accounting firm, found in its 2000 Organizational Integrity Survey that the ethical behavior of top executives affects employees' perception of their companies. Overall, 69 percent of the 2,390 employees of the companies surveyed believed that their current customers would recommend their company to others. But when employees believed management would uphold the company's stated ethical standards, that number shot up to 80 percent.

Important Elements in a Code of Ethics

Most banking codes of ethics include the following.

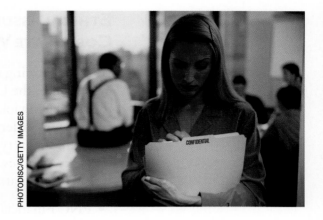

- **Confidentiality** Banking business is confidential, so only authorized individuals can receive information.

- **Dishonesty and fraudulent behavior** Such behavior will not be tolerated.

- **Representation of the institution** The behavior of employees must positively reflect the bank's integrity.

- **Gifts** Accepting gifts or money given to influence employees' performance of duties is strictly prohibited.

- **Financial management** All employees should practice wise financial management. Customers won't trust a bank to take care of their funds if its employees can't take care of their own money.

- **Conflict of interest** Employees must act with honesty and integrity, avoiding any personal activity, investment, or association that could appear to interfere with good judgment concerning the bank's best interests. A **conflict of interest** occurs when two interests are at cross-purposes. Employees are strictly prohibited from exploiting their position or relationship with the bank for personal gain.

- **Compliance with laws and regulations** Employees are required to provide full, fair, accurate, timely, and understandable disclosure in reports and documents that the bank files. Employees must perform their duties in accordance with all applicable laws and regulations.

- **Responsibility for violations** The conduct of employees can reinforce an ethical atmosphere and positively influence the conduct of their colleagues. Employees who are unable to stop suspected misconduct or discover it after it has occurred are required to report it immediately to the appropriate management.

When a bank develops its code of ethics, it must decide what it wants to stand for and then put appropriate information in writing (often in the company handbook or on the company website), discuss it with its employees, and then enforce it. This policy reflects the values that the bank has determined to be important.

 checkpoint

What is the purpose of a code of ethics?

ETHICAL ISSUES IN BANKING AND THE CORPORATE WORLD

At the beginning of the twenty-first century, a wave of corporate scandals broke out in the United States. A number of leading companies admitted that they had violated numerous regulations, including misstating their accounts, in order to project a positive impression of their status. In public companies, this type of "creative" accounting can be considered fraud. These companies violated both regulatory rules and accepted ethical practices. Unfortunately, the list could go on.

- PNC Financial Services Group Inc. reached a resolution with the Securities and Exchange Commission regarding charges that in violation of generally accepted accounting principles, PNC transferred from its financial statements approximately $762 million of volatile, troubled, or underperforming loans and venture capital assets. In addition, PNC issued a materially false and misleading press release that, among other things, overstated its 2001 full-year earnings per share by 52 percent.

- U.S. Bancorp settled a lawsuit brought by the Attorney General of Minnesota over the bank's sales of customer data to MemberWorks, a telemarketing company, for $4 million and a 22 percent commission on sales to those customers. The bank promised to end third-party sharing of information for marketing of nonfinancial products and provide customers the opportunity to opt out of affiliate-sharing of information for the purposes of selling additional company services.

- Citigroup Inc. agreed to pay $215 million to resolve charges that its Associates First Capital Corporation and Associates Corporation of North America had engaged in systematic and widespread deceptive practices designed to encourage borrowers to unknowingly purchase optional credit insurance products. It also participated in abusive lending practices.

- Enron Corporation, the energy trading and communications company based in Houston, Texas, used fraudulent accounting techniques that, when uncovered, caused it to become one of the largest corporate failures in history. It has become the symbol of institutionalized and well-planned corporate fraud.

- Merrill Lynch & Co., Inc., an investment banking company recognized as one of the world's leading financial management and advisory companies, reached an agreement in 2003 with New York State's attorney general on charges the firm's investment advice was influenced by conflicts of interest.

- Arthur Andersen, founded in 1913 and one of the Big Five U.S. accounting firms, was forced to cease business after accounting scandals involving Waste Management, Sunbeam, and Enron. Revelations of fraud in presenting Enron's financial statements and its felony conviction for obstructing justice for shredding tons of Enron documents led to the firm's demise.

Sarbanes-Oxley Act of 2002

On July 30, 2002, the *Public Company Accounting Reform and Investor Protection Act of 2002* (the *Sarbanes-Oxley Act of 2002*), also called SOX, was signed into law. It established a new Public Company Accounting Oversight Board with the power to set rules, investigate suspected wrongdoing, punish violators, and conduct regular inspections of accounting firms. The act gives broad new protections to corporate whistle blowers—employees who publicly report illegal activities occurring inside their company—and makes security fraud a criminal offense. A chief executive officer or chief financial officer who certifies false financial reports could get 20 years in prison and be fined $5 million. Shredding documents could result in a 20-year sentence. This act also places restrictions on loans by corporations to their executives. These restrictions strive to eliminate the interest-free loans that became a popular form of compensation for executives.

Ethics in Action

Billionaire-populist Warren Buffett is one of the richest men in the world and is chairman of the board and chief executive officer of Berkshire Hathaway Inc. In his 1998 letter to company shareholders, Mr. Buffett stated that "a significant and growing number of otherwise high-grade managers ... have come to view that it's okay to manipulate earnings to satisfy what they believe are Wall Street's desires. Indeed, many CEOs think this kind of manipulation is not only okay, but actually their duty. They also argue that in using accounting shenanigans to get the figures they want, they are doing only what everybody else does."

Think Critically

What ethical responsibility do employees at firms whose managers share this view owe to the company, the business community, and the public in general?

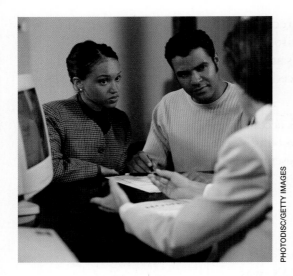
PHOTODISC/GETTY IMAGES

Everyday Ethical Dilemmas in Banking

The Sarbanes-Oxley Act addresses the behavior of corporate executives, but all bank employees, including tellers, accountants, loan officers, marketing directors, and customer service representatives, also face ethical dilemmas. Consider the ethical dilemmas in the following scenarios and the proper ethical action to take in each case.

- Luisa Sillas realizes that her immediate supervisor, who orders the bank's supplies, is taking kickbacks to order from several suppliers.

- Jerry Cappocci is a teller who processed the deposit of a rather confused customer for $1,600. The customer actually gave him $1,600 in checks and $75 in cash without realizing it.

- Several years ago while working with a client, Tanisha Higgins learned confidential information about the company's research. It is now planning to go public, and the information she learned indicates that purchase of its stock will be an excellent investment.

- Susan Issacs works for the marketing director of a large bank. She is sure that the facts of a new advertising campaign for bank loans are misleading but was told things were "okay."

Ethical Behavior as the Final Decision

Banking is an essential service like the supply of water, electricity, and police protection. As a result, ethics should be the ultimate factor in making decisions in the financial world. Banks must provide safe and convenient places for customers to take care of their financial needs. In providing essential services, bankers must be dedicated to giving advice based on the particular customer's financial position and situation in general, including loan and investment choices, willingness to take risks, and ability to assess the impact of the advice provided. Bankers should ensure that sufficient information about the bank's products and services is available to customers.

 checkpoint

What is it necessary to provide special protection to corporate whistle-blowers?

_____

_____

_____

assessment 11.2

Think Critically

1. Discuss how ethical dilemmas could involve making decisions between "right" and "right."

2. Why is confidentiality a critical element in banking?

3. Discuss the ethical implications of the ability of a bank to determine the interest rate for a loan.

4. Why did Congress and the President see the need for the Sarbanes-Oxley Act?

Make Academic Connections

5. **TECHNOLOGY**   Use the Internet to find out about ethical issues regarding online banking that are of concern to bank regulators. Present your findings to the class orally.

6. **RESEARCH**   Locate the websites of three commercial banks that have a code of ethics. List any elements not covered in this chapter.

7. **PROBLEM SOLVING**   As a supervisor, you must decide what to do about a loyal, honest employee who tries really hard but can't perform up to par, forcing coworkers to pick up the slack. You know that the employee is a single parent whose child has serious medical problems. What do you do?

11.3

goals

+ Identify types of fraud that are committed against banks.

+ Discuss mortgage-based scams.

terms

+ fraud

+ check kiting

+ forgery

+ check counterfeiting

+ scam

+ house flipping

+ straw buyer

Fraud and Scams

Banking Scene

Cheyenne Rainwater has learned from the news media that several people in her city have been victims of checking account scams. What can she do to protect herself from these crimes?

FRAUD RELATED TO BANKING ● ● ● ● ● ● ● ● ● ● ● ● ● ● ● ● ● ● ●

Although robbery is a concern for banks, far larger dollar values are lost through computer crime, vandalism, and various forms of fraud. **Fraud** is a deception deliberately practiced to secure unfair or unlawful gain. During 2007, it was estimated that the total amount of online fraud in the U.S. was about $240 million. The average victim lost about $2,500. The sheer volume of check and credit card transactions presents many opportunities for the unscrupulous. Various forms of fraud, some simple and some sophisticated, cost banks and consumers billions of dollars a year. Fighting and preventing these crimes is a never-ending part of the banking industry.

Fraud prevention occupies more resources of the banking industry than any other activity except routine processing. Bank administration is an important part of fraud prevention. Adhering to established procedures, including technology security rules, insisting on careful record keeping, conducting audits, and investigating suspicious activities of employees or customers are all part of an overall plan for security and fraud prevention.

Employee training may be the best return on investment for fraud prevention. Detailed checklists for ways to identify questionable or counterfeit checks, identification verification procedures, and frequent updates on new types of counterfeit and fraud schemes all help combat fraud on the front lines. Tellers, operations personnel, technicians, investment counselors, loan officers, and other personnel require training.

Consumer education is an effort that banks see as increasingly worthwhile. Most frauds are crimes of opportunity, and if consumers protect their checks, credit cards, identities, and account information more carefully, committing fraud becomes a more difficult task.

Counterfeit Currency and New Design

Counterfeiting money has been a crime throughout the history of the United States. It was a serious problem during the nineteenth century when banks issued their own currency. At the time of the Civil War, it was estimated that one-third of all currency in circulation was counterfeit. The adoption of a national currency in 1863 did not, as expected, solve the counterfeiting problem. On July 5, 1865, the United States

created the Secret Service to suppress counterfeiting. More recently, in 2006, an estimated $62 million dollars was lost in the U.S. due to counterfeiting. Nearly 4,000 people were arrested for crimes relating to the counterfeiting.

To address the continuing "funny money" problem, in 2003 the Federal Reserve began issuing redesigned bills. To date, the $5, $10, $20, and $50 bills have been redesigned. The most noticeable difference in the new $20 notes is the use of subtle green, peach, and blue colors featured in the background. The new $20 note design retains three important security features:

- The watermark, the faint image similar to the large portrait, which is part of the paper itself and is visible from both sides when the bill is held up to the light.

- The vertical strip of plastic making up the security thread—also visible from both sides when held up to the light—is embedded in the paper. "USA TWENTY" and a small flag are visible on the thread.

- The color-shifting ink—the numeral "20" in the lower-right corner on the face of the note—changes from copper to green when the note is tilted. The color shift is more dramatic and easier to see on the new notes.

Check Fraud

Statistics indicate the seriousness of check fraud. In a recent eight-month period, postal inspectors seized more than $2 billion of fake checks. The advancement of computer technology has made it increasingly easy for criminals, either individually or in organized groups, to manipulate checks to deceive unknowing victims. Desktop publishing and copying to create or duplicate an actual financial document are responsible for a significant amount of check fraud today. In most cases, these crimes begin with the theft of a financial document, such as a blank check, taken from your home or vehicle during a burglary, a canceled or old check you threw away, or a check you just put in your mailbox. Two of the most common schemes directed at banks are check kiting and money laundering. Other check fraud includes forgery, counterfeiting or alteration, and paperhanging.

Check Kiting   The fraud of **check kiting** requires opening accounts at two or more institutions and using "the float time" of available funds to create fraudulent balances. A person draws a check for an amount that exceeds the account balance at one bank and then deposits it at another bank. Before that deposit can be processed, the individual draws a check on the second bank to deposit at the first bank. Although neither bank account has

interesting *facts*

The National Consumers League is America's oldest nonprofit consumer group. In 1996 it launched Internet Fraud Watch to prevent online and Internet fraud by helping people recognize possible scams. The most common fraud signs on the Internet are incredibly low prices, extravagant promises of profits, guarantees of credit regardless of bad credit histories, or prizes that require payment to obtain. ■

enough money to cover the checks, the person may withdraw more than the collected balance from the first account.

Check kiting has become easier in recent years due to the Expedited Funds Availability Act of 1987, which requires banks to make funds available sooner. The Check 21 Act passed in October 2003 has probably helped counteract this problem. Instead of requiring physical possession of a paper check by the issuing bank before funds are transferred, the Check 21 Act allows the receiving bank to treat an electronic image of the check, called an Image Replacement Document (IRD), the same as the check itself. This significantly reduces the check clearing process time and has the power to help eliminate check kiting.

Money Laundering   The scheme of money laundering received its name because criminals use it to make money "clean." Criminals use the process to conceal illicitly acquired funds by converting them into seemingly legitimate income. Originally used to refer to the proceeds of organized crime, the term is now often associated with financial activities of drug dealers who seek to launder the large amounts of cash they generate from the sale of narcotics. Money laundering does not cause financial institutions a loss, but it makes large sums of money difficult to trace.

To help combat money laundering, Congress has passed several laws. The Bank Secrecy Act requires financial institutions to report suspicious transactions that may be a possible violation of law. This act creates a paper trail for currency so that money can not be deposited, invested, or exchanged in a way that conceals its illegal source. This discourages the use of banks to hide transfers or deposits of money derived from criminal activity.

The Patriot Act of 2001 prohibits financial relationships with banks that have no physical presence in their host county. Under this act, banks must use

Banking Math *Connection*

Many insurance policies currently will protect for losses caused by the acceptance in good faith of counterfeit money. Most pay from $500 to $1,000 for a loss. During a garage sale, a family unfortunately accepted $500 in counterfeit bills for a purchase. The family's insurance policy covered losses from counterfeit money up to $700 with a $200 deductible. Did the family experience a loss from this transaction? If so, how much?

Solution

Because the loss is less than the $700 ceiling, the formula for determining loss is

Amount of loss − Deductible = Amount covered

$500 − $200 = $300

The insurance covers $300, so the actual out-of-pocket loss is $200 ($500 loss − $300).

due diligence to determine the identity and source of transactions. The Patriot Act seeks to curtail the financing of terrorism with laundered money.

Forgery   Check **forgery**, or counterfeiting a check or other document with the intent to defraud, is difficult to spot. Criminals steal a check, endorse it with a forged or unauthorized signature, and, using fake identification, present it for payment at a retail location or a bank.

Counterfeiting and Alteration   Check **counterfeiting** can mean either entirely creating a check with desktop publishing equipment (personal computer, scanner, cutting-edge software, and top-grade laser printer) or simply duplicating a check with advanced color photocopiers. *Alteration* removes or modifies handwriting and information on the check with chemicals and solvents such as acetone, brake fluid, and household bleach.

Paperhanging   The act of purposefully writing checks on closed accounts or reordering checks for closed accounts is *paperhanging*. It is also known as *closed account fraud*.

Signs of Counterfeit Checks

Several signs can indicate a bad check. Telling signs are lack of perforations, a low number (such as 101 through 400 on personal checks or 1001-1500 on business checks), or no address for the customer or the bank. Stains or discoloration perhaps caused by erasures or alterations are other signs. Be alert to the Magnetic Ink Character Recognition coding number printed along the bottom: if it is shiny, if it does not match the check number, or if it is missing.

The first and probably most important line of defense against counterfeit checks is teller training. Knowing how to verify a check and what to look for on a suspicious one is the focus of training efforts.

Consumer Tips for Preventing Check Fraud

Checks are the most common negotiable instrument and should be treated as carefully as cash. Here are some steps to prevent check fraud.

- Use checks that have built-in security features. Many of these checks have a padlock icon on them to indicate the presence of enhanced security features such as watermarking and microprinting.

- Don't have your social security number imprinted on checks. Your SSN is enough for a criminal to get a credit card, bank account, or fake loan.

- Don't endorse a check until just before you cash or deposit it. It is better, in fact, if you sign the check in a teller's presence.

- Don't leave spaces on checks. Draw horizontal lines to fill any blank spaces, and write words close together, especially on amount lines.

- Reconcile your account regularly. Call your bank immediately if you notice any suspicious transactions on your statement.

- Shred statements, canceled checks, ATM slips, and credit card receipts, rather than just throwing them in the trash.

Conduct a poll of at least 10 people in your community about checking account scams. Have they experienced any attempts to obtain their checking account information that they thought were suspicious? If so, what were the circumstances?

- Be careful on the phone, in person, and on the Web. Never give out account information or numbers to anyone you don't know or of whom you are not certain. Don't be afraid to contact authorities.

How has computer technology affected counterfeit checking scams?

_____

_____

MORTGAGE-BASED SCAMS

Scam is a slang term for something that is fraudulent or a swindle. When a scam is perpetrated, trickery is used to intentionally dupe an individual or business into a transaction for the financial benefit of the thief. Available scams are limited only by the creativity of the thief.

Illegal Mortgage Practices

The recent mortgage and financial crisis put a lot of pressure on people throughout the economy. Businesses affected ranged from those who supply the raw materials to build a house through those that provide the décor for a finished home. Increased pressure to compensate for lost income due to tightened credit and reduced home sales has made many participants in the housing industry vulnerable to illegal schemes.

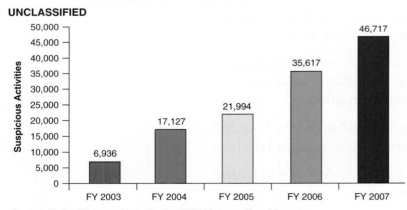

Mortgage Fraud Related Suspicious Activities

UNCLASSIFIED

Source: *Federal Bureau of Investigation 2007 Mortgage Fraud Report*

The FBI's *2007 Mortgage Fraud Report* highlighted common schemes. According to their research, between 2003 and 2007, reported instances of mortgage fraud rose from about 7,000 cases to about 47,000 cases. The graph provides a detailed overview of the increased incidents of fraud. Successful schemes resulted in financial losses to financial institutions. Some of the schemes are summarized below.

Illegal House Flipping House flipping commonly refers to the practice of buying a house for below market value and selling the house at or above market value. Oftentimes an increased sale price is obtained either because renovations were made to the home or because a distressed seller originally sold the house at below market value. This process becomes illegal if a fraudulent appraisal, which artificially inflates the value of the house, is used to secure a loan by a second buyer. In some schemes, a straw buyer is used to help with

flat world...

Scam Targets New Zealanders

In 2003, a slick online banking scam fooled New Zealanders into losing large sums of money. A website with a professional look and claiming to be business partners with all leading New Zealand banks was customized for New Zealand readers. The scam worked by convincing people to accept deposits into their bank accounts and then to send the funds minus a transaction fee to a third party. Of course, the initial deposit is then canceled. For example, a scam "associate" might deposit $14,000 into the account of a New Zealander, who then sends $13,500 on to someone else as soon as possible on the same day. The scammer then quickly cancels the $14,000 deposit. The result: The unlucky New Zealander has lost his or her own $13,500 sent to its perpetrators.

Think Critically   What do you think can be done to protect people from scams such as the one in New Zealand?

the scheme. A **straw buyer** is someone who agrees to use their personal information to buy the home at a falsely inflated price. The straw buyer agrees to state that they intend to live in the home even though their actual intent is to flip the home. Sometimes a straw buyer knows that they are participating in a fraudulent scheme and sometimes they themselves are victims.

Profits from illegal house flipping can be obtained by intentionally defaulting on a loan. For example, Buyer A purchases a house for $30,000 and then has it fraudulently appraised for $100,000. Buyer A solicits the help of Buyer B, a straw buyer, to purchase the house for $100,000 by obtaining a bank loan for $80,000. Buyer B does not plan to move in to the house and plans to default on the loan. An illegal profit of $50,000 is available to be shared between Buyer A and Buyer B. (An $80,000 loan minus the initial $30,000 investment in the house.) The bank is then left with a loss of $50,000. This loss arises because the bank has an $80,000 mortgage on a house that has a true value of $30,000. According to the FBI, if the loan was FHA-insured, then the loss is absorbed by the government.

Other Mortgage-Based Schemes   A variety of other schemes exploit the same concepts of illegally inflating the value of a house, obtaining financing to pay for the inflated value, and defaulting on loans for personal gain. Names of some of these schemes include *Builder-Bailout Schemes*, *Seller Assistance Scams*, *Short-Sale Schemes*, and *Foreclosure Rescue Scams*.

✔ checkpoint

What is the necessary step in the process to ensure that an illegal house flipping scheme achieves a profit?

assessment 11.3

Think Critically

1. How have $20 bills been redesigned to prevent counterfeit scams?

_____

_____

_____

2. Discuss how a person could commit check fraud on your account. When are you likely to first be aware that you've been a victim of the scam?

_____

_____

_____

3. How does mortgage fraud generate a profit for participants?

_____

_____

_____

_____

4. Why have mortgage-based schemes been rising over the last few years?

_____

_____

_____

_____

Make Academic Connections

5. **COMMUNICATION**   Talk to a local bank official about check fraud. Does the bank use any technological devices to identify counterfeit checks? If so, explain them in a one-page report.

6. **BANKING MATH**   If you accept counterfeit bills in payment for a $650 antique you sell at a flea market, what will be your actual loss if your insurance has a $900 limit and a $225 deductible?

_____

_____

_____

_____

Identity Theft

Banking Scene

Cheyenne was puzzled and embarrassed. While pumping gas, the attendant had said, over the loud speaker where everyone could hear, that her credit card had been declined. As she paid her bill in full and on time each month, she did not know why her credit card was declined. When she got home, Cheyenne called her bank. She was informed that her credit card had been closed due to suspicious activity that included charges in two separate states within hours of each other. Cheyenne then regretted not checking her voice mails promptly, as the bank had left her a message to call. Apparently, someone had obtained access to Cheyenne's account information and illegally used her identity. What should she do? Could she have prevented this?

goals

+ Explain the concept of identity theft.
+ Describe various identity theft methods.
+ Discuss identity theft prevention.

terms

+ spam
+ phishing
+ war driving
+ sniffer program
+ fraud alert
+ credit freeze

AN OVERVIEW OF IDENTITY THEFT

Identity theft occurs when someone intentionally obtains your personal information to use that information for personal gain. By illegally identifying themselves as you, they engage in financial transactions that enable them to receive goods and services that are charged to your accounts.

Categories of Identity Theft

In November, 2007, the Federal Trade Commission (FTC) released the *2006 Identity Theft Survey Report*. This report categorized identity theft by the severity of the harm caused by the identity thief. The *Existing Credit Card Only* categorization occurs when the thief only misuses one or more existing credit cards. It is the least serious category. The *Existing Non-Credit Card Account* categorization occurs when the thief accesses an existing account, like a checking or savings account, that is not a credit card account. The most serious category is *New Accounts and Other Frauds*. In this instance, the thief opens new accounts using the victim's identity. This type of identity theft can be difficult for the victim to catch. One way to catch this is to do an annual review of your credit report.

How Identity Theft Information Is Obtained

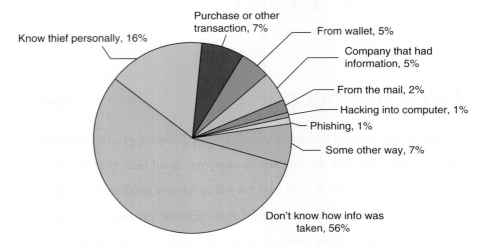

Purchase or other transaction, 7%

Know thief personally, 16%

From wallet, 5%

Company that had information, 5%

From the mail, 2%

Hacking into computer, 1%

Phishing, 1%

Some other way, 7%

Don't know how info was taken, 56%

Source: Federal Trade Commission — *2006 Identity Theft Survey Report*

Costs of Identity Theft

When identity theft occurs, victims experience financial costs, emotional costs, and loss of productive time. They have to use their time to resolve the many issues that arise from the identity theft.

According to the FTC's report, $500 was the median value of goods and services obtained by identity thieves. However, 5 percent of victims indicated that the thieves obtained at least $13,000 of products.

Fortunately, over half of the victims incurred no out-of-pocket expenses. Some victims, however, had expenses of $5,000 or more. Attorney fees, loss of salary, and paying for any charges attributed to the thief are among the potential costs. There is a variety of laws designed to protect consumers from out-of-pocket losses that result from identity theft.

Although the median amount of time victims spent resolving the identity theft was four hours, some victims spent at least 130 hours resolving the identity theft. The feelings of identity theft victims range from vulnerability to violation of personal privacy to anger to sadness. The emotional stress caused by identity theft adds to the overall fatigue victims experience when dealing with what can be a long process to thoroughly resolve all issues stemming from the theft.

 checkpoint

What are the three general categories of identity theft?

_____

_____

_____

METHODS FOR STEALING IDENTITIES ● ● ● ● ● ● ● ● ● ● ● ● ●

There is a variety of methods available for stealing identities. As technology evolves and as customer payment systems change, new methods of obtaining personal information become available. Some theft methods are manual and other methods are electronic.

Manual Ways to Commit Identity Theft

Identity thieves can be fairly creative. They have found ways to steal personal information through telephone scams, by using information from employment records, through stealing mail in residential mailboxes, by going through the trash, and through in-person observation. Once these methods are used to construct a false identity, the thief either steals the individual's funds or obtains credit in the name of the victim.

Telephone Scams   Many scams are committed using the telephone. The scam may begin with a postcard advertising easy credit approval or low credit card interest rates. When consumers call these phone numbers, someone asks for their checking account number, supposedly as part of a "verification process." Other scams involve con artists that call and claim to be from the person's bank, saying they need to verify certain information about the checking account for various reasons. Another common scam is to call people to tell them that they have won a prize. After a few minutes of pleasant chat, the thief requires the person to read the numbers off the bottom of a check to "confirm" that he or she "qualifies" for the prize. With checking account information, the con artist can issue a bank draft on the person's checking account.

©TYLER OLSON 2008/USED UNDER LICENSE FROM SHUTTERSTOCK.COM

Mail Theft   Some identity thieves steal mail from residential mailboxes. As about 700 million pieces of mail are delivered daily, thieves have ample opportunity to steal mail. Personal information, including credit card numbers and bank account numbers, can be obtained this way. Offers addressed to the resident for new credit or new loans can also be stolen. Once the thief obtains these documents, the information can be used to illegally establish accounts, apply for a loan, or access funds in existing accounts.

The U.S. Postal Inspection service works hard to prevent mail theft. According to their website, in 2007 they arrested more than 9,000 suspects for crimes relating to the mail. More than half of those arrests related to mail theft or identity crimes.

NETBookmark

The Federal Trade Commission (FTC) is dedicated to helping individuals and businesses avoid becoming victims of identity theft. Access www.cengage.com/school/pfinance/banking and click on the link for Chapter 11. Go to the Federal Trade Commission website. Review the content in the Hot Links section. What are some new identity theft schemes? How can you and your employer work to avoid them?

www.cengage.com/school/pfinance/banking

Trash Retrieval   Dumpster diving occurs when a thief goes through the trash of a business or individual with the specific intent of finding either personal identifying information or account information to construct a false identity.

Observation   In this day and age, it's hard to know who is watching you. Discrete image-taking devices, ranging from cell phone cameras to pocket-sized video recorders with micro button cameras, can record you discretely. Thieves can record an image of a credit card left exposed on a restaurant table or can photograph a customer entering a PIN in a retail store.

Electronic Ways to Commit Identity Theft

The Internet has streamlined financial transactions. It has also streamlined identity theft. The Internet allows individuals or companies to communicate with tens of thousands of people without spending much time, effort, or money. The Securities and Exchange Commission says that **spam**, or junk e-mail, allows "the unscrupulous to target more potential investors than cold calling or mass mailing." Spammers can use a bulk e-mail program to send personalized messages to thousands of Internet users at a time. In addition, anyone can also reach a large audience by posting a message on an online bulletin board. Fraudsters use spam to find investors for bogus investment schemes. Electronic methods for stealing identities abound.

Phishing   Common attacks on banks through the Internet include **phishing** ("fishing"), which is the act of sending a user an e-mail falsely claiming to be a legitimate enterprise in an attempt to solicit private information. The e-mail directs the users to visit a website onto which they are to update personal information, such as passwords and credit card, Social Security, and bank account numbers. The scammer commits identity theft using this information.

Hacking   Computer hackers that gain access to records or systems pose another threat to consumers and banks. Banks should use tools such as anti-virus software and *autobots*, programs that constantly monitor all transactions looking for abnormalities. *Firewalls*, programs that monitor and limit incoming and outgoing transmissions, have become increasingly important as banks allow access to records for online banking via the Internet. Banks must safeguard the technology that makes doing business possible.

Fraudelent HELOC Accounts   A HELOC loan enables borrowers to borrow against a home equity line of credit. Withdrawals against the credit can be made by check or credit card. An identity thief can open an online HELOC account using a false identity and then methodically withdraw funds from the account.

Fake Websites   There are multiple ways to extract personal information from fraudulent websites. One method is to develop a website that looks like an authentic business and prompt people to pay for a product or service from that website. When the victim enters identifying credit information, the thieves can use that information for their own purposes.

Another method exploits design weaknesses in the Domain Name System (D.N.S.). In the early 1980s, the D.N.S. was developed to provide Internet addresses. The system was not initially intended to safeguard transactions, like credit transactions, that required specific identity verification. Internet-savvy thieves can exploit the D.N.S. to redirect website visitors to nonlegititmate locations where their personal account information can be collected.

Personnel Data Theft   In the age of laptops and flash drives, it is fairly easy for confidential employee information to be lost or stolen. In recent years, electronic versions of personnel data has been stolen from a diverse array of organizations including the United States Veteran Affairs, Equifax, the District of Columbia, and Google. In many instances, an employer will offer employees a one-year free subscription to an identity-theft monitoring service after a data theft occurs.

Looking for Opportunities   Some thieves seek to abuse wi-fi systems used by stores to transmit customer credit information. **War driving** refers to the criminal practice of driving around to find retailers with weaknesses in their Internet security systems. Once a weakness has been found, **sniffer programs,** which are electronic programs that capture account numbers and PINs, can be installed.

One particularly effective example of this was widely reported during the summer of 2008. In this case, an international ring of thieves exploited weaknesses in the Internet security of major retailers including T.J. Maxx, Barnes & Noble, and OfficeMax. More than 41 million debit and credit card numbers were stolen. Sometimes the stolen numbers were sold online and sometimes they were used to manufacture fraudulent ATM cards. Cash could be withdrawn from victims' accounts with the fraudulent ATM cards.

List six ways to steal identity information electronically.

IDENTITY THEFT PREVENTION

There are a number of ways to proactively protect your personal information to try to avoid being an identity theft victim.

Common Sense Precautions

Keep your radar up at all times regarding any suspicious activities or inquiries. If someone unfamiliar is walking around your neighborhood and looking into mailboxes, keep an eye on them. If you think they are stealing mail, contact law enforcement authorities. Never provide account access codes, Social Security numbers, or other personal identifying information over the phone or online unless you are absolutely certain of the validity of the parties with whom you are interacting. Shred all documents containing personal identifying information—including offers for new credit that arrive in the mail.

Electronic Precautions

A **fraud alert** is an electronic warning placed on your accounts to monitor for suspicious financial activity. According to the FTC, you are legally entitled to two free types of fraud alerts. An *initial fraud alert* is good for 90 days and could be put in place if you suspect you may soon be a victim of identity theft. (If perhaps, your wallet was recently stolen.) An *extended fraud alert* lasts for seven years. An extended alert is a good idea if you have been a victim of identity theft. A copy of the Identity Theft Report must be submitted before an extended fraud alert can be placed on your account. A **credit freeze** prohibits access to your credit report. These electronic protections provide a good first step, but they do not necessarily prevent all types of identity theft.

Commercially Sold Identity Protection Packages

Many private companies offer a variety of services to help combat identity theft. Some companies offer services, like fraud alerts, that are actually available for free. Some companies may help you resolve complications resulting from being an identity theft victim. Carefully evaluate the services and costs of such programs. Determine the true value they offer before purchasing them.

 checkpoint

Distinguish between the two types of fraud alerts.

assessment 11.4

Think Critically

1. Identify financial costs associated with identity theft.

_____

_____

_____

2. Name four manual ways to commit identity theft.

_____

_____

3. How have electronic transactions and the Internet made identity thieves more efficient?

_____

_____

_____

4. List some ways to prevent identity theft.

_____

_____

_____

Make Academic Connections

5. **LAW ENFORCEMENT** The postal service is actively involved in trying to catch criminals. Go to their website at http://postalinspectors.uspis.gov/. Review the information on consumer awareness. List and define the types of fraud on the website that are not covered in this section. Be prepared to discuss your answers with the class.

_____

_____

6. **CURRENT EVENTS** Recently the post office made 77 arrests that spanned three countries to stop the flow of 666,000 fake checks. Research other recent arrests for fraud. Summarize the nature of the crime, the amount of the damage, and the agency that caught the thieves. Be prepared to share your research with the class.

_____

_____

chapter 11 assessment

Chapter Summary

11.1 Robbery Prevention and Response

A. Robbery prevention involves installing security equipment and training employees how to behave during a robbery.

B. During a bank robbery, employees should be concerned with the twin goals of safety and identification.

11.2 Ethics in Banking

A. Many banks provide written codes of ethics to help their employees know how to choose the "proper" behavior in specified circumstances.

B. Making the correct ethical decision for a company has become clouded recently with the concern for the "bottom line." Banks must be especially careful to make ethical decisions.

11.3 Fraud and Scams

A. Banking fraud has always occurred, but methods of performing bank fraud have increased with technological advances.

B. Checking account scams seek to find ways to illegally obtain money from the accounts of unsuspecting victims.

11.4 Identity Theft

A. Existing Credit Card Only, Existing Non-Credit Card Account, and New Accounts and Other Frauds are categories of identity theft.

B. Identity theft can be prevented.

Vocabulary Builder

a. bandit barrier
b. check counterfeiting
c. check kiting
d. code of ethics
e. conflict of interest
f. credit freeze
g. ethics
h. forgery
i. fraud
j. fraud alert
k. house flipping
l. phishing
m. scam
n. sniffer program
o. spam
p. straw buyer
q. war driving

Choose the term that best fits the definition. Write the letter of the answer in the space provided. Some terms may not be used.

____ 1. Another term for junk e-mail

____ 2. Act of sending an e-mail to a user falsely claiming to be an established legitimate enterprise to scam the user

____ 3. Process of determining standards and procedures for dealing with judgmental decisions affecting other people

____ 4. Situation in which two interests are at cross-purposes

____ 5. Using a fraudulent appraisal to extract value on a loan for a property you plan to default on

____ 6. Slang term for something that is fraudulent or a swindle

____ 7. Deception deliberately practiced to secure unfair or unlawful gain

____ 8. Name for bulletproof plastic shield at a teller's station

____ 9. Act of opening accounts at two or more institutions and using the "float time" of available funds to create fraudulent balances

____ 10. Statement adopted by management to guide employees in taking appropriate actions in critical situations that could reflect on the organization

Review Concepts

11. Discuss the way security can be described as robbery prevention.

_____

_____

_____

12. Name several actions that should be part of a "best practices" list for a bank.

_____

_____

_____

13. Why is training the key to preventing robbery?

_____

_____

_____

14. Discuss some actions that tellers should take during a robbery to help identify a suspect afterward.

_____

_____

_____

_____

_____

15. Explain how fraud related to banking may be committed.

_____

_____

_____

16. How does a credit freeze help prevent identity theft?

_____

_____

_____

17. Discuss the signs to look for that could identify counterfeit checks.

_____

_____

18. List and explain some steps to take to avoid becoming the victim of check fraud.

_____

_____

19. Describe what is involved in identity theft.

_____

_____

_____

20. What is the relationship between war driving and sniffer programs?

_____

_____

21. What is the Sarbanes-Oxley Act? What behavior does it seek to prevent?

_____

_____

_____

_____

Apply What You Learned

22. Why are the services of an appraiser critical for an illegal mortgage flipping scheme?

_____

_____

_____

23. Why do banks insist that employees not take any heroic measures during a robbery?

_____

_____

_____

24. What aspects of currency design can help prevent counterfeiting?

_____

_____

25. How has computer technology affected bank fraud?

_____

_____

_____

26. Give at least two examples of a conflict of interest or of a breach of confidentiality that could occur in banking.

_____

_____

27. What do you think caused the accounting scandals of the early twenty-first century?

28. Why should you be concerned about who is watching your financial transactions?

Make Academic Connections

29. **CRIMINOLOGY** Crooks can be quite clever. Use the Internet or other research materials to learn about some specific forms of fraud that are currently problematic. Present a report to the class about how they work and how they can be prevented.

30. **PROBLEM SOLVING** As the head of the HR department in your bank, you must develop screening procedures to be used during the hiring process. Create a list detailing the background information required of prospective employees and the steps to take to verify the information.

31. **ETHICS** Make a list of ethical dilemmas you have experienced during your daily life and describe how you handled each situation.

32. **COMMUNICATION** Do you believe that fraud can ever be effectively eliminated from the banking system? Explain your answer.

12

Bank Marketing

12.1	Define the Customer
12.2	Develop and Maintain the Customer
12.3	Public Relations
12.4	Customer Service
12.5	Marketing and Advertising

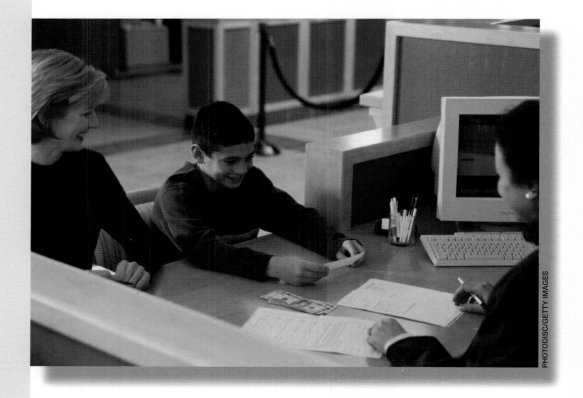

PHOTODISC/GETTY IMAGES

skills that pay dividends

Understanding Consumer Motives

People have a variety of reasons for buying products and services. Some of these reasons are based on thoughts and some are based on feelings.

Banking is a basic need in modern society. Intellectually, most people understand that they need a bank to deposit a paycheck, to hold their funds, to provide various checking and savings accounts, and to provide ATM services. How a bank is chosen depends on the personality and values of the customer.

An analytical customer may do a lot of research to compare products, service levels, and costs among competing banks. If an analytical customer values cost effectiveness and efficiency, they may select the bank that provides the best combination of both. This analytical customer takes a detached, objective approach to decision making.

Some customers take a more emotional approach when choosing a bank. A customer who either lived through the depression or who is worried about the lasting impact of the 2008 credit crisis may place a high premium on the security of their funds. This customer may gravitate to a bank with personnel that convey a strong sense of financial knowledge and financial responsibility. During banking transactions, this customer may often seek reassurance that their funds are safe.

A customer with a strong need either to feel like part of a community or to do business with people they know socially may place a higher premium on banking where one can develop strong personal relationships. This customer may not thoroughly comparison shop and may select, instead, to choose a bank where they feel they can trust the people they know.

When interacting with customers regarding product or service selection, ask them to rank what is most important to them in their selection process. Their answers will reveal whether they are more analytical, emotional, or a combination of both. Using their responses to frame your discussion, emphasize the qualities of your products or services that are most important to them. For example, efficiency- and value-driven customers might be influenced to buy from you if they hear about all of the free online services offered by your bank. Socially oriented customers might like to hear about outings to pro baseball games sponsored by your bank.

Customers make post-purchase evaluations. Followup with customers after a purchase to see if there's anything you can do to improve their satisfaction.

Develop Your Skill

In small groups, assign the role of an analytical customer and a social customer to group members. Assign the role of a bank representative, focusing on specific bank products, like a checking account or a CD, to other group members. The bank representatives should try to sell each type of customer their product by first asking the customer to list their decision priorities and then by framing the discussion around those priorities. Reflect on how the approaches and conversations are different based on the personality type of the customer. Be prepared to share your findings with the class.

PHOTODISC

12.1

goals

+ Understand customer characteristics.

+ Apply customer characteristics to banking customers.

terms

+ demographics

+ need

+ want

+ customer segmentation

+ target market

Define the Customer

Banking Scene

Yuan Liang is new to the city. He grew up in a small community where most people know each other, and he went to college in a nearby small town. He needs to find a bank where he can open checking and savings accounts. He knows what he expects from a bank, but he isn't sure how to identify one that meets his needs. He wants to be a valued customer at his bank. How can he find a bank that is interested in a customer who is just beginning his or her career?

CUSTOMERS ARE THE REASON BUSINESSES EXIST ● ● ● ● ● ●

All businesses exist to serve customers. Successfully defining current customers and accurately identifying targeted customers is critical to a business's ability to prosper.

Who is a Customer?

Marketing theories abound on how to best define a customer. However, there are common definitions of terms that describe characteristics of customers. **Demographics** refers to the specific shared characteristics that comprise distinct groups of consumers. Income, age, gender, race, profession, and home zip code are examples of specific customer characteristics. Knowing the demographic composition of your customers will help you decide which financial products to offer either nationally, regionally, or locally. For example, a bank branch located in a zip code with high net worth residents might elect to highlight investment options at that branch.

Customers have needs and wants. A **need** is a requirement for basic survival. Basic physiological needs include air, food, clothing, and shelter. A **want** is something that you would prefer to have but that you could live without if necessary. Wants may include Blackberrys, iPods, and designer clothes. In modern society, citizens have a basic need for money. If they want to have written records of their transactions, buy or rent a home, pay bills online, or put their money in a safe location, then they need the services of a financial institution.

Customer Segmentation

Banks recognize that they can't be all things to all people. **Customer segmentation** is the process of dividing customers into subgroups, each of which is identifiable by its specific preferences or needs, so that distinctive products can be developed for and sold profitably to these groups. As an example, all customers who need to open checking accounts are not the same but want and need different things from that account. Some want to write only a few checks a month, but others need to write unlimited checks and are willing to pay a fee for the service.

PHOTODISC/GETTY IMAGES

A **target market** is a preselected group of buyers for whom a product or service is created and to whom a marketing campaign is directed. For example, the target market for a small car that gets 60 miles to the gallon of gas won't be the same as the one for a large vehicle that gets 15 mpg.

 checkpoint

What is demographic information?

_____

_____

IDENTIFYING A BANKING CUSTOMER • • • • • • • • • • • • • • •

There are multiple ways to define, group, service, and sell to banking customers. The way that a bank defines its customers will impact how it provides products and services to those customers.

Individual Customers

Many bank customers are interested in services for themselves or their households. Ongoing products and services these customers need include checking accounts, savings accounts, CDs, insurance, and online banking. Lending products they need include mortgage, car, and home-equity and student loans. They may also seek credit cards, wealth management assistance, retirement planning, and trust planning. Within each of these categories of need there are multiple ways to approach the customer and multiple products from which each customer can choose.

branching out

Aisling

Banks have had branches in nontraditional locations, like grocery stores, for well over a decade. In addition to providing convenience to customers, these branches need to work to stay prominent in customers' minds. A variety of creative marketing approaches have been used by personnel at nontraditional branches. At one Ohio bank, tellers take to the supermarket aisles to interact with customers. By telling customers that they can receive $100,000 if they can identify the name of the bank located in the store, customers are prompted to recall the bank's name. If they correctly identify the name of the bank, the teller then gives them a $100,000 candy bar. Undoubtedly, receiving the candy sweetens their experience!

Think Critically How would you react if your grocery shopping experience included an individualized marketing effort by a bank? Do you think this is an effective way to engage customers?

Business Customers

Business customers have a variety of needs depending on their industry and business focus. Many banks serve a wide variety of business customers ranging from small businesses to large businesses. Businesses may vary from sole proprietorships to businesses with a few employees to multinational corporations. Industries that businesses participate in may range from house cleaning services to consumer products companies to agricultural businesses. Nonprofit groups, ranging from Girl Scout troops through various charities, need banking services. Religious institutions also need banking services.

New Immigrants

People who have recently immigrated to the United States, including those who do not speak English as a primary language, are a potential customer segment for banks. In the spring of 2008, it was estimated that there were nearly 12 million unauthorized immigrants living in the U.S. Between 2000 and 2007, it is estimated that the unauthorized immigrant population grew by 4 million. Specific banking programs are under development to address the needs of this population.

Various Approaches to Specific Customer Groups

There are many ways to approach individual groups that are in the targeted segment of a market.

Demographic Approach for Individuals Some financial institutions structure their sales approach and websites to appeal directly to specific age groups. For example, one credit union offers products to the following four distinct age groups: ages 20–34, ages 35–49, ages 50–64, and ages 65 and over. Advice on financial products is tailored to each age group. Customers in the ages 20–34 age group may be advised to focus on saving for a house down payment; customers in the ages 65 and over group may be advised to consider the ongoing income generated by their investments.

Business Approach A separate section of a bank's website may be dedicated to businesses. Categorizing products by basic business accounts, from checking accounts through loan lines, by services that will benefit employees, and by services that will help the business manage all types of routine transactions, from merchant services through payroll, is one approach.

Functionality Approach A national banking chain presents their products from a more functional standpoint. Their website breaks down personal banking services into the categories of earned income, loans, and savings accounts. Specific product offerings, from checking accounts through investment products, are positioned within these broad categories.

Product Approach A community bank prefers to offer product categories, from savings accounts through IRAs to loans, as direct product offerings. This is a straightforward approach that presumes that the customer has a basic understanding of products. This approach allows an educated customer to directly access specific products of interest.

 checkpoint

Why is identifying the age group of a customer an important consideration for a bank?

_____

_____

_____

assessment 12.1

Think Critically

1. Define customer segmentation.

2. What is a target market?

3. Why are banks interested in new immigrants?

4. How would your interaction with a customer be different for an analytical customer versus a customer with strong social needs?

Make Academic Connections

5. **ETHICS** Early in 2007 there was a great deal of media discussion about one bank's intended program to offer credit cards to customers without Social Security numbers. The program, which could potentially be used by illegal immigrants, caused concern on a number of levels. One concern was that the program would implicitly condone the status of illegal immigrants. Another concern was that the high fees associated with the cards could cause severe financial penalties to account holders. Research current offerings for nonauthorized workers. Summarize the required documentation standards for obtaining any type of account with a financial institution. Consider the benefits and risks to the consumer and the financial institution of the account. Be prepared to discuss your findings with the class.

6. **MARKETPLACE COMPARISONS** Have students visit three bank websites, one for a national bank, one for a community bank, and one for a credit union. Have them compare website organization relative to customer and product focus. Have them identify similarities and differences in how the banks identify and target their customers. Prepare a two-page report to share results with the class.

Develop and Maintain the Customer

12.2

goals

+ Discuss a strategic approach for developing and maintaining profitable customer relationships.

+ Explain how to keep customers in the midst of a highly competitive environment.

terms

+ customer relationship management (CRM)

+ cross-selling

Banking Scene

Yuan Liang is happy with his new bank. He looks forward to the occasional Friday when he can get a free hot dog lunch sponsored by his bank. Last summer he even got two free tickets to a professional baseball game from his bank. Yuan has taken advantage of the bank's online bill payment option and uses it to pay his regular bills. Some of his friends, who get a financial reward for referring new customers, are trying to get him to change banks. Yuan is hesitant to do so. What should he consider before changing banks?

CUSTOMER DEVELOPMENT

There's a popular business saying that says it is much less expensive to keep an existing customer than it is to obtain a new customer. Competition for banking customers is fierce. Traditional sources, like other brick-and-mortar banks, are a source of competition. Nontraditional sources that are part of the ongoing financial innovations in the industry, like automotive companies that offer financial products and online banks, also change the competitive dynamic within the industry.

Customer Relationship Management (CRM)

Customer Relationship Management (CRM) captures the idea that the most profitable way to view customers is not merely in terms of the current products or services they buy from you, but in terms of both the present and future potential value to your business as a customer. By fully understanding the customer's financial position, financial needs, and long-term financial goals, you can cross-sell customers into more lucrative financial products. **Cross-selling** occurs when you apply your understanding of your customer to suggest other products from which the customer could benefit. A quantitative way to understand your customer is through a thorough analysis of past buying patterns. *Customer relationship management software* can track customers' online transactions to garner up-to-date customer behavior information.

Strategically Developing Banking Customers

Banks, like all businesses, need a distinct business focus. Once banks have determined which products and services they want to sell, they need to develop methods for attracting customers from within their target market. They may align certain products to specific demographic groups.

Unique Product Benefits   Banks need to identify the unique, value-adding benefits of the products they offer. Highlighting these benefits to customers in all marketing, sales, and service interactions will help persuade customers that buying the product would be a good investment.

Keep Existing Customers   Banks need to strive to maintain all existing customers. Providing exemplary, proactive customer service is one way to do this. Offering customers structured ways to provide feedback, and then responding to that feedback, enables customers to help the bank continuously improve.

Expand Existing Customer Relationships   By cross-selling other products to customers, by servicing their accounts, and by forming partnerships with them to provide for their evolving needs, you can maintain customers.

Letting Go of Less Profitable Customers   Although this can be controversial, if a bank's business model or product offerings change, in some cases it may make sense to provide disincentives for a customer to continue in the banking relationship. For example, if current customers no longer fit the desired customer profile, then increasing the charges on their accounts may cause them to start to look for a new financial institution.

On the other hand, there are those who would argue that banks have fixed costs and the incremental cost of maintaining a less desirable customer is not that great. One financial institution consulting company, Peak Performance Consulting Group, states that banking is basically a fixed-cost business. Two hundred dollars per customer is an industry-accepted level of per customer cost. However, the marginal cost of each customer is only $35–$40. In essence this means that, on average, it is relatively inexpensive to keep a less profitable customer. This line of reasoning would further the line of thought that it is all right to keep a less profitable customer. A bank's decisions on overall profitability and its desire to maintain a rigid business focus will influence its decisions about whether to maintain less profitable customers.

 checkpoint

What is customer relationship management and why is it significant to the banking industry?

KEEPING CUSTOMERS ●

With abundant industry-wide competition and with customers' easy access to information, you will need to find innovative and cost effective ways to maintain your customers.

Providing Customers with Incentives to Stay

Financial institutions use a variety of customer incentive and loyalty programs. Reasons to use incentive programs may include increasing customer loyalty, elevating the bank beyond merely a business and into becoming part of a customer's social network, and to encourage purchase of specific products. A few of the programs are listed below.

Scorecard   This incentive program provides points for merchandise purchased with a bank card. The points can be redeemed for merchandise or travel. Financial institutions participate in this reward program.

Upromise   If you sign up for the Upromise program with your bank's credit or debit card, many retailers will make a donation to your children's college savings fund after certain purchases are made. Some banks offer an additional percentage contribution for the college fund.

Fun and Lively Customer Incentives   These can run the gamut from providing free lunches at branches on a rotating basis to offering sweepstake drawings for a month's free rent or mortgage payment to offering a chance to win a $100,000 sweepstakes to a lucky bank customer.

Referral Programs   Some banks offer a financial reward to customers who recommend the bank to friends or businesses. Each new account opened as the result of a referral can yield a cash reward of $25–$50 to the customer who made the successful referral. Reward levels vary by bank.

Exclusive Social Engagements for High-Value Customers   Customers with strong financial portfolios that provide ongoing, high-value business to a bank may also be invited to exclusive social engagements for the bank's top customers. This not only rewards customers for their business, but flatters them to know they are part of an exclusive group.

The Entrenched Customer

Automatic payroll deposit, online bill pay, and automatic monthly payments for repetitive, fixed-price bills all provide great convenience for customers. Although it may take a bit of time to set up each of these account options, once they are established they save customers a great deal of time for routine financial transactions. However, the thought of changing all of these transactions from one bank to another can become quite a disincentive for customers to change banks. Administratively it is very time consuming to make the necessary changes to both the vendor's account and the bank account. Avoiding this administrative time can provide an incentive for customers to maintain current banking relationships.

Competitive Threats

The best way to avoid losing customers to the competition is to not only know what the competition is currently doing, but also what they plan on doing. With a thorough knowledge of the competition, you can proactively address competitive programs and provide programs that will keep your customers with you. Below are some examples of some nontraditional competitors to the financial market.

Automotive Manufacturers Offering Mortgage Loans, Credit Cards, Personal Banking, and Insurance Products   Although financial companies have become accustomed to auto manufacturers offering car loans to customers, it was somewhat unusual to see General Motors (GM) offering mortgage loans to consumers. Although GM entered the market to offset the cyclical automotive loan business, the particular mortgages they provided tended to be high-risk loans where homeowners could pay only interest for the first few years. Many of the loans were also low-documentation loans. When the mortgage crisis of 2008 occurred, GM was forced to heavily invest to try to salvage the mortgage end of its business.

Through a subsidiary, BMW FS, BMW offers a variety of financial products. The credit card, personal banking, and home and auto insurance products they offer directly compete with traditional banking services. In their mission, vision, and values statement, BMW indicates they offer these services to enhance the BMW customer relationship by offering comprehensive banking and insurance services tailored for the BMW driver. BMW is cross-selling financial products to its customers.

Peer-to-Peer Lending   New lending opportunities are available for both borrowers and prospective lenders. With Internet sites to facilitate the borrower and lender matchmaking, a variety of streamlined financing methods are available. Although specifics vary, common options include using social networks to facilitate connections, allowing lenders to participate in earning interest at low risk (by offering a relatively small contribution as part of a larger loan), and selecting borrowers to finance by their personal narrative in addition to their credit ratings.

 checkpoint

Why might a customer with an established online banking relationship hesitate to change banks?

assessment 12.2

Think Critically

1. What is cross-selling and why is it important in banking?

_____

_____

_____

2. Why would a bank decide to let go of less profitable customers?

_____

_____

3. Why is peer-to-peer lending attractive to both lenders and borrowers?

_____

_____

_____

4. Provide five examples of customer incentive programs. Which program would appeal to you most? Why would you prefer that program?

_____

_____

_____

Make Academic Connections

5. **PARTICIPATING IN THE LENDING ECONOMY** Investigate peer-to-peer lending sites. Read the compelling narratives of potential borrowers. Do their stories move you? Would their personal stories influence your decision to lend to a prospective borrower? What factors would you weight most heavily in your lending decision making—earnestness, tough times, shared hobbies, shared political beliefs, volunteer activities, or others? How much of a competitive threat do peer-to-peer websites present to traditional banks? Summarize your thoughts and findings and be prepared to participate in a lively class discussion.

6. **MARKETPLACE COMPARISONS** An Ohio bank recently offered prospective customers $100 to open a new checking account. Search your local media, including newspapers, billboards, and the Internet. Are similar offers currently offered in your area? Are the customers who open such an account likely to be profitable customers to the bank? Why do banks provide customer incentives for new accounts? Summarize your findings and your thoughts. Be prepared to use the collected information to participate in a class discussion.

12.3 Public Relations

goals

+ Discuss the process of creating a public image.

+ Name the major tools used as part of a public relations effort.

terms

+ public image

+ public relations

Banking Scene

Yuan was surprised to learn of the philanthropic causes his bank sponsors. When he went to the local community theater production, he saw his bank helped sponsor the community theater troupe. Yuan wondered why the bank would be willing to donate money to such a cause. What do you think are some of the reasons?

CREATION OF A PUBLIC IMAGE

One of the most important assets a company has can't be found on its financial statements, but it can constitute a significant percentage of the company's value. Corporate *image* and *reputation* contribute to the bottom line in many ways—from attracting customers and investors to how successfully a company can recover from a crisis. A **public image** is the concept the public has of a business and should reflect its mission, values, and culture. You choose the businesses you frequent and the products you buy based on your image of the company. If the image is good, you buy; if it is negative, you don't. A bank's image or prestige is a critical factor in whether it will be able to attract and retain customers, sell its products and services, support its claims, attract the best employees, and satisfy its stockholders.

Steps in Creating an Image

It is important for a bank to consider the public image it wants to project. Many banks support local activities to keep their names before the public. They sponsor home and garden shows, fireworks displays, youth clubs, teen organizations, sport teams, playing fields, and even arenas, as well as cultural events such as theater, opera, ballet, and orchestra performances.

A bank must take a number of steps to create its public image, including the following.

Step 1 Analyze the image the bank wants to present. Does the bank want to be known for the services it offers? Perhaps it wants to be known as a community supporter.

Step 2 Determine its target audience of who it wants to be aware of its image.

Step 3 Determine the current image the bank has with its target market.

Step 4 Define the bank's goals in creating its image. Goals should be specific as well as being measurable within a specific time period.

Step 5 Develop a plan to accomplish the goal. It should consider the way the bank will communicate or reinforce its image. Many banks engage professional public relations consultants to implement this step.

Step 6 Track the results of the public relations campaign to create or revise the bank's image. Determine whether the bank achieved its defined objectives and goals.

PHOTODISC/GETTY IMAGES

 checkpoint

Why does a bank want to create a public image?

_____

_____

PUBLIC RELATIONS ACTIVITIES

An organization's reputation, profitability, and even its continued existence can depend on the degree to which its targeted "public" supports its goals and products. This support is often the result of the organization's public relations efforts. The Institute of Public Relations defines **public relations (PR)** as "the planned and sustained effort to establish and maintain goodwill and mutual understanding between an organization and its public." The term includes activities associated with areas such as customer relations, marketing, and advertising. PR work also includes keeping management aware of the attitudes and the concerns of the many individuals, groups, and organizations with which the company interacts. Effective public relations efforts are carefully planned and executed. The planning phase should address the following questions.

• What objectives will the PR program aim to accomplish?

• Is there a clear definition of the targeted audience or public? Have the methods to reach the targeted audience been clearly defined and described?

- Are employees prepared to support the activity? Will they need training?

- Do current forces, such as local, state, national, or international events, affect the message?

- What are the organization's current PR activities? Do they fit the plan?

- What does the budget allow?

- Who will implement the plan? Will outside help be needed?

In large banks, the key public relations executive, frequently a vice president, may develop the overall plans and policies with other executives. The public relations department employs specialists to write, research, and prepare materials for distribution, to maintain contacts, and to respond to

Ethics in Action

Because companies emphasize and expect immediate monetary benefits from their public relations programs, attention to ethics in this arena has increased in recent years. The Council of Public Relations has adopted a code of professional ethics for its members.

Think Critically

Do you see any problems with activities that businesses use to establish and maintain the public's goodwill toward them? Would you expect to find ethical problems in banks' PR efforts? Why or why not?

inquiries. In a small organization, there may be either one person or a few people who deal with all aspects of the PR job.

Public Relations Tools

The PR function uses various techniques to influence and direct the attention of the general public, interest groups, and stockholders to the company and its products. Public relations can and should use any media, including radio, television, the Internet, and print advertising, to gain a competitive advantage as well as to establish and maintain goodwill and mutual understanding between the company and the public.

Public relations activities can inform the public about facts relating to a bank such as its Community Reinvestment Act projects, a new branch, and the extension of its hours of business. News or press releases keep editors and readers up to date on positive developments including business news, technological advances, promotions and new hires, and special events. A bank submits written feature articles or "leads" to local and state news media about specific projects, industry trends, and so forth that involve the bank, suggesting that it is a leader in these areas. Brochures are PR tools that inform the reader about some aspect of the bank, such as its history, involvement in community events or special programs, interesting facts about its building architecture, and the details of its services. Brochures can also call attention to any special recognition the bank has received. Newsletters provide a valuable, ongoing channel for delivering a bank's message to current and potential customers.

Special events, such as anniversaries of doing business or winning an award for community reinvestment activities, offer the public and the media a reason to focus on the bank. Hosting professional organizations or associations can help a bank create the impression that it is well respected in the profession. Holding business seminars for customers allows a bank to explain new banking-related developments, trends, services, and products in detail, suggesting that it has expertise in these areas.

To whom are public relations activities addressed?

assessment 12.3

Think Critically

1. Why do you think a bank needs to be cautious and careful in creating its public image?

_____

_____

2. List and explain the first four steps in creating the public image of a bank.

_____

_____

3. What public relations tools may be used?

_____

_____

4. In your opinion, what are the most effective public relations tools discussed in the lesson?

_____

_____

Make Academic Connections

5. **ETHICS** Use the Internet to investigate ethical issues relating to public relations. Write a one-page report or prepare an oral presentation on your findings.

6. **COMMUNICATION** Collect at least four pieces of written documents or web-based documents such as brochures, news releases, newsletters, or a printout from the Internet for a local bank. What image do you believe the bank is trying to create through them?

_____

_____

7. **ECONOMICS** How do economic conditions affect the image a bank communicates?

_____

_____

_____

_____

Customer Service

Banking Scene

Yuan Liang was asked to participate in a customer service survey offered by his bank. The bank wanted to understand whether they were meeting customers' needs and expectations on service. Yuan reflected on the service he had received and thought about ways that service could be improved. What elements of service should he include?

CUSTOMER ASSISTANCE

In their classic book *In Search of Excellence,* Thomas J. Peters and Robert H. Waterman, Jr., listed eight characteristics of large, profitable companies. One was being "close to the customer." According to Peters and Waterman, profitable companies learn from the people they serve and provide unparalleled quality, service, and reliability. **Customer service** can be defined as the activities and programs a seller provides to make the relationship with its customers satisfying. Customer service is a concept that can be difficult to measure, but when it is good you know it, just as you do when it is bad.

Companies consider customer service to be a way they can differentiate themselves from competitors. The money that you receive from Bank A is the same as the money you receive from Banks B through Z. What distinguishes your experience in getting the money is service. In a 2008 survey reported in *Fortune,* respondents cited Apple, Berkshire Hathaway, General Electric, Google, and Toyota Motor as the top 5 of the top 20 firms that set the standard for service quality in the United States. In addition to Berkshire Hathaway, another investment company, Goldman Sachs Group, made the list. Banks did not make the top 20 list. Banks have become keenly aware of the importance of customer service to their image as well as their bottom line.

Meeting Customers' Needs

Financial institutions share common needs for developing strong customer loyalty, and offering outstanding customer service is a key component of customer loyalty. Before a bank develops its customer service program, it needs to consider customer preferences. Most customers want the following in their dealings with a bank.

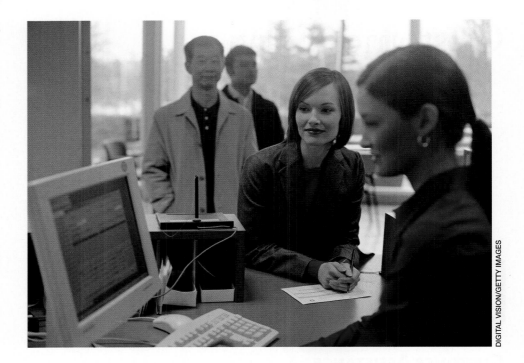

DIGITAL VISION/GETTY IMAGES

Responsive Service   You want your bank to be ready and willing to serve you promptly. Such responsive service makes it clear that the bank wants and values your business. You expect all bank personnel to be willing and ready to provide service, to answer your questions quickly and correctly, and to keep you informed about your accounts. To provide responsive service, banks must be sensitive to customer needs and help solve problems. Banks must also demonstrate flexibility, go "the extra mile," and follow up as needed. By proactively meeting customer needs, banks increase customer loyalty and good will.

Competent Staff   You expect all members of the bank staff to be professional and knowledgeable. Employees should have the skills to explain the bank's products and services accurately and clearly and be able to answer your questions. When staff members can assure you that they are trustworthy and competent, it increases your confidence in the bank.

Courteous Treatment   You want to hear "thank you" when you finish your business and "excuse me" if the bank employee needs to interrupt your service for any reason. You expect all bank staff to be considerate of your feelings and sensitive to your financial situation. You need assurance that you have the right bank that provides both courtesy and competence. The degree of caring and individual attention shown customers is known as **empathy**. A step beyond assurance, it demonstrates commitment to understanding customers' needs and finding the answer to exactly what they need. Empathetic service is caring and individualized. It is another way the bank lets you know that customer satisfaction is a top priority.

Customer Perspective   Bank employees should consider the customer's perspective. As the customer, you want a bank to communicate with you in clear, concise language that doesn't use banking "jargon." You don't want to have to decipher a lot of technical terminology. Bank employees can help acquire and secure business by making certain that the customer has a clear understanding of the product or service.

Reliable Service　The concept of reliability refers to a bank's ability to provide you what it promised in a dependable and accurate manner. In addition, reliability means that the bank will provide its services with consistency, dependability, and respect. Finally, reliability means that the bank will follow through when it says it will.

Easy Access to Staff and Funds　As a customer, you want your bank to make its services available when and where you need them. You need to access services without unacceptably long waits. Branches and ATMs should be conveniently located.

tech talk

Technology: Customer Service Asset or Problem?

According to a recent article in the Dallas *Morning News*, companies around the nation are beginning to recognize that technology can have both negative and positive effects on customer service.

Technology can be a huge asset for customer service. For example, Dallas-based 7-Eleven Inc. uses sophisticated software daily to identify which products sell and which don't. That way, the stores can keep what the customers want in stock. "By their purchases, we know what they want in their stores," said Margaret Chabris, a 7-Eleven spokeswoman.

Technology also can be advantageous in training. Sprint Corp. uses technology to put sales representatives through "hard-core training" with the use of simulations, according to Jed Dodd, vice president of training and development. Mad, angry customers have been filmed so that sales representatives get first-hand experience dealing with such customers. The video is a great training tool. It can be stopped as needed to discuss the best way to handle a situation.

In contrast, automated messages are prone to cause frustration for consumers. Frequently, the choices on the menus don't apply to their needs. At one point, Sprint used a computerized representative known as Claire, who was intended to help people through the interactive phone maze. But customers hated her, so the company "killed her," said Roxie Ramirez, a Sprint spokeswoman.

Think Critically
Search the Internet for examples of companies that are finding technology an asset or a problem for their customer service. Do you think the effect of technology on customer service is more positive or negative?

Professional Appearance   Both the banking environment and its employees should meet your expectations of professional appearance. The bank should be clean, uncluttered, and inviting, creating an atmosphere in which you expect safety for yourself and your funds. The employees should be dressed appropriately to convey a sense of professionalism. Employees that are dressed too casually or sloppily can project an apathetic image, which many customers may find disrespectful.

 checkpoint

How does the concept of reliability apply to customer service?

INAPPROPRIATE BEHAVIOR AND PROBLEMS

Sam Walton, founder of Wal-Mart, once said, "There is only one boss, the customer. And he can fire everybody simply by spending his money elsewhere." A typical dissatisfied customer will tell 8 to 10 people about the bad experience. One person in 5 will inform 20 or more. Some behaviors are certain to annoy or anger customers. These inappropriate behaviors may seem obvious to you, but they do occur and should be avoided.

- **Don't be rude to the customer.** Remember that you represent the bank to the customer. Remember to say "please," "thank you," and "excuse me"; make eye contact; avoid having a conversation with other employees or customers while serving the current customer; don't be abrupt; and never use rude or offensive language. Think about checkout clerks who mumble, "Have a nice day. Thank you for shopping at Blank Store" without ever looking at you and in a manner that suggests they really care nothing about you and where you shop but are required to memorize and repeat this phrase.

- **Don't argue with the customer.** Even if you are absolutely certain you are correct, arguing will insult and embarrass the customer without solving the problem and will likely make it worse.

- **Don't ignore a customer.** Ignoring the person basically treats him or her as a nonperson.

- **Don't make excuses or use negative phrases.** Avoid the phrases "I don't know," "It's not my job," "I can't help you," or "You'll have to wait." Instead, use phrases such as "I'll get that information for you," "Rick can help you with that," or "I'll be happy to help you as soon as I finish this transaction." Be helpful in recognizing what the customer needs and quickly find an answer or solution.

- **Don't criticize, condemn, or complain.** You should never criticize the bank, any employees, or customers. Avoid condemning bank policies or complaining about anything while with a customer.

- **Don't be condescending.** Never treat a customer as if he or she is not your equal. Don't "talk down" to them, treat them as if they are incapable of understanding, or give them "pat" answers.

- **Don't leave customers on the telephone.** If talking to clients on the telephone is part of your job, be constantly aware of them when they are on hold. Check with them frequently to let them know that you are still working with them. Apologize for delays.

Responding When Things Go Wrong

Some days are simply difficult, and things will go wrong no matter how you try to prevent problems. These are some steps you can take to salvage the situation.

- **Apologize.** Start by saying you are sorry, even if you believe the customer is at fault.

- **Listen and ask questions.** Listen carefully to the customer, show empathy, and ask questions that will allow you to gain and keep control.

- **Correct the problem quickly and fairly.** Tell the customer how you are going to solve the problem.

- **Keep your promises.** Be realistic about what you can and cannot do. Don't promise something just to pacify the customer.

- **Follow up on the problem.** Check with your customer to ensure that what was wrong has been addressed and corrected.

 checkpoint

Why should an employee not argue with a customer?

_____

_____

_____

assessment 12.4

Think Critically

1. It has been said that profitable companies learn from their customers. Explain in your own words what this means.

2. Why is it important that employees convey a sense of assurance?

3. Why do you think an empathetic attitude is important in dealing with a bank's customers?

4. What do you think is wrong with using the phrases "I don't know" and "I can't help you" with a customer?

Make Academic Connections

5. **HISTORY**   Investigate the Malcolm Baldrige National Quality Award. Identify the criteria for this award. Make a list of firms that have received this honor. Do you see any consistency in the service standards among these companies?

6. **PROBLEM SOLVING**   Inappropriate employee behavior may seem obvious to you, but customers encounter it all too often. Suggest ways that businesses can prevent this behavior.

Marketing and Advertising

Banking Scene

Yuan Liang now knows what he expects from a bank in terms of customer service. What are some ways that banks market their services to potential customers like Yuan?

goals

+ Explain how banks create a target market.

+ Identify the way banks advertise their products and services.

terms

+ marketing
+ social responsibility
+ advertising
+ cybermarketing
+ search engine optimization (SEO)
+ direct marketing
+ viral marketing

TARGET MARKET

Many people think that marketing is only about advertising or selling goods and services. However, advertising and selling are just two of many marketing activities. **Marketing** is the process of planning and executing the conception, pricing, promotion, and distribution of goods, services, and ideas to create exchanges that satisfy individual and organization objectives. A bank can identify the goals of its marketing plan by answering the following questions: Where is the company now? Where does it want to go? How will the company get where it wants to go? How will the company know when it gets there? Marketing objectives for a bank should be measurable, flexible, and complement its financial objectives. The marketing plan also needs to stretch the entire bank to a higher level of performance. The plan should include the "4 Ps" of marketing—*p*roducing [developing], *p*ricing, *p*romoting, and *p*lacing [distributing]—which classify the controllable elements of a marketing plan.

- **The bank should have the same goals as its target market.** If the target market is teenagers, advertisements for mortgage lending would be inappropriate.

- **Its target market should be consistent with its resources.** A bank without an adequate computer system and technical support should not advertise online banking services.

- **Its target market should generate sufficient profit.** The selected market must provide profits that warrant the effort.

- **Its target market should be adequate in size.** A market in which many competitors are already present is difficult to enter. Thus, it's important that the customer base is large enough to support all participants.

Extensive research is required in identifying a target market. Banks generally hire companies that specialize in developing this information to direct the research.

Marketing Planning

The American Bankers Association (ABA) reported that banks spent more than $3.8 billion on marketing in 2001. Its Bank Marketing Planning Survey Report investigated how banks planned to spend their marketing money in 2004. Survey highlights include the following:

- On average, banks anticipate increasing their marketing budgets by 7 percent.

- Internet initiatives such as website development and bill payment top the list of marketing initiatives that banks are planning to pursue.

- More than three-fourths of banks with less than $100 million in assets use market segmentation, up significantly from 2001 when less than one-third did so.

Successful marketing encompasses many aspects of a business, from front-line customer service, backroom operations, and human resource management to advertising and other corporate communications. As in other companies, banks need to recognize that effectively integrating and coordinating marketing activities is based on a simple truth: The people who work for them are the business. A bank markets itself every time a customer interacts with an employee. A courteous and efficient teller gives the impression that those characteristics apply to the bank as a whole. Integrating the marketing concept effectively throughout the bank increases the likelihood that all bank jobs will be performed in a manner consistent with that concept.

Marketing and Social Responsibility

Social responsibility is the obligation to profitably serve employees and customers in an ethical and law-abiding manner. Like other respected institutions in the community, banks are expected to take an active, socially responsible role in civic affairs. This is especially important because banks provide somewhat of a public service. Financial institutions frequently require their officers to be involved with local service organizations and give them time to do so.

 checkpoint

What is the purpose of marketing?

ADVERTISING

Advertising permeates society in the twenty-first century. One estimate suggests that the average person encounters 1,500 to 1,800 ads a day! This is an enormous number, but you have learned to "turn off" most of these ads. **Advertising** is the paid description or presentation of a product, service, idea, or organization to encourage individuals to buy, support, or approve of it. It is one element in a firm's marketing plan.

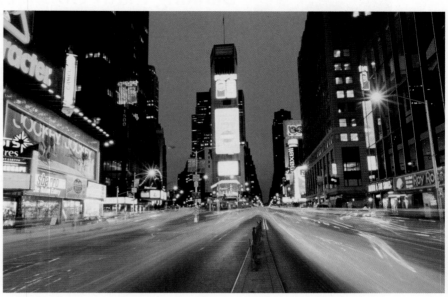

Organizations use a variety of media to send their messages. Ad distribution can occur via the Internet, print media, broadcast media, outdoor media, mobile media, and through direct marketing. An effective advertising campaign uses a combination of these.

Cybermarketing and Search Engine Optimization

Some estimates predict that online business will either triple or quadruple in the future. As Internet usage displaces print media, advertising on the Internet has transformed into a highly effective way to reach customers. **Cybermarketing** is a carefully planned and sustained effort to advertise a company, its products, and/or services through the Internet by using the most practical, effective, and up-to-date strategies. Public relations information, marketing materials, and online data transactions can all take place on the Internet.

Search engine optimization (SEO) is the most effective way to drive Internet business to your site. A *search engine* is a software program that indexes web content so that it can be referenced in Internet searches. There are complicated mathematical formulas, called *algorithms*, that are used by search engines to select relevant data in response to an Internet search. The selection algorithms are being continually tweaked. There are precise methodologies available to optimize how valuable your website is relative to other websites. Developing intriguing web content that will increase web traffic to your site, either through direct hits or via links from other websites, is a bit of an art and a science. Training staff to do this or outsourcing this work to a qualified vendor will greatly improve your marketing presence online.

Banking Math *Connection*

Financial success in a business is far more likely if the projects in which it invests provide a return on its investment. Assume that Third State Bank is considering two marketing opportunities. One is a newspaper advertising campaign budgeted at $75,000 and estimated to have a positive benefit of $11,000 in the first year. The other is a series of television commercials that will cost $200,000 in the first year with an expected return of $33,000. Using the return on investment (ROI) formula below, what return on investment from each option can the bank expect?

ROI = Average annual net benefit ÷ Initial costs

Solution

The newspaper ads will have the following return:

ROI = $11,000 ÷ $75,000 = 15%

The TV ads will have this return:

ROI = $33,000 ÷ $200,000 = 17%

These figures indicate that although it involves a considerably larger investment, Third State Bank should choose the television campaign.

Print Media

Look in any Sunday newspaper, and you will find advertisements for a number of banks. The ads describe the characteristics of checking accounts, mortgage and home equity loans, free Internet banking and online bill payment, and extended lobby and drive-up hours.

Although circulation is declining, newspapers are still common in U.S. homes. By advertising in local newspapers, a bank can target a specific geographic area. Newspapers provide a quick turnaround for ad distribution for ads that highlight bank promotions. Ads that promote a bank's image can be found in other printed materials including programs at theater, orchestra, opera, and dance events.

Broadcast Media

In the early years of the twenty-first century, commercials for banks seemed to saturate television and radio advertising. Banks use these media to emphasize their low lending rates, especially those on home mortgages and home equity loans. Although broadcast media is more costly than print media, broadcast media is better at reaching the target market. For example, the bank may target a certain age group by selecting a radio station that caters to those specific age demographics. A bank may want to target young families by running television advertisements during family-oriented shows.

Outdoor Media

Many of you may have become somewhat immune to outdoor advertising, but because people now spend much more time in their vehicles than ever before, it is experiencing a resurgence. A billboard may be the most obvious form of an outdoor ad, but its style has changed in recent years. Computer technology enables the modern "billboard" to present supersize digital images that can be changed on a daily or even hourly basis. A tri-vision billboard allows up to three advertisements to rotate at various intervals on a single billboard.

People tend to notice moving objects when they are driving. Bus ads are eye-catching and unique and therefore memorable. Full-wrap and tail-wrap ads on buses and even cars are so distinctive that people often remember them after only one viewing.

Advertising at airports and subways offers a range of opportunities. It includes signage along an airport's concourses or at subway entrances and stops.

Outdoor advertising also includes large banners such as those draped around the entrance to a museum stating, "Treasures of the Orient Presented by City National Bank."

Direct Marketing

Another form of advertising, **direct marketing** is a promotion technique that delivers the materials individually to a target market via direct mail, telemarketing, or other direct means. Its purpose is to generate a revenue-producing response. Direct mail campaigns generally consist of printed material such as flyers, brochures, or letters that appear to be first-class mail. These documents offer low-cost checking accounts, interest rates on auto loans, and limited-time specials. In the last few years, consumers have become so bothered by telemarketers that the United States has implemented a national "do-not-call" list intended to block most phone sales pitches.

Viral Marketing

Viral marketing is intentionally using ordinary people to help spread the word about a product or service. Referral programs are one form of viral marketing. Some websites are so intriguing and entertaining that you are inclined to share them with your friends. One online bank even developed an animated website complete with games to draw people to it. Finding a specific, unique, or fun attribute associated with your product or service is another way to promote viral marketing.

Digital Signage

Some banks are using digital signs, which can resemble flat-screen TVs, to provide continually updated information to customers visiting branches. Updated information can pertain to rate changes, referral incentives, or new product offerings and can be programmed to change based on typical traffic patterns in the bank. Some digital signs have embedded RFID technology to record what products a customer picks up from a shelf. Digital ads that are shown can be changed in response to RFID signals to reflect the interest of customers in the branch.

Advertising Spending By Media

Media	Jan–June 2007 (Millions)
Television Media	**$31,627.7**
Network TV	$11,835.9
Cable TV	$8,3790.0
Spot TV	$7,287.6
Spanish Language TV	$2,127.5
Syndication—National	$1,997.7
Magazine Media	**$14,551.7**
Consumer Magazines	$11,501.9
B-To-B Magazines	$1,858.9
Sunday Magazines	$860.0
Local Magazines	$228.5
Spanish Language Magazines	$102.4
Newspaper Media	**$12,916.60**
Newspapers (local)	$11,091.1
National Newspapers	$1,653.5
Spanish Language Newspapers	$172.0
Internet	**$5,519.0**
Radio Media	**$5,139.8**
Local Radio	$3,516.2
National Spot Radio	$1,161.0
Network Radio	$462.6
Outdoor	**$1,903.9**
Free Standing Inserts	**$934.7**
Total	**$72,593.4**

Advertising Budget

An old adage says that at least 50 percent of all advertising is a waste of money. This may be true, and anyone who can figure out which half is useless can revolutionize the industry with that knowledge. According to TNS Media Intelligence, advertising expenditures during the first half of 2007 were as shown in the table.

 checkpoint

What is advertising and how does it relate to marketing?

assessment 12.5

Think Critically

1. What are the "4 Ps" of marketing?

2. Why should banks engage in socially responsible activities?

3. Banks often support community cultural activities. In your opinion, what does this say about their target markets?

4. What is search engine optimization (SEO) and why is it important to banking?

Make Academic Connections

5. **ADVERTISING**   Design a newspaper ad for a bank. The size should be 5¾″ × 4″. Identify the target market for the ad.

6. **BANKING MATH**   Woodstown Bank is considering investment in several advertising projects. Ads in the local orchestra's programs will cost $5,000 and have an expected return of $400 in the first year. The other is to build a playground at the local park. This project will cost $9,000 with an expected first-year return of $900. Which project will have the higher return on investment? List any nonfinancial considerations that could affect this decision.

7. **COMMUNICATION**   Work in teams to conduct a poll of at least 20 people. Find out how many can recall an ad from any medium in the last month. Which medium did most people name?

chapter 12 assessment

Chapter Summary

12.1 Define the Customer
A. Demographics, customer segmentation, and target markets provide an organized method for grouping customers.
B. Customer characteristics drive product recommendations.

12.2 Develop and Maintain the Customer
A. Customer relationship management provides a methodology for viewing the long-term potential value of a customer.
B. Banks need to provide customers with incentives to maintain their existing banking relationships.

12.3 Public Relations
A. Banks need a positive public image to attract and retain customers.
B. Public relations strategies are used to create and maintain goodwill between an organization and the public.

12.4 Customer Service
A. Banks must provide exemplary customer service.
B. Banks must ensure that their employees understand the importance of customer service and avoid behaviors that are inappropriate.

12.5 Marketing and Advertising
A. The 4 Ps of marketing are producing, pricing, promoting, and placing.
B. Multiple advertising methods should be used.

Vocabulary Builder

a. advertising
b. cross-selling
c. customer relationship management (CRM)
d. customer segmentation
e. customer service
f. cybermarketing
g. demographics
h. direct marketing
i. empathy
j. marketing
k. need
l. public image
m. public relations
n. search engine optimization (SEO)
o. social responsibility
p. target market
q. viral marketing
r. want

Choose the term that best fits the definition. Write the letter of the answer in the space provided. Some terms may not be used.

____ 1. The public's concept of a business
____ 2. Degree of caring and individual attention shown to customers
____ 3. Paid presentation of a product, service, idea, or organization
____ 4. Promotion technique that delivers materials directly to targeted individuals
____ 5. Activities and programs a business provides its customers to satisfy them
____ 6. Preselected group of buyers who are the focus of marketing efforts
____ 7. Company's effort to advertise through the Internet
____ 8. Planning and executing a program to create exchanges that satisfy the objectives of both an organization and individuals
____ 9. Division of customers into subgroups
____ 10. Effort to establish goodwill with the public
____ 11. The most effective way to drive Internet traffic to your website
____ 12. Viewing the customer in terms of their total present and future value to your company

Review Concepts

13. Why are banks interested in recent immigrant demographic information?

14. What is public relations, and how does it relate to customer service and marketing?

15. Name four components of a plan to strategically develop customers.

16. You can choose to do business with any number of banks. How does customer service affect your decision of which bank to use?

17. List five types of customer incentive programs.

18. What is empathy? Why is it an important part of customer service?

19. How can offending a customer affect a bank's public image?

20. List competitive threats to traditional banks. Why are banks concerned about the competition?

_____

_____

_____

_____

21. What activities make up the marketing process?

_____

_____

_____

_____

22. What is customer segmentation?

_____

_____

_____

23. Describe cybermarketing.

_____

_____

_____

_____

Apply What You Learned

24. Why is it important that a bank identify the audience for its public relations activities?

_____

_____

_____

25. In what ways does corporate or public image contribute to a bank's bottom line?

_____

_____

_____

26. Why is search engine optimization critical to the effective use of an Internet advertising budget?

_____

_____

_____

27. What does responsive service entail?

_____

_____

_____

28. Why is viral marketing important?

_____

_____

_____

29. Do you think that banks should use computer popup ads? Why or why not?

_____

_____

_____

_____

Make Academic Connections

30. **PROBLEM SOLVING**   As a bank teller, you have an obviously upset customer because the bank has returned checks to the telephone and utility companies due to nonsufficient funds in her account. The customer believes this is a bank error. She states that the bank has ruined her credit rating and that she must now pay late fees plus "excessive" bank fees for the returned checks. Write a one-page paper discussing how to appease this customer.

31. **BANKING MATH**   Use the Internet to find the financial statement of a bank that shows its marketing budget. This information may be listed under various headings such as advertising and promotion, marketing, and so on. Calculate the percentage of sales/revenue this amount represents. (*Hint:* Divide advertising/marketing expense by net sales/revenue.)

_____

_____

_____

32. **COMMUNICATION**   Use the Internet to investigate one of the companies that *Fortune* listed in its 2008 survey that set the standard for customer service. Describe the characteristics of the customer service policies of one of these businesses

33. **RESEARCH**   In 1982, Johnson & Johnson, the highly respected U.S. pharmaceutical company, faced a crisis. One of its major products, Tylenol, the leading painkiller medicine in the United States, was at the time responsible for $1.2 million in annual revenue. However, Tylenol was linked to seven poisoning deaths in the Chicago, Illinois, area. Research this classic case. Find out how the company reacted to protect both its image and its customers, and present your findings to the class.

CHAPTER

13

Employment Opportunities

13.1	Organizational Structure
13.2	Human Resources
13.3	Employee Evaluation

©MONKEY BUSINESS IMAGES 2008/USED UNDER LICENSE FROM SHUTTERSTOCK.COM

climbing the ladder

From Teller to District Manager

After her first morning of college classes, Beth went to work her shift as a part-time teller. As she had demonstrated a solid understanding of the job and a good work ethic while working at the bank during the summer, the bank had agreed to schedule her for about 20 hours a week. This flexibility enabled her to schedule her classes efficiently.

As a part-time customer service representative/teller (CSR), Beth's responsibilities ran the gamut from processing routine customer transactions, maintaining consistent balances at her station, developing a strong customer rapport, to helping the branch achieve its sales goals by promoting banking products.

After her first four quarters of college, Beth enrolled in the college's cooperative education program. By alternating a quarter of classes with a quarter of full-time professional work, Beth was able to expand her responsibilities at the bank.

During her first two co-op quarters, Beth worked as a lead customer service representative (LCSR). She was responsible for assisting with opening new accounts and safe deposit boxes, training new tellers, delegating daily projects, and finding solutions to customer issues. To address the fears customers had after the credit and mortgage crises, Beth also proactively provided customers with information on the bank's overall stability.

Upon graduation, Beth accepted a position at her bank as an assistant branch manager. In support of the branch manager, her duties included helping the branch staff meet and exceed sales goals, selling to individual customers, meeting compliance requirements, and assuming operational responsibility for the branch in the manager's absence.

After a few years, Beth accepted a cross-town transfer to become a branch manager. Her new duties included achieving financial goals for the branch, expanding her involvement in the community to develop relationships that would bring new business to the branch, managing sales, service and operations for the branch, and protecting the branch's assets and the assets of its customers.

Beth enjoyed working as a branch manager, but believed she had the talent to perform similar functions on a larger scale. Consequently, she applied for and obtained a position as a district manager. In lieu of focusing on a specific branch, her new duties focused on a specific territory. Beth was now responsible for overseeing the sales, service, expenses, operations, and credit controls for her district. With an eye on future business, she was also responsible for community leadership, human resources planning, and developing short- and long-term business objectives for her area.

Upper Rungs to Consider

Although Beth's role as a district manager was challenging, gratifying, and lucrative, she decided to develop a tentative series of new jobs to target. Positions included on that list are private banking relationship manager, senior relationship manger, or a senior sales and leadership coach. Each of the targeted jobs would enable her to make broad-based contributions that would help improve the bottom line of the bank.

Preparing for the Climb

As promotions occur, a broader overview of the business is required. How would obtaining a broad range of experience including assignments dealing with automotive lending, credit card services, retail lending and commercial lending help a candidate prepare for higher-level jobs?

PHOTODISC

13.1

Organizational Structure

goals

+ Explain how banks organize their business by department.

+ Identify jobs that provide operational support at banks.

terms

+ operations

+ departmentalization

+ customer service representative (CSR)

+ integrity

+ teller

Banking Scene

Nathaniel Bryant has just graduated from high school and is looking for a job. He isn't interested in just any job. He wants something that will provide an entry-level position leading to a career. His aunt suggested that he apply at one of the local banks. He wonders what skills are needed for bank jobs. What research should Nathaniel conduct on job opportunities in banking?

DEPARTMENTS IN A BANK • • • • • • • • • • • • • • • • • • •

Commercial banks experienced many changes in the last decades of the twentieth century. Some became huge entities operating throughout the country and offering a complete line of financial services. Others remained small, serving only one community and offering highly personalized services. Information and communications technologies created new strategic possibilities. Today's commercial banks are more diverse, although they continue to provide the three traditional deposit-gathering, loan, and trust functions. The deposit-gathering functions establish checking and savings accounts. The deposit and loan functions are closely linked because the deposits provide the funds to lend. The trust area's funds come specifically from the fees it charges customers. Each of these areas may have marketing and operations components. **Operations** provides support services such as bookkeeping.

No matter how big or small the bank or how many services it offers, it must have some type of organizational structure. This **departmentalization**, or division of the bank into departments, can vary as widely as the products and services the bank offers.

Functional Departments

Banks can have many different departments that make up the traditional business of banking. These departments work to meet consumer and business needs. Smaller banks may not have as many departments or offer as many services as larger banks.

Individual or Personal Banking   The name of the personal banking department varies from bank to bank. Personal banking, consumer banking, and personal services are some names of the departments that meet the needs of individual customers. In this department, new account personnel or **customer service representatives (CSRs)** help customers open checking and savings accounts, obtain debit and credit cards, and learn the various options available, such as how to bank, whether in person, through an ATM, by phone, or online. CSRs may also direct customers to departments that offer other services.

Small Business and Consumer Lending Consumer loan specialists, loan officers, financial services representatives, and underwriters explain products to customers interested in starting a small business, buying a new car, buying a home, or financing college tuition. These departments are also called business banking, business services, and small business lending. Some banks have departments dedicated to serving relatively new entrants into the market, including women and minority businesspeople.

Trust Funds In the trust department, sometimes known as wealth management, the trust officer, personal trust administrator, or trust account officer manages assets placed in trust with the bank according to clients' wishes. The assets vary greatly from real estate to money to securities to artwork.

PHOTODISC/GETTY IMAGES

Brokerage Brokers, investment assistants, and financial planners are just a few of the titles of employees who provide financial and investment services to individuals and institutional customers.

Insurance Some banks offer a full-service, independent insurance agency dedicated to serving the needs of their customers. Agents advise personal and business clients about various services and policies to meet their insurance needs.

Operational Departments

Other departments in a bank provide "behind the scenes" operational support for the basic functional departments. In small banks, one or two individuals may provide the operational support. Large banks have entire departments dedicated to various operational activities.

Accounting/Finance Accountants, auditors, and controllers provide critical support. They prepare financial reports and budgets. They also write, analyze, and verify financial reports containing current financial information and check that the records are accurate.

Human Resources The recruiters, job analysts, benefit coordinators, compensation specialists, and trainers in this support area are responsible for hiring and training employees. They also design compensation/benefit programs and maintain personnel records. The responsibility for firing employees, when necessary, also falls to this department.

Operations   Proof operators, bookkeepers, wire transfer specialists, account research and reconcilement specialists, and statement processors provide "back office," or operations, support. These employees provide assistance to other employees as needed to help manage customer accounts.

Treasury Management   Financial experts in this department manage the bank's monetary assets/liabilities and financial risks. They manage the bank's cash and funds in reserves on deposit at the Federal Reserve and in interbank loans to minimize interest expense and maximize interest income. This department is also responsible for placing and liquidating investments and managing foreign exchange and interest rate exposures.

Public Relations/Marketing   Marketing coordinators, public relations representatives, and marketing specialists now work at banks to sell the various products and services. They perform market research, set marketing strategy, create advertising and promotions, and inform the public of the bank's policies, activities, and accomplishments.

Technical   Computer operators, programmers, analysts, and support specialists provide critical technological support for the products and services the bank offers. The employees program and service the computers that allow banks to store and manipulate the vast amount of information the bank processes.

Maintenance, Purchasing, and Security   These departments provide the support you would expect. Engineers, custodians, plumbers, and so on pro-

vide the day-to-day upkeep of the building. Purchasing agents monitor the supplies, from office furniture and computer monitors to paperclips, and purchase them as needed. Security guards or officers patrol and inspect property to protect against fire, theft, vandalism, and illegal activity.

Bank Officers   Although these positions don't really represent a department in banks, officers fulfill the necessary management/oversight function. Large banks may have officers known as president, chief executive officer, chief financial officer, chief operating officer, controller, and vice presidents. Smaller banks will have fewer of these positions.

What is the difference between functional and operational departments?

JOB POSITIONS WITHIN A BANK'S DEPARTMENTS • • • • • •

There are several job positions within a bank's many departments. While the tasks and responsibilities that come with these positions may vary, all bank employees are held to the highest employment standards. Honesty and integrity are two characteristics that are especially important for bank employees. **Integrity** is the steadfast adherence to a strict moral or ethical code. An important factor for all bank employees to remember is that banking revolves around people. Thus, good people skills are a must. Detailed below are a few of the more common positions available at banks.

Bank Teller

The **teller** position is the most common one at banks. Tellers are likely to have the most contact with customers. They perform the following duties:

- Balance the cash drawer daily by adding deposits and subtracting withdrawals from the opening cash funds

- Process customer transactions (checking and savings deposits, check cashing, and savings withdrawals)

Banking Math *Connection*

Bank tellers accept credit card deposits from local merchants. Some merchants submit charges to customers' credit cards electronically. The credit card companies automatically deposit funds from the sale into the seller's bank account. This service isn't free. Credit card companies charge vendors a percentage of the sales for providing this convenience.

On Valentine's Day, Noble's Flowers and Gifts electronically charged $2,200 of sales transactions. The card companies charge Noble's a 5 percent service fee. How much was deposited in Noble's account from these credit card sales?

Solution

The formula for finding the amount is

Amount deposited = Amount of sales − (Amount of sales × Fee rate)
$$= \$2,200 - (\$2,200 \times 0.05)$$
$$= \$2,200 - \$110$$
$$= \$2,090$$

In this example, the 5 percent fee amounts to $110. This amount is subtracted from the $2,200 total sales charged to arrive at a total of $2,090 deposited in Noble's account.

- Sell money orders, travelers' checks, and savings bonds

- Accept credit card, mortgage, loan, and utility payments from individuals and bank card deposits from merchants

- Prepare currency and coin for retail customers

- Balance automated teller machines, replenish their cash, and process deposits and withdrawals made through them

- Promote banking services and answer customer inquiries

Other Bank Positions

Space limitations prohibit the listing of all possible jobs in a bank. The following are brief descriptions of common bank positions.

- **Customer service representatives (CSRs)** work directly with customers. CSRs open deposit accounts, interview clients to obtain financial information, explain available services, and help clients solve account problems.

- **Credit analysts** evaluate the financial condition of individuals and businesses seeking credit or a loan. Analysts research the applicant's credit record to gauge whether or not to approve the loan.

- **Trust officers** manage billions of dollars in assets placed in trust with the bank according to clients' wishes. Officers direct trust disbursements according to the terms of the trust or the beneficiary's needs, invest surpluses as the trust directs, and negotiate with public agencies, such as the Social Security Administration, to combine all eligible assets into a trust.

branching out

Tending To Financial Ills

Many banks have expanded their retail presence by establishing branches in nontraditional locations. Some banks put branches in children's hospitals. Providing convenience of services to hospital staff as well as families of patients is a benefit of these branches. From servicing high net worth individuals, including hospital staff who may earn large salaries, to providing loans to families who may need money to help with medical expenses, these branches can offer the same gamut of services as traditional branches. Some hospital websites feature the branch information on their website. This has the dual benefit of reassuring incoming families that they can access financial information during their stay and provides good publicity for the bank.

Think Critically
Why would a bank choose to place a branch in a hospital? How do you think hospital staff feels about having a branch in the hospital? How do you think patient families feel about this?

- **Auditors** maintain and examine the bank's financial records to verify their accuracy. They also look for areas of waste, mismanagement, or fraud. For example, the auditor might check tellers' cash boxes to determine whether their transactions and records are accurate.

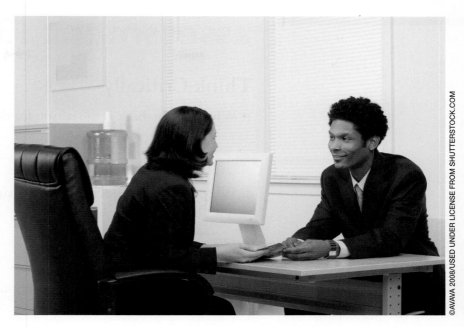

- **Job analysts** perform the human resources role of investigating the duties performed in the various banking positions in order to write an accurate, detailed job description. Information in the description details the skills and training required for the job.

- **Accounting clerks** provide operational support to the bank by keeping its financial records, either in books called *ledgers* or in computer documents. They also prepare financial statements that report its assets and liabilities, which summarize how much the bank earns and spends.

- **Public relations specialists** publicize information about the bank, such as an award it received, a new service it provides, or an educational program it sponsors. They also prepare film, slide, or other visual presentations for meetings.

- **Computer operators** install, modify, clean, and repair computer hardware and software, and they monitor equipment operation. These troubleshooters analyze and fix problems. They also may train computer users to use computer hardware and software.

- **Chief financial officers (CFOs)** are the top financial officers who direct all of a bank's accounting and financial activities. The CFO makes financial plans, such as examining the impact of proposed new functions on the bank's earnings, sets policies, and brings together other managers to develop creative solutions to problems.

checkpoint

What does "balancing a cash drawer" mean?

_____

_____

assessment 13.1

Think Critically

1. What do you think is the reason for departmentalization in banks?

2. What are some characteristics that bank customer service representatives must have?

3. Why do banks need the services of public relations specialists?

4. Which bank jobs described in this lesson do you think may require college degrees?

Make Academic Connections

5. **BANKING MATH**   Happy Trails is a backpacking adventures outfit that accepts credit cards for only those credit card companies that have waived the service fee. In the past year, Happy Trails has noticed that quite a few of its customers have wanted to use a certain credit card that Happy Trails doesn't accept. Happy Trails is reconsidering its policy and making an exception for this card company, which charges a 3 percent fee on sales. Assuming sales for the year charged under this new credit card are estimated to be $5,600, what is the additional expense that Happy Trails would incur by accepting this card and how much would actually be deposited in its bank account?

6. **MEDIA**   Collect want ads for banking jobs in the Sunday edition of a local newspaper and on the Internet. List all of the skills required. Make a poster that graphically illustrates various categories of skills.

Human Resources

Banking Scene

Nathaniel Bryant sees a newspaper ad about an opening for a bank teller at Farmers Bank. He applies and lands an interview. How can he use the information in the job description from the newspaper ad to prepare for the interview? What skills should he emphasize in discussing his qualifications for the position? What else should he do to prepare? How should he dress?

goals

+ Identify the steps that a human resources department takes to hire new bank personnel.

+ List the information that an employee's record should include.

terms

+ job description
+ benefit
+ telecommuting
+ merit-based employment
+ job fair
+ orientation

THE HUMAN RESOURCES DEPARTMENT

The heart of any organization is its employees. Employees "put a face on a bank" by answering the questions, accepting the deposits, investing the money, and recording the numerous transactions processed. With today's emphasis on providing quality customer service, banks seek to hire people who have both technical expertise and the ability to work well with customers at all levels. Most banks seek to fill entry-level positions with people who have good basic math and communication skills, enjoy public contact, and feel comfortable handling large amounts of money. The human resources (HR) department, sometimes called the *personnel department,* establishes the bank's policies and procedures for hiring, training, and evaluating employees, as well as compensation and benefits. In doing so, HR must be in compliance with government rules and regulations pertaining to hiring and employment practices.

Job Analysis and Description

The human resources (HR) department analyzes each job in the bank. The analysis involves reviewing the position's responsibilities, the skills required to perform it, its supervisory relationships, and how it fits in the bank's organizational structure. Using this information, HR then prepares the **job description**, the formal document that factually and concisely identifies the job, responsibilities, work involved, and education required. The multi-purpose job description is used in advertising openings, interviewing applicants, orienting new hires, evaluating employee performance, and making promotions. As an example, a loan officer job description might read as shown on the next page.

Commercial Loan Officer

General Responsibilities: Generating and servicing a wide variety of commercial loans; aggressively seeking and obtaining quality new business through client and prospect calls, referrals, and cross-selling efforts; building and maintaining relationships with a high degree of customer satisfaction.

Job Requirements: Skills and experience in applicant interviewing and perceptive character judgment, loan structuring, credit analysis, and monitoring credit performance; a bachelor's degree and four to five years of credit-associated lending.

Salary: $40,000-$55,000

Benefit Establishment

Banks offer competitive benefits. Human resources sets the policies for benefits as instructed by the bank's board of directors. **Benefits** involve matters such as hours of employment and time off for vacation, illness, holidays, and jury duty. Benefits cover health insurance policies, including dental and vision coverage, disability and unemployment insurance, and retirement plans. To become competitive in attracting high-quality employees, large banks have recently offered benefits such as child and elder care, wellness and fitness programs, and flexible benefits plans. Other new benefits include **telecommuting**, which lets employees do some work from their homes via computer. HR managers must be knowledgeable about changing government regulations and legislation that affect the benefits the bank offers.

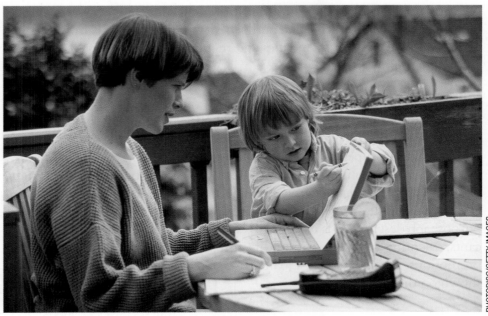

PHOTODISC/GETTY IMAGES

Compensation Determination

The human resources department sets and maintains policy to ensure that employees receive fair and equitable pay rates. Setting the rates could involve conducting surveys to see how the bank's rates compare with those of other banks. HR also conducts research to ensure that the bank's pay scale complies with changing laws and regulations. In addition, the department oversees the performance evaluation system, and it may design reward policies such as pay-for-performance plans. The Bureau of Labor Statistics reported the following median hourly pay for these banking occupations in 2006.

Occupation	Depository Institutions	All Industries
General and operations managers	$40.89	$40.97
Financial managers	34.89	43.74
Loan officers	23.51	24.89
First-line supervisors/managers of office and administrative support workers	19.66	20.92
Executive secretaries and administrative assistants	18.05	17.90
Loan interviewers and clerks	14.35	14.89
Customer service representatives	13.68	13.62
New accounts clerks	13.60	13.65
Office clerks, general	11.82	11.40
Tellers	10.63	10.64

The Hiring Process

The human resources department is in charge of hiring new employees for the bank. It sets policy for **merit-based employment**, that is, selecting the person with the best qualifications for a specific position. The hiring process is somewhat detailed and, depending on the size of the bank and its need, can be long. It begins when an opening is identified.

Advertising   The first step in hiring is to advertise the position, both inside and outside the bank. Depending on the specific job, banks may advertise in newspapers, professional publications, or on the Internet. Information about the job in the ad is based on the job description. Some banks hold **job fairs**, which are public employment events at which they can present employment opportunities, requirements, and personnel benefits to a large number of people at one time. Interested fair attendees can apply for a position during the fair or at a later time.

Reviewing Applications   After the *closing date*, which is the last day applications are accepted, they are reviewed and screened. Candidates who are most qualified are identified and invited to interview for the position.

Accountant/Bookkeeper

Center City Bank, a leader in banking in the state, has an opening for an accountant/bookkeeper, 8 AM–5 PM, M–F. Accounts payable, accounts receivable, general ledger, and Excel experience required. Competitive salary matched to experience. Apply by March 25. Send resume to Center City Bank, 1504 Riverside Drive, Center City, Attn: Human Resources
An equal opportunity employer

Ethics in Action

Many human resource departments face ethical issues concerning their personnel files. Space constraints create the need to dispose of them after employees leave the firm. Also, many companies now require any documents relating to an employee's medical history be removed from the personnel file.

Think Critically

What are the ethical concerns regarding the disposal of personnel files, which are confidential? Why do you think medical-related documents should not be in the personnel file?

Interviewing Depending on the individual bank's practice, the interview may be conducted by a human resources representative, the manager of the department in which the job is located, or both. The interview focuses on the elements in the job description, which include the position's responsibilities, requirements, reporting relationships, salary, benefits, and advancement opportunities. Only job-related questions that help assess the candidate's experience, skill, and training may be asked. The applicant discusses his or her qualifications for the position and any related experience. Persons applying for the position should be prepared to ask specific questions about the bank, working conditions, special training required, and so on.

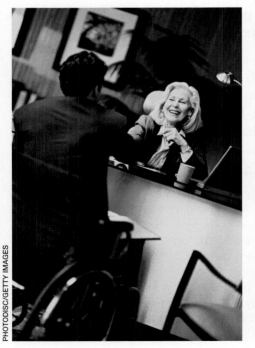

Conducting Preemployment Testing Banks may require applicants for certain jobs to take tests as part of the process of determining job suitability. Some tests determine a candidate's current level of skills, and others evaluate the person's aptitude or potential ability to perform the duties required. The test should be carefully prepared to ensure that it focuses on the skills and knowledge required to perform the job. For example, tellers might be tested on their mathematical ability. Results of such tests help the employer make unbiased decisions and distinguish between similarly qualified applicants.

Verifying Application Information and Checking Backgrounds
Before making hiring decisions regarding employment at any level in the bank, the human resources department will check an applicant's references. The inquiries are made in a professional manner and may request only factually verifiable and job-related information. As technology has advanced, it is fairly common for the hiring process to include browsing personal information in publicly available online formats. Be prudent in online information that you post. Before posting any online personal information ask yourself "how would a prospective employer regard this information"?

Orienting New Hires   The next step in the hiring process is **orientation**, which welcomes new employees to the bank and helps them understand its policies and how it operates. The orientation will reflect the individual bank's personality. A general session covers the bank's philosophy, a detailed explanation of the various benefits it offers its employees, and the bank's expectations of its employees. At this time, a bank that has a written employee handbook may distribute copies to the employees. The presentation of its expectations should include these topics:

- Importance of customer service and other areas that the bank emphasizes

- Rules concerning attendance and punctuality

- Standards of performance

- Performance review process, including the frequency with which an employee's performance is evaluated

- Training opportunities

- Promotion

- Salary increases

- Safety and security measures

Training   New employees learn the procedures, rules, and regulations that apply to their jobs through a combination of formal instruction and on-the-job training. They are often paired with an experienced employee who instructs them in the steps and processes required in the position. More formal instruction is provided through workshops, seminars, and training sessions, which can be held on-site or off-site.

Banks in general encourage employees to advance their careers by developing their job skills and learning new ones by taking approved courses. Some banks offer their own programs, such as those that lead to *teller certification.* Other banks provide opportunities for employees to take courses through the Center for Financial Training (CFT), a nationally recognized training group. There are many CFTs around the country, offering a wide variety of public and distance learning programs. Many CFTs are associated with community colleges, offering courses with transfer credit arrangements. Bank employees can locate the CFT office closest to them by visiting the national website at www.cftusa.org or calling toll free 888-628-5238 or 888-NATLCFT.

 checkpoint

Why is checking an applicant's job and educational background important?

MAINTAINING EMPLOYEE RECORDS

Keeping proper records is a requirement for employers. It makes good business sense to have accurate and organized information when needed. In addition, federal and state governments require certain employee data to be kept on record. The human resources department fulfills a critical organizational and legal function by keeping a personnel file for each employee. The file is updated as needed. The file typically includes the original or a copy of these items:

- Personal information including employee's full name, address, telephone number, Social Security number, and name of person to contact for emergency purposes

- Application information (resumes, references, and so on)

- Wage or salary information, including the basis on which wages are calculated (hourly or weekly, for example), the pay rate, pay record by pay period including overtime earnings if applicable, and all additions to or deductions from the employee's wages

- Job description of original and any new position as well as any changes in responsibilities

- Education information (transcripts, certificates, credentials, training)

- Federal/state documents (forms W-4 for tax withholding, I-9 regarding immigration and naturalization), and any later changes

- Performance evaluations, including the required documentation signed by the employee and supervisor

- Benefits forms

Human resources specialists must understand all legal regulations governing today's workplace. They must know, for example, the types of questions they can and cannot ask during an interview, the privacy issues concerning the employee personnel folder, and the appropriate uses of the information in the folder.

 checkpoint

Why would HR want to include education information in an employee's personnel folder?

assessment 13.2

Think Critically

1. From an employer's perspective, what are some advantages of allowing employees to telecommute?

_____

_____

2. What is the importance of merit-based hiring in the employment process?

_____

_____

3. What are the problems that could result from "beefing up" or exaggerating duties of a job when the company advertises it? What would the company hope to gain by this practice?

_____

_____

_____

4. Why is the process of setting employee pay rates a crucial activity?

_____

_____

_____

Make Academic Connections

5. **PROBLEM SOLVING**   Working in groups, list the characteristics that you believe a human resources specialist in a bank should have. Then design a form to be used during an interview to help uncover an applicant's strength in those areas.

6. **CONSUMER AFFAIRS**   On the Internet, find at least three banks that offer call center services. What do these centers do? What department would supervise the call center? Summarize your findings.

_____

_____

_____

_____

13.3

goals

+ State the objectives of employee performance evaluations.
+ Describe the employee discipline process.

terms

+ performance standard
+ evaluation form

Banking Scene

Nathaniel Bryant has been hired as a teller at Farmers Bank. All new employees are hired on a probationary period and are evaluated six months after their hire date. How might Nathaniel prepare for the performance evaluation process?

EMPLOYEE PERFORMANCE EVALUATION

One way to ensure that employees are meeting the bank's goals is to make sure that they understand their responsibilities and are performing at an expected level. Banks, like other businesses, periodically conduct formal employee reviews. These reviews should come at regularly scheduled intervals, such as every six months or every year, or at the end of the probationary period if the employee is on probation. Of course, effective supervisors bring obvious problems to an employee's attention as they occur rather than waiting for a formal assessment.

Employment performance evaluation can be a sensitive area. Although both the evaluator and the employee might feel awkward or uncomfortable, the review is a crucial part of the employment process. It is only fair for supervisors to let employees know how they are performing and what they need to do to improve.

Objectives

In general, employee performance evaluations have these objectives:

• To assess actual performance and accomplishments against the duties, responsibilities, and standards of the employee's position as stated in the job description

• To identify the employee's potential and interests and assist her or him in setting goals for job improvement and professional growth

• To provide a written record of employee performance to support future personnel decisions related to salary, promotion, increased responsibility, reassignment, transfer, reemployment, or disciplinary action

• To provide a communication tool through which to recognize the employee's special talents, capabilities, and achievements and identify any areas of job performance that need to be improved

Performance Standards

To ensure that evaluations are fair and objective, standards must be established related to job duties and responsibilities. **Performance standards** define for both supervisors and employees the expectations for completing a job's essential functions and tasks. For example, bank tellers may be evaluated on their ability to count money, keep the cash drawer in balance, and process customer transactions accurately. An understanding of the standards provides the basis for ongoing feedback and performance counseling between assessments as well as for formal evaluation.

Numerous methods can be used to develop standards. Traditionally, the human resources department identifies the standards in consultation with management. A collaborative approach involves both supervisors or HR personnel and employees. Employees bring valuable insight about their jobs to the process, and they are more likely to support the final standards that they helped define. Specific standards focus the discussion on specific elements of the employee's performance.

Evaluation Forms

In an effort to make their performance evaluations fair and objective, many banks use standardized forms, called **evaluation forms**, on which to record employee assessments. It is probably best for a bank to develop its own form so that it reflects that bank's standards, but many different versions are available for sale. An effective form includes the following:

- Employee's name and job title

- Name and position of person making the evaluation

- Scale used for evaluation, such as outstanding, very good, satisfactory, development needed, or a scale of 1 to 10

tech talk

Virtual Tellers

IBM recently introduced interactive bank kiosks. Tellers at brick-and-mortar banks can remotely service customers with the help of webcams. With technology conveying the voice and image of both the teller at his or her workstation and the customer at a kiosk, the majority of customer-to-teller services can be performed via the virtual teller. Cash transactions cannot be handled through the virtual teller. Current expectations are that virtual tellers will provide an additional service option for customers. It is not expected that virtual tellers will replace live tellers.

Think Critically What type of customer is mostly likely to seek the help of a virtual teller? How will bank personnel react to this new technology?

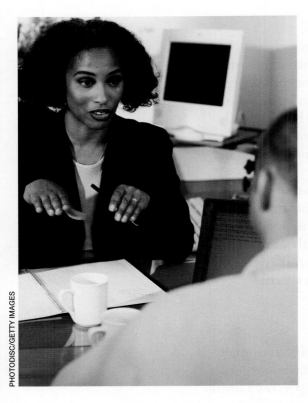

PHOTODISC/GETTY IMAGES

• List of performance standards for the job title

• A section allowing space for listing suggested steps to take for improving performance

A sample performance appraisal is shown on the next page. At the end of the review, both the employee and the supervisor should sign the form, indicating their agreement as to the information it contains. Employees who disagree with anything in the review should have a specific procedure through which to appeal the process.

Appeal Process

Banks should establish standard procedures by which employees can appeal some or all of their performance evaluation. These procedures are generally detailed in the bank's employee handbook. Appeals may be made verbally or in writing, although it is generally preferred to have a written statement. A written appeal states the reason for which the employee is contesting the evaluation and any supporting information or documentation. The appeal advances through the established channels until it is resolved.

✔ **checkpoint**

Why do you think it is better to appeal a job evaluation in writing?

_____

_____

EMPLOYEE DISCIPLINE •

Most employers are careful to provide employees detailed descriptions of their job duties and responsibilities and the proper way to perform them. Banks are no exception. Many of them provide handbooks or other written documents that explain the behavior and performance expected of their employees. These documents also explain disciplinary procedures and reasons for termination. Discipline can include informal warnings, formal written warnings, suspension without pay, and termination if the employee does not solve the problem.

Informal Warning

Minor problems, such as tardiness, failure to cooperate with employees, or forgetting to sign documents, can result in a verbal warning after the supervisor has discussed the problem with the employee. Although this is considered informal, it is recorded in the employee's personnel file.

Performance Appraisal—Teller I

Employee's Name _____

Supervisor's Name _____

Performance Review Date_____

Rating   Performance Level

7   **Outstanding:** Outstanding total performance. Consistently completes duties in an outstanding manner.

6   **Exceptional:** Very good performance; exceeds standards generally and expectations continuously.

5   **Very good:** Performance above standard at times.

4   **Satisfactory:** Overall satisfactory performance meeting the job's requirements.

3   **Borderline:** Performance unacceptable at times and requires improvement.

2   **Poor:** Performance often below expectations; inconsistent and unacceptable in many areas.

1   **Unsatisfactory:** Consistently unacceptable performance.

Standards

____   Demonstrates understanding of job requirements and implements that knowledge in performing duties

____   Balances the cash drawer daily

____   Is able to process customer transactions (checking and savings deposits, check cashing, and savings withdrawals)

____   Sells money orders, travelers' checks, and savings bonds

____   Accepts credit card, mortgage, loan, and utility payments from individuals and bank card deposits from merchants

____   Prepares currency and coin for retail customers

____   Balances automated teller machines, replenishes their cash, and processes deposits and withdrawals made through them

____   Promotes banking services and answers customer inquiries

____   Demonstrates customer-service orientation in working with customers

For areas rated 1–3, these specific actions should be taken to improve performance _____

_____

Improvement required by (date) _____

Employee Signature_____   Supervisor Signature_____

Formal Warning

When an employee commits a serious breach of the bank's policy or fails to show improvement after an informal warning, the supervisor discusses the problem with the employee, citing specific occurrences. The employee may explain any special circumstances regarding the violation. The supervisor considers the facts and may decide that a formal warning is warranted. The supervisor explains the reason for the decision, describes in detail the performance changes necessary to correct the situation and a timeframe in which the performance must change, and the consequences if the employee does not meet the expectations, including dismissal. A copy of the formal warning is placed in the employee's personnel file.

Suspension or Dismissal

An employee who does not improve his or her performance or repeats the offensive action within the specified time may be suspended or dismissed. A hearing including members of the management team, the personnel department, and the immediate supervisor is generally held. All special circumstances are considered. If the decision is to suspend the employee, employment will be discontinued for a time specified by the bank's policy. The written notice is added to the employee's file.

If the decision is made to dismiss the employee, he or she is given the reasons. This decision is confirmed in writing, and the employee is given a termination notice. Some misconduct is so serious that the required disciplinary action is immediate dismissal. This gross misconduct includes:

- Refusal to comply with an instruction

- Failure to follow safety rule(s)

- Theft, fraud, or deliberate damage to bank property

- Alcohol or drug intoxication on bank property

- Violent behavior or threats to coworkers, management, or customers

Appeal

Disciplinary procedures must be followed to protect the employer from charges that its actions are either unfounded or performed improperly.

Procedures also serve to protect the employee from having unjustified action taken against him or her. An employee who has been given a formal warning, a suspension, or a termination notice has the right to appeal the decision according to the policies that the bank has established.

 checkpoint

Why is a standardized process needed for disciplining and dismissing employees?

assessment 13.3

Think Critically

1. Why is it unwise for a supervisor who is aware of an employee's performance problem to wait to bring it to the worker's attention until the formal job review?

2. In what way does an employee evaluation act as a communication tool?

3. Why is it important for job descriptions to be updated regularly?

4. What is the purpose of using suspension without pay as a disciplinary measure?

Make Academic Connections

5. **RESEARCH**   The Bureau of Labor Statistics is an excellent source of information about the banking industry. Use information you obtain from its website to prepare a one-page report on the working conditions in banking.

6. **ECONOMICS**   Analyze the impact of the use of online services on the banking industry.

chapter 13 **assessment**

Chapter Summary

13.1 Organizational Structure and Employees

A. Banks are organized by departments. Titles of departments vary. A typical bank is structured around the deposit-gathering, loan, and trust functions. Other departments support these functions.

B. Many different positions provide the services that banks offer. A wide range of skills and responsibilities is involved.

13.2 Human Resources

A. Human resources departments at banks establish the policies and procedures related to hiring, training, evaluation, compensation, and benefits.

B. The HR department maintains confidential employee records according to legal requirements and bank guidelines.

13.3 Employee Evaluation

A. To ensure that employees understand their responsibilities, perform them as required, and have a gauge as to their performance level, banks conduct periodic employee assessments.

B. From time to time, a bank must discipline and even dismiss an employee. In doing so, it must follow specific steps and perform certain procedures aimed at protecting the employer and the employee.

Vocabulary Builder

Choose the term that best fits the definition. Write the letter of the answer in the space provided. Some terms may not be used.

a. benefit
b. customer service representative (CSR)
c. departmentalization
d. evaluation form
e. integrity
f. job description
g. job fair
h. merit-based employment
i. operations
j. orientation
k. performance standard
l. telecommuting
m. teller

____ 1. The most common position at banks
____ 2. Provides support to all functional departments
____ 3. A form on which to record employee assessments
____ 4. An event at which banks present information about employment to a large group of people
____ 5. Involves policies concerning hours of work, vacation and sick time, and insurance and retirement plans
____ 6. The adherence to a strict moral or ethical code
____ 7. States a job's duties and the skills and education required to perform those duties
____ 8. Creates an organizational structure for a bank by dividing it into departments
____ 9. Defines the expectations for completing a job's essential functions and tasks
____ 10. Allows an employee to work from home via computer
____ 11. A process that occurs at the beginning of employment that welcomes new employees and helps them understand a banks policies
____ 12. Selecting the most qualified candidate for a specific position
____ 13. Account personnel that help customers open a variety of new accounts

Review Concepts

14. List three primary activities or functions of a bank.

_____

_____

_____

15. What is the difference between the functional and operations areas of banks?

_____

_____

_____

16. What is a financial statement?

_____

_____

_____

17. List the various uses of a job description.

_____

_____

_____

18. What is a job fair?

_____

_____

_____

19. What is the reason for preemployment testing?

_____

_____

_____

20. List the documents that a personnel file typically includes.

_____

_____

_____

21. What are the objectives of employee evaluation?

_____

_____

_____

_____

22. What is the purpose of performance standards?

_____

_____

_____

23. What are the stages in employee discipline?

_____

_____

_____

24. List three actions for which an employee could be dismissed immediately.

_____

_____

_____

_____

Apply What You Learned

25. Why is integrity an essential characteristic for all bank employees?

_____

_____

_____

_____

26. Why must all bank employees have good "people" skills?

_____

_____

_____

_____

27. Why is it improper for an interviewer to ask a job applicant about his or her child care arrangements?

_____

_____

_____

_____

28. Why should the personnel file be kept confidential?

_____

_____

_____

29. What do you think is the purpose of having an employee sign the employee evaluation form?

_____

_____

_____

_____

30. What should employees do if they believe their performance evaluation contains inaccurate information?

_____

_____

_____

_____

31. Give examples of what employee issues would prompt an informal warning and then what problems would necessitate a formal warning.

_____

_____

_____

_____

Make Academic Connections

32. **RESEARCH**   Choose one of the job positions discussed in Lesson 13.1. Investigate the job tasks, salary, and job outlook. Write a two-page report on what you learn.

33. **BANKING MATH**   At the beginning of the work day, a teller's cash drawer has a total of $5 in loose change, 50 one-dollar bills, 50 tens, 30 twenties, 10 fifties, and 10 hundreds. During the day, the teller had deposit transactions totaling $3,150 and withdrawals of $4,300. At the end of the day, the drawer contains $1,060. Is the drawer in balance?

_____

_____

_____

34. **COMMUNICATION**   Use the Internet to find samples of resumes. Compile a resume that you can use when applying for banking jobs.

35. **CAREERS**   Interview a bank's auditor or accountant about the position's responsibilities. Learn about the person's daily business activities and recent technological advances that have affected the job. Present your findings to the class in an oral report.

GLOSSARY

A

Adjustable rate mortgages (ARMs) mortgages in which the interest rate and payments are fixed for a period of time at the outset but then change according to an index value (p. 228)

Adjusted balance method payments made are subtracted during the billing cycle, however new purchases are not included (p. 209)

Adverse feedback loop occurs when financial disruptions cause investment and consumer spending to decline (p. 72)

Adverse selection concept that the borrowers who are most willing to accept a high interest rate are the same borrowers who are most likely to default on their loans (p. 188)

Advertising paid description or presentation of a product, service, idea, or organization to encourage individuals to buy, support, or approve of it (p. 387)

Aggregate measures the collective components of the money supply that are used to estimate the size of the money (p. 101)

Annual percentage rate (APR) nominal rate on which interest is calculated per year (p. 132)

Annual percentage yield (APY) represents the effect of compounding (p. 132)

Annuity series of payments, often to a retired person, of a set amount from a capital investment; it is paid at a specified frequency and for a set number of years or until the annuitant's death (p. 314)

Asset anything of value (p. 19)

Asset transformation refers to using deposits to generate revenue by putting deposits to work via loans (p. 187)

Automated teller machines (ATMs) fee-based mechanism by which bank customers can perform banking transactions without the aid of a bank teller (p. 23)

Average daily balance method credit card balances for each day of the billing cycle are added and then divided by the number of days in the billing cycle to yield an average figure on which the finance charge is calculated (p. 210)

B

Balance of payments record of all the exchanges of goods and services that occur between two countries for a specified time period (p. 88)

Balloon mortgage mortgages in which the interest rate and payment stay fixed, but at some specified point, perhaps five years, the entire remaining balance of the loan is due in one single "balloon" payment (p. 228)

Bandit barrier bulletproof plastic shields that can be positioned in front of each teller's station (p. 333)

Bank business which sells services to earn money; they manage and market those services in a competitive field (p. 4)

Bank run occurs when many people try to withdraw their money at once (p. 49)

Bearer instrument instrument which is payable to the whomever holds it (p. 154)

Beneficiary person for whose benefit the property is held (p. 321)

Benefit involves matters such as hours of employment and time off for vacation, illness, holidays, and jury duty; also covers health insurance policies, including dental and vision coverage, disability and unemployment insurance, and retirement plan (p. 406)

Bill of exchange negotiable and unconditional written order, such as a check, draft, or trade agreement, addressed by one party to another (p. 155)

Blank endorsement signature of the holder which is the least secure of the four main types of endorsement, but it is also the most negotiable (p. 161)

Bond debt instrument issued for a period of more than one year with the purpose of raising capital through borrowing (p. 313)

Bridge loan form of short-term loan used to cover expenses until long-term financing is in place (p. 268)

Brokerage brings together parties interested in making a transaction, such as buying and selling shares of stock (p. 313)

Buy-down mortgage mortgages in which the borrower buys down, or prepays, part of the interest in order to get a lower rate (p. 230)

C

Call Report quarterly report of income and financial condition that all U.S. commercial banks are required to file with their federal and state regulatory agencies (p. 82)

CAMELS system examiners use to evaluate six criteria of safety and soundness of banks. Each letter stands for one of the criteria: capital adequacy, asset adequacy, management, earnings, liquidity, and sensitivity to risk (p. 83)

Captive borrower consumer with a weak credit history (p. 189)

Cash card commonly used at an automated teller machine (ATM) at which consumers can get cash, make transfers and deposits, or perform almost any other banking function at the machine by inserting the card and entering a personal identification number (PIN) (p. 172)

Central bank government banks that manage, regulate, and protect both the money supply and the banks (p. 6)

Certificates of deposit (CDs) certificates issued by banks that guarantee the payment of a fixed interest rate until a specified date in the future (p. 127)

Charge card card that specifies that consumers must pay the account in full at the end of the month (p. 171)

Charter legal approval to operate a business as a bank (p. 82)

Check 21 federal legislation effective in October 2004 that created a new category of negotiable instrument, and allows banks to process check information electronically (p. 123)

Check counterfeiting can mean either entirely creating a check with desktop publishing equipment or simply duplicating a check with advanced color photocopiers (p. 347)

Check kiting requires opening accounts at two or more institutions and using "the float time" of available funds to create fraudulent balances (p. 345)

Code of ethics is a statement adopted by the management and board of directors of businesses to guide employees in taking appropriate actions in critical situations that could reflect on the organization (p. 338)

Collateral item that secures a loan (p. 194)

Commercial bank institutions commonly thought of as banks (p. 6); bank owned by stockholders who expect a profit on their investments (p. 26)

Commercial lending lending to business enterprises (p. 264)

Commodity money money based on some item of value—for example, gold or precious stones (p. 102)

Compound interest process of adding interest to the principal and paying interest on the new total (p. 131)

Conflict of interest occurs when two interests are at cross-purposes (p. 339)

Consumer reporting agency (CRA) company that compiles and keeps records on consumer payment habits and sells these reports to banks and other companies to use for evaluating creditworthiness (p. 202)

Corpus property that is held (p. 321)

Correspondent bank acts as points of contact for other banks that do not have a branch, agency, subsidiary, or corporation in the host country (p. 301)

Country risk entire range of political, legal, social, and economic conditions that may put international business at risk (p. 301)

Credit card card that allows consumers to pay all or part of their bills each month and finance the unpaid balance (p. 172)

Credit default swap (CDS) swap designed to transfer the credit exposure of fixed income products between parties (p. 288)

Credit freeze prohibits access to your credit report (p. 356)

Credit rationing occurs when banks refuse to provide a loan, or when they lend less than the customer requested (p. 189)

Credit risk a bank's estimate of the probability that the borrower can and will repay a loan with interest as scheduled (p. 216)

Credit union savings and loan institution owned by depositors who share a common type of association, such as employer (p. 27)

Creditworthy customer with a good credit rating, sufficient collateral for loans, and ongoing income (p. 14)

Cross-selling occurs when you apply your understanding of your customer to suggest other products from which the customer could benefit (p. 369)

Currency all media of exchange circulating in a country (p. 38)

Currency risk risk posed by variations in exchange rates between countries (p. 301)

Customer Relationship Management (CRM) captures the idea that the most profitable way to view customers is not merely in terms of the current products or services they buy from you, but in terms of both the present and future potential value to your business as a customer (p. 369)

Customer segmentation process of dividing customers into subgroups, each of which is identifiable by its specific preferences or needs, so that distinctive products can be developed for and sold profitably to these groups (p. 365)

Customer service activities and programs a seller provides to make the relationship with its customers satisfying (p. 379)

Customer service representative (CSR) helps customers open checking and savings accounts, obtain debit and credit cards, and learn the various options available, such as how to bank, whether in person, through an ATM, by phone, or online; also directs customers to departments that offer other services (p. 399)

Cybermarketing carefully planned and sustained effort to advertise a company, its products, and/or services through the Internet by using the most practical, effective, and up-to-date strategies (p. 387)

D

Debit card transfers money from a person's designated account to the account of the retailer (p. 172)

Debt ratio the total obligations compared to the total income (p. 272)

Debt service coverage ratio (DSCR) compares net operating income to the total cost of debt (p. 273)

Demand deposit type of transaction account that is payable on demand whenever the depositor chooses (p. 122)

Demographics refers to the specific shared characteristics that comprise distinct groups of consumers (p. 364)

Departmentalization division of a bank into departments (p. 398)

Depositor people who put money into banks (p. 17)

Depository intermediaries financial institutions that get funds from the public and use them to finance their business (p. 26)

Depreciation change in value (p. 265)

Deregulation loosening of government control (p. 21)

Direct marketing promotion technique that delivers the materials individually to a target market via direct mail, telemarketing, or other direct means (p. 389)

Discount rate rate of interest that the Federal Reserve charges banks for short-term loans (p. 68); interest rate that the Federal Reserve sets and charges for loans to member banks (p. 113)

Disintermediation of funds occurs when depositors take their money out of bank accounts and invest those funds directly into capital markets (p. 136)

District Reserve Banks twelve regional banks in the Federal Reserve System that carry out banking functions for government offices in their area, examine member banks in the district, decide whether to loan banks funds, recommend interest rates, and implement policy decisions of the Board of Governors (p. 61)

Donor person who creates a trust (p. 321)

Draft order signed by one party (the drawer, or drafter) that is addressed to another party (the drawee) directing the drawee to pay to someone (the payee) the amount indicated on the draft (p. 155)

E

Edge corporation financial corporations that are federally chartered and allowed to engage only in international banking or other financial transactions related to international business (p. 301)

Elements of negotiability a written, signed, unconditional promise or order to pay a fixed amount on demand or at a defined time (p. 158)

Empathy degree of caring and individual attention shown customers (p. 380)

Equal Credit Opportunity Act (ECOA) prohibits creditors from discriminating against applicants on the basis of race, color, religion, national origin, sex, marital status, and age (pp. 75, 239)

Equity represents net assets, or total assets, minus total liabilities (pp. 20, 231)

Escrow amount of money lenders require to be paid to them in advance, from which they pay the real estate taxes (p. 235)

Estate total property, real and personal, that an individual owns (p. 322)

Ethics process of determining standards and procedures for dealing with judgmental decisions affecting other people; also refers to beliefs that help people distinguish right from wrong (p. 338)

Evaluation form standardized form on which employee assessments are recorded (p. 413)

Excess reserves reserves held by a bank beyond its reserve requirement (p. 106)

Executor person named in the will to administer the estate who must identify and determine the value of all assets in the estate including securities, business interests, and retirement plans (p. 323)

F

Factoring form of asset-based lending which advances cash to a business in exchange for its receivables (p. 268); practice of buying debt at a discount (p. 319)

Fair Credit Reporting Act (FCRA) promotes accuracy, fairness, and privacy of information in the files of consumer reporting agencies (pp. 75, 239)

Fair Debt Collection Practices Act (FDCPA) protects consumers from unfair collection techniques (p. 76); prohibits abusive practices by debt collectors (p. 239)

Fannie Mae Federal National Mortgage Association (FNMA) was created during the Great Depression in 1938 to help lenders find funds to make available for mortgages (p. 247)

Federal Deposit Insurance Corporation (FDIC) guarantees deposits against bank failures up to $100,000 per depositor, per bank, and sometimes even more for special kinds of accounts or ownership categories (p. 49)

Federal funds rate rate at which banks borrow from each other (pp. 67, 113)

Federal Open Market Committee (FOMC) makes discount rate decisions (p. 68)

Federal Reserve Act of 1913 created a system to stabilize the banking system

Federal Reserve System Open Market Account (SOMA) account in which the Fed maintains international reserves (p. 89)

Fiat money money that is deemed legal tender by the government and it is not based on or convertible into a commodity (p. 102)

FICO score three-digit number that credit granters can use in making a loan approval decision (p. 204)

Financial intermediary institution, firm, or individual who mediates between two or more parties in a financial context (p. 5)

Fixed exchange rate occurs when the monetary valuation of one country's currency is tied to the valuation of another country's currency (p. 88)

Fixed rate mortgages loans with a fixed interest rate for the life of the loan (p. 227)

Flexible exchange rate enables currencies to fluctuate based on market conditions (p. 88)

Float funds that are on deposit at two institutions at the same time due to inefficiencies in the collection system allowing a person or firm to earn extra income because the two institutions are paying interest on the same funds (p. 168)

Foreclosure occurs when a mortgage is not paid and the creditor seeks a court-ordered sale of the property (p. 227)

Foreign exchange rate value of one currency in terms of another (p. 303)

Forgery counterfeiting a check or other document with the intent to defraud (p. 347)

401(k) plan allows employees to make tax-deferred contributions to a trust and direct their funds to be invested among a variety of choices, getting their money back at departure or retirement (p. 322)

Fractional-reserve system (FRS) monetary policy at the basis of the modern banking system (p. 103)

Fraud deception deliberately practiced to secure unfair or unlawful gain (p. 344)

Fraud alert electronic warning placed on your accounts to monitor for suspicious financial activity (p. 356)

Freddie Mac Federal Home Loan Mortgage Corporation buys home mortgages from banks and other lending institutions and combines them into large groups, selling interest in the groups to investors (p. 248)

Full endorsement transfers a check to another specified party (p. 162)

G

Ginnie Mae Government National Mortgage Association is part of the Department of Housing and Urban Development (HUD); it backs securities issued by holders of pools of mortgages (p. 249)

Governing documents formal set of documents that outline customer rights, the policies and rules of a bank, and how customers can expect their bank to operate (p. 141)

Government Accountability Office (GAO) the auditing arm of Congress that helps ensure that federal laws and policies are implemented properly (p. 79)

Grace period amount of time you have to pay the bill in full and avoid any finance charges (p. 197)

Great Depression the worst and longest economic crisis of Western industrialized nations during the twentieth century; it began in 1929 and extended worldwide until about 1939 (p. 48)

H

Holder in due course person or financial institution that acquires a check or promissory note received in good faith as payment and who is entitled to payment by the drawer of the check or note (p. 158)

House flipping refers to the practice of buying a house for below-market value and selling the house at or above-market value (p. 348)

I

Identity theft occurs when someone intentionally obtains your personal information to use that information for personal gain (pp. 11, 351)

Inflation occurs when rising prices decrease the value of money (pp. 50, 71)

Installment loan loan for which the amount of the payments, the rate of interest, and the number of payments (or length of term) are fixed and are repaid on a periodic basis (p. 193)

Integrity steadfast adherence to a strict moral or ethical code (p. 401)

Interbank transaction transactions that occur when banks make or receive deposits from each other or from the Fed (p. 136)

Interest price paid for the use of money (pp. 17, 130, 235)

IRA individual retirement account in which funds are invested on a before-tax basis, which allows the earnings on the investment to compound (p. 322)

J

Job description formal document that factually and concisely identifies the job, responsibilities, work involved, and education required to perform a job (p. 405)

Job fair public employment events at which they can present employment opportunities, requirements, and personnel benefits to a large number of people at one time (p. 407)

Joint account checking account that has two or more owners, each of whom has equal and independent access to the account (p. 123)

Joint tenancy type of joint checking account used by two or more persons wishing to have co-owner accounts with others; allows each co-owner to make deposits and withdrawals independently (p. 123)

K

Keynesian economics economic policy in which expanded demand causes industries to manufacture more products, hire additional employees, and invest in new buildings and equipment (p. 70)

L

Letter of credit instrument given by a bank on behalf of a buyer (applicant) to pay the bank of the seller (beneficiary) a given sum in a given time provided that documents required by the letter are presented to the issuing bank

Liability a cash obligation (p. 19)

Lien legal claim to the property to secure a debt (p. 195)

Liquid asset anything that can readily be exchanged, like cash (p. 19)

Liquidity measure of how quickly things may be converted to something of value like cash; liquidity is variable, depending on the nature of the asset or liability (p. 99)

Liquidity risk risk that a bank will have to sell its assets at a loss to meet its cash demands (p. 216)

Living trust legal document that provides an expedient way to transfer property at a person's death (p. 324)

Loan-to-value (LTV) value of the loan compared to the value of the asset (p. 236)

M

Manufacturer business engaged in manufacturing some product (p. 270)

Margin stock bought for a fraction of its price and resold at a profit without the full purchase price of the stock ever having been paid (p. 48)

Marketing process of planning and executing the conception, pricing, promotion, and distribution of goods, services, and ideas to create exchanges that satisfy individual and organization objectives (p. 385)

Market risk risk that an investment will decrease in price as market conditions change (p. 216)

Medium of exchange an agreed-upon system for measuring the value of goods and services (pp. 4, 38)

Member bank any bank that is part of the Federal Reserve System (p. 61)

Merchandiser businessperson engaged in retail trade (p. 269)

Merit-based employment selecting the person with the best qualifications for a specific position (p. 407)

Modern portfolio theory (MPT) states that within any portfolio of investments, diversification should be used to spread out risk (p. 187)

Money laundering deposit, invest, or exchange money in such a way as to conceal its illegal source (p. 302)

Money market deposit accounts (MMDAs) time deposits that offer a higher rate of interest than regular savings accounts and usually require a higher initial deposit to open (p. 127)

Money supply liquid assets held by banks and individuals (p. 98)

Moral hazard occurs when a borrower takes greater risks if they think the harm they will incur from those risks will somehow be minimalized (p. 189)

Mortgage a note, usually long-term and secured by real property, that places a lien on the property and is not released until the debt is paid (p. 227)

Mortgage-backed securities businesses that pool individual loans and sell them as a group to other investors; any risk associated with a specific loan becomes part of the collective risk of the pool of loans (p. 254)

Mortgage origination new mortgages (p. 226)

Multiplier effect expansion of the money supply that results from a Federal Reserve System member bank's ability to lend significantly in excess of its reserves (p. 106)

Mutual fund investment companies that pool money from many savers who have small amounts to invest (p. 314)

N

Need requirement for basic survival; basic physiological needs include air, food, clothing, and shelter (p. 364)

Negative equity occurs when the amount owed on a home is more than the current value of the home (p. 256)

Negotiable instrument written order or promise to pay a sum of money, either to a specified party or to the person who holds it (p. 152)

Niche market targeting particular customers in defined locations or by particular services (p. 21)

Nondepository intermediaries financial institutions that do not take or hold deposits (p. 26)

O

Open-end loan loan that is flexible, as is the term; the longer the loan is used, the more will be paid (p. 197)

Operations provides banking support services such as bookkeeping (p. 398)

Orientation employer-sponsored event which welcomes new employees to their new workplace and helps them understand its policies and how it operates (p. 409)

Outsourcing practice of having an outside party supply a product or service that the firm had been producing or performing itself (p. 317)

P

Performance standard defines the expectations for completing a job's essential functions and tasks for both supervisors and employees (p. 413)

Person-to-person (P2P) payments online systems that allow consumers to pay each other directly for a product (p. 173)

Phishing act of sending a user an e-mail falsely claiming to be a legitimate enterprise in an attempt to solicit private information (p. 354)

PITI principal (p. 234)

Point a value equal to 1 percent of a loan (p. 230)

Post-dated check check which is dated later than when it was written (p. 143)

Predatory lending occurs when lenders create problems for consumers by making credit too easily available without regard to the borrower's ability to pay (p. 212)

Previous balance method the amount owed at the beginning of the billing cycle with calculated interest on that figure, regardless of payments or charges (p. 209)

Primary reserves consist of cash on hand and the required percentage amounts on deposit in the Federal Reserve District Bank (p. 105)

Prime rate interest rate that banks charge their best and most reliable customers (p. 113)

Probate court proceeding that settles an estate's final debts and formally passes legal title to property from the decedent to his or her heirs (p. 322)

Profit what's left of revenue after costs are deducted (p. 18)

Promissory note written promise to pay at a fixed or determinable future time a sum of money to a specified individual (p. 155)

Public image concept the public has of a business and should reflect its mission, values, and culture (p. 374)

Public relations planned and sustained effort to establish and maintain goodwill and mutual understanding between an organization and its public (p. 375)

Q

Qualified endorsement attempt to limit the liability of the endorser without limiting an instrument's further negotiability (p. 162)

R

Radio frequency identification (RFID) uses a transponder to convey identifying information including the account holder's account or balance information and the fees being assessed to the account by the business for products or services (p. 174)

Recession occurs when there is a decline in total production lasting a minimum of two consecutive quarters (at least six months) (p. 51)

Redlining illegal banking practice in which banks refuse to lend to residents of certain neighborhoods (pp. 113, 241)

Reserve liquidity ways to convert reserves readily to cash (p. 47)

Restrictive endorsement limits the use of the instrument to a means specified by the endorser (p. 161)

Retail bank thrift institutions such as mutual savings banks, savings and loans, and credit unions, developed to help individuals who are not served by commercial banks (p. 6)

Returned check check written on an account that does not have adequate funds to cover it and which is returned unpaid to the person who deposited it (p. 169)

Return on assets (ROA) the ratio of net income to total assets (p. 20)

Return on equity (ROE) measures how well a bank is using its equity (p. 20)

Reverse mortgage occurs when a homeowner receives a sum from the lender secured by the value of a home and does not pay the loan back as long as he or she lives there (p. 232)

Revolving credit line of credit that has a maximum limit and can be used on an ongoing basis until the limit is reached (p. 207)

Risk averse investor who would prefer to invest in a product that has very little risk of failure (p. 286)

Risk preferrer investor who seeks a high level of return on investments (p. 286)

ROCA score composite score of foreign bank performance in four distinct areas are: risk management, operational controls, compliance, and asset quality (p. 87)

S

Savings and loan association (S&L) depository intermediary that receives most of its deposits from individuals who receive shares of the company (p. 27)

Scam slang term for something that is fraudulent or a swindle (p. 348)

Search engine optimization (SEO) software program that indexes web content so that it can be referenced in Internet searches (p. 387)

Secondary reserves bank reserves including securities the bank purchases from the federal government and deposits that are due from other banks (p. 105)

Secured loan loan in which some item of value backs the loan in case the borrower defaults on the loan (p. 194)

Share certificate time deposit held in a credit union that is equal to a certificate of deposit in a regular bank (p. 128)

Shared appreciation mortgage mortgage which can lower interest rates for borrowers who agree to share profits with the lender when the house is sold (p. 230)

Share-draft account account held in a credit union that operates like a checking account in a regular bank (p. 128)

Short-term loan loan, usually for a year or less, used by businesses to finance expenses for seasonal or cyclical business costs, such as increasing inventory or maintaining the business until predictable receivables arrive (p. 266)

Small Business Administration (SBA) offers a number of financial, technical, and management programs to help businesses (p. 279)

Smart card credit, debit, or other type of card that has an embedded microchip (p. 23)

Sniffer program electronic programs that capture account numbers and PINs that can be installed on a computer via computer spyware (p. 355)

Social responsibility obligation to profitably serve employees and customers in an ethical and law-abiding manner (p. 386)

Sovereign wealth fund funds are segregated from the country's official currency reserves and can be used to generate profit for a country by making investments (p. 300)

Spam junk e-mail (p. 354)

Speculation occurs when people make investments based on anticipated or hoped for outcomes, without having an ownership stake in the asset being insured (p. 288)

Spread difference between what a bank pays in interest and what it receives in interest is the (p. 17)

Stagflation condition of slow economic growth and high unemployment (p. 51)

Stale check check which is dated six months or more before it is presented for payment or deposit (p. 143)

Statement savings account provides a monthly or quarterly computerized statement detailing all account activity, including interest credited and fees charged (p. 126)

Stock capital raised by a corporation through the issuance of shares entitling holders to an ownership interest, or equity, in the corporation (p. 313)

Straw buyer someone who agrees to use their personal information to buy the home at a falsely inflated price (p. 349)

Strength of Support Assessment (SOSA) reflects how well a foreign bank is able to provide appropriate guidance, oversight, and financial backing to its U.S. offices (p. 87)

Subprime rates rates that are higher than normal to offset the increased risk represented by a less-than-perfect borrower (p. 201)

Sum-of-digits method method of calculating finance charges that takes the total finance charge, divides it by the number of months in the loan term, and assigns a higher ratio of interest to the early payments (p. 208)

Synthetic financial product products that lack an underlying value in their assets (p. 289)

System to Estimate Examinations Ratings (SEER) automated system that analyzes and compares historical supervisory ratings of banks with their Call Report data and provides an additional method of capturing changes in financial performance that may require supervisory intervention (p. 83)

T

Target market preselected group of buyers for whom a product or service is created and to whom a marketing campaign is directed (p. 365)

Taylor rule provides ideas for how to use short-term interest rates to achieve the goals of a central bank, including keeping the economy stable and controlling inflation (p. 69)

Telecommuting allows employees to work from their homes via computer (p. 406)

Teller bank position whose duties include balancing the cash drawer daily by adding deposits and subtracting withdrawals from the opening cash funds, and processing customer transactions (p. 401)

Tenants in common type of joint checking account that is frequently used by business partners in which the approval of all owners is required to make withdrawals (p. 123)

Term loan finances permanent working capital, equipment, real estate, business expansion, or acquisition of another business; terms and rates vary with the asset securing the loan or the expected life of the asset (p. 266)

Time deposits deposits including savings accounts, money market deposit accounts, certificates of deposit (CDs), and various bonds that are held for or mature at a specified time (p. 126)

Transaction account account that allows transactions to occur without restrictions on the frequency or the volume of transactions (p. 122)

Transit number 9-digit number that identifies the bank that holds the checking account and is responsible for payment (p. 168)

Trust arrangement by which one party holds property on behalf of another party for certain defined purposes (p. 321)

Truth in Lending Act (TILA) Title I of the Consumer Credit Protection Act of 1968; was landmark legislation guaranteeing that all information about cost of a loan is provided in writing to consumers (p. 74); promotes informed use of consumer credit by requiring disclosures about its terms and costs (p. 239)

Truth in Savings Act of 1991 requires banks to disclose the interest rate paid and the fees charged on deposit accounts to enable consumers to make informed decisions (p. 143)

U

Underwriting process of reviewing a loan for soundness (p. 200)

Unsecured loan loan backed only by the reputation and creditworthiness of the borrower (p. 195)

U.S. Treasury Exchange Stabilization Fund (ESF) account in which the Treasury maintains international reserves (p. 89)

V

Variable annuity combines the opportunity for tax-deferral with a choice of portfolios and the flexibility to vary annual contributions according to the investors' needs or market conditions (p. 322)

Viral marketing involves intentionally using ordinary people to help spread the word about a product or service (p. 389)

W

Want something that you would prefer to have but that you could live without if necessary (p. 364)

War driving criminal practice of driving around to find retailers with weaknesses in their Internet security systems (p. 355)

Wholesale banks commercial banks that specialize only in business banking (p. 26)

Will document by which the individual gives instructions as to what is to happen upon his or her death in regard to property and remains (p. 322)

World Bank lends money to developing countries and expects the loans to be repaid (p. 299)

INDEX

A

AAA bond rating, 255
ABA number, 168
Acceleration clause, 198
Accommodation endorsement, 162
Accounts, 202, 317
Adjustable rate mortgages (ARMs), 228–229
Adjusted balance method, 209
Adjustment interval, 229
Adverse feedback loop, 72
Adverse selection, 188–189
Advertising, 387, 390, 407
Aggregate measures, 101
Agreement corporations, 301
Alternative Motor Vehicle Credit, 59
American National Standards Institute (ANSI), 159
Annual percentage rate (APR), 132, 195, 208–211
Annual percentage yield (APY), 132
Annuity, 314
Appreciation, 230
Asia Pacific Economic Cooperation (APEC), 90
Asset transformation, 187
Asset, 19
Asset-based loans, 268
Automated clearing houses (ACHs), 177, 318
Automated teller machines (ATMs), 8, 23, 125, 172, 175, 191, 355
Automatic identification and data capture (AIDC), 174
Availability of Funds and Collection of Checks regulation, 144
Average daily balance method, 210

B

Balance of payments, 88
Balance sheets, 190–191
Balloon mortgage, 228
Bandit barriers, 333, 334
Bank(s)
  additional sources of revenue for, 190–191
  asset management and, 187
  assets and liabilities, 19
  best practice to deter robberies, 333
  business of, 4–6
  changes traditional services of, 21–22

consumer lending theory and, 188–189
in crisis, Great Depression and, 48–49
deposits in, 120–128
faulty investment strategies of, 20
foreign, 300. *See also* International banking
income sources of, 18–19
lending and, 13–15
managing portfolios of, 186–187
mergers and, 7
modern portfolio theory (MPT) and, 187
movement of money and, 12–13
new services of, 22–24
in new United States, 43–44
off-balance sheet activities of, 190–191
predatory lending and, 212
risk management and, 199–200
robbery and prevention, 332–336
role in the economy, 10–12
security and, 331–333
test of profitability of, 20
types of, 5–6
Bank collection services, 318
Bank currency, 38
Bank departments, functional
  brokerage, 399
  individual or personal banking, 398–399
  insurance, 299
  small business and consumer lending, 399
  trust funds, 399
Bank departments, jobs within
  accounting clerks, 403
  auditors, 403
  bank teller, 401–402
  chief financial officers (CFOs), 403
  computer operators, 403
  customer service representatives (CSRs), 402
  human resources. *See* Human resources
  job analyst, 403
  public relations specialists, 403
  trust officers, 403
Bank departments, operational
  accounting/finance, 399
  bank officers, 400
  human resources, 399

maintenance, purchasing, and security, 400
operations, 400
public relations/marketing, 400
technical, 400
treasury management, 400
Bank holiday, 49
Bank for International Settlements (BIS), 90
Bank loans
  consumer loans, 185–198
  cost of credit, 207–211
  granting and analyzing credit, 199–206
  impact of credit and, 211
  policy and, 214–219
  role of banks and, 212–213
  See also Loan(s)
Bank run, 49
Bank Secrecy Act of 1970, 302, 346
Banking
  before 1913, 43–46
  business of, 2–35, 138
  competition effects on, 8
  customers and. *See* Customers
  deregulation and, 52
  fees, 18
  how the system works, 17–25
  inflation and, 50–51
  interest bearing accounts, 130–134
  introduction to, 4–9
  marketing and. *See* Marketing
  modern, 47–57
  other financial institutions, 26–31
  public relation activities and, 375–376
  role of in the economy, 10–16
  society and, 15
  spread, 17–19
  steps in creating a public image, 374–375
  technology effects on, 8
Banking account rules
  account statement policies, 143
  check policies, 143
  deposit collection, 142
  Federal Reserve Regulations and, 143–144
  minimum balance/service charges, 142
  opening and closing accounts, 142
  other policies, 143
  overdraft policies, 142
  providing governing documents, 141
  resolution form, 142

signature policies, 141
waivers, 143
withdrawal policies, 142
Banking Acts of 1933 and 1935, 49
Banking and deposit account
documents, 140–141
Banking crisis, 81
Banking Math Connection (feature)
balance your checkbook, 156
calculate debt ratios, 275
calculate fee percentages, 319
calculate money created from a
deposit, 106
calculate one year spread, 18
calculate simple interest, 131
calculating interest payment, 209
inflation, 50
insurance and counterfeit money, 346
marketing, 388
private mortgage insurance, 235
rate of currency exchange, 87
vendor credit card fees, 401
Banking stability, 81–83
Banking system
development in the U.S., 36–41
how it works, 17–20
maintaining balance in, 83
regulations that facilitate private
investment, 84
trust and, 83
Banking, ethics in
code of ethics, 339
ethical behavior, 338, 342
everyday ethical dilemmas in, 342
issues in the banking and corporate
world, 340–341
Sarbanes-Oxley Act of 2002, 341
Banking, fraud and scams
check fraud, about, 345–346
counterfeit currency, 344–345
Bank of the United States, 43–44
Basic checking accounts, 123–124
Beneficiary, 321
Bernanke, Ben, 62
Big Five U.S. accounting firms, 341
Bill payment services, 173
Bills of exchange, 155
Biometrics, 174–175, 177
Blank endorsement, 160–161
Bond, defined, 313
Boom economy, slowing the, 70–71
Branching Out (feature)

Aisling, 366
Credit Card Kiosks, 190
Financial Matchmaking with
CDARS, 283
Skip the Bank, Come to the Store, 71
Tending to Financial Ills, 402
Wal-Mart, 128
Bridge loans, 268
Broadcast media, 388
Brokerage, 313, 399
Brokerage houses, 29
Brokerage services, 313-314
Brokers, 29
Buffet, Warren, 341
Builder-bailout mortgage schemes, 349
Bump-ups, 127
Bureau of Economic Analysis, 298
Bureau of Engraving and Printing, 105
Bureau of Labor Statistics, 407
Business
approach to customers, 367
characteristics of profitable, 379
customers, types of, 366
international, and trade financing,
303–305
manufacturers, 270
merchandisers, 269–270
Business insurance, 311–313
Buy-down mortgage, 230

C

Call report, 82
Capacity, 201, 237
Capital investments, 319
Capital services, and cash management,
318–319
CAPLines loan program, 283
Captive borrower, 189
Car loans, 194
Cash cards, 172
Cash flow, 218
Cash management, 316-319
Central bank, 6
Certificate of Deposit Account Registry
Services (CDARS), 283
Certificates of deposit (CDs), 127–128
Charge cards, 171
Charitable remainder trust (CRT), 324
Charter, 82
Chartered financial analyst (CFA), 121
Check 21, 123, 178, 166, 346

Check advance loans, 29
Check alteration, 347
Check fraud, 345-348
Checking account
asset management and, 125
ATM fees and, 125
Automated transfer service transac-
tions and, 125
basic, 123–124
defined, 122–123
electronic funds transfer and, 125–126
free, 124
mobile banking and, 125
no-frills, 124
no service charge, 124
online banking with, 125
returned check, 169
Checking account, types of, 123–126
Checks, 154
Checks, legal structure of payment
system
Check 21, 166
Electronic check conversion, 166
Expedited Funds Availability Act
(EFAA), of 1987, 166
Federal Reserve Act of 1913, 165–166
Uniform Commercial Code (UCC) of
1958, 166
Checks, payment and processing of,
167-169
Chief financial officers (CFOs), 403
Circulation of money, 107–108
Clearing House Interbank Payment
System (CHIPS), 177
Closed account fraud, 347
Closing, 201, 237
Coins, 39–40, 102
Collateral
about, 194–195
use of, 201, 215, 218, 237
Collections, international, 304
Colonial cash, 39
Commerce Department, 302
Commercial bank, 6, 26
Commercial credit analysis, 272–274
Commercial lending, 264–291
Commercial loans, 264-268
Commercial paper, 156
Commodity Futures Trading Commis-
sion (CFTC), 65, 79
Commodity money, 202
Common stock, 313

Communicate (feature)
  conduct poll about checking account scams, 347
  conduct survey about consumer attitudes, 137
  government rescues of banks, 82
  interview a bank employee, 8
  interview bank officers, 308
  interview entrepreneurs, 282
  interview people about banks and social responsibility, 386
  interview people about the value of money, 103
  interview someone about the Great Depression, 48
  poll homeowners, 227
  take a poll about forms of credit payment, 166
  use Internet and PowerPoint to explain banking regulations, 143
  use Internet to investigate employee discipline problems, 416
  use Internet to research free credit reports, 204
Community Reinvestment Act (CRA), 218, 240–241, 377
Competition in banking, 8
Compound interest, 131
Comptroller of the Currency, 45, 47, 49, 82
Consumer Credit Protection Act of 1968, 74–75
Consumer protection, 64, 74–79, 81, 83
Consumer Reporting Agency (CRA), 202
Consumers, 72, 75–78, 133
Contract financing, 268
Conventional mortgage, 227
Correspondent banks, 167, 168
Council of Economic Advisors, 68
Council of Public Relations, 376
Counterfeit currency, 344-346
Country risk, 301–302
Coverdell Education Savings Accounts (CESAs), 322
Credit analysis, 402
Credit cards, 14, 22-23, 172, 197
Credit, analyzing, 202-205
Credit, cost of, 208-210
Credit, granting, 199–201
Credit, impact of, 211-212
Credit-approval process

application, 200
documentation, 200
processing, 200
underwriting, 200–201
Credit counseling, 213
Credit default swap (CDS)
  about, 287–288
  complicating factors of, 288–289
Credit freeze, 356
Credit insurance, 309
Credit life, 309
Credit Repair Organization Act, 78
Credit reputation, 201, 237
Credit risk, 216
Credit transaction protection, for consumers
  Credit Repair Organization Act, 78
  Equal Credit Opportunity Act (ECOA), 75
  Fair Credit Billing Act, 77
  Fair Credit and Charge Card Disclosure Act, 78
  Fair Credit Reporting Act (FCRA), 75–76
  Fair Debt Collection Practices Act (FDCPA), 76
  Gramm-Leach-Bliley Act, 78
  Home Equity Loan Consumer Protection Act, 78
  truth in lending, 74–75
Credit union, 27–28
Creditworthiness, 14–15
Cross-selling, 369
Currency
  additional functions of, 41
  classifying, 38
  coins as early American medium of exchange, 39–40
  coins as oldest form of, 102
  colonial, 39–40
  counterfeit, 344–345
  creation of a national, 38–39
  defined, 38
  foreign exchange of, 304–305
  gold as, 103
  shifting meaning of, 38–39
  U.S., after Revolutionary War, 40–41
Currency exchanges, 30
Currency risk, 301
Currency values, stabilizing, 87–88
Customer(s)
  business, 366

competitive threats, 372
defined, 364
entrenched, 371
how to treat, 382–383
individual, 365
keeping, with incentives, 371
new immigrants, 366
perspective, 380–381
public relations with, 374–377. *See also* Public relations
segmentation, 365
specific approaches to, 366–367
strategically developing, 369–370
Customer Relationship Management (CRM), 369
Customer service, 379-383
Customer service representatives (CSRs), 399, 402
Cybermarketing, 387

D

Debit cards, 172
Debt buyers, 308
Debt ratio, 272–273
Debt service coverage ratio (DSCR), 273–274
Delinquent accounts, 202
Demand deposit, 122
Demographics, 364
Departmentalization, 398
Department of Commerce's Office of Small Business, 279
Department of Housing and Urban Development (HUD), 247, 249
Department of Veterans Affairs (DVA), 249–250
Deposit accounts
  savings, 126–127
  transaction accounts, 122–126
Deposit check loans, 29
Deposit currency, 38
Deposit regulations, 140-145
Deposit services, outsourcing of, 318
Depositors, 17
Depository intermediaries, 26–28
Deposits, 19, 135-138
Depreciation, 265
Deregulation, 21, 52
Digital signage, and marketing, 390
Direct deposit, 176
Direct express, 177

Direct marketing, 389
Disability insurance, 310, 312
Disclosure statements, 141
Discount rate, 68, 113
Disintermediation of funds, 136
District Reserve Banks, 61–62
Diversification, 187, 314
Documentation, for loan, 236
Documented Management Systems
(DMS), 51

E

Economic Injury Disaster loans, 283
Economics and banks, 10–12
Economy and banking
about, 135–136
Federal Reserve and, 137–138
EDI implementation, 169
Electronic check conversion, 166
Electronic Data Interchange (EDI), 318
Electronic funds transfer, 88, 125–126,
144, 176, 177
Electronic wallets, 174
Elements of negotiability, 158-160
Emergency Banking Act of 1933, 49
Emergency Economic Stabilization Act
of 2008, 336
Employee, 380, 382
Employee performance, 412-416
Endorsement, 159-162
Endorsing, 152
Environmental Protection Agency
(EPA), 59
Equal Credit Opportunity Act (ECOA),
29, 75, 239
Equifax, 202, 203
Equipment loans, 265, 267
Equity, 20, 231
Escrow accounts, 242
Estate, 322-324
Ethical dilemmas, 338, 342
Ethics, 225, 338-342
Ethics in Action (feature)
accurate financial statements, 276
bank customers' rights and obliga-
tions, 323
blank endorsement, 163
consumer protection laws, 77
credit, 29
credit card teaser rates, 197
ethics in public relations, 376

Federal Reserve, 48
governing documents, 142
human resources, 408
redlining, 113
unethical lending, 240
Warren Buffet on ethics, 341
Evaluation forms, 413–414
Excess reserves, 106
Exchange, foreign currency, 304–305
Existing Non-Credit Card
Account, 351
Expedited Funds Availability Act
(EFAA), of 1987, 166, 346
Express checking accounts, 124
Express loans, 282–283
Extended fraud alert, 356

F

Factoring, 268, 319
Fair Credit Billing Act, 77
Fair Credit and Charge Card Disclosure
Act, 78
Fair Credit Reporting Act (FCRA),
75–76, 203, 239
Fair Debt Collection Practices Act
(FDCPA), 76, 239
Federal Deposit Insurance Corporation
(FDIC), 49, 79, 126, 300, 336, 240
Federal Financial Institution Examina-
tion Council (FFIEC), 82
Federal funds rate, 67, 113, 253
Federal Housing Administration
(FHA), 245–246, 249
Federal mortgage programs, 231,
245–250
Federal National Mortgage Association
(FNMA). Federal Open Market
Committee (FMOC), 68, 89
Federal Reserve
adjusting the money supply,
137–138
automated clearing houses, 177
banking business, 138
banking regulations and, 143–144
check payment and processing, 167
Check 21, 178
counterfeit currency, 345
deposit account documents, 140–141
Fedwire, 177
fiat money, 108–109
foreign banks, 300, 301

impact of on interest rates, 112–113
monetary policy and, 114
Federal Reserve Act of 1913, 40, 45,
47-48, 165–166
Federal Reserve Bank, 240, 253
Federal Reserve Bank Open Market
Operations, 113
Federal Reserve Board
about, 47, 49, 82
HOEPA rules and, 243
Federal Reserve District Bank, 105
Federal Reserve Note, 102
Federal Reserve System, 6, 15, 18
board of governors, 62
chair of, 62–63
consumer protection and, 74–78
District Reserve Banks, 61–62
enforcement of consumer protection
and, 79
fiscal policy of, 70–72
functions of, 63–64
international banking and, 86–90
keeping the dollar strong, 89
member banks, 61
monetary policy of, 67–69
oversight responsibilities of, 81–84
President's Working Group on
Financial Markets (PWG), 64–65
regulation of foreign banks, 87
reorganization of, 65
review process and, 82
structure of, 60–66
Federal Reserve System Open Market
Account (SOMA), 89
Federal Savings and Loan Insurance
Corporation (FSLIC), 52
Federal Trade Commission, 29, 79, 240,
309, 351, 354
Fedwire, 177
Fees, banking, 18, 190–191, 196
FHASecure, 247
Fiat money, 102–103, 108–109
Fiat system, 286–287
Fidelity National Information Services,
317–318
Fiduciary, 323–324
Finance charge, 29, 196, 208–211
Finance companies, 29
Financial crisis of 2008
credit default swap (CDS), 287–289
cumulative effects of, 290
ineffectiveness of self-regulation, 290

mortgage-backed securities, 287
profit motive, 286–287
revenue generation from assets of
dubious value, 287–289
synthetic financial products, 289
Financial institutions, types of, 26–30
Financial Management Service
(FMS), 176
Financial risk, 301
Fiscal policy, 70-72
Fixed exchange rate, 88
Fixed rate mortgage, 227–228
Fixed rate, 195
Flat World (feature)
Export-Import Bank of India, 303
Global Biometrics, 175
The International Impact of the
U.S. Mortgage Crisis, 256
The Bank of England, 44
The European Union and the
Euro, 13
Scam Targets New Zealanders, 349
U.S. Currency Abroad, 108
Flexible exchange rate, 88
Flex line, 191
Float, types of, 168
Flood Disaster Protection Act of
1973, 78
Foreclosure, 227
Foreclosure rescue mortgage scams, 349
Foreign Bank Supervision Enhance-
ment Act of 1991 (FBSEA), 87
Foreign Corrupt Practices Act of
1977, 302
Foreign currency exchange/rates, 87–88,
304–305
Foreign Intelligence Surveillance Act
(FISA), 77
Forgery, check, 347
Formula, 229
401(k) plan, 322
Fractional-Reserve System (FRS), 103
Fraud, 284, 344, 256
Freddie Mac, 248, 249
Free checking accounts, 124
Full Employment and Balanced Growth
Act of 1978, 100
Full endorsement, 161–162
Functionality approach to
customers, 367
Funding, 201
Futures and securities, 65

G

Glass-Steagall Act of 1933, 49,
307–308
Global economy, and interdependence,
86–87
Globalization, 86
Gold, as currency, 103
Governing documents, 140–142
Government Accountability Office
(GAO), 79
Government currency, 38
Government-sponsored enterprise
(GSE), 249
Grace period, 197
Gramm-Leach-Bliley Act of 1999, 78,
240, 241, 308
Great Depression, 15, 21, 48, 70, 81,
247–248, 290, 307–308
Greenspan, Alan, 290

H

Hacking, identity theft and, 354
Health insurance, 311–312
HELOC loans, fraudulent, 354
Holder in due course, 158
Holdover float, 168
Home Equity Loan Consumer
Protection Act, 78
Home equity loans, 23, 194, 231
Home loans, 14. See also Loan(s)
Home Mortgage Disclosure Act
(HMDA), 241
Home Ownership and Equity
Protection Act (HOEPA), 78,
241–243
Homeowners insurance, 311
Homeowners' Protection Act of
1998, 243
House flipping, 348–349
Housing demand and the mortgage
crisis, 253
Housing Finance Agencies (HFAs), 250
Human resources (HR), 399, 406–408
conducting preemployment
testing, 408
interviewing for jobs, 408
job analysis and description, 405–406
maintaining employee records, 410
orienting new hires, 409
reviewing applications for hiring, 407

training new employees, 409
verifying application and background
information, 408
Humphrey-Hawkins Act, 100

I

Identification, 11, 163
Identity theft
categories of, 351
commercial protection
packages, 356
common sense precautions
against, 356
costs of, 352
covert observation and, 354
defined, 11
electronic phishing, 354
electronic precautions against, 356
fake websites, 355
fraudulent HELOC accounts, 354
hacking and, 354
how information is obtained, 352
mail theft, 353
personal data theft from electronic
devices, 355
security of major retailers and, 355
telephone scams, 353
trash retrieval, 354
wi-fi systems and, 355
Identity Theft Enforcement and
Restitution Act of 2007, 353
Identity Theft Report, 356
Image Replacement Document
(IRD), 346
Immigrants, as customers, 366
Incentive programs, for banking
customers, 371
Income, 321
Independent Treasury System, 45
Index, 229
Indexed rates, 195
Individual account, 123
Individual retirement account.
See IRA
Inflation, 50-51, 71
Initial fraud alert, 356
Installment loans, 193–194, 210–211
Insurance, 235, 309-311, 399
Insurance and brokerage 307–309
Interbank transactions, 136
Interest, 17, 130, 195, 235

Interest-bearing accounts, 124, 130–133
Interesting Facts (feature)
  ACH payments, 176
  computing compound interest, 132
  Council of Economic Advisors, 68
  credit bureau errors, 202
  currency, 100
  employment in the banking
    industry, 402
  Federal Reserve, 64
  Federal Reserve notes, 100
  first ATM, 5
  first checks, 152
  foreign assets of U.S. banks, 299
  Great Depression, 49
  Identity Theft Enforcement and
    Restitution Act of 2007, 353
  Internet Fraud Watch, 345
  leasing, 268
  Malcolm Baldrige National Quality
    Award, 380
  misrepresentation of academic
    credentials, 409
  mortgage crisis and pet
    abandonment, 253
  NeighborWorks America, 236
  origin of word *bank*, 21
  rate of homeownership, 246
  Sara Lee, 317
  spending of young adults, 196
  tax free college savings, 322
  time deposits, 126
Interest-only loans, 254
Interest rates, 68, 111–115
Internal Revenue Service, 63, 232
International banking, 87–90,
  298–302
International Banking Act of 1978
  (IBA), 87
International Monetary Fund (IMF),
  90, 300
Internet
  banking marketing initiatives
    and, 386
  cybermarketing and search engine
    optimization, 387
  fake websites for identity theft, 355
  First Internet Bank of Indiana, 312
  hacking and identity theft, 354
  identity theft and, 354–355
  investigate employee discipline
    problems using, 416

online banking, 24, 136
online help for entrepreneurs, 267
online identity verification, 203
online transfers, 177
  peer-to-peer lending and, 372
  person-to-person payments and,
    173–174
  as public relations tool, 377
  safe Internet banking, 125
  security of major retailers and identity
    theft, 355
  viral marketing and, 389
Internet Fraud Watch, 345
Intranet, 23
Investment strategies, faulty, of
  banks, 20
Investment, mortgages as, 252–253
IRAs, types of, 322

J

Job analysts, 403
Job description, 405
Job fair, 407
Joint account, 123
Joint tenancy account, 123

K

Keynesian economics, 70
Kiting, checks, 345–346

L

Lead customer service representative
  (LCSR), 397
Leasing, 268
Ledger entries, 108
Lending, 13-15, 23, 217, 254-255,
  299, 399
Letters of credit, 303–304
Leverage, 218
Liability, 20
Lien, 195
Life insurance, types of, 310
Lifeline checking accounts, 124
Lifetime cap, 229
Lines of credit, 197, 231, 267
Liquid asset, 19
Liquidity, 215, 218
Living trusts, 324

Loan(s)
  auto manufacturers', 372
  bridge, 268
  CAPLines, 283
  check advance, 21
  commercial. *See* Commercial loans
  consumer, 188–189, 194–197. *See also*
    Installment loans
  credit and market risk, 216
  decisions and trade-offs, 215
  Economic Injury Disaster, 283
  income and, 214–215
  interest only, 254
  liquidity and, 215
  loan policy committees and,
    217–218
  micro, 283
  No Income No Asset loans
    (NINA), 255
  No Income, No Asset, No
    Employment loans, 255
  operations, 265
  payday, 29–30
  post-dated check, 29
  prequalifying for a, 252
  SBA express, 282–283
  7(a) loan guaranty, 282
  short-term, 266
  simple, 231
  special programs, 283–284
  Stated Income State Assets loans
    (SISA), 255
  Stated Income Verified Assets loans
    (SIVA), 254
  stated income, 242
  term, 266
  types of, 23
  who owns?, 255
Loan documentation, 236
Loan guaranty program, of the
  SBA, 280
Loan policy committee, 217, 218
Loan theory, consumer, 186–
Loan-to-value (LTV), 236,
  254, 273
Lockbox services, outsourcing of, 318

M

Magnetic Ink Character
  Recognition, 347
Mail theft, of identities, 353

Malfunction float, 168
Marketing, 22, 385-390, 400
Market risk, 216
Maturity date, 127
Media, as public relations tool, 377
Medium of exchange, 4–5
Merchandisers, 269–270
Metallic currency, 38
Minimum payments, 210
Mint Act of April 1792, 40
Mobile banking, 24, 125
Modern portfolio theory (MPT), 187
Monetary Control Act of 1980, 52
Monetary policy, 67-69, 71-72, 114
Money
    creation and circulation of, 105–110
    defined, 4–5
    as fiat system, 286–287
    guaranteeing, 15
    history of storing, 10–11
    interest and, 96–119
    as medium of exchange, 38, 286–287
    nature of, 102–103
    safeguarding, 10–12
    at work, 17–20
Money laundering, 302, 346–237
Money market deposit accounts
    (MMDAs), 127
Money market mutual funds, 127
Money supply, 98-101, 137-138
Mortgage(s), 14, 226–227, 230, 236–237,
    242–250
Mortgage-backed securities,
    253–255, 287
Mortgage-based scams, 348-349
Mortgage crisis, 252-256, 276-277
Mortgage disability insurance, 311
Mortgage legislation, 239-243
Mortgage lending, types of, 227–232
Mortgage origination, 226
Mortgage Origination Commission
    (MOC), 65
Multiplier effect, 106–107
Mutual funds, 97, 314
Mutual savings banks, 27

N

National Banking Act of 1864, 40, 45, 47
National Consumers League, 345
National Council of State Housing
    Agencies (NCSHA), 250

National Credit Union Administration
    (NCUA), 79, 82
National Currency Act of 1863, 40
Negative equity, 256
Negotiable instruments, 151–152,
    158–163
Negotiable instruments, types of, 154,
    155–156, 158–179
Net Bookmark (feature)
    automated human resource
        functions, 410
    automating payments, 300
    federal funds rate, 112
    identity theft, 354
    interest rates, 15, 112
    mortgage crisis, 255
    MyMoney Facebook application, 372
    national identity cards in Britain, 177
    OCC annual report on bank
        lending, 277
    safe Internet banking, 125
    solutions for the underbanked, 218
    tax incentives, 77
    United States Mint, 41
Net charge-off, 199
Net income, 18
Net interest income, 17
Newspapers, and marketing, 388
Niche markets, 21
No Income No Asset loans (NINA), 255
No Income, No Asset, No Employment
    loans, 255
No service charge checking
    accounts, 124
No-frills checking accounts, 124
Nondepository intermediaries, 26, 28–30
Nonsufficient funds check (NSF), 169
North American Free Trade Agreement
    (NFTA), 283, 298
North American Industry Classification
    System (NAICS), 279
Note passing bank robberies, 336

O

Office of the Comptroller of Currency
    (OCC), 79, 276, 300
Office of Housing, 247
Office of Thrift Supervision, 65, 79
Open-end loans, 197
Open endorsement, 160–161
Open market operations, 67

Operations, 398, 400
Operations loans, 265
Opt-out, 308
Organizational Integrity Survey, 338
Orientation, 409
Outsourcing, 317-318
Overdraft, 142
Overdraft protection, 190–191
Overextension, 211
Overseas Private Investment Corpora-
    tion (OPIC), 305

P

Paper currency, 38, 40
Paperhanging, 347
Passbook savings account, 126
Patriot Act, 77, 302, 346–347
Payable on demand, 159
Payday loans, 29–30
Payee, 154, 304
Payment(s), consumer, 171–175
Payroll, outsourcing, 317
Peer-to-peer lending, 372
Periodic cap, 229
Personal banking services, 398–399
Personal identification number
    (PIN), 172
Personal loans, 193
Personnel department, 405
Person-to-person payments (P2P),
    173–174
Phishing and identity theft, 354
Physical security, 332-333
PITI, 234–235
Point-of-sale (POS) transaction, 172
Post-dated checks, 29, 143, 169
Predatory lending, 212
Preferred stock, 313
Premium, 309
President's Working Group on Finan-
    cial Markets (PWG), 64–65
Previous balance method, 209
Pricing, 385
Primary Dealer Credit Facility
    (PDCF), 69
Primary dealers, of securities, 67
Primary reserves, 105
Prime rate, 113
Principal, 195, 234, 321
Print media, and marketing, 388
Privacy-policy, 308

Private mortgage insurance, 235, 243, 254
Probate, 322–323
Profit, 18
Profit and loss statements (P&L), 268, 274, 282
Profit motive, 286–287
Promissory notes, 155–156
Promoting, 385
Property insurance, 313
Public image, 374
Public records, 202
Public relations, 375-377, 400, 403
Purchasing, as bank operation, 400

Q

Quantitative skills, 97
Quarterly Banking Profile, 186, 191

R

Radio frequency identification (RFID), 174, 390
Rate chasers, 133
Real estate, commercial lending and, 265, 267
Real Estate Settlement Procedures Act (RESPA), 78, 243
Recession, 51
Reconstruction Finance Corporation (RFC), 279
Recording mortgages and deeds of trust, 237
Redlining, 113, 241
Refinancing, 230–231
Regulations, banking, and the federal reserve, 143
Request for proposal (RFP), 297
Reserve liquidity, 47
Reserve requirement, 137–138
Reserves, 47, 105–106
Resolution form, 142
Restrictive endorsement, 161
Retail bank, 6
Return on assets (ROA), 20
Return on equity (ROE), 20
Returned check, 169
Revenue, 19
Reverse mortgages, 23, 232
Revocable trust provision, 324
Revolutionary War, 40
RFP. *See* Request for proposal

Right of survivorship, 123
Risk adverse, 286
Risk-based pricing, 76
Risk management, in granting credit, 199–200, 216
Risk preferrer, 286
Robbery Description Form, 335
Robbery prevention, 332-336
ROCA score, 87
Roosevelt, President Franklin D., 49, 246
Roth IRA, 322
Routing number, 168

S

Safeguarding money, 10–12
Sarbanes-Oxley Act of 2002, 341–342
Savings accounts, 126–127
Savings and loan associations (S&Ls), 27
Scorecard, banking incentive program, 371
Search engine optimization (SEO), 387
Secondary endorsement, 161
Secondary reserves, 105
Secretary of the Treasury, 47, 49
Secured loan, 194–195
Securities
    mortgage-backed, 253–254
    primary dealers of, 67
    treasury, 109
Securities and Exchange Commission (SEC), 65, 79, 309, 340
Securitization of loans, 189
Segmentation, customer, 365
Self-regulation, ineffectiveness of, 290
Seller assistance mortgage scams, 349
SEPA Credit Transfer Scheme (SCT), 299
Share account, 128
Share certificate, 128
Shared appreciation mortgage (SAM), 230
Share-draft account, 128
Short-sale mortgage scams, 349
Short-term loans, 266
Signature, 154
Signature loan, 195
Signature polices, 141, 159
Single account, 123
Single Euro Payments Area (SEPA), 299

Single-premium whole life insurance, 310
Skills that Pay Dividends (feature)
    convey a professional image, 331
    ethics at work, 225
    public speaking and persuasion, 151
    quantitative skills, 97
    understanding consumer motives, 363
    understanding public policy and its impact on business, 59
Small Business Administration (SBA), 279–284
Small Business Investment Company (SBIC) program, 283–284
Small business loan programs, SBA, 279–280
Small business practices, 11–12
Smart cards, 23–24
Social responsibility, marketing and, 386
Software, for customer relationship management, 369
SOMA. *See* Federal Reserve System Open Market Account
Sovereign wealth fund, 300
SOX. *See* Sarbanes-Oxley Act of 2002
Special endorsement, 161–162
Split deposit, 161
Spread, 17, 133
Stagflation, 51
Stale check, 143
Standby letter of credit, 304
Stated income loans, 242
Stated Income State Assets loans (SISA), 255
Stated Income Verified Assets loans (SIVA), 254
Statement savings accounts, 126
Stock, 313
Stock market crash, of 1929, 48
Strength of Support Assessment (SOSA), 87
Subprime mortgage crisis, 51
Substitute check, 123
Sum-of-digits method, 208–209
Synthetic financial products, 289
System to Estimate Examinations Ratings (SEER), 83

T

Target market, 365, 385–386
Taxes, 235

Taylor rule, 69
Tech Talk (feature)
    Documented Management Systems
        (DMS), 51
    EDI Implementation, 169
    Electronic Funds Transfer, 88
    Fannie Mae DU and Freddie Mac
        LP, 248
    First Internet Bank of Indiana, 312
    Cup of Java, 136
    Intranet, 23
    Measuring Nontraditional Forms of
        Money, 100
    Online Help for Entrepreneurs, 267
    Online Identity Verification, 203
    Taking Technology To the Limits To
        Prevent Robberies, 334
    Technology: Customer Service Asset
        or Problem, 381
    Virtual Tellers, 413
Tenants in common, 123
Term Auction Facility (TAF), 69
Term loans, 266
Term Securities Lending Facility
    (TSLF), 69
Testamentary trusts, 324
Time deposits, 126-128
Time-delay locks, 333
Title insurance, 311
Trade agreements, 298
Trade financing, 303–304
Transaction accounts, 122–126
Transfers and circulation of money,
    107–108

Transit number, 168
Transportation float, 168
Transportation security, 333
Treasury securities, 109
Trust companies, 5, 29
Trust funds, as banking service, 399
Trust officer, as banking job, 402
Trustor, 324
Trusts, 321-324
Truth in Lending Act (TILA),
    74–75, 239
Truth in Lending Statement, 194
Truth in Savings Act of 1991, 143

U

Underwriting, 200–201, 236-237, 248,
    276-277
Uniform Bank Performance Report,
    82–83
Uniform Commercial Code (UCC) of
    1958, 166
Universal life insurance, 310
Unsecured loan, 195
U.S. Community Adjustment and
    Investment Program
    (CAIP), 283
U.S. Department of Agriculture
    (USDA), Rural Housing
    Service, 250
U.S. Department of Energy
    (DOE), 59
U.S. Department of the Treasury, 176
U.S. Export-Import (Ex-Im) Bank, 305

U.S. Mint, 41
U.S. Postal Inspection service, 353
U.S. Small Business Administration
    Office of the Inspector General
    (OIG), 284
U.S. Treasury Exchange Stabilization
    Fund (ESF), 89

V

Variable annuity, 322
Variable life insurance, 310
Variable rates, 195
Variable universal life insurance, 310
Vault cash, 105
Vehicle loans, 194
Viral marketing, 389

W

Wall Street Journal Prime Rate (WSJ
    Prime), 280
Want, 364
Whole life insurance, 310
Wholesale banks, 26
Will, 322
Wires, 304
Workers' Compensation, 313
World Bank, 299

Z

Zero-balance accounts
    (ZBAs), 318